CISTERCIAN STUDIES SERIES: NUMBER ONE HUNDRED–THIRTEEN
BOOK TWO

Hidden Springs
Cistercian Monastic Women
Book Two

Medieval Religious Women III

The genealogical tree of Saint Humbelina (key to picture on page 813)

CISTERCIAN STUDIES SERIES: NUMBER ONE HUNDRED–THIRTEEN

BOOK TWO

HIDDEN SPRINGS

CISTERCIAN MONASTIC WOMEN
BOOK TWO

MEDIEVAL RELIGIOUS WOMEN
VOLUME THREE

Edited by
John A. Nichols and Lillian Thomas Shank ocso

CISTERCIAN PUBLICATIONS INC.
1995

The work of Cistercian Publications is made possible in part
by support from Western Michigan University to
The Institute of Cistercian Studies

Acknowledgements
The editors of Cistercian Publications express their appreciation to
Sheed & Ward Publishers, Kansas City, Missouri
for permission to quote from
The Selected Poetry of Jessica Powers (1984).

Library of Congress Cataloging-in-Publication Data
(Revised for volume 3)

Medieval religious women.

    (Cistercian studies series ; no. 71–72, 113)
    Includes bibliographies and indexes.
    Contents: v. 1. Distant echoes – v. 2. Peaceweavers – Hidden
springs.
    1. Cistercian nuns–History. 2. Monasticism and religious
orders for women–History–Middle Ages, 600–1500. 3. Spirituality–
History. I. Nichols, John A., 1939–   . II. Shank, Lillian
Thomas, 1933–   . III. Series: Cistercian studies series ; no. 71–
72, 113.
BX4210.M345   1984   271'.9'000902   83-2111
ISBN 0-87907-871-5 (v. 1)
ISBN 0-87907-971-1 (pbk. : v. 1)

Library of Congress Cataloging-in-Publication Data

ISBN 0-87907-887-1 (v. 2)
ISBN 0-87907-986-X (pbk. : v. 2)
ISBN 0-87907-613-5 (alk. paper : v. 3)
ISBN 0-87907-913-4 (pbk. : alk. paper : v. 3)

Printed in the United States of America

TABLE OF CONTENTS

PART ONE
THE HISTORY OF MEDIEVAL CISTERCIAN NUNS

PART THREE
CONTINUING THE TRADITION

viii   *Contents*

Epilogue

Ida of Léau, or,
The Inconveniences of Ecstasy

Chrysogonus Waddell ocso

As a doe longs for running streams,
so longs my soul for you, my God.
Ps 42:1

A MORE APPROPRIATE BIBLICAL QUOTATION could hardly have been found by Sister M. Colman to serve, in the very opening line of her study of Ida of Léau,[1] as a summary statement of the life and spirituality of that remarkable flemish cistercian nun. Nor is the title of Sister Colman's contribution, 'Ida of Léau: Woman of Desire', any less apposite. It might even not be going too far to suggest that, had Pope Saint Gregory the Great never written a single word about desire for God, little would have been lost, since the *Vita* of Ida of Léau could be substituted as a living illustration of almost every aspect of Gregory's doctrine about desire.

The comprehensive nature of Sister Colman's contribution dispenses any future commentator on the *Life of Ida* from having to deal with questions concerning Ida's background, the historical setting, the sociological conditions of her milieu, or even her spirituality and her message for today.

What follows, then, is little more than a somewhat naive record of one twentieth-century monk's growing friendship with the thirteenth-century Ida of Léau. Sister Colman obviously meant her study of Ida to encourage this kind of personal rapport with the subject of her enquiry, and the following pages should be considered as no more than a personal testimony appended to Sister Colman's wonderfully objective and well-rounded synthesis of the life and spirituality of Ida of Léau.

445

MY DIFFICULTIES WITH THE AUTHOR

The *Life of Ida* is to be found in two extant MSS, the one at the Brussels Bibliothèque Royale, MS 8895–8896, written at Ida's own monastery of la Ramée towards the end of the thirteenth century; the other at the library of the University of Liège, MS 230, and dating from the fourteenth century. For his edition of this Life in the Bollandist *Acta Sanctorum* (Oct. XIII: pp. 107–124), Father de Buck, SJ, established his text on the basis of the first MS, but collated with the second. The *Life* had been published earlier by the Cistercian Chrysostom Henriquez, in his *Quinque Prudentes Virgines*,[2] but with a considerable amount of editorial bowdlerizing. Simone Roisin notes that the author (a monk of Villers?) 'handles Latin with ease and correctly'.[3] I wonder. True, the obviously corrupt state of the text is probably due at least in part to an error-prone scribe who sheds little luster on his or her profession; but the style itself is nothing if not tangled. It is normal to toss in word-fillers for the sake of rhythm and to balance off one statement with its parallel. This author is just wordy. He heaps up commonplaces which add next to nothing to the point under discussion, and, in spite of the verbiage, really meaningful biblical and liturgical references are in short supply. With the help of a mere word or two from a contextually important passage of Holy Writ, the better authors know how to make a hagiographical narrative resonate with new levels of significance. This technique is by no means ignored by our author, but really meaningful instances of its application are hard to find. The less discerning reader is likely to be fooled, too, by some of the author's misguided attempts at literary effect. Take, for instance, these excerpts from the second sentence of the Prologue:

Ideoque nihil dubium est quín amator hominum,		
a quo	et ex quo	et per quem
intellectus	et mens	et ratio
producuntur,	et sunt,	et permanent . . .
ut abyssus	et fons	et pelagus . . .

The 'by-whom, from-whom, through-whom' smacks obviously, does it not, of the doxology in Romans 11:36 (*ex ipso, et per ipsum, et in ipso*)? or is it perhaps inspired by one of the texts from the Trinity Office? And that parallel line-up of the intellectual faculties—intellect, mind, reason. Surely our author must here be dependent on some theologian or school of theologians of whom this combination is characteristic? And may we not see in the following trio of verbs a carefully nuanced progression: 'They are brought forth', 'and they are', 'and they remain in being'? This becomes all the more exciting if we align these verbs respectively with the 'abyss', 'fount', and 'ocean' of the final group, which imply yet another progression: depths from which—water wells up—to form a vast ocean. But the moment readers begin attempting to coordinate these threesomes with each other and with the members of the Blessed Trinity, I wish them the joy of their efforts. My own impression is that the author has let himself get carried away by the presumed exigencies of rhetoric, as he clearly does elsewhere. He is a bit of a literary magpie: he clutters up the text with showy trifles that contribute little to the solidity of the structure.

This is not to say that all the biblical and liturgical allusions and the rhetorical figures should be disregarded. Rather, one has to evaluate each case as it comes along, even if this very often leads to nothing very positive.

Then, too, we have to remember that we are dealing less with Ida herself than with an interpretation of Ida. This is nothing new. The same is true of most modern-day biographies; and I for one am more comfortable reading about Ida as portrayed by, perhaps, a near-contemporary monk of Villers than I am reading about Thomas Merton as portrayed by a Monica Furlong. Besides, I myself am not particularly interested in a plethora of secondary historical details. As important as Ida is in herself, perhaps even more important is the Ida loved and appreciated in her cistercian milieu. She obviously articulated something that was considered important for those monks and nuns. She therefore stands for something, and it is this 'something' which lies behind the author's choice and arrangement and exposition of his material. So in telling us about Ida, our author is also telling us about the ideals and aspirations of those monks and nuns who provided the milieu in which Ida attained to the fullness of her life in Christ. We must not look to our author, then, to supply us with bits and pieces of information which might be interesting to us, but which would interest little if at all the author and his contemporary readers. I would like, of course, to know about the business Ida's father ran. But what in the world does this have to do, the author asks, with the writing of a *Life* of Ida?

I admit to not having some of the difficulty with our author that many others experience. Simone Roisin's utterly splendid study of cistercian hagiography around thirteenth-century Liège is punctuated, for instance, with expressions of regret at the naive credulity of these pious but, oh, so uncritical biographers. There seems to be something about visions and locutions that is, for us moderns, in definitely poor taste—and raises, moreover, the whole question of veracity and historicity. Perhaps my own lack of critical sense here is conditioned in part by the experience of people I have come to know and love. Just a few months ago, for instance, I was in a little village near Roanne, St-Victor-sur-Rhins, where, after a morning spent with a manuscript kept for safety in the mayor's office, I had lunch at the home of the deputy mayor and his wife. Their two youngest boys, both now in their early twenties, were what we now call 'exceptional children', and what the French call *inadaptes*. This had meant much suffering for the parents, but their lives had been touched deeply by their contact with a stigmatic visionary from a neighboring region, Marthe Robin. A few days later, in passing through Basel train station on my way to Italy, I thought of the late Adrienne von Speyr, a townswoman of the place, and something of a latter-day Hildegard von Bingen minus a cloister. Unlike Hildegarde, however, Adrienne had a Hans Urs von Balthasar to vouch for the authenticity of her charism—and Urs von Balthasar was neither naive nor uncritical. The next day, in Milan, I made a visit of devotion, as I have often done, to the tomb of the holy Benedictine Cardinal Schuster whose body, after all these years in a fissured casket in a water-clogged crypt, remains incorrupt. A day or two later I was chatting with a young priest who, like his spiritual mother, has permission to carry the Blessed Sacrament with him in a pyx—only *her* consecrated Host gives off a quite wonderful fragrance. She gets by on an hour of sleep each day and her prayer life is rather lively—visions, locutions, that sort of thing. In another day or two I was at Vitorchiano, where the list of Blessed Maria Gabriella's authenticated first-class miracles is growing apace. Life in my own community is considerably more humdrum. Granted that a good part of the accounts of paramystical phenomena relative to our thirteenth-century cistercian mystics may be exaggerated or in specific instances even false, I for one am not about to mumble apologies over Lutgard's homely conversations with the Lord or Aleydis' Good Friday shewing of the Passion. Modern-day critics sometimes have their own brand of naivete and credulity.

THE PROLOGUE

The prologue is about as useless as are most prologues to second-rate *Lives*. Ida is a lamp whose light ought not remain hidden; the author, unworthy as he is, writes only in response to the insistence of others; his style is unbearably uncouth (a statement rendered invariably in as elegant a Latin as the author is capable of penning); he is ever so honest; the impeccability of his sources should stop the mouths of detractors. All this we have read before, countless times. There is one single detail of interest, however: witnesses are left unspecified by name, since so many of them are still alive. This places the redaction of the life within the living memory of those who best knew and loved Ida. So, with Simone Roisin, we may assign the redaction of the *Life* to sometime during the last quarter of the thirteenth century.[4]

THE TABLE OF CONTENTS

Father de Buck's Table of Contents[5] is an editorial interpolation, but a useful one. It is composed of the seventeen unnumbered section-headings contained in the Brussels MS, which otherwise has none of the six chapter-divisions or chapter-headings of the De Buck edition. A separate listing of these sections indicated in the MS is helpful in that it provides us with a clue as to the structure the author intended his work to have. This is not to say that the actual contents of a particular section will necessarily correspond all that well to the section-title. On the contrary, the final sections of this *Life* seem to form a somewhat haphazardly arranged series of vignettes. But it is clear that our author meant to provide some kind of structure to the *Life* as a whole. The first five titles concern her life in the world: the town she comes from (1), her father Gilbert and her sister, the cistercian Katherine (2), her childhood (3) and subsequent life in the world (4), and her spirit of compassion (5). Sections 6 to 17 relate her life in the cloister: her entrance into religion followed by her first consolation (6); this is, however, the consolation given beginners, and is therefore followed by a period given over to temptations, the practice of patience, and further adversities (7). An increase of ascetic toil and patience leads to an increase of grace (8); this takes the form of keen spiritual understanding and mirth (9) and further expands into an excess of sheer joy (10). This then leads to acts demonstrative of practical love of neighbor and to an initial rash of miracles (11). Visions follow, together with an experience of the Real Presence and a loftier degree of contemplative prayer(12). Section 13 concerns further visions, but also Ida's humility and compassion, while the final four sections seem to suggest an ever loftier kind of contemplative prayer: her rarified spiritual knowledge (14), her raptures (15), the full abundance of her understanding and consolation (16), and, last of all, in true hagiographical style, the death which she herself foretells (17).

But if we are looking for some kind of a directory for our own spiritual ascent, we shall be disappointed. The structure suggested by the section-headings corresponds only imperfectly with the contents from section 9 onwards.

Sections 1–3 (Vita, pp. 109–110)

The terminology of these initial three sections deserves attention: *praise* of the diocese of Liège, and Ida's birthplace (1); *praise* of Ida's father, Gilbert, and the vocation of her sister Katherine (2); *praise* of Ida, and of her childhood. Praise is one of the hallmarks of cistercian spirituality. It is noteworthy, then, that our author makes his introduction to our cistercian mystic into a veritable hymn of praise. So long as God continues to exist and the human race does not become extinct, there will always be question of a man-God relationship, with the consequent possibility of emphasizing differently at different times one of the two terms of the relationship. In the twelfth and thirteenth centuries there was no doubt that God came first. If the monk was concerned with his own perfection, this was chiefly in order to be able to praise God the more perfectly. The renaissance vision, borrowed from greek antiquity, of man as measure of the universe, has long affected the nature of our spiritual strivings, even at times within christian contemplative communities. Too often God has become a mere means for the attainment of our perfection. Occasional relics of a past age have survived like so many dinosaurs into the present age—the late Karl Rahner, for instance:

> I want, wish for, and expect a Church—can I say it?—of exceptionally strong spirituality, of much livelier piety, a Church of prayer, a Church that praises God and does not think that God is there for us, but is convinced rather, in theory and in practice, that we are here to adore God, that we have to love him for his own sake and not only for ours.
> [Reporter:]
> But hasn't this been the Church's mistake somewhat, that she always gave people the impression that they were principally there for God? . . . Shouldn't the other side be emphasized much more, namely, that God is there for us, unconditionally there for us?
> [Rahner:]

> Well, it is certainly true that God is our salvation, that God loves us, and that God extends his arms to us in a special way to take us up into his eternal life. But just as you can only really become happy with another person if you love this person for his or her sake alone and not for your own happiness, so there is a similar relationship between the human person and God. We must love God for His own sake—love—because He is the eternal, holy, blessed incomprehensible. . . . The strange thing is that one can find something only when one does not seek it directly and for one's own sake. I'd like to say that this is a basic structure of human existence.[6]

This is, in particular, a basic structure of cistercian spirituality, whether in cloisters of monks or of nuns. Talk about mysticism in any context other than that of love and desire of God because God is God, and you pervert the cistercian experience in its very essence. Praise, no less than charity, is the very form of cistercian existence. Work at the contemplative experience in any other context, and you will end up frantically whirling in ever diminishing circles around the still point of your own little ego.

Our author is right to praise Liège. The place was exploding with christian vitality. Living there in the mid-thirteenth century must have been like living at the center of an on-going Pentecost. It was not a matter of a single noteworthy phenomenon, such as the efflorescence of cistercian houses of women, or the multiplication of augustinian communities, or the re-birth of benedictine abbeys, or the rise and lightning-like spread of the beguine movement. Everything was happening at once. There was a common vision, a shared experience. And though each particular milieu had its own distinguishing marks, the depth and intensity of the overall reality of reform and renewal cut across all religious particularism and insularism. It was a great time for friendships between religious and laypeople, a great time for fruitful sharing and exchanges between beguines and canonesses and nuns; between Cistercians, Benedictines, Augustinians, Dominicans; between male religious and female religious.

There is special praise meted out for Ida's parents, whose marriage seems to have been one of those made in heaven. Ida is 'a sweet pledge [of their union], a lovable covenant, a delectable bond, and a strengthening and knotting together of sweetness and love'. Rhetorical hyperbole aside, the importance of this description of the family should not be overlooked. This was no feudal aristocratic family. Affection could be shown and demonstrated between parents

and children. Relationships between the parents were not governed
by a strict formal code. There was no separation of the sexes within
the same household, or separation of boys and girls at an early
age, under the remote tutelage, respectively, of father or mother.
More importantly, a surplus of children did not mean that the
supernumerary youngsters were to be shipped off to the local abbey
or priory, so as to avoid the division of family property among too
many heirs; or that most of the funds available for dowries was to be
reserved for only one or two of the girls, the better to maintain their
rank in high society, while the daughters less amply provided for
would have to withdraw to a convent. Consequently, if a youngster
from a family of the merchant class embraced the monastic state,
this was more often than not in response to a personal attraction
rather than to a social exigency. Ida's family seems to have belonged
to just this privileged stratum of society. For Ida, our author tells us,
came from a family of average condition (*mediocri prosapia*), and was
therefore free from having to cope with the problems caused either
by excess poverty or excess wealth. At the same time, the various
branches of the family were wealthy enough to adopt a life-style
from which Ida stalwartly distanced herself. The family to which Ida
belonged seems to have been not too many notches below the kind
of family we meet in *The Buddenbrooks*, Thomas Mann's great novel
about well-off merchant families in nineteenth-century Lübeck.

Only two of Ida's sisters are mentioned: the one, Katherine, becomes a cistercian nun in a community remarkable for its spiritual
vitality; the other, who remains anonymous, is a little worldling who
serves as Ida's harshest (and perhaps only) critic in what seems to
have been an otherwise happy household.

The period of Ida's life at home is divided into two sections,
the first relating to her early childhood, the second to her young
girlhood. Each section begins with a litany of praise and is rounded
off by a vignette which catches Ida in a characteristic moment.

The first encomium (*Vita*, pp. 109–110) tells us that Ida is a pretty
child (most children are), remarkable for her gentleness, innocence,
sweetness. She is never a bother to anyone. We are uneasy when we
read that she does not like to play, but the term here used suggests
not the quiet play of a little girl with her doll but rowdy horse-play,
jocis sacularibus. For the medieval, one's outward comportment was
of a single piece with one's interior physiognomy. What for us is no
more than a child's expression of healthy high spirits would be, for
the medieval, irrational behavior that betrays a fractured interior
life. This litany of praise ends on a monastic and contemplative

note. The characteristic adjectives and nouns are: *constans et stabilis, et omino tranquillis residens et quieta . . . morum conversio, constans maturitas, stabilisque modestia . . .*, and the author notes that it was as though Ida were already living in the cloister. We easily recognize references to two of the three benedictine 'vows', that is, conversion of manners and stability. The absence of any reference to the third of these, obedience, is perhaps significant—this is not to suggest that obedience was not one of Ida's strong points. Here the author is concerned with stressing the specifically contemplative dimension of monastic life. The vignette which follows supports this. At the age of around seven, Ida began attending the local school. Learning, which she loved passionately, came easily. Rather than miss school when the winter snow was too high or the mud too deep, the little girl had herself carried to school. There is a lovely characteristic scene of her getting up at break of day (*summo diluculo surgens*), arriving at school early (*mane praeveniens*), and quietly sitting (*quiete residens*) at the school door, waiting for the janitor to unlock the door. How could the author have resisted the temptation to refer us here to Wisdom's exhortation in Proverbs 8:34—'Blessed is the man that heareth me, and that watcheth daily at my gates, and awaiteth at the posts of my doors'? That Ida's love of learning was solely in function of her desire for God is too obvious a point to need development. We are far from the atmosphere of contemporary theological disputes over the relative superiority of the will or of the intellect, the relative superiority of loving or of knowing. To know God, to love God—in practice, it comes to the same thing in the context of monastic spirituality, provided, of course, that we invest the word 'to know' with the full meaning given it in biblical, patristic, and liturgical usage.

Sections 4–5 (Vita, p. 10)

A second description of Ida shows her at an age when many a young girl begins getting clothes-conscious and boy-crazy. Stress is laid on Ida's maturity. Despite her many social virtues, she loves solitude; she also follows an ascetic regime which includes taking the discipline. There is, however, relatively little that is remarkable about her ascetical program: no bloody macerations, no extraordinary fasts, no all-night vigils. This section ends with a second vignette with the curious title, 'About the fervor of her *compassion*'. I say 'curious', because few of us would offer the same incident as illustrative of the theme of compassion. It seems as though the

author, who feels obliged to adumbrate in Ida's early life the themes
which were later to be featured in her life in the cloister, here had to
find something that would pass as 'compassion'. Ida, in the company
of her wearisome sister, is on her way to visit one of the recluses
or beguines whose company she so enjoys. On their way, the two
girls come across a dance going on in or next to the thorough-
fare. The author's description reminds one of the rowdy peasant
dancing scenes later depicted by Brueghel with characteristic brutal
earthiness. Confronted with this scene, Ida is so overwhelmed that
she runs back home as fast as she can. Though we can understand
this visceral reaction in a sensitive girl suddenly confronted with
a scene of drunken carousing and suggestive behavior, we would
probably not describe it in terms of 'compassion'. The author, however, claims that Ida sees all this as an insult to her Beloved, and
that she is filled with compassion for the foolishness of her erring
neighbors. She is 'transfixed by the sword of charity, wounded no
little by the darts of love, strangled by the noose-snare of compassion
(*compassionis laqueo suffocata*)'. In brief, Ida has a sudden flash of
insight into the human condition immersed in the frantic trivialities
of an existence without meaning or direction.

Sections 6–7 (Vita, p. 112)

Ida entered the cistercian monastery of la Ramée at the age of
thirteen. The description of her early formation there is typically
benedictine. She is 'thirsting and desiring to fight for the King of
kings more freely and expeditely'—a phrase based on the opening
paragraph of the Rule of Benedict (Prologue 3); and the description
of the monastic exercises into which she is initiated is similarly based
directly on the Rule. It is a fact, however, that 'fighting for the King
of kings' does not mean for the author, as it did for Benedict, chiefly
the life-long practice of obedience. Instead it meant love, desire,
mystical experience. It is, moreover, perfectly in keeping with the
ascetical program outlined in the Rule; just as Chapter Seven of the
Rule ends with that perfect love that casts out all fear and totally
transforms the monk from within, so also this paragraph about Ida's
initiation and progress in monastic *praxis* ends with a description of
what the section-title calls Ida's 'first spiritual consolation'—what we
moderns would be more inclined to call her first mystical experience.
Christ is speaking to the heart of Jerusalem, calling to Ida from
within. He comes to visit her, offering her paradisiacal drinks (this
suggests a return to the innocence of Eden). Ida is inundated by a
flood of spiritual mirth (jocundity) and divine sweetness. Her heart's

joy expresses itself even outwardly. The stream of the river makes the city of God joyful, as the most high, the most subtle Consecrator hallows his own tabernacle (see Ps 45:5). Still, this is merely an initial 'consolation'. Love grows, so does desire; and this means a painful purging away of everything in Ida that is incompatible with absolute Love. Ida's attitude is a sensible one: better purgatory now than later.

In keeping with the experience of most pilgrims of the spirit, temptations and adversities come apparently to obstruct Ida's further progress. In point of fact, these trials and temptations of diabolical origin are the condition for Ida's growth, or, as the author has it, their purpose is 'that she might receive fruit in greater abundance'. This period, marked by frequents bouts with chronic insomnia, lasts for a year and a half. Ida's surest defense against the wiles of the Enemy is the Eucharist. This she asks to receive 'frequently'. Through the Eucharist, Christ becomes Ida's tower of refuge, the castle where she finds protection; and she herself becomes his Sion, the city of his strength, whose wall and bulwark are the Saviour himself (see Is 26:1). By this time, the positive aspects of trial and temptation, which result invariably in her closer dependence on the Lord, are so evident and so appreciated, that Ida, during occasional periods of respite from trial, fears this might be a sign that Christ loves her less. Ida is another Job, but also another Judith. The devil gives up. The only result of his campaign against Ida has been that the Lord, whose delight is to be with the children of men is, indeed, uninterruptedly abiding with his beloved. And this, really, is the last we hear of the Enemy. There will be future trials for Ida, but none of them of diabolical origin.

Section 8 (Vita, p. 113)

The title of the next section, *On Her Toil, Patience, and Increase of Grace*, is somewhat inaccurate. The toil and patience belong to the preceding section. This section concerns, rather, the fruit of the former toil and patience. For the increase of grace means here the grace of contemplation. Ida has been the blear-eyed Leah long enough—Leah being, of course, the traditional symbol of the life of ascetic striving. With Rachel, Ida now experiences the delights of nuptial love. Here the biblical vocabulary is drawn chiefly from those texts most often used by Origen, Gregory the Great and Bernard of Clairvaux in their descriptions of the union between Bride and Bridegroom.

This is not to say that Ida has abandoned life in the body. The author refers to her Sunday Communions—Sunday Communion being still the norm for the reception of the Eucharist in at least some cistercian monasteries of the period.[7] He mentions, too, her activity as a scribe—the point here being that even Ida's external pursuits brought her into contact with the Word of God and things sacred. The author also remarks that, during worktime, Ida worked harder than the other sisters. But his chief focus is, of course, on Ida's life of the spirit.

This brings us to the author's description of a phenomenon which somewhat escapes the category of either toil or trial of patience. Ida is unable to make her Sunday Communion without falling into at least a partial swoon. Other nuns in the community had the same difficulty, and the problem must have been widespread enough for the General Chapter to require that nuns unable to receive Communion without derogation to the rubrical prescriptions must abstain.[8] So Ida abstained. Our author notes that the sisters concerned grieved mightily over the deprivation, but Ida soon found she had little to complain about. 'You know, o good Lord, that I dare not approach you, but *you* can come to me easily enough.' For an entire year, the Bridegroom paid a Sunday visit to his bride with all the overwhelming effects which had theretofore accompanied his visits to her in sacramental Communion. Ida even composed a couplet (in the vernacular) which, in another context, might be taken as smacking of anti-sacramentarianism, or as an example of the kind of fuzzy thinking that did so much to compromise the reputation of the beguines and beghards:

> The draughts Christ's people [= priests] give are good,
> 'tis clear;
> but better by far are those God himself gives.

We here run directly into the problem that will plague Ida throughout the whole of her monastic life. Her mystical graces threaten to remove her from the mainstream of community life. Here it might be well to skip ahead to an episode which the author places in the final months of Ida's life.[9] One Sunday she loses her perception of God's grace at work within her. She is devastated. But when one of her sisters suggests that this may simply be a trial sent by God to test her heart, Ida answers (by sign-language, no less), that 'So long as it entails no fault on my part, God knows that I do not particularly want to have this grace'. And the biographer goes on to explain that this was not said in disdain of the special graces received, but out of her thirst to be able to observe along with all the other sisters the Order's statutes. Since the author here refers to the grace 'with which the divine goodness visited her for a long while every Sunday', it seems likely that this comment, recorded in the final paragraphs of the Life, belongs by right to the earlier period when Ida had to give up her Sunday Communions.

This comment of Ida's provides matter for thought when we read, for instance, Father Thomas Merton's perceptive remarks about Ida's flemish contemporary, Lutgard of Aywières:

> ... these thirteenth-century Cistercian mystics ... do not represent the pure Cistercian spirituality that characterized the first century of the Order's history. In St. Lutgarde we find practically nothing of that beautiful and simple zeal which was the very foundation stone of the Order—the zeal for the Rule of St. Benedict in its purity, the zeal for labor in the fields, silence, solitude, community life, monastic simplicity, and that concern with doing ordinary things quietly and perfectly for the glory of God, which is the beauty of pure Benedictine life. Of course, St. Lutgarde was Cistercian and Benedictine in her spirituality, in her love of the Divine Office, in her love of Christ above all else; but she lacks this Benedictine *plainness*, and this Cistercian technique of humility which consists in a kind of protective coloring, by which the monk simply disappears into the background of the common, everyday life, like those birds and animals whose plumage and fur make them almost indistinguishable from their surroundings.[10]

It was obviously not Ida's fault that her mystical life took the turn it did. She loved the Rule; she was a hard worker (when work was possible for her); she loved solitude as well as community life. Then, too, the community in which Ida had to cope with the less than welcome effects of ecstasy and rapture was itself a community which one could describe in the same terms Father Merton used to describe the twelfth-century cistercian ideal. Indeed, Father Merton's observation is just a trifle ironic, coming as it does from a man who tended to approach the Cistercian Fathers by way of Saint John of the Cross, and one of whose earliest studies of Saint Bernard dealt precisely with Saint Bernard and the point of transforming union.[11] Indeed, if we wish to understand what is happening to our reluctant mystic, Ida, we could do worse than to take up a manual of ascetical and mystical theology based on John of the Cross and Teresa of Avila, and turn to the description of ecstatic union or spiritual espousals, one of the distinguishing features of which is a suspension of the activity of the exterior senses corresponding to the absorption of the soul in God. This suspension of the exterior senses admits of varying degrees, but there is no need go into such matters here. Let me say, however, that one pleasant and relatively harmless way of passing a long winter Sunday afternoon would be to take the *Life* of Ida and skim through the various descriptions of her spiritual experiences. Itemize the phenomena described, both spiritual and physical, and then check these against the descriptions of the various states of prayer dealt with in Book III, Chapter Two, 'Infused Contemplation', in that most neglected of all once standard manuals, the Very Reverend Adolphe Tanquerey's *The Spiritual Life. A Treatise on Ascetical and Mystical Theology.*[12] You will see that now Ida is experiencing simple ecstasy; now she is in a state of rapture; now she is soaring in a flight of the spirit.

It would, of course, be a bit silly to take all this too seriously, especially since the descriptions of Ida's experiences come to us second-hand. But it would likewise be somewhat foolish not to recognize the fact that what our author is describing is what anyone with an eye to clinical detail would be describing in the case of persons called to a form of union with God that falls short of the spiritual marriage or transforming union described by Madre Teresa or John of the Cross. One of the characteristics of this state is the absence of rapture and of the concomitant suspension of one's faculties, interior and exterior. It would seem, then, that Ida still has further heights of divine union to which she can be raised. Had she attained to the fullness of transforming union, she could have gone about hoeing the turnip patch and washing up after supper without much fear of the inconvenient side-effects of a sudden fit of rapture.

The objection may be voiced that, when we are dealing with a thirteenth-century cistercian nun, it is bad methodology to mix spir-itualities by bringing in carmelite mystics and carmelite spirituality. But we are not in the least mixing spiritualities. It is simply a matter of clinical analysis. Benedictines, Premonstratensians, Carthusians, Franciscans, laymen and laywomen, even Cistercians, had raptures long before John of the Cross came on the scene. It is just that this Carmelite has provided convenient categories for understanding the phenomenon in question, and situating it in its proper context of the unfolding of one's life in the Spirit. The experience of spiritual espousals is not spirituality-specific. Any who wishes to use instead the categories of analysis provided by this or that contemporary school of depth psychology is free to do so—even though some of the practitioners of analytical psychology occasionally make the back-bush witchdoctor look sophisticated by comparison. Here we are simply trying to understand something about Ida's experience; and, thanks to Madre Teresa, we can see that we are dealing simply with a 'normal' case of ecstatic union.

Section 9 (Vita, p. 9)

The next section bears the title: *About Her Understanding and Her Increase of Mirth (Jocundity)*. We see her first in conversation with an unidentified 'spiritual person'. Ida leads the conversation to topics such as 'the modes and degrees whereby the light inaccessible of the Godhead transfuses itself to the angels'. We here may justifiably suspect that Ida has been reading that *vade-mecum* of so many theologians of mysticism, *Denis Hid Divinity*, that is, the *Celestial Hierarchy* of Pseudo-Denis, with its description of the outflowing of light and understanding from God through the hierarchy of spirits into the created cosmos, and the return of all back into God in the inverse direction. Ida has wonderful things to say, too, about 'that ineffable unity of the Trinity'. If Jan Van Ruysbroek had been born earlier than 1293, one might almost think that Ida, under his influence, was attempting to speak of that unity or divine rest in which the soul is said to dwell rather than in the Trinity, since it is to the Trinity that the divine operations are ascribed, and since it is in the underlying Unity that the divine repose of the Three Persons appears to subsist. If this sounds recondite and seems to be skirting dangerously close to unorthodoxy, it probably is. But whatever it was that Ida was trying to communicate, she failed to do so, utterly. Her discourse tended to center on the sweet humanity of Jesus Christ from the time of his blessed infancy onwards.

The text goes on to note that Ida's Sunday state of spiritual inebriation (accompanied by bodily weakness) began now on the preceding day. A year later the experience was beginning immediately after Friday None. This is more remarkable than it might sound. The experience of spiritual joy coincides with the moment of Christ's death on the cross and extends throughout the whole of Sunday. For flemish piety of this period, the period between the death of Christ and his resurrection was a time of joy: the soul of the Saviour went victorious to the place of departed spirits, smashed the gates of hell, and led the waiting souls of the just in triumphal procession into heaven. We are used to mystics suffering with our Lord during his Good Friday agony. We are less used to mystics sharing his paschal joy during the interval between his death and resurrection.

We should note that Ida's mystical experiences are coordinated with the saving events of the Mystery of Christ. We note, too, that however lofty her spiritual experiences, there is nothing the least bit discarnate about her piety. The next paragraph of the Life has her 'sitting solitary' (*sedebat solitaria*, see Lam 3:28)—the vocabulary of contemplation—in a spot in church from where she can view the reserved sacrament. Absorbed as she is in her prayer, she nevertheless is able to answer a summons to speak with someone at the grille.

Section 10 (Vita, pp. 114–115)

The next section, *On the Excess of Her Joy*, is doubtless meant to mark yet another stage in Ida's spiritual itinerary. She is flooded with so much joy that it seems impossible for her to go on living; and yet it is equally impossible for her to die. She is clearly no *illuminata*, since she here depends on the advice of others to help her. The remedy proposed is the reception of the Eucharist. 'I will kill and I will make to live; I will strike and I will heal' (Deut 32:39), quotes the author, explaining that the alternation of states was for the purpose of making Ida's love well up the more, while at the same time keeping it within due measure. A glance here at our trusty Tanquerey will suggest that a painful seesawing that affects both mind and will is characteristic of the night of the spirit:

> . . . God sends intervals of relief, during which one experiences a sweet peace in the enjoyment of divine love and familiarity. But such moments are followed by counter-attacks . . . This is the anguish of spiritual derliction.[13]

It is interesting to note, then, that Ida's mystical experiences result in her more direct insertion into the sacramental life of the Church.

That Ida had the complete understanding and sympathy of her superiors, her sisters, and the monastery clerics is a presupposition that lies behind many of the vignettes painted by our author. In the present section, for example, we are told how, on one of the feasts of general Communion, Ida was so overwhelmed during Lauds by her desire for the Eucharist that she was unable to wait any longer. Normally the nuns received Communion at the major Mass late in the morning; laysisters and a few others at the matutinal Mass after Prime. The priest anticipated by bringing the Blessed Sacraments to Ida (presumably lying some place outside the church) before Prime. Ida's state by now was such that she was unable to complete her Communion, and the priest had to return to church with the consecrated host. Ordinarily, we are told, Ida was able to pray during the matutinal Mass, but not at the major Mass later in the day. Mass was followed by Sext, then dinner. Ida's absorption in God carried through into the refectory, where eating so soon after Communion became a virtual impossibility. For anyone returning to consciousness after an experience of ecstatic union with God, this kind of physical reaction is normal enough. In this context mention is made of one instance where Ida broke silence in refectory by spontaneously bursting out with 'Wi here min harte', 'O Lord, my heart, my heart . . .'

The author waits till now to give us an example of Ida's insight and prayer on behalf of others. Ida would have been a rather strange kind of nun had she not prayed on behalf of others, and this habitually. Perhaps it is because charity towards the neighbor is one of the effects of the prayer of union that the author waits till now to record the following incident where, admittedly, the emphasis is less on Ida's compassion than on her supernatural insight. One of the sisters is worrying over a fallen augustinian canoness. Ida prays over the matter, and on the third day is able to console the sister. This sickness is not unto death. The canoness' fall will become the occasion for her receiving a new lease on life.

Section 11 (Vita, pp. 116–117)

This incident leads into the next section, *On the Virgin's Love for Her Neighbors, and about Certain Miracles*. Two stories used to illustrate Ida's love for neighbor concern two of her own sisters in the convent, both of them laboring under some hidden vice. The first tells Ida what the problem is, and receives the advice to go to Communion on such and such a day, and to tell our Lord that Ida sent her. In the second case, Ida herself takes the initiative of approaching a sister, identifying her secret fault, and urging her to correct it. In a third instance Ida restores 'a certain person' from a state of languor to health, though it is far from clear whether this is a state of physical languor or of spiritual.

In the single 'miracle-story'—one of the Saint Scholastica type[14]— Ida had arranged (by signs) for a sister to help her receive Communion privately—Communion being accompanied, of course, by ecstasy with all the unwanted physical side-effects. At the last minute the sister is called away on an errand of obedience. What is Ida to do? A sudden downpour forces the postponement of the errand long enough for Ida to receive Communion.

Next comes a series of vignettes which, despite the title of this
section, have little to do either with Ida's love for neighbor or with
miracles.

In the first scene, Ida is seated off by herself (*solitaria resideret*, Lam
3:28 again). A sister asks her if she is feeling sick or weak. Ida answers
that 'This grace that I have does not make me weak', and thereupon
is unable to say another word. This is probably just another instance
of Ida's experience of ecstatic union. Since the suspension of one's
senses in this state is gradual, there is nothing remarkable about
Ida's answering the question before falling into greater absorption
in God. Her insistence that this kind of experience does not leave
her weak agrees with Madre Teresa's observation that this condition, which should naturally weaken the body, rather imparts to it
new energies. The mystic does indeed feel a certain fatigue at the
moment of returning to 'normalcy', but this is followed by a sense
of renewed vigor.

In the second incident, it is harvest time, and the community
is away in the fields. Ida takes advantage of the absence of the
community to receive Communion privately. But she swoons right
there at the altar. The poor priest and his (male) assistants hesitate
to pick her up. The priest finally gets someone (a female) to remove
Ida from the sanctuary, but attempts to put Ida in a sitting position
prove unavailing. She finally has to be put in bed, where her sleep
lasts till after None.

In the third incident, we find Ida frustrated of her expectation of
receiving Communion at the Sunday major Mass. The community
had gone for this Mass to a newly constructed building at some
distance from the monastery; there, for some rubrical or other
reason, Communion of the sisters was not allowed. On her way
back to the monastery, the disappointed Ida falls to the ground
in a state of sudden ecstasy. The sister who stays behind to look
after her agrees, for the price of two rosaries, to lift Ida's veil so
that some nosy by-stander can see what the poor woman looks
like in ecstasy. Ida soon recovers the use of her faculties, and on
the following Tuesday, when asked whether she would like to go to
Communion, answers that the graces received the preceding Sunday
are all she needs.

On another occasion, Ida has been talking with her sisters about
the child Jesus. One of the nuns asks: Which is more important, that
the Lord should be born, or that he should suffer? 'If the Lord had
not been born,' answers Ida, 'he could not have died; but given the
fact of his birth, it behooved him to suffer the punishment of death.'

Ida's acute perception of the Real Presence was reflected in her face, now pale, now ruddy, every time she had occasion to cross the area in front of the 'priests' choir' (that is, the sanctuary), where the Blessed Sacrament was reserved.

Section 12 (Vita, pp. 117–118)

The next section, *About a Christmas Vision, and about the Virgin's Recognition of [Christ's] Presence, and about Her Contemplation,* for the first time mentions a vision. This is a bit surprising, since imaginative and intellectual visions of our Lord's sacred humanity and of our Lady are standard concomitants of ecstatic union, and there seems little doubt but that Ida's experience of ecstatic union were frequent. The vision took place during the Christmas Night Mass, as Ida, 'agonizing with delight', was lying expectantly abed in the infirmary. Three details are noteworthy about the description of this vision:

> 1. Mary gives the Babe not just to Ida, but to Ida and the *community*. This solidarity between the individual charismatic and the community is typically Cistercian.
> 2. The vision has trinitarian resonances perceived 'in an all-perfusive divine light': the Father is experienced as present and 'co-inhering' with the Son, and even speaking to Ida. The description here is somewhat confused, and it is uncertain whether this is an intellectual vision of the kind usually reserved for those radically purified individuals who have at last reached the state of transforming union. This is unlikely in Ida's case, even though afterwards she feels so light-filled within that, were her body to be suspended in mid-air, it would suffice to illumine the whole world. (In intellectual visions of the Trinity, the Persons habitually manifest themselves 'in a cloud of extraordinary brightness'.)[15] Despite the extraordinary nature of this vision, however,
> 3. Ida is still able to ask questions about a number of different persons, and about one in particular. This, too, is noteworthy. Even in ecstasy Ida has present to her a love and concern for others.

Upon returning to herself, Ida realizes that the *Agnus Dei* is being chanted in church. Unable to wait any longer, she has to have Communion brought her—one of the Hosts consecrated at the Night Mass. (The author takes for granted that the reader knows that the Communion Mass is the one celebrated in the late morning, and that Communion at the dawn Mass is allowed only in special circumstances.)

Like John the Baptist, Ida felt the hidden presence of Christ, and knew when the ringing of the sacring bell at Mass was too early or too late.

The further remarks contained in this section add little to our knowledge of Ida's inner life. From Spy Wednesday until Low Sunday,[16] she loses her appetite—a hardly surprising phenomenon for someone in an intermittent state of ecstasy. She has the gift of reading hearts, and knows the spiritual state of those going to Communion. And at times ecstasy comes upon her so suddenly that she cannot finish swallowing the morsel in her mouth. It would be harmful, at such times, to attempt to arouse her.

Section 13 (Vita, p. 118)

From this point on the author heaps up vignette after vignette arranged, apparently, in no particular order. In the section *On the Night Office Vision, and about Her Humility and Compassion*, we read first of the well-known story in which Mary hands Jesus to Ida during the chanting of the Night Office. All goes well until Ida has to chant the verse of the responsory assigned her. The rubrics call for her to stand with her arms hanging at her side. 'Lord, you will have to look out for yourself . . .' So she sang the verset with the Child clinging to her neck.

Mystic though she is, Ida does not disdain spiritual 'gimmicks'. When discoursing on things spiritual, she adopts a rather kaballa-like pedagogy by assigning various letters of the alphabet a symbolic meaning. As for her spiritual graces, these were no more hers in any real sense than was the rosary she was holding in her hand. Perhaps more meaningful for us than all the descriptions of her ecstasies taken together is the spiritual help she gives an otherwise unidentified person in deep spiritual trouble. So long as that person agrees to a change of life, Ida will gladly exchange all her own past good deeds for all the past sins of that person.

Sections 14–15 (Vita, pp. 120–121)

In the next section, *About Her Insight and Spiritual Knowledge*, we have yet another hotchpotch of disconnected scenes. By assigning each letter of her name a significance, Ida manages to invest it with the meaning 'One who loves God keenly'. There is here an unexpected reference to Ida's death which was to take place three years later on a Sunday, as she had hoped. Death on a Friday, in union with the dying Jesus, is a familiar theme; or on a Saturday, the day dedicated to our Lady. But death on a Sunday? This strikes a less accustomed note, but one that is fairly consonant with the general picture of Ida which has been emerging. When she receives Communion on Sunday, she spends almost the whole day in prayer; when she cannot herself receive Communion, she urges others to do so. In a rapid series of examples of her spiritual insight about the interior state of others, the most important detail is perhaps found in Ida's remark: 'I sleep less often than I used to,' that is, she falls into ecstasy less often. She continues: 'For I asked the Lord for this slumber to be taken away from me'. If we take our Tanquerey seriously, this probably suggests a genuine advance in Ida's spiritual progress; for the spiritual marriage generally has as one of its effects the cessation of ecstasies.[17] As Mother Teresa explains it in the *Spiritual Castle*, Mansion VII, ch. 3: 'If they [raptures] come at all, it is very seldom, and almost never in public.' Still, after giving yet another instance of Ida's knowledge of others gained through supernatural communication, the biographer records one more instance of Ida's ecstatic Communions. She and a friend had agreed to go to Communion together. But since Ida was sure to fall into rapture and thus be unable to pray for her friend expressly, this shrewd companion, desiring as she did Ida's intercession, asked her to delay her Communion until she had first offered up her intercessory prayers. It is, of course, quite possible that this incident dates from a time before her ecstasies tapered off. But can the same be said for the several incidents related in the next section under the rubric: *About Her Frequent Rapture*?

There is yet another account of Ida falling into ecstasy while trying to eat: this time it is after Compline in the infirmary, and the prioress is trying to help Ida take some little sustenance. Another day Ida sits at a table in refectory, deep in ecstasy, and stays there in contemplation till time for Vespers—frequent occurrence, notes the author. On another occasion Ida is carried off to bed after one of her ecstatic Communions; the efforts of one of the nuns to arouse the slumbering Ida prove disastrous till our Lord allows Ida to fall once more into the mystic sleep that lasts till Vespers. Another time, on one of her Communion days, Ida remains in church after the community thanksgiving after dinner; and the efforts of one of the nuns to awake her from her sleep of contemplation prove unavailing. More interesting, perhaps, is Ida's response to one of the nuns who gently chides her for failing to take the wine ablution customary in the cistercian rite after receiving the Eucharist under both kinds at the altar.[18] 'Sweetest Sister,' answers Ida, 'when I feel the Trinity rejoicing in me, and the Godhead jubilating in [my] mind, and my own spirit becomes one with the Beloved, how do you think I could receive the chalice from the sacristan, or taste it?'

The author adds that Ida had other things to say about something that had happened to her, but these he omits in deference to us intellectual simpletons. Since Ida's distinction between the rejoicing of the Trinity and the jubilation of the Godhead is already straining the limits of orthodoxy, one suspects that it is less our stupidity than the boldness of Ida's formulation that gives the author pause. We think, of course, of Meister Eckhart and the difficulties occasioned by his theological formulations. His disciple, the sweet Suso, insisted that these admitted of an orthodox interpretation. But not everyone was as convinced of this as Suso. Here, however, we may note that Ida's reception of the Body and Blood of Christ has become a specifically *trinitarian* Communion. Asked on one occasion to comment on the union of her spirit with the Spirit of God, she compared it to a drop of water in a wineskin filled to the full with wine. It is possible, of course, to give this traditional image a perverse theological twist; but the author specifically notes that this simply means that there is no possible common measure between the infinite God and the finite created being.

Section 16 (Vita, pp. 121–122)

The next to final section, on Ida's *Understanding and the Abundance of Her Spiritual Consolation*, begins with the rather disgusting behavior of one of the sisters, who opens again and again Ida's closed eyelids during one of her ecstasies. Each time Ida's eyelids fly shut, 'because,' she later explains, 'my own spirit was not yet separated from the Spirit of God'. The clinical analyst of mystical phenomenon would suggest, as a more likely explanation, that Ida's eyes were probably closed at the moment she entered into ecstasy, and that in this state the body preserves the attitude in which it was when seized by the ecstasy. As for her intermittent inability to eat, Ida asks how eating is possible when one feels oneself so filled with God's sweetness that not so much as a hair could be ingested. A further query about the alternation of Ida's complexion between an extreme pallor and a ruddy glow during times of ecstasy is given a somewhat disconcerting answer: Ida's pallor suggests she is contemplating the Trinity; her ruddiness means she is contemplating the Sacred Humanity. The important thing to remember here is not her psychosomatic mutations of color, but rather the fact that hers is not a zen-type experience. There is an object of her contemplation. Her attention is not focussed on herself or on her psychological states or on nothing at all. She is wholly centered on God. When asked about what she experiences at the moment of Communion, she speaks of a reception of God (rather than simply Christ) into her soul, while at the same time she has absolute certitude that the true humanity and the perfect divinity are indwelling her mind and sweetly communicating themselves to her spirit. If the author's credentials were better than they are, we might ask if he intends a distinction between 'soul', 'mind', and 'spirit'. But, given the inconsistency of his terminology elsewhere, we would do well not to examine his terms too closely.

And now a reassuring note about the sister who has been acting as Ida's interlocutor. She claims that her nearness to Ida during her ecstasies strengthens her in her own efforts towards spiritual progress. This effect of Ida's contemplation on at least one member of the community should be noted. The same sister had further questions to ask about the overflow of spiritual delight into the bodily faculties. As for Ida herself, her invariable practice was to be reserved as to the content of her mystical experiences. The mere use of the word 'One' by Ida's companion, in conversations about the Trinity, was enough to plunge Ida into a state of silent meditation. Meanwhile, eating seems to have become more and more of a torture. There follows a reference to the episode already touched upon earlier, when the 'loss' of the usual Sunday grace resulted in Ida's claim not to be all that attached to graces of this sort in view of her deeper desire to live the ordinary life to the full. The final vignette shows us Ida lying abed shortly before Christmas, being overwhelmed by the trinitarian passages in Saint Augustine's treatises. The reference here is probably to the two sermons read on Thursday of Advent Ember Week, Pseudo-Augustine, *Sermon* 245, and Quodvultdeus, *Sermon* 4.[19] The same lessons read in church would have been read also in the infirmary by the sister appointed to read the Office aloud for the sake of the infirmary denizens.

Section 17 (Vita, pp. 123–124)

The death of Ida is wholly unremarkable. The final section is captioned *About the Ailing Virgin's Vision before Her Death, and about Her Death*. The section begins with some observations about Ida's physical transformation; it seemed at times that the onlooker could gaze straight into her inward being, whose light was breaking through the limitation of corporeity. When asked whether it would help her to talk about divine things during periods of spiritual torment from so much joy, Ida answered frankly that it would drive her mad. Only Communion could still the violence of what she was experiencing from within. Even so, insomnia became more and more chronic a problem. There is, in keeping with hagiographical tradition consecrated by long usage, a final diabolical apparition, but one easily disposed of. This fleeting appearance of the Evil One provides the author with the opportunity to describe briefly an earlier encounter of Ida with the Enemy, one of little consequence; and another, rather more dramatic one, in which her fervent prayers at the death-bed of an otherwise unidentified person resulted in the personal intervention of the Mother of mercy, Mary, and the consequent liberation of the moribund sufferer from the clutches of the Evil One. There is a final mention of Ida's personal reserve: she refuses to divulge at large certain things communicated privately to 'a certain man who was a religious', for fear of winning a reputation for being holy.

And so, knowing in advance the day of her death, she asks one of the nuns to lower her veil for her after her final Communion. The sister does so, but notes as she kneels beside the bed and moves the veil aside slightly, that Ida's eyes remain fixed upon some invisible object. She dies on the morrow, after fierce physical pain, but with her spirit of perfect devotion wholly unimpaired. That is all. She simply dies, in a manner as unremarkable as she would have liked to have lived. Ida's biographer has presented us with one of the most anti-climactic death-scenes in the whole of thirteenth-century hagiography.

CONCLUSION

Though I have already suggested in the opening page of this re-reading of the *Life* of Ida, that Sister Colman's study dispenses us from any need to sum up Ida's message for today, I wish to touch once more on the strange apparent contradiction that runs throughout much of this *Vita*: Ida is a woman eager to remain within the mainstream of quite ordinary day-to-day cistercian living, even while she is being swept up into a type of mystical experience over whose concomitant paramystical phenomena she has no control. One of the things that comes through with clarion-like intensity in almost all medieval cistercian sources is the conviction that the quite ordinary cistercian life is of itself an efficacious sacrament for one's total immersion in the mystery of Christ. In such a context, ecstasy can be inconvenient, even unwelcome. Still, not every monk or nun has lived in such a way as to be a convincing witness to this common doctrine of the first Cistercians. Most of us need the witness of someone like Ida: someone like ourselves in most respects, but one who has been touched in a more particular way by God as a sign of his presence and action in the lives of individuals and of communities. People like Ida seem to experience in a more plenary manner what is actually the substance of our own life in Christ. Such persons have not only returned to something of the first innocence of Eden, they are already tasting the fruits of the Kingdom already accessible to us here and now, even if not yet in all its fullness.

Towards the end of C. S. Lewis' Narnia chronicle, *The Voyage of the Dawn Treader*, there is a lovely passage where the talking beast, the fabled mouse Reepicheep, symbol of the true contemplative, passes beyond the World's End into the uttermost East. As Lewis explains it, Reepicheep's *pascha* is somehow a condition for breaking the enchantment that holds certain lords of Narnia in a deep sleep of oblivion. But there is a sleep of obliviousness that casts a spell over our own world, and we need our Reepicheeps and our Idas who are willing and eager to pass beyond the World's End and to help make us more aware, in our moments of greater lucidity and wakefulness, of the presence and action of Christ in our lives and in our communities. For, in the final analysis, this is what Ida was for the sisters of la Ramée: a sign of the seriousness of God's love; a sign of the seriousness of his intention to draw us experientially into the fullness of his life; a sign, for our greater comfort and encouragement, that even here and now, in the midst of the ordinary, Christ is present and acting.

NOTES

1. 'Ida of Léau: Woman of Desire,' in this same volume, pp. 415–443.

2. *Quinque Prudentes Virgines* (Antwerp, 1630) 440–458.

3. L'Hagiographie cistercienne dans le diocèse de Liège au XIIIe Siècle (Louvain-Bruxelles, 1947) 60.

4. Roisin, *L'Hagiographie*, p. 60.

5. De Buck, pp. 108–109. All references are to the edition in the Bollandist *Acta Sanctorum*.

6. Karl Rahner, *I remember. An Autobiographical Interview with Meinold Krauss*, trans. H. D. Egan, sj (New York: Crossroad, 1985) 107–108.

7. But see J.-M. Canivez, *Statuta Capitulorum Generalium Ordinis Cisterciensis* 2 (Louvain, 1934), anno 1260, stat. 6, p. 462, where the norm is a minimum of seven communions a year (the same number prescribed for laybrothers).

8. *Vita*, p. 113, Col. 1, para. 19–20. Cf. Henriquez, *Quinque Prudentes Virgines* (Antwerp, 1630) 448.

9. *Vita* (in *Acta Sanctorum* Oct., XIII), p. 122, para. 52.

10. Thomas Merton, *What are These Wounds?* (Milwaukee: Bruce, 1950) 158–159.

11. Thomas Merton, 'The Transforming Union in St Bernard and St John of the Cross', first published in a series of installments in *Collectanea O.C.R.* (April and July, 1948; January and October, 1949; January, 1959), and later published anew in *Thomas Merton on Saint Bernard*, CS 9 (Kalamazoo: Cistercian Publications, 1980) 161–240.

12. A. Tanquerey, *The Spiritual Life. A Treatise on Ascetical and Mystical Theology*, trans. H. Branderis (Westminster, Md: Newman Press, 2nd ed., s.d.).

13. Tanquerey, p. 690.

14. Gregory the Great, *Dialogues*, Bk II, ch. 33.

15. Tanquerey, p. 685, n. 1456 a.

16. Wednesday of Holy Week until the Sunday after Easter.

17. Tanquerey, p. 693.

18. After the receiving the sacrament from the chalice, the communicant drank a wine ablution, as prescribed by the Usages (*Ecclesiastica Officia*), Chapter 58: Regredientibus ab altari sacrista stans incapite sinistri chori noviciorum ninum propinet . . . ; 'Let the sacristan, standing to the left at the head of the novice's choir, offer wine to those returning from the altar. . . . ' See also Fulgence Schneider, ocr, *L'Ancienne Messe Cistercienne* (Tilbourg, Netherlands: Abbaye N.-D. de Koninghoeven, 1929) 206.

19. PL 39:2196–2198; PL 42:1123–1127.

Gertrud of Helfta: Her Monastic Milieu and Her Spirituality

Miriam Schmitt OSB

AMERICAN BENEDICTINE PRIORESSES in their contemporary monastic document, *Of All Good Gifts*, affirm that the central elements of monastic life are community and contemplative vision, the inner power to 'see with the heart of Christ'.[1] The spirituality of Gertrud of Helfta (1256–1301/2), a benedictine mystic known also as Saint Gertrud the Great, focuses on precisely this seeing and loving with the heart of Christ.

This study begins by examining the contemplative environment of Helfta which shaped Gertrud: its origin and founders, the extant writings of its members, the forces making it unique, and the mysticism which characterized it in the thirteenth century. Next, I will locate Gertrud in this setting, describing her early life in the monastic community and her own account of her conversion experience. Most importantly, I will focus on her contemplative spirituality—an integration of Scripture, liturgy, and mysticism with the teachings of the Rule of Benedict—as exemplified in her writings, *The Herald of God's Loving-Kindness* and *Spiritual Exercises*.[2]

HELFTA AND ITS SPIRITUAL LEGACY

The Origins of Helfta

The monastery of Saint Mary, later to be at Helfta, was founded in Saxony in 1229 by Elizabeth of Schwartzburg and her husband Burchard, count of Mansfeld, within their castle precincts. Cunegunde, abbess from 1229 to 1251, came to Mansfeld to establish the new foundation with seven companions from the nearby monastery of Saints James and Burchard at Halberstadt. During this time of baronial feuds, proximity to any castle was hazardous. In 1234, at the suggestion of Countess Elizabeth, now widowed, the community moved to safer and more suitable surroundings in nearby Rodarsdorf. Shortly afterward, the countess herself came to live there and remained until her death in 1240.

Because the rapidly growing community needed more adequate water resources and additional space to accommodate new members, Abbess Gertrude of Hackeborn,[3] who succeeded Cunegunde in 1251, moved the community seven years later from Rodarsdorf to Helfta near Eisleben, on land donated by her two brothers, Albert and Louis. On the Sunday following the feast of the Holy Trinity in 1258, Bishop Vulrad of Halberstadt, in the presence of Rupert, archbishop of Magdeburg, and many other prelates, as well as relatives and friends of the nuns, dedicated the new church to Mary and the monastery to Saint Benedict.[4] During his visit Vulrad presided at the reception as novices of Sophia and Elizabeth, granddaughters of the founders, and he also received the profession of vows of some novices during the eucharistic celebration.[5] The new site proved to be an environment conducive to contemplation and allowed the community to be relatively self-sufficient. Their land was fertile, gently sloping, and blessed with streams flowing into the lake of Seeburg.

For centuries the question has been debated: was the Helfta community benedictine or cistercian? Contemporary scholars of medieval monasticism now generally agree that Helfta was firmly inserted into the benedictine tradition. Charters and other documents prove that Helfta could not have been officially incorporated into the Cistercian Order: a statute of 1220 specifically decreed that no more monasteries of women be added; and in 1228, the year before Helfta was founded, the Cistercian General Chapter reiterated this prohibition in even more precise terms.[6] The cistercian emphasis on nuptial mysticism and on asceticism influenced Helfta's spirit, however, especially in the community's early years.

The Extant Writings of Helfta

Four literary works written at Helfta in the late thirteenth century constitute the largest body of extant mystical literature produced by women of this period. In some twelve hundred pages are found the visionary experiences of three mystics: Gertrud the Great and her two friends, the nun Mechtild of Hackeborn and the beguine Mechtild of Magdeburg. *The Flowing Light of the Godhead* echoes the mystical experiences of Mechtild of Magdeburg.[7] The life and revelations of Mechtild of Hackeborn are recorded in *The Book of Special Grace*.[8] The other two literary works, *The Herald of God's Loving-Kindness* and *Spiritual Exercises*, depict the life and mysticism of Gertrud.

The Herald of God's Loving-Kindness is a collaborative work attributed to Gertrud, although of its five books only the second came from her pen. In these pages, Gertrud not only counsels readers outside the cloister but also shares her mystical insights with present and future Helfta members. The first book is a memorial tribute to Gertrud, written by one of the Helfta nuns after her death. In the second, Gertrud recorded her spiritual autobiography. At the behest of Christ, she describes her visionary encounters over a period of nine years.[9] The final three books, compiled by one or several Helfta nuns, are dictated notes and recollections. They present Gertrud's mystic union with God (Book Three), her reflections on the liturgical feasts and seasons (Book Four), accounts of the preparation for death made by Mechtild of Hackeborn and by Gertrud, and an explanation of the Great Psalter as an intercessory prayer for the deceased nuns and benefactors of Helfta (Book Five).

The *Spiritual Exercises*, composed entirely by Gertrud, is her masterpiece. These seven devotional exercises, an artistic blend of meditations, ritual prayers, psalms, antiphonal chants, hymns, and litanies, are rooted in the liturgical rites that formed the core of her spirituality. Its principal themes echo the decisive events in her vocation as a Christian and a Benedictine: the renewal of her christian initiation; her monastic investiture, profession, and consecration as a nun of Helfta; a celebration of spiritual nuptials based on the canonical hours and expressed in her own hymns of joy and praise, the *benedicat* and *jubilus*;[10] and, lastly, her meditation on death, a face-to-face encounter with God in glory.

Gertrud composed these *Spiritual Exercises* for her own yearly use, but they were quickly adopted by others. In a sense this masterpiece, 'a true jewel among medieval spiritual prose pieces',[11] is a classic not only because of Gertrud's insights on prayer but also because of her exquisite literary style.

Gertrud's uniquely feminine approach to God is relevant in our age, when the Church is experiencing an unprecedented interest in feminist theology and, appropriately enough, a new appreciation of the writings of medieval women mystics. With rare creativity,

Gertrud provides exemplary approaches to prayer for us today. Through a profusion of imagery—biblical, catholic, and lovingly bold in language—she shows her readers how to pray in forms which transcend sexist, temporal, or spatial limits. Her contemplative vision is the fruit of her urgent desire 'to see with the heart of Christ'.[12]

Formative Influences on the Spirituality of Helfta

Aside from Scripture, the preeminent source of all christian life and prayer, the Rule of Benedict doubtless exercised a pivotal influence on the Helfta Benedictines. In Gertrud, as her writings attest, the Rule inspires contemplative prayer, the resting in God which Benedict describes as 'pure prayer'.[13] Here Benedict has borrowed from the writings of John Cassian (c 360–435) on 'pure' and 'fiery' prayer of the heart, *oratio pura*.[14] Cassian repeatedly emphasizes that 'purity of heart' is the immediate goal of monastics and 'life eternal' their ultimate end.[15] In fixing their gaze steadily on the proximate aim as if on a definite mark or prize, monastics strive to direct their course as straight as possible toward God, their ultimate end.[16] Benedict links purity of heart with tears of compunction as absolute requisites for approaching God in prayer when he writes, 'We know that God regards our purity of heart and tears of compunction, not our many words'.[17] He also exhorts the entire community during 'Lent to keep its manner of life most pure'.[18] Since Benedict twice urges his monks to read the *Conferences* and *Institutes* of Cassian,[19] it is plausible that Gertrud was acquainted with these writings; at least she knew implicitly of Cassian's teaching regarding 'purity of heart' because of her familiarity with the Rule.

Gertrud's prayer, whether liturgical, devotional, or contemplative, emphasizes a similar singleminded intentness on God through 'purity of heart'.[20] Her plea for this gift is mentioned frequently, not only in *The Herald*, but also in all seven Exercises.[21] In renewing her milestones of christian initiation, monastic investiture, and consecration as a nun, Gertrud desires purity primarily as a 'chaste freedom in the spirit' applicable to body, soul, mind, and heart.[22] Gertrud compares her desire to empty and rivet her heart on God with the freedom of doves 'wheeling in flight' which she observed in Helfta's courtyard:

> Moreover, if I looked down on the things of earth and, in free flight like the doves, sought the things of heaven, and if my outer self with its bodily senses were held aloof from hustle and bustle,

my mind would be completely at your disposal and my heart would offer you a dwelling-place with all that is pleasant and joyful.[23]

Her *Exercises*, particularly her ritual in preparation for death, contain numerous petitions, for the gift of a singlehearted intent on God. She entreats Jesus repeatedly to be totally cleansed at the moment of her crossing over into eternity:

> My cherished one, by the pure tears of your brightest eyes, wash away all spots of the sins of my eyes, that, at the termination of my life, without hindrance and with the clean eye of my heart I may see your most dulcet face in the mirror of the Holy Trinity, for you alone are the one I desire with all my heart.[24]

From explicit and implicit references in the writings of all the Helfta mystics, it is evident that they knew some of the writings of Bernard of Clairvaux (1090–1153).[25] These Helfta nuns, or some of them, reverenced Bernard's teachings on bridal mysticism, *brautmystik*, found primarily in his sermons *On the Song of Songs*.[26] Gertrud often voices admiration and love for Bernard, above all when he appeared to her on 20 August, his feast;[27] she indicates, however, that not all the other Helfta nuns shared her admiration for his teachings. Even though some parallel aspects are evident in their mystical writings based on the Song of Songs, Gertrud's spirituality is singularly liturgical and markedly benedictine in orientation. Unique to Gertrud is her fusion of the liturgical with the biblical and the mystical. In her use of explicit bernardine quotes and frequent allusions, she manifests neither a dependence on nor an undue influence by Bernard but develops her own gertrudian style and meaning of mystical texts with a distinctive freedom of heart. As an example, she quotes Bernard directly in describing God's relentless pursuit of her during the brief time when she experiences the loss of God's presence for an eleven-day period:

> As we flee you pursue us; we turn our backs and you run to meet us face to face; you plead but are scorned. But no embarrassment or scorn can turn you aside or stop you from acting unwearyingly to draw us to that joy which eye has not seen, not ear heard, and which has not risen into the heart of man.[28]

A recent study of the relationship between the writings of Bernard and Gertrud, regarding their emphasis on nuptial mysticism, concludes that: 'In the absence of further evidence or better judgment, . . . direct literary influence from Bernard was neither significantly present nor significantly absent' in the work of Gertrud.[29]

The four extant literary works of the Helfta mystics make frequent
allusions to other writers as well: Origen (c 185–c 254), Augustine
(354–430), Gregory the Great (540–604), Bede (673–735), Hugh
of Saint Victor (1096–1141), and even Thomas Aquinas (1225–
1274) and Albert the Great (1200–1280).[30] Regarding the two last
mentioned, Thomas and Albert, the Helfta community may well
have imbibed their teachings because of the dominican friars who
probably ministered to them toward the end of the thirteenth century. One reason for this was the proximity of Helfta to Halle and
Magdeburg, two centers from which the Dominicans traveled to
surrounding areas. A second reason is an order of Pope Innocent
III (1254), a decree of the Chapter of Florence (1256), and the
recommendation of Herman of Minden, provincial of the Friars
Preachers from 1286 to 1290—all three required that learned friars
be the spiritual directors, not only of dominican nuns, but also those
of other orders.[31]

Principal Mentors of Gertrud in the Helfta Community

Gertrud's writings indicate her sense of indebtedness to three
members of her benedictine community for her own spiritual formation. These were: Abbess Gertrude of Hackeborn (1232–1291);
Gertrude's sister, Mechtild of Hackeborn (1241/2–1298); and the
beguine Mechtild of Magdeburg (1207?–1282). In varying ways,
all influenced Gertrud—the first by her guidance as abbess, and
the other two by their encouragement, friendship, and exemplary
mysticism.

The first of her mentors, Abbess Gertrude of Hackeborn, entered Rodarsdorf before she was sixteen; the exact date is uncertain.
When Abbess Cunegunde died in 1251, this nineteen-year-old was
unanimously elected abbess of the monastic community she was
to govern for forty years. As we have indicated, the first years of
Helfta's existence were rather unsettled because of the frequent
moves to safer locations, together with the anxiety and risk the nuns
experienced in the civil and ecclesiastical turmoil surrounding them.

As in most other german monastic houses of that day, Helfta's
members were, with few exceptions, daughters or kinswomen of
highborn saxon and thuringian families. Surnames such as Mansfeld, Halberstadt, Hackeborn, Wippra, Schwartzburg, Querfort, and
Stolberg occur frequently in historical accounts of Helfta.[32] Nobility
of birth played an important role in medieval monasteries: it affected
acceptance of members, the selection of superiors, abbatial elections,

and even the economic, social, and political status of monasteries generally.

The forty-year reign of Abbess Gertrude, considered the golden age of Helfta, was remarkable for a flowering of nuptial mysticism. Under her wise and courageous leadership, Helfta became an intellectual and cultural center renowned for its love of learning manifested in the nuns' mastery of the latin classics, schooling in the seven liberal arts, and appreciation of Scripture. The abbess 'was known to say that if the study of letters should be neglected, soon the Scriptures would no longer be understood and monastic life would begin to decay'.[33] Her vibrant monastic community, the 'crown of German cloisters',[34] quickly gained a reputation for its liturgical celebrations, eucharistic piety, and devotion to the humanity of Christ Jesus.

The abbess inspired in the Helfta nuns a fidelity to the monastic practices of *lectio divina* and *oratio*. She urged them to memorize biblical texts, including the entire Psalter. They were to ponder, savor, and treasure the Scriptures to nurture their prayer life. Because she encouraged the spiritual development of her sisters, she left a deep imprint on the contemplative spirit at Helfta and particularly on her most renowned disciple, Gertrud. That the cultivation of biblical study and monastic prayer bore fruit in Gertrud of Helfta in the thirty years she lived under the direction of Abbess Gertrude, will be illustrated later.

Mechtild of Hackeborn was the second Helfta member who significantly influenced Gertrud by her friendship. Mechtild came with her mother to Rodarsdorf at the age of seven to visit her sister Gertrude, who was nine years her senior and who would within three years be elected abbess. Little Mechtild insisted on remaining there and was allowed to enroll as a student at Rodarsdorf in 1248. Years later, she made her monastic profession; the exact date is not known. Because of her musical gifts, Mechtild became known as the 'Nightingale of Christ'. Duly appointed *Domna Cantrix* (Lady Chantress), Mechtild served her community not only as choir director for forty years, but also as instructor of novices, teacher and counselor.[35]

When Mechtild was seriously ill during her fiftieth year (1291), she recounted her mystical experiences to two confidantes. Without her knowledge or approval, Abbess Sophia, who governed Helfta from 1291 to 1298, commissioned the pair to compile Mechtild's lyrical outpourings in a manuscript now known as *The Book of Special Grace*. Later, when Mechtild learned of its existence, she gave her consent to the disclosure of these intimate exchanges, but only after she had conversed with Christ on the matter.[36] The book's literary style and latinity are so similar to those found in the writings of Gertrud that she is today considered to have been its principal compiler.[37] The writings of both saints reveal that Mechtild of Hackeborn was not only Gertrud's well-loved teacher and mentor, but continued to be a cherished lifelong friend.

Thirdly, there is Mechtild of Magdeburg, who renounced her status as a member of the nobility to become a fiery yet humble beguine. She is a remarkable character, although not honored in the calendar of benedictine saints as are Mechtild of Hackeborn and Gertrud of Helfta. The beguines, originating as a lay movement in the Low Countries, had by the end of the twelfth century developed into semi-religious communities without dowry or cloister. They lived an austere communal life, but took no vows and had no common rule. Consequently, they were free to own property, leave the community at will, or marry. Theirs was a twofold goal: contemplative prayer and ministry to the needy.

Mechtild was moved to denounce the irreligious living and moral laxity of the clergy and religious of Magdeburg, and so provoked their hostility. Forced to flee Magdeburg in 1285 when she was seventy-five, she took refuge with the Helfta nuns for the last twelve years of her life.

The Flowing Light of the Godhead, written by Mechtild on loose sheets of paper in a low german dialect, describes her mystic union with God. In its seven sections, we find in both prose and verse, accounts of her visions, revelations, thoughts, and correspondence. The first six books were completed by Mechtild between the years 1265 and 1285, while she was a beguine at Magdeburg. Henry of Halle, her dominican friend and a former student of Albert the Great, is believed to have served as her spiritual director, since it was he who compiled and arranged her notes—but not chronologically.[38] He also translated them from 'the original *barbara lingua* [low german] into latin,' and circulated the first six parts of her book during her lifetime.[39] Because Mechtild became blind shortly after coming to Helfta, she dictated the seventh book there, with the encouragement of her dominican director and her benedictine friends.

Since Mechtild of Magdeburg had been formed in a non-monastic milieu under Dominicans, mendicant preachers committed primarily to apostolic ministry, her *brautmystik* differs from that of Gertrud the Great and Mechtild of Hackeborn. Their lives had been shaped in the monastic environment of Helfta, where they had lived since the ages of five and seven respectively. Caroline Bynum seems correct in observing that medieval monastic women who entered the cloister as children tended to develop 'a poised, self-confident, lyrical female mysticism', whereas those who entered religious life as adults were 'influenced by the contemporary stereotype of women as morally and intellectually inferior'.[40]

However dissimilar her background and brief her stay with the Helfta nuns, Mechtild of Magdeburg left a deep imprint on their spirituality during those twelve years. Her mysticism is, in comparison with that of the other Helfta mystics, erotic in its nuptial imagery. In her lyrics, she uses the romantic language of courtly and chivalrous love to describe her ecstatic union with God. Her focus is on the apocalyptic and prophetic, in the visionary tradition of Hildegard of Bingen (1098–1179) and Elizabeth of Schönau (1129–1164). It contrasts, therefore, with the mysticism of Gertrud of Helfta and Mechtild of Hackeborn, which, though nuptial in imagery, employs the biblical and liturgical symbols dear to monastic spirituality and echoes the lyricism and language found in the Song of Songs.

LIFE AND CONVERSION OF GERTRUD THE GREAT

Gertrud's Early Life at Helfta

Gertrud of Helfta, born on Epiphany, 6 January 1256, was entrusted at the age of five to the care of Abbess Gertrude of Hackeborn, and enrolled in the cloister school at Helfta. Nothing at all is known of her family roots or the circumstancess which prompted her to come to Helfta; her writings vaguely imply that she may have been an orphan.[41] Her friendship with the two Hackeborn sisters, Mechtild and Abbess Gertrude, provided a dynamic force in forming the intellectual vision of the brilliant young student. She was outstanding for her love of study, especially of the literary classics of her day. Her closeness to Mechtild, even though there was an age difference of fifteen years, grew ever stronger as they shared their lives as cenobites, their choir duties as cantors—Gertrud was second chantress—and their mystical experiences.

Since Gertrud lacks a recorded surname, she was, in all probability, of peasant origin and, therefore, an exception to the elitist monastic practice of admitting only highborn women.[42] This may well have contributed to the later incorrect though pervasive identification of Gertrud with Abbess Gertrude of Hackeborn. The error, originating in the sixteenth century, is still prevalent in printed works and in iconography that depicts her with an abbatial staff.[43] Jean Leclercq offers a probable reason for this posthumous elevation of Gertrud into an abbess with the unique designation of 'the Great'—a title accorded to no other woman in Germany:

> It seems very likely that St Gertrud the Great, in the second half of the thirteenth century, could not become abbess at Helfta because she was not of noble birth. This did not, however, prevent her from having lofty spiritual experiences and a great theological message. Thus the value of what she wrote did not come from any secular influence she might have had but from her intrinsic gifts as a common sister. As this was almost unthinkable, however, she was made a posthumous abbess in the sixteenth century, thanks to an easy confusion with her own abbess, Gertrude of Hackeborn, and in the romantic nineteenth century, she was considered 'the great abbess' (*die grosse Abtissen*).[44]

The exact dates of Gertrud's reception into the benedictine community at Helfta, of her monastic profession, and of her consecration are not known. Monastic profession usually occurred around age sixteen;[45] it always preceded the consecration rite, a solemn ceremony permitted only after reaching the age of religious maturity, generally at the completion of the twenty-fifth year.[46] In Gertrud's own account, written years later, she tells of her conversion and describes herself as having been a nun in name and appearance only until her conversion: too long, she says, she had given priority to intellectual and literary pursuits over contemplative prayer.

Gertrud's Conversion

In Advent of 1280, when Gertrud experienced unrest because of her deviation from the benedictine ideal through 'vainglory, curiosity, and pride',[47] there came a dramatic shift. It marked the beginning of a truly spiritual journey. Her conversion is presented to readers in a progressive series of events: initiated in Advent, deepened on Epiphany—6 January, her twenty-fifth birthday—and decisively consummated two months later, on 27 January 1281.[48] It is conceivable that this conversion experience coincided with her consecration, since Gertrud was now of the requisite age for this rite, and Epiphany was one of the recommended feasts for the celebration of this ceremonial blessing.[49] At least one thing is clear: her lifelong love for the feast of Epiphany.

After Compline on 27 January, Gertrud later relates, in a vision she beheld Christ, 'a lovable and fine-featured youth of about sixteen years', placing his right hand in hers and confronting her because of her sadness, mediocrity, and laxity: 'You have licked the dust with my enemies, and you have sucked honey amidst thorns'.[50] Christ continued, however, with this reassuring promise: 'Return now to me—I will receive you, and inebriate you with the torrent of my celestial delights'.[51] As Christ lifts Gertrud over the thorny and otherwise insurmountable hedge separating them, she noticed the wounds in his hands. She writes of her ensuing awareness of the immanent presence of Christ: 'a friend living with a friend or a bridegroom with his bride'.[52] Following this unforgettable encounter, Gertrud begins using the vocatives, 'God of my heart' and 'God of my life', invocations which later become her 'mantras', repeated frequently in her writings. This mystical event changed Gertrud from a seeker of intellectual delights into an ardent Godseeker, ever yearning to behold the face of God.

Contemplative Environment of Gertrud at Helfta

Gertrud's writings are evidence that after this conversion experience, her attitude was transformed; she regarded Helfta no longer as an intellectual and cultural center, but rather as a house of contemplative prayer. The monastic setting became the environment which nurtured her God-experience.

Gertrud's perspective on time and place also changed. All places now were sacred to her; all times and activities holy, not only those involving worship. Even though her visions often occurred in the oratory, they also took place in the garden, the dormitory, the chapter room, and the refectory. Gertrud experienced these mystical encounters before, during, or immediately after liturgical celebrations; sometimes they came as she performed her assigned work; they occurred even when she was ill. Various prayerful activities—chanting psalmody, singing antiphons or hymns, pondering the Scriptures, reflecting or praying silently—often served as preludes to her visions.

CHARACTERISTICS OF GERTRUD'S SPIRITUALITY

Use of Biblical Sources and Imagery

We have located Gertrud within the contemplative setting of Helfta and seen the transformation effected by her conversion-crisis. We are now ready to explore in greater depth her prayer and spirituality: an integration of the biblical, liturgical, and mystical

within the context of her cenobitic life. We begin with the biblical
Word of God, the wellspring of her contemplative vision.

Gertrud the Great quotes Scripture extensively in *The Herald*
but even more frequently in the *Spiritual Exercises*.[53] Numerous
direct references, as well as allusions to and paraphrases of biblical
passages, indicate the breadth of her knowledge. One of the Helfta
nuns, in a tribute to Gertrud, praises her for having shared the fruit
of her intense study of Scripture and patristics with others: 'The
basket of her heart she packed to the very top with the more useful,
and honey-sweet, texts of holy Scripture, so that she always had at
hand an instructive and holy quotation'.[54]

Gertrud's appreciation for the Psalter is evident in the *Exercises*;
all but two, the second and third, are rife with quoted psalms.
She cites more than sixty of them, and incorporates seven in their
entirety.[55] There are thirteen other psalms she quotes frequently,
having selected them as milestones of her spiritual journey.[56] Three
chapters in the final book of *The Herald* are devoted to the Great
Psalter: the efficacy of praying the entire Book of Psalms, and
its intercessory value in suffrages for the deceased.[57] The Great
Psalter was Gertrud's term for all one hundred fifty psalms with
introductory and concluding prayers, as well as refrains alternating
with every verse of each psalm. Gertrud recommended praying the
entire Psalter in times of adversity (the threat of an armed attack on
Helfta)[58] and on joyous occasions (the feast of St. Benedict).[59]

Since Gertrud's visions and contemplative experiences are couched
primarily in nuptial imagery, it is not surprising that she frequently
quotes the Song of Songs. She refers to this book in all seven of
the *Exercises*, but particularly in the third and fifth: 'Dedication of
the Self' by espousals and consecration; and 'Mystical Union' in
divine love. Both emphasize the tradition of *brautmystik* in Gertrud's
renewal of her ritual consecration to Christ.

The most lyrical passages in her writings center on two themes:
the Trinity; and the mediation of Christ. Gertrud depends mainly
on the New Testament, particularly Revelation, Matthew, Luke,
and John, for a variety of inclusive and complementary images for
God. Through an apt selection of biblical symbols, she emphasizes
now the transcendent and again the immanent dimensions of God's
presence; at times she interweaves them, in accord with her God-
experience.

Her prayers addressing the transcendent God include an abundance of abstract nouns juxtaposed to superlative adjectives, and
numerous concrete biblical names and symbols. Among her favorite

expressions for the *God-Beyond* is the phrase, 'the ever-peaceful, refulgent, and resplendent Trinity'.[60] The Father is frequently addressed as the 'abyss of omnipotent power',[61] the Word as 'inscrutable wisdom' or 'abyss of uncreated wisdom',[62] and the Spirit as 'amazing charity',[63] 'ocean of charity',[64] or 'uncreated love'.[65]

Gertrud emphasizes the nearness of God in Jesus Christ by using light, fire, and creation-centered imagery such as 'eternal solstice', 'continual fountain of inestimable pleasures', 'eternal springtime', 'Paradise of unchanging delights',[66] and 'imperial morning star, fulgent with divine brightness'.[67] Cyprian Vagaggini, commenting on the pendulum-like swing between Christ and the Trinity exemplified in her prayer, writes:

> The center and apex of Gertrud's attention is not simply Christ, nor simply the Trinity; her mind follows a Christological-Trinitarian movement. Gertrud's mental process goes ceaselessly from Christ to the Trinity, in respect to which she makes frequent use of the formula *fulgida semperque tranquilla Trinitas*, and to which she likes to make reference in terms of the liturgical formulas of the feast of the Trinity.[68]

Because benedictine spirituality is dependent upon *lectio divina* and is centered in the scriptural-liturgical celebrations of Word and Sacrament, we expect to find scriptural imagery in Gertrud's writings. In composing her seven *Spiritual Exercises*, Gertrud integrated the symbolism derived from pondering the biblical Word with her liturgical experiences, transforming them into pure *oratio*. Her literary works are molded by the benedictine tradition of monastic spirituality which, until the thirteenth century, found in Scripture and liturgy its source of eucharistic piety, imagery, and mysticism. The *Spiritual Exercises* and *The Herald* are formed around the liturgy with its various rites and rituals; even the chapter headings indicate this inspiration and integration. The qualities of monastic prayer described by Benedict in his Rule—purity and humility of heart, a singlehearted intent on God, a heart expanded by love, compunction of heart manifested in tears—all these permeate Gertrud's devotional writings.[69]

In composing her prayer rituals, Gertrud employs imagery rooted in the sensory experiences of her familiar monastic environs. This is not surprising, since she never stepped beyond the boundaries of Helfta after her entrance at age five. A sampling of the concrete, everyday images permeating her writings include: 'roses without thorns, lilies white as snow and fragrant violets',[70] 'clear and flowing stream',[71] a dove making 'its nest in the crevice of the rock',[72] and 'wax softened by fire, impressed like a seal upon the bosom of the Lord'.[73]

Gertrud's use of biblical symbolism, although frequently oriented to her yearning for face-to-face communion with God, sprang from the reality in which she lived: 'Make me completely whatever you want me to be so that after this life, having left behind the cloud of my body, I may in jubilation see your mellifluous face'.[74]

In the jubilantly lyrical canticles of the sixth *Exercise*, Gertrud integrates bridal imagery with song and instrumental music appropriate to the joyful sound of cithara, cymbal, lyre, psaltery, and organ. These hymns are marked by parallel passages and a refrain of either *benedicat*, 'bless the Lord', or *jubilet*, 'praise the Lord', in anaphoras blessing God or proclaiming joyous praise. The mystical *jubilus*—jubilant praise and thanksgiving for God's goodness—'anticipates the eternal radiant praise before the face of the Lord'.[75] The *jubilus* can be partially illustrated in the following lines, excerpted from one of the more than twenty-four hymns, uniting the entire universe in extended jubilation of God:

> May all your miraculous works, whatever is grasped within the
> circumference of heaven, earth, and the abyss, be jubilant to you
> and forever give you that praise which, going out from you, flows
> back into you, its source.[76]

Biblical Personages Envisioned During the Liturgy

Gertrud often writes of her mystical encounters with biblical characters of both covenants, and also with saints whose feasts are celebrated in the liturgical calendar. Their frequency gives her visions a cosmic dimension and unites her with the celestial throng and the earthly pilgrim church. Her ponderings range from Abraham, the first biblical patriarch, to John the Beloved. They include saints of christian times, beginning with John the Baptist and including not only Thomas Aquinas, her contemporary, but also recently deceased members of her own Helfta community. With each yearly recurrence of the liturgical seasons and feasts, Gertrud immersed herself ever more deeply in the paschal mystery of Christ in his members now glorified. By pondering the holiness of her God mediated to her through his saints, she had a foretaste of the celestial liturgy while still on earth. In the examples cited below, I will focus on biblical characters rather than on her visions of saints or of deceased contemporaries unfamiliar to us in the twentieth century.

Gertrud identifies with three matriarchs of hebraic times and four New Testament women. Of the former, she points to the unique blessedness of Rachel for her loving kindness and of Lia for her fruitfulness;[77] more frequently, she dwells on Esther for her 'incredible beauty' and her power of supplication.[78] She admires Martha and Mary offering hospitality to Jesus at Bethany;[79] Mary Magdalen searching for the God she loved passionately;[80] and of course, Mary, the glorious Mother of Jesus and the 'Empress of Heaven'.[81]

Gertrud notes the similarities of her own mission to that of the messianic prophets—Jeremiah, Isaiah, and Elisha—[82] and the apocalyptic prophet, Ezekiel.[83] Beginning with Noah, she finds exemplars in many biblical patriarchs, including Isaac, Jacob, Joseph, and Benjamin.[84] Because Gertrud desired to work zealously to extend the reign of God and to see God face to face, she prays to Moses, blest with a singular face-to-face vision of God,[85] and to Aaron, whose rod of power[86] signifies for her that good zeal which all Benedictines should radiate.[87] Aware of her need to be ever grateful to divine goodness, she likens herself to David and Solomon.[88] Gertrud, a cloistered gentile commoner and a woman, does not hesitate to compare herself to the royal heroes of ancient Israel.

Her mystical encounters with apostles, disciples, and evangelists—countless friends of Jesus—impelled her to compose hymns of praise emphasizing the unique relationship of each person with the Saviour. Gertrud favored as particularly significant Joseph, the spouse of Mary and protector of Jesus, and John the Baptizer, the zealous preacher of repentance for the conversion of sinners.[89] She implored a blessing from Peter and Paul, apostles and mediators of God, that she might receive some measure of their power to forgive.[90] Lastly, Gertrud had a special devotion to John the Beloved, whom she saw as a paradigm of the disciple's love of Christ. As she explains, John not only received the gift of highest contemplation, but also exercised profound humility when entrusted at the death of Jesus to be a filial protector of Mary, Jesus' mother.[91] Gertrud identifies with John primarily because he was her contemplative model, resting his head on the heart of Christ at the Last Supper; she sees her own loving communion with God as a mystical bonding.[92] The exchange of hearts[93] between Christ and Gertrud is described in a vision wherein Christ shows Gertrud his heart, saying: 'My beloved, give me your heart', and even promises to use her 'heart as a canal' to pour forth torrents of compassion on all seeking help from him through her.[94] Gertrud writes of this mutually abiding indwelling:

You have also granted me your intimate friendship, by opening the sacred ark of your divinity—I mean your divine heart—to me in so many ways, as to be the source of all my happiness; sometimes imparting it freely, sometimes, as a special mark of our mutual friendship, exchanging it for mine.[95]

The Transforming Effects of the Liturgy

Gertrud's fidelity to *lectio divina* provided both a continuous preparation for the liturgical celebrations of Helfta and also the fountainhead from which her mysticism flowed. Her prayer of the heart is intertwined with the liturgical life observed at Helfta. Faithful to their benedictine heritage, these nuns regarded the Eucharist and the Liturgy of the Hours as privileged actions, forming the symbolic summit of their cenobitism. Gertrud, mindful of the maxim in the Rule, 'Indeed, nothing is to be preferred to the Work of God',[96] shows concern that her devotional life be in harmony with the liturgy.[97] She even asks for the gift not to be so lost in ecstasy as to be unable to follow the community's rituals.[98]

Formed by the sacramental rites and rhythms of the liturgy, Gertrud was also transformed by their grace and sense of mystery. Liturgical celebrations constituted the framework of her spiritual experiences and set the rhythm of the day and week, culminating in the festivity of Sunday. The liturgical year, with its dual temporal and sanctoral cycles—seasons and feasts of saints—formed the framework of Helfta's monastic *horarium*. Even the accounts of their mystical experiences are arranged by both Gertrud and Mechtild of Hackeborn according to the events of the church year. Sundays and feasts are often named according to the first two latin words of the antiphon sung at the Eucharist or at a canonical hour. Some examples are *Esto Mihi* Sunday,[99] *Oculi* Sunday,[100] *Laetare* Sunday,[101] and *Ecce sponsus venit*, the Feast of the Eleven Thousand Virgins.[102]

The temporal cycle, with its dual focus on the yearly recurring Advent-Christmas-Epiphany and Lent-Easter-Pentecost mysteries, set the seasonal and annual rhythm for Helfta and therefore for Gertrud. Even though the Easter cycle is preeminent in the liturgical year, for Gertrud the celebration of God's Incarnation in Jesus at Christmas enjoyed particular significance because of her devotion to the humanity of Christ. As we have noted, she experienced her second conversion—and many subsequent graces—during this festal season.

Moving to the sanctoral cycle, we find that Gertrud's visionary experiences of the saints, recorded in the fourth book of *The Herald*, follows the same sequential pattern of the liturgical seasons as the temporal cycle. The feasts of saints, interwoven through the Sundays as they occur in the church calendar, were the occasions of numerous mystical graces for Gertrud.

For Gertrud, the liturgy revealed and also concealed, the central theme of her prayer, Christ, the incarnate deity. The celebration of Christ's paschal mystery in the Eucharist was, without a doubt, the apex of her mysticism, as it is of the christian life. The Eucharist as sacrifice is prominent in her thinking, yet she perceives it also as a meal, often in such figures as the festal banquet or the nurturing pelican.[103] When viewing the Mass as a sacrificial banquet, she lovingly offers herself with Christ as an oblation to God the Father for the members of the Helfta community and for the entire Church, especially sinners.

The moment of communion was often a mystical experience.[104] Repeatedly, as she participated at the eucharistic liturgy in Helfta's chapel, Gertrud, rapt in ecstatic vision, was conscious of her presence at the mystical Mass offered by Christ Jesus in the celestial court of heaven.[105] Gertrud could thus unite her contemplative prayer with the community's liturgical celebrations so that each enhanced and fructified the other. Cyprian Vagaggini describes Gertrud's intuitive apprehension of God as Love the 'mystical invasion' by the divine.[106]

Gertrud was deeply aware of the ordinary demands of community life at Helfta; after her conversion, she experienced a different mindfulness of God and union with Christ which 'all the eloquence in the world' could not adequately describe: 'I can neither fully express it by my feeble words, nor altogether pass it over in silence'.[107] She receives praise from Christ for her unique 'liberty of spirit'; it readies her to accept God's gifts at every moment and 'prevents her from attaching her heart to anything' which could either impede or displease him.[108] A renowned nineteenth-century liturgist characterizes Gertrud's inner journey as a constant tension between the abyss of humility and the summits of love:

> Sometimes she stops short in her sublimest flights, and she who almost rivals the seraphim descends to earth, but only to prepare herself for a still higher flight. It is as though there had been an unending struggle between the humility which held her prostrate in the dust and the aspirations of her soul, panting after Jesus, who was drawing her, and who had lavished on her such exceeding love.[109]

Gertrud's Mystical Graces

In the second book of *The Herald*, written over a period of nine years (1281–1290), Gertrud considers her conversion (described above) as her first mystical grace. Subsequently, she was to be granted an awareness of God's continuous indwelling of her spirit. Gertrud refers to her habitual awareness of God's presence in such terms as 'amazing charity', 'commerce of charity', 'ineffable charity', and 'amiable presence'.[110] This abiding, loving consciousness deserted her only once during the nine years—for eleven days before the Feast of John the Baptist (24 June). She attributed this loss to a worldly conversation, and confesses that she reached a 'pitch of madness' during this brief but painful relapse.[111]

Two other spiritual favors elicited deep gratitude to God from Gertrud: the imprint of Christ's wounds in her heart—sometimes referred to as spiritual stigmata—and the piercing of her heart by an arrow of divine love,[112] a phenomenon known to mystics as 'the wound of love'.[113] Gertrud recounts how she received the interior imprint of the five wounds of Christ while she was sitting in the refectory after Vespers, some time during the winter of the first or second year after her conversion experience:

> I perceived in spirit that you have imprinted in the depth of my heart the adorable marks of your sacred wounds, even as they are on your body; that you cured my soul, in imprinting these wounds on it; and that, to satisfy its thirst, you gave it the precious beverage of your love.[114]

It was seven years later, after she had received communion on the third Sunday of Advent that Gertrud received the initial stage of her second gift, the piercing of her heart by an arrow of divine love, 'as a ray of light like an arrow coming forth from the wound of the right side of the crucifix'.[115] On the following Wednesday, again after having received the Eucharist, she was meditating on the Incarnation and Annunciation when she experienced fully the transfixing of her heart. Of this experience she writes: 'Suddenly you came before me, and imprinted a wound in my heart';[116] and, 'You have truly and deeply pierced this same heart with the wound of your love'.[117] So great was her esteem for these graces that she wrote: 'You have conferred such happiness on me by these two alone, that even if I lived for a thousand years, I should find hourly more consolation, thanksgiving, and instruction than I could possibly contain'.[118]

Some years afterwards, when confined to her bed by severe illness on the Feast of the Presentation (2 February), Gertrud experienced an imprint of divinity on her soul similar to the impression of a seal upon soft wax. Exuberant in her praise of the 'ever-peaceful Trinity', she uses images of flame and peace to express the consuming love and consummate union which overwhelmed her: 'ardent fire of my God', 'consuming fire which even amid ardent flames imparts sweetness and peace to the soul', and 'burning furnace in which we enjoy the true vision of peace'.[119]

In the years following her conversion, Gertrud, though deeply grateful for her acute awareness of God's abiding presence, longed in a spirit of humility for still another favor: the gift of tears. She associated 'tears' with her continual, deeply felt need for compunction of heart, because she sensed the abyss between God's holiness and her own frailty apart from the Creator. She feared that she might somehow, albeit inadvertently, have sullied the purity of God's gifts through negligence or inadequate gratitude. Gertrud was troubled at her inability to force even one tear from her eyes. She felt further confusion when, instead of bestowing the gift of tears, Christ, parched with thirst, approached her with a cup in his hand, asking her for a drink. As she took the cup he presented to her, she felt her heart melt into 'a torrent of fervent tears'.[120] In this vision Gertrud seems to associate tears with two concepts: compunction of heart, and a desire for the salvation of sinners—this latter symbolized as the assuaging of the Saviour's thirst.[121]

On three different occasions—Gertrud gives no reference to the dates—at Christmas, on the Sunday before Lent (*Esto Mihi* Sunday), and on the first Sunday after Pentecost, Gertrud enjoyed a suprasensible, intimate exchange with Christ. In the language of mystics, this is the nuptial kiss of spiritual marriage. Gertrud writes of this loving intimacy: 'You have ravished me to so close a union with yourself, that I marvel more than at a miracle how I have lived since then as a creature among creatures'.[122] In her gratitude for these extraordinary graces, Gertrud usually pens canticles resembling the Song of Songs, to the accompaniment, as it were, of Christ's divine heart, to which she refers as the organ, or lyre, of the Trinity.[123]

Of a purifying experience in her heart on the Vigil of Pentecost, Gertrud's Helfta biographers wrote: 'She appeared to be plunged into this cave [her heart] to be regenerated therein, so that she came forth purified from every stain, and whiter than snow'.[124] Unlike mystics of later centuries who in their devotion to the humanity and/or the heart of Jesus emphasize his excruciatingly painful sufferings and focus on reparation for sins, Gertrud is noted for her exultant joy in the loving exchange of hearts between herself and

Christ.[125] She repeatedly expresses her gratitude for the mutuality of this mystical grace: Gertrud abiding in the divine heart of Christ as in a mystical ark[126] and Christ reposing in the heart of Gertrud.[127]

Another visonary experience which Gertrud records centers on Mary. It occurred, like many others, on the Feast of the Presentation. Christ directs his Mother to be a special advocate for Gertrud, who then exclaims: 'You have given me your sweetest mother, the Blessed Virgin, for my advocate, and you have lovingly recommended me to her many times with the same ardor as a faithful bridegroom would recommend his beloved to his own mother'.[128]

Gertrud also refers to drinking mystic liquors in the wine cellar of her Beloved; such expressions of intimate and intoxicating love she has doubtless borrowed from the Song of Songs.[129] On occasion, too, she writes of experiencing Christ's caresses: 'You have often, during a single Psalm, embraced my soul many times with a kiss which far surpasses the most fragrant perfumes or the sweetest honey; and I have often observed you look on me favorably in the condescending caresses you gave to my soul'.[130]

Not surprisingly, Gertrud is very appreciative of her Tabor experience, the ineffable grace of beholding the face of the transfigured Jesus. She writes of this mystical encounter, which occurred on Transfiguration Sunday, the Second Sunday of Lent (no year noted) while the community was singing the processional antiphon, *Vidi Dominum facie ad faciem*:

> A marvellous and inestimable coruscation illumined my soul with the light of divine revelation, and it appeared to me that my face was pressed to another face, as Saint Bernard says: 'Not a form, but forming; not attracting the bodily eye, but rejoicing the heart; giving freely gifts of love, not merely in appearance but in reality'.[131]

Gertrud never forgot the adorable face, the transfixing eyes of that enchanting vision: 'Nothing touched me so much as this majestic look of which I have spoken'.[132] She resorts to an image of annihilation in her attempt to convey the effects of his penetrating glance, for which words are totally inadequate:

> It appeared as if the marrow were taken from my bones; then, my flesh and bones appeared annihilated; so much so, it seemed as if my substance no longer had any consciousness save that of divine splendor, which shone in so inexplicable and delightful a manner that it was the source of the most inestimable pleasure and joy to my soul.[133]

Gertrud gratefully enumerates seven privileges conferred on her by Christ. Several relate to situations in which people were seeking her counsel: (1) her discernment in assisting those too timid to approach Christ in communion; (2) her wisdom in appraising guilt or innocence in those who contritely and humbly exposed their faults to her; and, in this context, (3) her power to forgive the sins of those who confessed to her. She is promised by Christ (4) that her prayers for others will be fruitful, (5) that those who seek her help will be either edified or consoled, and (6) that anyone who prays for or performs good works on her behalf will die in God's grace. Finally, (7) she is promised by Christ that after her death, all who 'recommend themselves humbly' to her prayer will be heard, subject to a twofold proviso: that they make reparation for their faults and negligences and thank God for the special graces given to Gertrud.[134] As a confirmation of these favors, Gertrud is told to place her hand in the 'mystical ark' of Christ's heart. Upon withdrawing her hand, she discovers that a golden ring adorns each finger, with three on her signet finger.[135] She perceives that with these rings Christ has ratified his sevenfold covenant with her, the privileges listed above.[136] Reference to this covenant occurs in an antiphon of monastic Lauds for her feast: 'With seven rings my Lord Jesus Christ espoused me'.

Gertrud concludes the account of mystical experiences conferred on her with a prayer to God, 'the Almighty Dispenser of all good things', that her readers be 'transformed into his image' through the power of the Spirit of Love until they behold 'the glory of the Lord with unveiled countenance';[137] she continues her prayer asking for God's blessings upon all who ponder her writings:

> Grant to all who read this account in humility, gratitude for your generosity, compassion for my unworthiness and compunction at their own progress. Out of the golden censers of their loving hearts may so sweet an odor ascend to you that it may make abundant recompense to you for my every failure of ingratitude and negligence.[138]

Gertrud of Helfta, as we have seen, fixes her contemplative gaze on Jesus, object of her love, ever aware that it was he who first loved her. So mutual was their attraction in holy intimacy that the Office for Gertrud's feast (17 November) fittingly opens with a revelation which Christ is said to have granted one of Helfta's nuns, probably Mechtild of Hackeborn: 'In the heart of Gertrud you shall find me'.[139]

NOTES

1. Conference of American Benedictine Prioresses, *Of All Good Gifts: Upon This Tradition* III (Erie: Benet Press, June, 1980) 5.

2. *The Life and Revelations of Saint Gertrude, Virgin and Abbess of the Order of St. Benedict*, tr. M. Frances Clare Cusak (1865; reprint, Westminster: Christian Classics, 1990); hereafter cited as *Life* and quotations noted with book and chapter numbers. Gertrud the Great of Helfta, *The Herald of God's Loving-Kindness*, Books One & Two, tr. Alexandra Barratt, Cistercian Fathers Series 35 (Kalamazoo: Cistercian Publications, 1991); hereafter cited as *Herald* and quotations noted with book and chapter numbers. Gertrud the Great of Helfta, *Spiritual Exercises*, tr. Gertrud Jaron Lewis and Jack Lewis (Kalamazoo: Cistercian Publications, 1989); hereafter cited as *Exercises* and quotations noted as either introduction or exercise and page numbers. I have concentrated mainly on the *Spiritual Exercises* and Book II of *The Herald* since these constitute what are generally accepted to be the most authentic writings of the gertrudian corpus. Quotations from *Life* have been slightly modified to change archaic terms and the pronouns 'thy' and 'thee' to 'your' and 'you' when referring to God.

3. Since Gertrud of the monastery of Helfta has no surname, I have chosen to keep her proper name, the germanic form Gertrud traditionally used for her; and I use Gertrude for Helfta's Abbess Gertrude of Hackeborn, in order to distinguish the abbess from her disciple.

4. *The Life of St. Mechtildis* (Rome: Vatican Press, 1899) 30–31; hereafter cited as *St. Mechtildis*.

5. Mary Jeremy Finnegan, *The Women of Helfta: Scholars and Mystics* (Athens: University of Georgia Press, 1991) 3.

6. Sally Thompson, 'The Problem of the Cistercian Nuns in the Twelfth and Early Thirteenth Centuries,' *Medieval Women*, ed. Derek Baker (Oxford: Basil Blackwell, 1978) 238–40.

7. *The Revelations of Mechtild of Magdeburg* or, *The Flowing Light of the Godhead*, tr. Lucy Menzies (London: Longmans, Green and Co., 1953).

8. *The Booke of Gostlye Grace of Mechtild of Hackeborn*, ed. Theresa A. Halligan (Toronto: Pontifical Institute of Medieval Studies, 1979). This is a fifteenth-century translation of an abridged version of Mechtild's *Liber specialis gratiae*.

9. *Life*, 1.3; 2.5, 10, 23, 24; 5.29.

10. See 'The Mystical *Jubilus*: An Example from Gertrud of Helfta (1256–1302),' tr. Gertrud Jaron Lewis, *Vox Benedictina* 1:4 (October 1984) 237–47.

11. *Exercises*, Gertrud Jaron Lewis, 'Introduction,' 10–11.

12. *Of All Good Gifts*, 5.

13. *The Rule of St. Benedict in Latin and English with Notes*, ed. Timothy Fry (Collegeville: Liturgical Press, 1981) 20:4; hereafter cited as RB with chapter and verse numbers.

14. John Cassian, *Conference* 1, 9 and 10 with special emphasis on 9.25, 26 and 10.11, 14 taken from *A Select Library of Nicene and Post-Nicene Fathers of the Christian Church* 11, ed. Philip Schaff and Henry Wace (Grand Rapids: Wm. B Eerdmans, 1982) 296–7; hereafter cited Conf., number, and chapter number. See Terrence Kardong, 'John Cassian's Evaluation of Monastic Practices,' *The American Benedictine Review* 43:1 (March 1992) 82–105 on purity of heart as the goal of monastic practices as well as the strength and weakness of the evagrian/cassianic approach to 'purity of heart' as a monastic practice.

15. Cassian, Conf., 1.4, 5, 6, 7, 14; 9.2, 4, 8, 19; 10.11; See Richard Byrne, 'Cassian and the Goals of Monastic Life,' *Cistercian Studies* 22:1 (1987) 3–16 for a fuller explanation of the nature of Cassian's teaching on 'purity of heart' in relation to evagrian *apatheia*. Byrne holds that for Evagrius '*apatheia* is the gateway to love,

which is the gateway to contemplation'. Cassian's 'purity of heart' includes but goes beyond evagrian *apatheia* in that it is 'not simply the gateway to charity' but 'its very counterpart' as he 'equates purity of heart with charity'; Cf. Adalbert de Vogue, *The Rule of Saint Benedict: A Doctrinal and Spiritual Commentary*, Cistercian Studies Series, 54 (Kalamazoo: Cistercian Publications, 1983) 253–256.

16. Cassian, Conf., 1.4; Cf. Terrence Kardong, 'Aiming for the Mark: Cassian's Metaphor for the Monastic Quest,' *Cistercian Studies* 22:3 (1987) 213–220.

17. RB 20:3, 4.

18. RB 49:2.

19. RB 42:3, 5; 73:2, 5.

20. See my article, 'Freed to Run with Expanded Heart: The Writings of Gertrud of Helfta and RB,' *Cistercian Studies* 25:3 (1990), 223–225, which illustrates Gertrud's consciousness of 'purity of heart'.

21. *Exercises*, 1.27; 2.37, 39; 3.43, 45, 50; 4.61; 5.75; 6.108, 110, 114; 7.135, 141, 142, 143, 144.

22. *Exercises*, 1.27; 2.37, 39; 3.43, 45, 50; 4.63.

23. *Herald*, 2.3.

24. *Exercises*, 7.142.

25. *Herald*, 1.5; 1.6; 1.7; 1.9; 1.11; 1.16; 2.3; 2.21.

26. Bernard of Clairvaux, *On the Song of Songs*, 4 volumes, tr. by Kilian Walsh and Irene Edmonds, Cistercian Fathers Series, 4, 7, 31, 40 (Spencer,Kalamazoo: Cistercian Publications, 1971, 1983, 1979, 1980). Except for the direct citations of Gertrud from *On the Song of Songs*, it is not known how many of the eighty-six sermons by Bernard of Clairvaux were familiar to her.

27. *Life*, 4.50.

28. *Herald*, 2.3.

29. Michael Casey, 'Gertrude of Helfta and Bernard of Clairvaux: a Reappraisal,' *Tjurunga* 35 (September 1988) 17.

30. Cf. *Gertrud die Grosse: Gesandter der göttlichen Liebe*, tr. Johanna Lanczkowski (Heidelberg: Lambert Schneider, 1989) 574–575, listing other probable latin and greek influences.

31. Finnegan, *Women of Helfta*, 6–7.

32. Finnegan, *Women of Helfta*, 1–2, 11; *St. Mechtildis*, 16–17, 191.

33. Finnegan, *Women of Helfta*, 11–12; Mechtild of Hackeborn, *Le Livre de la Grace Speciale: Revelations de Sainte Mechtilde Vierge de l'Ordre de St. Benoit*, tr. Nuns of Wisques from the Latin edition of Solesmes (Tours: Mame, 1928) 6.1, 362; hereafter cited as *Livre* with book, chapter and page numbers.

34. Finnegan, *Women of Helfta*, 1.

35. Finnegan, *Women of Helfta*, 26–28; *St. Mechtildis*, 45–47, 192.

36. Finnegan, *Women of Helfta*, 28; *Livre* 2.43, 187–88; 5.31, 357–58.

37. Caroline Walker Bynum, *Jesus as Mother: Studies in the Spirituality of the High Middle Ages* (Berkeley: University of California Press, 1982) 178, 210–11; Halligan, *Gostlye Grace*, 37.

38. Odo Egres, 'Mechtild von Magdeburg: Exile in a Foreign Land,' *Goad and Nail*, Studies in Medieval Cistercian History 10, ed. E. Rozanne Elder (Kalamazoo: Cistercian Publications, 1985) 138–40; Odo Egres, 'Mechtild von Magdeburg: *The Flowing Light of God*,' *Cistercians in the Late Middle Ages*, Studies in Medieval Cistercian History 6, ed. E. Rozanne Elder (Kalamazoo: Cistercian Publications, 1981) 19–20, 27, 34; Finnegan, *Women of Helfta*, 20.

39. Mechtild von Magdeburg, *Flowing Light of the Divinity*, tr. Christiane Mesch Galvani, ed. with an Introduction by Susan Clark (New York: Garland Publishing, 1991) 'Introduction,' xii; Menzies, *Revelations of Mechtild of Magdeburg*, 'Introduction' xix, xxii–xxiii; Odo Egres, *Goad and Nail*, 139–140.

40. Bynum, *Jesus as Mother*, 185.

41. *Life*, 1.4; 2.23; 3.26; *Exercises*, 3.42; Finnegan, *Women of Helfta*, 62.

42. Bynum, *Jesus as Mother*, 175, 180; Stephanus Hilpisch, *History of Benedictine Nuns*, tr. Joanne Muggli (Collegeville: St. John's Abbey Press, 1958) 36; Jean Leclercq, 'Medieval Feminine Monasticism: Reality versus Romantic Images,' *Benedictus: Studies in Honor of Saint Benedict of Nursia*, ed. E. Rozanne Elder (Kalamazoo: Cistercian Publications, 1981), 55–56.

43. P. Doyere, 'St. Gertrud the Great,' *The New Catholic Encyclopedia* (New York: McGraw-Hill Book Company, 1967) 451, portrays Gertrud of Helfta with an abbatial staff; Book One of *The Life*, 1990 reprint, confuses her in art and text with Abbess Gertrude of Hackeborn.

44. Jean Leclercq, 'Medieval Feminine Monasticism,' 55–56.

45. Hilpisch, *History of Benedictine Nuns*, 36, gives the approximate age for profession as fifteen. Gertrud Jaron Lewis in *Exercises*, 'Introduction,' 14, gives twelve as the age permitted for profession until the Council of Trent and twenty-five for consecration; Columba Hart, 'Consecratio Virginum: Thirteenth-century Witnesses,' *The American Benedictine Review* 23:2 (June 1972) 259 gives sixteen as the approximate age for monastic profession and the completion of the twenty-fifth year as the age for the consecration rite.

46. See the *Ceremonial for the Consecration of Virgins According to the Roman Pontifical* (Clyde: Benedictine Convent of Perpetual Adoration, 1952) p. 1, a reprint of the directive given in the Roman Pontifical requiring the consecrating prelate to interview each candidate the preceding evening prior to the ceremony to ascertain whether she had completed her twenty-fifth year; David R. Kinish, in 'The Consecration of Virgins,' *The American Benedictine Review* 4:2 (Summer 1953) 126–127 points out that the traditionally required age in the Roman Pontifical is the completion of the twenty-fifth year, but that variations occurred throughout the centuries; Roland Behrendt, in *The Consecration of Virgins: Conferences to Benedictine Sisters*, multilithed copy (Collegeville, St. John's Abbey, 1964) p. 66 states that the rite of consecration presupposed a certain age of religious maturity in the candidate.

47. *Life*, 2.1.

48. *Life*, 2.1, 23.

49. *Ceremonial*, 1; See *The Exercises of Saint Gertrude*, Introduction, Commentary and Translation by a Benedictine Nun of Regina Laudis [Columba Hart] (Westminster: Newman Press, 1956) 27–32 for a brief history of the rite of consecration at Helfta during the time of Gertrud; See also Columba Hart, 'Consecratio Virginum,' 258, 268–270 suggesting the rationale for linking Gertrud's conversion-crisis with her consecration.

50. *Life*, 2.1.

51. Ibid.

52. *Life*, 2.23.

53. See 'Index of Scriptural Citations,' *Exercises*, 147–51.

54. *Herald*, 1.1.

55. Psalms (Jerusalem Bible numbering) 23, 24, 34, 51, 91, 103, 145.

56. Psalms (Jerusalem Bible numbering) 4–5, 17–19, 45, 63, 66, 71, 73, 84, 116, 119.

57. *Life*, 5.16–18.

58. *Life*, 3.40.

59. *Life*, 4.20.

60. *Life*, 2.7, 11: 4.2, 20, 43.

61. *Life*, 2.1.

62. *Life*, 2.1, 6, 9; 4.61.

63. *Life*, 2.1, 23.

64. *Life*, 2.6.

65. *Life*, 2.23.

66. *Life*, 2.8.

67. *Exercises*, 5.74.

68. Cyprian Vagaggini, *Theological Dimensions of the Liturgy*, tr. Leonard J. Doyle and W. A. Jurgens (Collegeville: Liturgical Press, 1976) 761.

69. RB 7:8, 62–63; 20:2–4; 49:4; 52:4; See Schmitt, 'Freed to Run with Expanded Heart,' 219–232.

70. *Life*, 4.49.

71. *Life*, 2.3.

72. *Life*, 2.4.

73. *Life*, 2.7.

74. *Exercises*, 7.139.

75. *Exercises*, Gertrud Jaron Lewis, 'Introduction,' 10, 16–17.

76. *Exercises*, 6.110.

77. *Life*, 2.10.

78. *Life*, 2.23; 3.70; 4.23, 36, 59.

79. *Life*, 4.23.

80. *Life*, 3.8, 11; 4.31, 47; 5.28; *Exercises* 4.63.

81. *Life*, 2.15–17; 3.1, 18, 19; 4.1, 2, 3, 49.

82. *Life*, 1.3; 3.26; 5.24.

83. *Life*, 1.3; 3.26; 4.3, 21; *Exercises*, 4.58.

84. *Life*, 3.26; 4.17, 25, 61.

85. *Life*, 2.22; 4.2; *Exercises* 4.61.

86. *Life*, 1.5.

87. RB 72:2–3.

88. *Life*, 4.13; *Exercises*, 4.61.

89. *Life*, 4.4, 21, 44; *Exercises* 4.61.

90. *Life*, 1.31; 4.45, 61; *Exercises*, 4.62.

91. *Life*, 4.4.

92. *Life*, 4.4, 13, 34, 49; 5.28; *Exercises*, 4.62.

93. *Life*, 1.4; 2.3, 14; 4.11, 23, 40, 59.

94. *Life*, 3.55, 62.

95. *Life*, 2.23.

96. RB 43:3.

97. *Life*, 4.17.

98. *Life*, 4.12.

99. *Life*, 2.8.

100. *Life*, 4.17.

101. *Life*, 4.18.

102. *Life*, 4.55.

103. *Life*, 3.17.

104. *Life*, 3.17, 32.

105. *Life*, 3.16; 4.51; See Rv 4:1–11; 5:1–14; 7:9–17; 19:1–8.

106. Vagaggini, 777–8.

107. *Life*, 2.22.

108. *Life*, 1.2.

109. Prosper Gueranger, 'Preface,' *The Exercises of St. Gertrude, Virgin and Abbess of the Order of St. Benedict*, tr. Thomas Alder Pope (London: Burn Oates and Washbourne, 1921), 'Introduction,' xix–xx.

110. *Life*, 2.23.

111. *Life*, 2.3.

112. *Life*, 2.4, 5, 23.

113. See 'The Living Flame of Love' (Stanzas 1 and 2) in *The Collected Works of St. John of the Cross*, tr. Kieran Kavanaugh and Otilio Rodriguez (Washington, D.C.: Institute of Carmelite Studies, 1973) 577–600 for a commentary on the 'wound of love'. For other medieval mystics with this phenomenon, see Harvey D. Egan, *Christian Mysticism: The Future of a Tradition* (New York: Pueblo Publishing Company, 1984) 314–318, 200–202.

114. *Life*, 2.4.

115. *Life*, 2.5.
116. Ibid.
117. *Life*, 2.23.
118. Ibid.
119. *Life*, 2.7.
120. *Life*, 2.11.
121. Jn 19:28–30.
122. *Life*, 2.23.
123. *Life* 2.23; 3.41; 4.11, 43, 51.
124. *Life*, 4.40.
125. For a summary of the proponents of devotion to the Sacred Heart beginning with the early Church and ending with Margaret Mary Alacoque (1647–1690), see Gilbert Dolan, *St. Gertrude the Great*, (London: Sands, 1916) 'Preface,' ix–xxxiv.
126. *Life*, 2.23; 4.11.
127. *Life*, 2.3, 14.
128. *Life*, 2.23.
129. Sg 1:2, 4; 4:10; 8:2; *Life*, 2.6, 8, 9, 19.
130. *Life*, 2.22.
131. Ibid.
132. Ibid.
133. Ibid.
134. *Life*, 2.20.
135. *Life*, Introduction, xxxi–xxxiv. The signet ring is one to which a signet, or monogram has been affixed, for use in sealing documents. Portraits of rulers and prelates of the late medieval era reveal that officials' signet rings were worn on the index finger of the left hand. *The Oxford-Duden Pictorial German-English Dictionary* indicates the fourth finger was customarily the ring finger. For women, the ring finger associated with matrimony, was the fourth finger of the left hand. Gertrud does not explain the significance of three rings on her signet finger, nor which finger it was. She regards the seven rings on her hand with three on her signet finger as a ratification by Christ of his sevenfold covenant with her. An antiphon for the Office of Lauds mentions these seven rings as symbols of her spiritual marriage to Christ. In *The Life of St. Mechtildis*, 219–21 (based on *Liber specialis gratiae* 4.50), Mechtild describes the significance of the five fingers including the ring finger (fourth finger) in her correspondence with a 'woman of the world'.
136. *Life*, 2.21.
137. *Life*, 2.24.
138. *Herald*, 2.24.
139. *Life*, 1.1.

The Scriptures and Personal Identity: A Study in the *Exercises* of Saint Gertrud

Maureen McCabe, OCSO

'WHEN WILL YOU LIGHT the lamp of my soul that it may nevermore go out, and kindle it anew in yourself, causing me to know myself in you even as I am known?'[1] So prayed Gertrud of Helfta, the nun and mystic of the late thirteenth century. Her writings remain for us a source of blessing and light. Her prayer expresses a thirst for knowledge that cannot be acquired by introspection and can only be received as a gift—the self-knowledge which preoccupied the Cistercian Fathers and of which William of Saint Thierry wrote, 'The soul will never know itself (what it is and what it is capable of) unless it finds itself in this light', that is, in the light of 'God's countenance'.[2] This brief study will explore the theme of self-knowledge in Gertrud's *Exercises* in relation to a specific path to knowledge, the Sacred Scriptures. More precisely, I will probe her personal experience of the Scriptures as a guide to her deepest self known in the school of the Spirit, in being called by name, and in the experience of the fecundity of the word.

Gertrud, like all those men and women who lived according to the Cistercian tradition, walked and wrestled with the word of God and unreservedly opened her life to it in *lectio divina* and liturgy. For her it was a word of fire.[3] Her *Exercises*, so thoroughly impregnated with biblical images, gives eloquent testimony to the word's intrinsic power to shed light, to cleanse, to renew, and to heal, functions to which the Scriptures themselves bear witness:

497

Is not my word like fire, says the Lord, like a hammer shattering
rocks? (Jer 23:29)
The word that goes from my mouth does not return to me
empty without . . . succeeding in what it was sent to do. (Is 55:11)
You are clean already by means of the word that I have spoken to
you. (Jn 15:3)

This devotional work likewise reveals a woman who has made the
word her own and who has, so to speak, come into her own through
the word.

GERTRUD AND THE SCHOOL OF THE SPIRIT

'Grant,' Gertrud prays, 'that in this life I may so perfectly learn
your scripture, full of love, that to fill up your charity in me, not one
iota may be wanting'.[4] She leaves no doubt here about the course of
study she intends to pursue her whole life long. But like her Father,
Saint Benedict, she is aware that such a goal demands a suitable environment, a school of the Lord's service. To this end she prays in the
second exercise, in which she recalls her reception of the holy habit,
that she may be received by the Lord into the cloister of love as into
the school of the Holy Spirit.[5] School, curriculum, instructor—this
delightful pedagogical imagery, which Gertrud develops in detail,
is on the one hand a tribute to the zeal of her abbess, Gertrude of
Hackeborn, in promoting studies that would ultimately result in a
deeper understanding of the Scriptures. It is, on the other hand, the
natural expression of her own strong intellectual bent. In *The Herald
of God's Loving-Kindness*, Gertrud's account of her conversion to the
interior life, she praises God not only for detaching her from her
excessive love of profane studies, but also for 'composing a beverage
suitable to my temperament', a temperament which retained an avid
thirst for knowledge and adeptness in acquiring it.[6] By 'beverage'
she evidently meant the knowledge and love of the things of God
that now claimed her entire being. Her thirst to learn rooted itself
in the end in total docility to the Spirit, in the conviction that she
was the student of this most perfect Instructor and of our Lord who
had anointed her with the Spirit.

Anointing is a spiritual reality dear to Gertrud. Several times in
the *Exercises* she alludes to the text of 1 Jn 2:27: 'The anointing he
gave teaches you everything'. In the first exercise commemorating
baptism, as in the fourth on monastic profession, she exhorts her
readers to pray to the Lord that the anointing of his Spirit may

teach them all things; in the second exercise she aspires to rapid advancement in the school of the Spirit by means of two aids: the discipline of grace and the anointing that teaches all things. In the fifth exercise she advises:

> Pray to the Lord, the most perfect of all masters, that, by the anointing of his Spirit, he may teach you the art of love, accepting you as his own disciple, that under his tutorship you may be exercised unremittingly in the virtue of charity.[7]

Always her heart is intent on comprehending the most excellent lesson, the most profound mystery, that of love. She determines to 'examine, consider, learn, know, and recognize' each letter of the alphabet of love[8] and prays ardently that her understanding be surrounded with the light that only love sheds.[9] Clearly Gertrud had experienced the anointing of the Spirit. John wrote that only the person who loves knows God (1 Jn 4:8), and it is the Spirit, anointing the hearts of all the baptized, who ceaselessly labors to bring each to that loving communion with God in which one may truly cry out, 'I know him'. Here is a knowledge that has much less to do with rational thought processes than with connaturality, that is, with an inner likeness to the God who is love.

With the Spirit as her tutor and the Scriptures as her text, Gertrud commited herself wholeheartedly to this path of knowledge—to knowing the Lord and 'herself in him'—with the second aspect, self-knowledge, the fruit of the first. The conviction that Gertrud expressed in simple, scattered prayers Saint Bernard once related in a single exhortation that clarifies the point:

> Let us return now to ourselves, let us examine our paths; and in order to accomplish this in truth, let us invoke the Spirit of truth, let us call to him from the deep into which he has led us, because he leads us on the way by which we discover ourselves.[10]

I HAVE CALLED YOU BY NAME

In leading Gertrud into her own truth, the Spirit seems to have uncovered hidden treasure for her in the scriptural notion of 'name'. A prayer she addresses to Jesus hints at the depth of meaning she finds in this term: 'Your face is winning and beautiful, radiant with the fairest dawn of the Godhead. In the color of your cheeks is written in red the wondrous name Alpha and Omega'.[11]

To reveal the nature of the bearer, whether God or a person, was precisely the function of a name in biblical times. It was never a mere label. As Gerhard von Rad remarks, 'Certain words were thought of as having power inherent in them, as for example people's names. A man's name was not looked on as something additional to his personality, something that could be changed at will; on the contrary, it contained an essential part of his nature'.[12] Another scholar has expressed such revelation in an especially beautiful way:

> A name . . . is intended to characterize the real nature of a person or thing, and, in a sense, to complete the singularity of the bearer of the name. We may say that a person's name is a part of his creation.[13]

Delving into this rich biblical tradition, Gertrud played with the possibilities of her own name, or, more precisely, with the symbolic name(s) that express her deepest meaning. Certain key passages reveal the centrality of this theme in her understanding of herself as she addresses the Holy Spirit and Jesus:

> O holy and almighty Paraclete, in that love whereby you have sealed me for yourself by a spiritual name, grantthat I may love you with my whole heart, cleave to you with my whole soul, expend all my strength in loving and serving you.[14]
> O sweetest Jesus, set down my name beneath your glorious name in the book of life. Say to my soul: You are mine; I your salvation have called you by name. Now you shall no more be called 'Forsaken' but you shall be called 'My delight in her' that my inheritance may be with you for ever in the land of the living.[15]
> There you keep me for yourself, written upon your hands and your feet and upon your most loving heart, that you may never forget my soul which you have redeemed and made yours at such great cost.[16]

What is immediately discernible in even a cursory reading of these, and indeed of most of Gertrud's, prayers is the total way in which the Scriptures have taken root in her, allowing her to move rapidly from one allusion to another. Jean Leclercq describes this literary phenomenon as *reminiscence* 'whereby the verbal echoes so excite the memory that a scriptural phrase will suggest quite naturally allusions elsewhere in the sacred books'.[17] Thus, taking the prayers as a whole, we find there are actually two closely related themes that tend to evoke each other: 'seal' and 'name'.

Gertrud speaks several times of being sealed or marked by God. For her this seal expresses God's exclusive possession of her person:

'He has put a mark upon my face, that I may admit no lover other than himself'.[18] Only in the first prayer above, however, does she explicitly link seal and name. The allusion seems to be a spontaneous joining of two texts whereby the seal who is the Spirit (Eph 1:13) himself seals Gertrud with a name (Rev 7:3, 14:1). What was this 'spiritual name'? Since it occurs within the context of the seal, I think Gertrud refers here primarily to God's name, that is, to the name of Christ and of his Father (cf. Rev 14:1) written upon her face as upon the faces of all his servants:

> Then I saw another angel rising where the sun rises, carrying the seal of the living God; he called in a powerful voice. . . . Wait before you do any damage on land or at sea or to the trees, until we have put the seal on the foreheads of the servants of our God (Rev 7:2–3).
>
> His servants will worship him, they will see him face to face, and his name will be written on their foreheads (Rev 22:4).

This application accords well with Gertrud's understanding of a seal as a mark of ownership; God's name upon a person symbolizes 'private property' or 'consecration' (cf Is 44:5). Yet the term also has a deeper implication for her, one bearing upon her experience of her personally unique name. An analysis of the other two prayers quoted above will help bring this to light.

Gertrud's first exercise, in which she gratefully recalls the reception of her baptismal name, provides the context of her second prayer. She takes as her source Second (and Third) Isaiah. The prophet of divine consolation again and again rouses Israel to the hope that Yahweh is about to create her anew; that she need no longer recall the past; that her future is secured in his redeeming love. But if Israel is to be a new creation, her new identity will demand, according to biblical thought, a new name (Is 62:2). Just as Jacob the 'Supplanter' (Gn 25:26), after his mysterious struggle with the divine, became 'Israel' or 'he who has been strong against God' (Gn 32:39), so the metaphorical names that Isaiah applies to the entire people of Israel designate a similar change in identity and destiny. She is no longer 'Forsaken', the old name for the old identity, but Yahweh's 'Delight' whose land will be called the 'Wedded' (cf. Is 62:4). The Gertrud who could not rest content with knowing the Lord by the mere 'syllables of his name', so great was her desire to know him with 'understanding',[19] was drawn by this text to probe the depths of her own name. Freely combining Psalm 35 with Isaiah 43:1, she first rejoices to know that God has called her by her name. Then her mind immediately leaps to the essence, the spiritual sense of the term. God has called her not only by the syllables of her name but, in naming her, he has identified her, understood her, interpreted her. That she is his 'Delight' is part of the revelation of her inmost being.

The third prayer articulates another aspect of the mystery. Skillfully adapting the text to the image of the crucified Christ, Gertrude alludes to Isaiah 49:15–16. It is he who, like a mother cherishing her child, will never forget her. Her name is branded on the palms of his hands—and on his feet and heart. Could there be a more apt way of expressing that one's identity is hidden in God than to speak of oneself as being written on the wounded body of Christ?

This image, I feel, provides the key to the bond between seal and name in Gertrud's thought. Christ is the bond, and the name of every child of God is a name of Christ. In him Gertrud's name is written on God and God's name on Gertrud. To be identified with Jesus, a reality she rejoices in continually, is to find one's deepest meaning. So Gertrud prays to be engulfed by and buried in Jesus's Spirit:

> Jesus . . . , engulf my spirit in your Spirit so powerfully and so deeply that I may in truth be entirely buried in you, abandoning myself in union with you, that the place of my burial may be known to your love alone.[20]

Abandoned in her union with Christ, Gertrud loses herself in God. She has died and lived again:

> My God and my King, who are in your holy place, in whom my life is hidden with Jesus, behold, the deluge of your chaste delights has flowed over me. I am already lost unto myself in you, and living I have died.[21]

Finally, the last vestige of an acting self in Gertrud freely extinguishes itself in union with Christ's consuming love:

> Jesus, I offer you as a holocaust of praise yourself in me and myself in you; naught more do I possess.[22]

Nothing of this, of course, is meant to suggest that one may actually know Gertrud's name. This, as the glorified Christ in the Book of Revelation assures us, is her secret: 'I will give the hidden manna and a white stone—a stone with a new name written on it, known only to the person who receives it' (Rev 2:17). Even so, these

passages give us a glimpse of Gertrud's understanding of name as
spiritual identity and of her longing to find her place in God, an
experience captured in these words of a contemporary theologian:

> What we truly are he alone can say, and the word he spoke to the
> weeping Magdalen at the grave is enough: 'Mary!' This proper
> name coming from the mouth of eternal life is each man's true
> idea: it is the true I in God, given and uttered to the believer
> through pure grace and remission of sins, but accompanied with
> the compelling might of the love which, of its very nature, de-
> mands and appropriates all.[23]

From this consideration of the spirituality of name we may proceed towards a more practical question. How did Gertrud use the
Scriptures in order to find her deepest self, her 'spiritual name'?

MY WORD DOES NOT RETURN TO ME EMPTY

In reading or praying the *Exercises,* I find myself constantly
charmed by Gertrud's fluency in scriptural language. She had
learned to *think* scripturally, and her biblical vocabulary is so vivid
that she often surprises the reader by uncovering or playing upon
obscure or unexpected passages. She identifies, for instance, with
the crafty steward in her efforts to gain God's compassion. Since
she cannot dig and is too ashamed to beg, she artfully persuades
'Compassion' to agree to this pact with her: 'You and I shall have but
one purse between us!'[24] The reference, to a rarely quoted passage
of Proverbs (1:14), concerns very crafty dealing indeed.

Yet within this broad compass of references, Gertrud displays
a definite selectivity. She consistently prefers certain themes and
passages to others and identifies with particular images and models
personally and deeply. The most striking pattern of selection appears
in Gertrud's association with creaturehood, frailty, littleness. From
the Law to the Prophets, from the Wisdom writings to the New
Testament itself, she finds her rest in the images that express this
reality. Like Mary she is a poor handmaid, like Abraham dust and
ashes (Lk 1:38; Gn 18:27). She thirsts for life as does the Samaritan
woman (Jn 4:15). She is the hungry one begging at Wisdom's door
(Pr 8:34 and 9:5). In considering the parable of our Lord, she identifies with the beaten and bruised man on the road to Jericho, the
woman of Canaan whose place was 'among the dogs', the dishonest
steward, the man who buried his talent (Lk 10:30; Mt 15:27; Lk

16:1–8; and Mt 25:25). She loves to describe her poverty in the diction of the biblical images of nature: the dried-up branch which has not observed its time of pruning; the least seed of God's true sowing; the unfruitful tree (Jn 15:2, 6; Mt 13:32; and Lk 13:6).

Gertrud realized, however, that these did not give a complete picture of her identity. God has lifted her up from the dust (Ps 113:7, a favorite image) and by his word has given her a *new* name. She expresses this newness most frequently by the symbol of the Bride. Here, of course, cultural influence was strong, for in the thirteenth century 'nuptial' vocabulary (*Brautmystik*) dominated mystical writings.[25] Yet she combines with it the freshness of the Scriptures, drawing not only from the Song of Songs but also from Isaiah, Hosea, and the Gospels. As the Lord hastens to betroth her to himself, so she hastens to meet him, clad in a wedding garment and with lamp alight.

Gertrud also loved to reflect upon the great pauline theme of adoption. She is God's 'adopted daughter', a title which she relates to her role as student in the school of divine wisdom: 'Come, O Love, immerse my spirit so deeply in your charity, that through you I may become a child gifted with understanding, and you yourself may be in truth my Father, Teacher, and Master'.[26] This adoption, she believed, united her to the entire family of God with whom she experienced deep communion. Hers is an identity discovered within the community, not apart from it, as she indicates several times by her desire 'to be counted with Israel'.

The narrative of Jacob's meeting with God at Penuel particularly attracted Gertrud. Like the patriarch she struggles to obtain a blessing from the God whom she can name as Jesus, but unlike him she refuses to let go even after the blessing is bestowed!

> I hold you by my love, most loving Jesus, and I will not let you go, for your blessing is in nowise enough for me unless I may hold you and possess you as my best part, all my hope, and all my expectation.[27]

Gertrud shows a similar virility of spirit in her descriptions of herself as a warrior. She prays the Lord will gird her with the sword of the Spirit and train her fingers for war (cf. Ps 18:34). With such protection she will not fear if armies stand up against her (cf. Ps 27:3).

Psalm references like these spring up frequently and spontaneously in the *Exercises*, revealing how deeply the psalmody had become a part of Gertrud. Again it is the poor and humble—those who look to

God for everything, especially himself—whom Gertrud meets and with whom she prays and identifies in these songs of the Church, songs ancient yet new, human yet divine, capable of expressing the full range of that which is most base and needy and most purified and sublime in us.

At work in all of Gertrud's spiritual self-discovery is a process which is at the very heart of monastic life, a process of internalization, as Jean Le Clercq has pointed out. If, Leclercq recommends, we are receptive to the living, active word of God, it opens our lives to a world of images and models that are capable of being recreated, reactivated.[28] Just as the human imagination of Jesus was full of the images of the Scriptures, images which he revived in himself—the Exodus, the new David, the new Joseph—so Gertrud, following our Lord and the whole monastic tradition, gave free entry to these images, allowing them to grow like a living seed in her heart. She lived them, she became them, yet always in the light of their perfect fulfillment in Jesus.

The very power of the Scriptures makes such profound internalization possible. The word which is light and a creative force not only reveals me to myself; it 'gives me to myself'.[29] In other words, it transforms me, enabling me to be the person I am called to be. Again I turn to William of Saint Thierry who offers a penetrating description of the process:

> Now that the soul understands, the Spirit speaks of mysteries; the Word of God speaks of himself, and his word runs swiftly to its fulfillment, since in him to whom it is spoken, the things heard with understanding come to pass efficaciously.[30]

As we have seen, Gertrud made a personal and selective internalization, called as she was, and as we all are, to unfold the mystery of Christ in a unique way, in a truly unrepeatable way.[31] Here an insight of Adrian Van Kaam may prove useful:

> How does my unique call make itself known to me? For most of us the core meaning of life only bit by bit reveals itself in the act of living without any sudden orientation. As I live in prayerful presence to what happens to me, in me, and around me, slowly a certain line may emerge. I see a certain direction, a hidden consistency makes itself known.[32]

Although van Kaam is speaking of life experiences in general, I feel that it is equally true to say that a 'hidden consistency' makes itself known in a person's reading of the word of God. The Spirit who leads us into our unique selves speaks in various ways to various people. Therese of Lisieux, for example, confided at the close of her life that the texts of Isaiah 53 were the foundation of her whole piety, for these texts led her into the mystery of the name she bore: 'Therese of the Child Jesus and of the Holy Face'.[33] In like manner, the pattern that reveals itself in the *Exercises*—a consistent joining of confident frailty with ardent strength, of the humility of a poor woman with the loving daring of a bride—perhaps comes closest to disclosing to us the mystery of Gertrud's 'spiritual name'.

Centuries after Gertrud's death, Dietrich Bonhoeffer, a theologian in very different circumstances from hers, penned words that summarize a marvellous lesson we may learn from Gertrud in her *Exercises*:

> If we wish to pray with confidence and gladness, then the words of Holy Scripture will have to be the solid basis of our prayer. For here we know that Jesus Christ, the Word of God, teaches us to pray. The words which come from God become, then, the steps on which we find our way to God.[34]

It was on these steps of the Scriptures that Gertrud began to discover her unique self in God. She can provide a light on the path of each person's search for identity so deep and lasting that it transcends, without excluding, the cultural elements of identity posed in distinctions such as male/female, Jew/Greek, slave/freeman (cf. Gal 3:23). The ultimate liberation is to experience what she so longed to experience—'to know myself in you even as I am known'; it is to be called by name and in his calling to recognize the Lord and oneself.

Sister Maureen McCabe, ocso
Mount Saint Mary's Abbey
Wrentham, Massachusetts 02093

NOTES

1. Gertrude of Helfta, *The Exercises*, translated by a Benedictine Nun of Regina Laudis (Westminster, Maryland: Newman Press, 1956) p. 126. All references are to this edition which is somewhat modernized and updated. A more recent translation was published after this essay was composed: Gertrud the Great of Helfta, *Spiritual Exercises*, Cistercian Fathers Series Number 49, translated by Gertrud Jaron Lewis and Jack Lewis (Kalamazoo, Michigan: Cistercian Publications, 1989).

2. William of Saint Thierry, *Exposition of the Song of Songs*, translated by Columba Hart osb, Cistercian Fathers Series Number 6 (Spencer, Massachusetts: Cistercian Publications, 1970) p. 54.

3. *Exercises*, p. 96.

4. *Exercises*, p. 97.
5. *Exercises*, p. 20.
6. *The Life and Revelations of Saint Gertrude*, translated by M. Frances Clare, PC (Westminster, Maryland: Newman Press, 1952) p. 73. Also translated by Alexandra Barratt, *The Herald of God's Loving-Kindness*, Cistercian Fathers Series Number 35 (Kalamazoo, Michigan: Cistercian Publications, 1991).
7. *Exercises*, p. 95.
8. *Exercises*, p. 97.
9. *Exercises*, p. 70.
10. Bernard of Clairvaux, *SC 17, On the Song of Songs* 1, Cistercian Fathers Series 4, translated by Kilian Walsh, ocso (Spencer, Massachusetts: Cistercian Publications, 1971) 132.
11. *Exercises*,p. 86.
12. Gerhard von Rad, *Old Testament Theology* (New York: Harper and Row, 1965) I:83.
13. Myles Bourke, *The Book of Exodus: Old Testament Reading Guide* (Collegeville, Minnesota: Liturgical Press, 1968) p. 72.
14. *Exercises*, p. 21.
15. *Exercises*, p.10.
16. *Exercises*, p. 117.
17. Jean Leclercq, *The Love of Learning and the Desire for God*, translated by Catherine Misrahi (New York: Fordham University Press, 1961) p. 91.
18. *Exercises*, p. 44.
19. *Exercises*, p.98.
20. *Exercises*, p.70.
21. *Exercises*, p. 139.
22. *Exercises*, pp. 111–12.
23. Hans Urs von Balthasar, *Prayer*, translated by A. V. Littledale (New York: Sheed and Ward, 1961) p. 22.
24. *Exercises*, p. 165.
25. Francois Vandenbroucke, *The Spirituality of the Middle Ages, A History of Christian Spirituality* 1 (New York: Desclee, 1968) 377.
26. *Exercises*, p. 96.
27. *Exercises*, p. 103.
28. Jean Leclercq, lecture given to the cistercian nuns of Mount Saint Mary's Abbey, Wrentham, in November 1980. Thomas Merton's *Opening the Bible* (Collegeville, Minnesota: Liturgical Press, 1970) also offers a description of this process.
29. Von Balthasar, *Prayer*, p. 21.
30. *Exposition of the Song of Songs*, p. 130.
31. Pope John Paul II, *The Redeemer of Man*, Vatican translation (Boston, Massachusetts: Saint Paul Editions, 1979) p. 26.
32. Adrian Van Kaam, *In Search of Spiritual Identity* (Denville, New Jersey: Dimension Books, 1975) p. 139.
33. Thérése of Lisieux, *Her Last Conversations*, translated by John Clark, ocd (Washington, DC: ICS Publications, 1977) p. 13.
34. Dietrich Bonhoeffer, *Psalms: The Prayer Book of the Bible*, translated by James H. Burtness (Minneapolis, Minnesota: Augsburg Publishing House, 1970), p.11.

Taste and See the
Goodness of the Lord:
Mechtild of Hackeborn

Ann Marie Caron RSM

> When she had received the Body of Christ the Lord said to her:
> 'Do you see how I am in you and you in me?' Then she saw the
> Lord as a transparent crystal, and her soul as pure and brillant
> water which flowed through the whole Body of Christ. She was
> in admiration of this favor and the astonishing goodness of God
> in her regard . . . 'what you are by grace you are in me'.[1]

THIS PASSAGE from the thirteenth-century *Book of Special
Grace*[2] expresses in personal terms an experience of liturgi-
cal prayer and contemplation. It identifies encounter with
Christ in the liturgy as the source of Mechtild of Hackeborn's
prayer. A century earlier Saint Bernard of Clairvaux (c.1090-1153)
had written: 'Read in your heart. Become aware of your need of
God whose love never ceases to meet your need, to answer your
expectations. Because the heart of Christ is the heart of the Father.'[3]
Mechtild of Hackeborn experienced this union with the heart of
Christ in the heart of the Father. This woman, spoken of as a
'prophetess of divine praise', shared her spirituality to help others
understand and experience God's special graces. Mechtild was more
than fifty years old and in poor health in 1291, when she confided
her revelations to her friend and confident Gertrud the Great. Her
revelations reflect her experience of prayer over these many years.
Initially, she was disturbed that Gertrud and another nun in the
community transcribed her revelations. Only when Mechtild realized this was God's will did she consent[4] to the transcription of *The
Book of Special Grace*. The compilers of this work believed that the

great graces Mechtild received were given not so much for herself as for 'us and for those who will come after us'.[5] In other words, the transcription of the revelations was to benefit the nuns in the Helfta community and all who were in contact with them. In a recent study Caroline Bynum made a similar observation.

> It is clear that the words of Mechtild of Hackeborn and Gertrude not only in fact reveal the spiritual orientation of the whole group of Helfta nuns but also were a conscious effort to establish and hand on to a next generation of sisters and to readers outside the cloister a spiritual teaching and a collective reputation.[6]

Book One of the *Book of Special Grace* seems to confirm Bynum's insight. For of its seven books or parts, Book One seems to set forth devotional teaching.[7] It provides a stylized description of Mechtild's graces of prayer through an account of her lived experience of the mysteries of Christ. Its thirty-five subdivisions correspond to feasts and seasons of the liturgical year. Her prayer is centered on Christ in the liturgy. And the liturgy, in turn, is seen in terms of the liturgical year and the monastic community.

This paper will examine Mechtild's experience of liturgical prayer in the accounts of her revelations. From these we can begin to identify and appreciate the rich liturgical-theological content which nourished her spiritual life. To establish the context for this discussion I will first present a brief introduction to Mechtild of Hackeborn and the Helfta monastery.

MECHTILD OF HACKEBORN IN THE MILIEU OF THE HELFTA MONASTERY

Mechtild of Hackeborn (1241-1298)

Little is known about the life of Mechtild of Hackeborn save what we glean from *The Book of Special Grace*. At the age of seven, she accompanied her mother to the monastery at Rodarsdorf, where her sister, Gertrude of Hackeborn, was a nun. That day Mechtild asked to stay. In 1258 she followed her sister Gertrude, now the abbess, to the new foundation of Helfta, near Eisleben, Germany. There she assisted in administration, was first chantrix, directed the choir, trained novices, and taught young children in the monastery school. Mechtild of Hackeborn was a well-loved counselor, friend, and guide to the nuns and to many outside the convent.[8]

The Helfta Monastery

During her forty-year administration, Abbess Gertrude of Hackeborn encouraged the development of the intellectual and spiritual gifts of her nuns. In addition to Mechtild of Hackeborn and Gertrud the Great, Helfta was also, at that time, home to Mechtild of Magdeburg, the thirteenth-century beguine and author of *The Flowing Light of the Godhead*. Within the lifetime of abbess Gertrude of Hackeborn Helfta became a center of mysticism in Germany. Its influence radiated in all directions.[9]

Dominican friars offered spiritual guidance to the nuns. Yet, the spirituality of the community was most influenced by the Rule of Saint Benedict and the Constitutions of Citeaux. 'Though the monastery was not juridically joined to the Cistercian order,' Cypriano Vagaggini noted, 'it is none the less certain that the spirit and influence of Saint Bernard were felt most strongly in the spiritual tone of that house.'[10]

Monastic spirituality has as its center a concentration of attention on divine praise through the liturgy. A balanced life of prayer and work is characteristic of benedictine and cistercian monasteries. And so, in the Helfta monastery the hours of the Divine Office gave a rhythm to each day, and the liturgical feasts to the entire year. Humanistic studies were held in high honor, for in the monastic tradition such studies were understood as preparation for *lectio divina*. By *lectio*[11] we understand the specifically monastic endeavor of a prayerful reading of the Scriptures, the Fathers, and more recent authors in relation to the great themes of the spiritual and liturgical life. Monastic *lectio* was considered a direct and continual preparation for living the liturgical life in depth. The passage from *lectio* to *oratio* and, if God willed, to *contemplatio* was regarded as a natural and continuous experience. This way of uniting reading, meditation, prayer and contemplation, or this 'meditative prayer', as William of Saint Thierry called it,[12] had great influence on religious psychology in the Middle Ages. *Lectio* occupied and engaged the whole person in whom Scripture took root, later on to bear fruit.

The rhythm of the nuns' life in the Helfta monastery was created by the balance of *Opus Dei* (liturgical prayer), work, and *lectio divina*. The liturgy with its cycles of feasts and seasons through which the nuns celebrated the transforming mysteries of Christ was the wellspring of the 'special graces' recounted in Book One of the *Book of Special Grace*. The revelations of Mechtild of Hackeborn, as recounted in Book One, are descriptive of ordinary graces of liturgical prayer for someone nurtured in the monastic environment. The *Book of Special Grace* witnesses to the remarkable spirituality of the thirteenth-century monastery at Helfta.

THE BOOK OF SPECIAL GRACE, BOOK ONE

An Overview

The narrative in Book One of the *Book of Special Grace* follows the medieval liturgical calendar from Advent through the feast of the Dedication of the Church. Several of the revelations are related to mysteries in the life of the Blessed Virgin Mary and the saints. Angels and heavenly choirs are frequently mentioned. The accounts are rich in dialogue and in biblical and medieval symbolism and imagery, not least in the evocation of colors. The unfolding liturgical calendar awakened in the reader an understanding of the Mystery of God disclosed in the liturgy. At the same time, the celebration of the sacred mysteries throughout the seasons and feasts fruitfully grounded the spiritual life of the nuns in theology and fostered religious affections.[13] These accounts of the revelations of Mechtild's special graces of liturgical prayer leave no doubt that her spiritual life was centered in the liturgical mystery. In the liturgy she encountered Christ in his mysteries and was transformed by grace.

Mechtild's visions and revelations did not take place in one single year. The transcriptions reflect special graces of prayer Mechtild had received up to her fifty-first year. Nor should these revelations be taken to mean sensible visions. The word vision, used here, simply meant graces of prayer. Jean Leclercq, in his *Love of Learning and the Desire for God*, offered an understanding of the meaning of vision when he explained biblical imagination:

> [Biblical imagination] permitted them to picture, to 'make present', to see beings with all the details provided by the texts: the colors and dimensions of the people, the clothing, bearing and actions of the people, the complex environment in which they move. . . . The words of the text never failed to produce a strong impression on the mind.[14]

This textual richness of color, feelings, and symbols pervade the revelations of Mechtild in Book One. Her privileged experiences of prayer increased Mechtild's interior sensitivity when she celebrated the liturgy.[15] Everything in liturgy became more vivid. At Helfta the liturgy, always a communal action, was usually chanted by the nuns. Here was a source for deep, personal prayer that was sustained by *lectio divina*. Indeed the environment of the Helfta monastery fostered prayer that gradually became 'prayer of the heart'. Hence, we find in the revelations of Mechtild a continuous interchange between liturgy and personal devotion.[16] The liturgy, understood in this full sense, fostered the transformation of christian life.

Praying the Liturgy

Clearly, Mechtild of Hackeborn's heart and mind were attuned to Christ present in the liturgy, which is basically a trinitarian prayer of praise and thanksgiving—in, with, and through Christ, to the Father, in the unity of the Spirit. Her contemplative experience during the liturgy most often involved visual imagination: 'I saw the Lord.' The vision came to her as she participated in the liturgical action through chant, song, ritual activity such as procession, and communion or as she listened to the scriptures being proclaimed. Book One gives numerous examples. Those which follow have been selected to illustrate: 1) the pattern of the experience of prayer, 2) the influence of the seasons of the liturgical year and the effect of the mysteries of Christ upon her heart and mind, and 3) the content of its teaching.

The Mystery of the Incarnation: Advent

In the transcription of her revelations entered on the Saturday in the fourth week of Advent[17] we notice Mechtild's prayerful response to the communion antiphon, 'come and behold'. While she was praying for all those who ardently desired to see the face of God, she saw the Lord standing in the middle of the choir. His face, more radiant than the sun, illuminated each person present. She asked the Lord, 'why his face appears as radiant as the sun?' He responded, 'because the sun has three properties: it warms, gives life, and gives light'. She understood that these properties were illustrative of the work of Christ, the Son of God, in the souls of the faithful. Later, the text tells us she recalled psalm eighteen (in the Vulgate numbering): 'High above he pitched a tent for the sun who comes out of his pavilion like a bridegroom exulting like a hero to run his race.' The communion antiphon mentioned above, this psalm, and the end of the Advent season were combined in her prayer.

As her vision unfolded, she saw Christ as a tall young man, handsome, with a lively walk. He wore a cincture of red, green, and

white silk. She interpreted the colors allegorically: 'red for his passion which surpasses all other martyrdoms; green and white reflect
the innocence of his humanity and holy life.' She understood that
Christ was the bridegroom, the hero of the psalm eighteen. His
course or path she understood as the redemption of humankind.
The Lord seemed to teach her that those who carry a treasure also
bind themselves to press on without losing sight of the finish. The
incarnation is the mystery, or event of salvation which this liturgy
proclaimed. In the past, as today, Jesus carries a 'noble treasure'
which is our human nature. 'I have carried in my heart,' said the
Lord to Mechtild, 'all ransomed souls.'

Near the end of this revelation, when Mechtild was to receive
Holy Communion, she saw the same Lord now under the aspect of
a magnificent king. He took the place of the priest. In her vision, the
sisters, approaching Holy Communion, held burning oil lamps as
they ran to meet the Lord. The Holy Spirit let her understand the
meaning of her vision. Again the interpretation is allegorical. The
lamps symbolized their hearts; the oil, the loving kindness (*pietas
divinae cordis*) of the divine heart; and the flame of the lamp, the
ardor of love. The revelation teaches that the holy Sacrament of
the Eucharist communicates to those who receive it the devotion
(*pietas*) to sustain their daily lives. Thus the grace of the Mass sets
them afire with divine love.

This text illustrates the patterns of prayer and teaching found
in Book One as well as its theological content. When she prayed
the communion antiphon of the Mass, Mechtild united her prayer
with 'all who seek the face of the Lord'. In this attitude of prayer
she saw the Lord. That is, through this experience, God graced
her with deeper insight into the mystery of the incarnation. The
revelation is easily seen to be didactic. Christ carried the treasure
of humanity so that human beings might become participants in
God. The Eucharist celebrates and effects anew this divine exchange
between God and humanity. In Mechtild's revelation, the word
pietas, loving kindness, seems to convey the outpouring of God's love
through Christ, which transforms those who celebrate the saving
mystery of the Eucharist. The resultant increase in devotion (*pietas*)
is expressed in one's daily living. The text, cited for the Fourth
Sunday of Advent expresses this liturgical-theological doctrine in an
allegorical manner, using the biblical and eschatological symbolism
of burning oil lamps. One is reminded of Saint Bernard's teaching
on the three comings of Christ.

> The third lies between the other two. It is invisible, while the
> other two are visible. In the first coming he was seen on earth,

dwelling among us. . . . In the final coming all flesh will see the salvation of our God and they will look on him whom they have pierced. The intermediate coming is the hidden one; in it only the elect see the Lord within themselves and they are saved. . . . In his first coming our Lord came in our flesh and in our weakness; in the middle coming he comes in spirit and in power; in the final coming he will be seen in glory and majesty. Because this coming lies between the other two, it is like a road on which we travel from the first coming to the last.[18]

It is possible that the nuns of the Helfta community were familiar with this sermon. The image of the 'third coming' seems to be central to Mechtild's revelation.

The Nativity of the Lord

It seems to have been monastic custom on the vigil of Christmas[19] to chant the martyrology proclaiming the birth of the Lord at the Hour when the community assembled in the Chapter Room. During this ritual Mechtild recounts in her revelation[20] that she saw angels carrying torches accompanying each of the sisters as they entered the Chapter Room. The Lord appeared also, in the place of the abbess, seated on an ivory throne. She saw a rush of water, like a river, that flowed from Christ. The water washed away every flaw from the faces of the sisters as they recited the first response, 'Have mercy O God'. At the second refrain of 'Lord have mercy', they all moved toward the Lord, to offer Christ the prayers which they offered at this hour for all the Church. At the third 'Lord have mercy', the Lord with his own hand offered the golden chalice to those who had been mentioned in the sisters' prayers.

This portrait of the community gathered on the vigil of the solemn feast of the Nativity may reflect how literal and incarnational their spirituality was. The abbess holds the place of Christ.[21] The 'rush of water, cleansing water' may be an illusion to the rite of blessing and sprinkling with holy water during which the abbess, in the name of Christ, blesses the community gathered at prayer.

While at Mass on the Sunday within the Octave of Epiphany[22] Mechtild saw the Lord Jesus as a beautiful child of twelve years. The altar was his throne. He said: 'Here I am with my divine virtue, ready to heal all your offenses.' Mechtild desired to offer perfect praise to God. Yet she experienced a groaning, a suffering because she was unable to praise God as she desired. This vision taught her that the Lord supplies for the soul's imperfections and powerlessness. The Lord heals our weaknesses.

The Mystery of Redemption: Lent and the Spiritual Journey

As the liturgical year moves into the lenten season of forty days and forty nights of fasting and prayer, the Church ponders the mystery of human Redemption through the passion and death of the Lord. The biblical image of journey, the spiritual journey of the soul, is a familiar theme in Christian spirituality and well suited to Lent. It appears here in the revelations of Mechtild. On *Quinquagesima Sunday*[23] Mechtild heard Jesus, the 'beloved of her soul', murmur in her ear this sweet invitation: 'Would you come to dwell with me on the mountain during these forty days and nights?' 'Oh, willingly my Lord,' she answered, 'this is all I want and desire.'

Then the Lord showed her a high mountain which extended from east to west with seven plateau to ascend and seven fountains. This description suggests traditional teaching on the spiritual life as well as images which seem to be particular to Mechtild. At the end of the transcription she desired to 'offer satisfaction' for members of the Church who 'gravely insulted her Beloved'.[24]

The first plateau represents humility; the waters of the fountain purify the soul of all her sins. The second plateau is called the degree of sweetness; the fountain, 'patience'. Its waters purify the soul from any faults of anger or passion. The third degree is that of love and the fountain is charity. The soul is washed of all sins of hatred. 'At this stage, the Lord paused several times with the soul. She prostrated herself at the feet of Jesus; the gentle voice of Christ resonated as an organ.' She spoke to the Lord using words from the Song of Song.

> Arise my love, let me see your face' (Song 2:14). All the angels and saints surrounded the mountain, chanting in unison with God the sweet healing prayer of love. The chant was so sweet, the modulation so gentle, that no human tongue would be able to repeat it.[25]

This portion of the vision, with its reference to music, seems to be particular to Mechtild, the chantrix.

The fourth plateau represents the degree of obedience and the fountain, holiness. Its waters purify the soul of all faults committed by disobedience. The fifth degree is moderation and the fountain liberality. Here the soul is purified of sins committed by avarice—using creatures or things with no view to the glory of God or for personal advancement. The sixth plateau represents chastity. Its fountain purifies the soul of all inordinate carnal desire. At this stage

Mechtild saw the Lord dressed in a white robe. Finally arriving at the seventh stage, spiritual joy, the fountain was called 'heavenly joy'. The soul is purified of all faults committed by disgust for things spiritual. This fountain did not gush like all the others. It 'flowed slowly, drop by drop, because heavenly joy is not able to be grasped fully by the person in this life. On earth one receives only a taste which is nothing in comparison with the reality.'[26]

As her vision continued, the Lord, whom Mechtild calls 'Beloved', ascended to the summit of the mountain 'with his beloved' Mechtild. At the summit of the mountain were a multitude of angels and two thrones: one of the Holy Trinity; the other of the Blessed Virgin Mary. These are described in detail in the *Book of Special Grace*. The "throne of the Trinity" was surrounded by a golden baldachin embellished with precious stones. The image shifts to a royal feast, the celestial banquet, where

> the Son of the Virgin came herself to offer for them a delicious food, that is to say, his adorable body, bread of life and of salva-tion, . . . He also offers the chalice filled with pure wine, that is to say, the blood of the immaculate lamb, who purifies the heart from all defilement. The Lord said: 'Now I have given to your soul with all its goodness, what I am . . . you in me and I in you; you will never be separated from me.'[27]

After the royal feast Mechtild prayed to the Blessed Virgin Mary to offer praise to her Son for her. The vision describes Mary, accompanied by the choir of all the heavenly hosts, chanting praise. The Lord invited Mechtild to chant with them. She intoned the beautiful response: 'You, O Lord, are holy'. The Lord then lifted her in adoration to himself and placed her sweetly on his bosom. After this vision, Mechtild said to the Lord, 'O my unique Friend, what would please you so that all people may know you?'[28] The Lord answered, 'My goodness and my justice.' Mechtild prayed to understand how she could offer satisfaction for the members of the Church who had so gravely insulted her Beloved. In order to repay the injustices she understood she was to pray three hundred and fifty times the antiphon: 'All praise, honor and thanksgiving to you, Most Blessed Trinity.'

The teaching of this lengthy pre-lenten meditation highlights the nature of the spiritual journey of the soul with her Lord, its virtues and purifications, the special graces of contemplative prayer Mechtild was given, the centrality of the eucharistic mystery as the memorial of the mystery of redemption. At the summit of the mountain the vision of the throne of the most Holy Trinity surrounded with heavenly hosts and choirs of angels emphasizes the present, eschatological and cosmic themes of the Eucharist. We notice also the role of the Blessed Virgin Mary, seated to the right of her Son, our intercessor.

The Mystery of the Resurrection

Though several other visions are transcribed in the *Book of Special Grace* for the lenten liturgical season, we turn our attention now to the great mystery of the Lord's resurrection. On the night of the resurrection,[29] Mechtild, the servant of Christ, saw the Lord as he lay in the sepulcher. She knew by divine inspiration that the Father had conferred all his power on the humanity of Christ in his resurrection, that he had given the Son this glorification which he had eternally from the Father, that the Holy Spirit had poured out his gentleness, his goodness, and his love on Christ's glorified humanity. During the Mass of the Resurrection, while singing the *Gloria*, she wanted to thank God for these new graces. The Lord said to her: 'If you desire to praise me become one with this glory by which I honor the Father . . .'[30]

On another occasion during the same Easter feast the Lord showed her a splendid house, extensive and noble.[31] In this house she saw a smaller one made of cedar wood, lined on the interior with silver walls. The Lord dwelt there. She recognized without difficulty that the house was the divine heart because 'she had seen it more than once under this symbol'.[32] The Lord said to her, 'Your soul is always enclosed in my heart and mine in thee.' Mechtild then prayed to the Lord that she might prepare worthily to receive his most precious body in Holy Communion. 'The Lord said to her, "When you desire to receive Communion, examine with care the house of your soul in order to see that the walls are neither unclear nor deteriorating."'[33] A teaching, similar to an examination of conscience before Holy Communion, was given. Some of the points for consideration were zeal or negligence in all that regarded God, fidelity to the Church, actions towards her neighbor, devout prayer for sinners. 'Immediately after the divine teaching [Mechtild] entered into the house and sat at the feet of the Lord.' The Lord lifted her up, placing her on his heart, and kissed her three times saying: 'I give you the kiss of peace, with all my strength, all my wisdom, and all my unchanging goodness.'[34]

THE FEAST OF PENTECOST: GIFT OF THE HOLY SPIRIT

Several entries for the Vigil of the Feast of Pentecost enable us to see how images drawn from the Pentecost season's readings and liturgical actions formed the dispositions of her heart and prayer under this aspect of Christ's mysteries: the gift of the Holy Spirit and the birth of the Church.[35] Like the apostles, Mechtild aspired to become the dwelling place of the Holy Spirit. She understood that the Holy Spirit effected three things in the Apostles: a transformation from fear and weakness which enabled them to become strong and full of love; a purification by fire which sanctified them; and a transformation, as the psalm verse reflected: 'I say, "You are gods, sons of the Most High, all of you;"'.[36] Thus, in the third of these activities the Holy Spirit fashioned the apostles in the true image, the divine image. This led Mechtild to ask the Lord to permit the Holy Spirit to complete the same operations of knowledge in her soul.

At another time, also on the vigil of Pentecost, during the Divine Office, Mechtild saw the King of Glory, the Lord Jesus Christ, sitting in the church with a multitude of angels and saints.[37] From his heart rays illuminated the saints. When she chanted a responsory verse taken from the prophet Isaiah and containing the image of the vineyard of the Lord, she said to the Lord in an outpouring of love: 'God be pleased to grant that my heart would always be a chosen vineyard agreeable to your heart'. The Lord responded, 'I am doing all that you desire'. And immediately she saw herself within his sinless heart. There she walked as in a magnificent vineyard which the angels, like a wall, protected. In the middle of the vineyard was a fountain beside which the Lord was seated. From his sacred heart, as from a source, water poured rapidly into this fountain where it seemed to draw her so that he might pour out on humankind desire for spiritual rebirth.

COMMEMORATION OF THE SAINTS

After the close of the Pentecost season the entries found in Book One correspond to feasts of the Blessed Virgin Mary, several saints, the angels, and lastly the Feast of the Dedication of the Church. One example, from the transcription for the *Feast of Saint Mary Magdelene*[38] demonstrates how Mechtild prayed with the help of the saints. On the Feast of Mary Magdelene, Mechtild saw the Lord walk through the choir holding Saint Mary Magdelene gently in his arms. On seeing this she was not surprised because of the word from the Book of Wisdom 6,20: 'incorruptibility brings near to God'.[39] The Lord said: 'The intensity of love which she had for me on earth is proportionate to the union which associates her with me in heaven'. Mechtild prayed: 'O most sweet God, teach me how I would be able to praise you with your lover, Mary Magdelene.' Thus with Mary Magdelene, Mechtild was taught to offer praise to Christ through his five wounds.

SUMMARY

These examples, drawn from Book One of the *Book of Special Grace*, help us to see how Mechtild's prayer was both fashioned by the season of the liturgical year and formed by the mystery of Christ. Usually each transcription began with a specific text or image drawn from the liturgy. To 'see the Lord' was to experience and know the Lord's presence in her heart and in the community gathered to celebrate the liturgy. Dialogue between Mechtild and Christ and Christ and Mechtild demonstrated the degree to which Mechtild made this communal, liturgical prayer her own. It also was the source of her intercession for others. She spoke freely to Christ her petitions, questions, prayer and praise. Vision and dialogical prayer offered her, and through her, her companions, new understanding of spiritual experience and doctrine celebrated in the liturgy and carried over to daily living. Often she came to the depth of insight, that is, she understood the grace she either desired or received, by an association of images. Frequently these were echoes of biblical images drawn from antiphons, responsories, gospel pericopes, or ritual actions found in the liturgy of the day.

The theological-liturgical content of these revelations is christocentric, trinitarian, and eucharistic. The liturgy of the Church bears witness to the one mystery of Christ in the unfolding story of salvation which the liturgy celebrates. The Blessed Virgin Mary is seen in her role as bearer of Christ and intercessor with Christ.

We close with a final transcription. It is cited in the *Book of Special Grace* for the second day of Easter.[40] At Mass, during the reading of the lucan Gospel account of the Emmaus story, (Luke 24:29), the disciples' words 'Remain with us' drew Mechtild to the Lord. She said to him, 'O my unique sweetness, remain with me

I pray, because the day of my life is inclined toward evening.' The Lord responded: 'I will remain (*manebo/resterai*) with you.' This revelation provides a beautiful meditation on the experience of how the Lord 'remains' with us. It is interesting to notice in the French translation,[41] that two different words, *rester* and *demeurer* each translating the Latin verb *manere*, 'to remain', express degrees of a single spiritual experience. In her vision Mechtild heard the Lord relate four examples of how He dwelt with the soul. They were enumerated as follows.[42]

First, the Lord said 'I will remain (*resterai/manebo*) with you as a father with his son and give you part of the celestial heritage that I have acquired by my precious blood and that I accomplished for you during my years on earth.' Second, 'I will remain (*resterai/manebo*) with you as a friend with his friend, those who have found a faithful friend have found a refuge . . .' Third, here the word in the French edition shifts to *demeurer*, 'I will remain with you (*demeurerai*) as a spouse/husband with his spouse/bride; . . . no separation is possible between us, because there is an indissoluble marriage and eternal union. Fourth and last, 'I will remain (*resterai/manebo*) with you as a pilgrim with his companion . . .' Mechtild then prayed for pardon and forgiveness.

She spoke to the Lord, addressing him with the words 'life of my soul, sweet guide'. Mechtild asked for pardon of her sin because she 'has little good in her in comparison with her noble companion and spouse'. The Lord told her she is forgiven and that he will dwell[43] (*demeure/manebo*) with her until the end of her life. At that time he will receive her soul in the same manner as he commended his own spirit into the hands of his Father, and he will present her to his heavenly Father. Hearing the Lord's promise, she prayed for a person who had been her faithful friend. 'Immediately she saw this person in the presence of Christ. . . . Her heart was carried to highest praise for the Lord's kindness'.[44]

She then saw a splendid feast. The Lord was dressed in a wedding garment that was 'green with golden roses'. The heavenly family of the Lord wore the same garments as the Lord did. When the banquet was ready the Lord asked, 'Who would have the place of the minstrel?' And immediately he took Mechtild into his divine hands and began to dance with her. All the guests saw this and experienced a new increase of joy. They thanked the Lord for showing himself so graciously lovable with this soul. Mechtild, joined to Christ in the embrace of love, was guided before the table of those invited. She then saw a light, a marvelous splendor radiating from the divine face of the Lord, and overflowing from the cup. His radiance flooded the royal table in light and illuminated the heavenly court. The teaching of this vision is explained. The clarity of Christ's lovable face was their reassurance, their joy, and their delight. He is the good Lord who gives himself without tiring as satisfaction for our sins. This vision of Christ is a joy without end; the joy of eternal gladness. Therefore during such a feast, there would be praise and honor to the sweet Son of the Virgin.

CONCLUSION

Mechtild of Hackeborn died approximately eight years after confiding her revelations to her confidant, Saint Gertrud the Great. Though Mechtild is said to have endured intense physical suffering during her lifetime, her whole prayer experience, like the liturgy, was characterized by joy, praise, entry into the mystery of Christ and union with the Trinity in divine indwelling. What Cypriano Vagaggini wrote about the purpose of Gertrud the Great's visions is similarly true of the revelations of Mechtild of Hackeborn as transcribed by Gertrud the Great and another nun in Book One of the *Book of Special Grace*. 'Besides the simple reason of giving praise to God, it was for this precise purpose of leading others, by means of these imaginal descriptions, as by means of painted portraits, to taste one day of those higher intimacies of divine union.'[45] Book One of the *Book of Special Grace* invites the reader to taste and see the goodness of the Lord.

NOTES

1. The *Book of Special Grace*, chapter XVIII *Revelationes Gertrudianae ac Mechtildianae*, II, ed. Dom Ludwig Paquelin, *Sanctae Mechtildis: Liber Specialis Gratiae* (Paris, 1875–1877). Traduites sur l'édition latine des Pères benedictins de Solesmes (Paris: Tours, 1920). All translations are my own.

2. See note 1.

3. *In dedicatione ecclesiae*, 5:4–5; *SBOp* 5 (Rome, 1968) 391; *Super Cantica* 62:5; *SBOp* 2 (Rome, 1958) 158. Also from Jean Leclercq, 'Lectio Divina,' *Worship* 28:3 (May, 1984) 248.

4. See Book Five of the *Book of Special Grace*, chapter 24, 'How the Book Was Composed' (*Qualiter hic liber sit provisus*), pp. 356–358. Also chapter 22 'On the truth of this book, one may see special grace' (*De veritate hujus libri. Videlicet specialis gratiae*), pp. 353–355. See also the 'Preface' in *Revelations de Sainte Mechtilde* Vierge de l'Order de Saint-Benoit. Traduites sur l'édition latine des Pères benedictins de Solesmes (Paris: Tours Maison Alfred Mame et Fils, 1920) p. vii.

5. See Book Five of the *Book of Special Grace*, chapter 30, On the Admirable Life of this Virgin [Mechtild of Hackeborn], (*De laudabili conversatione hujus virginis*) pp. 363–369, especially pp. 368–369.

6. Caroline Walker Bynum, *Jesus as Mother Studies in the Spirituality of the High Middle Ages* (Berkeley: University of California Press) 180.

7. The *Book of Special Grace* is composed of seven parts sometimes called books. The first book, which we are considering, describes Mechtild of Hackeborn's graces of liturgical prayer over the course of the liturgical year. The second book is another accounting of her special graces. Books three and four are concerned with conventual life, and the fifth book with the afterlife. Books six and seven give information about the deaths of Mechtild of Hackeborn and Gertrud the Great.

8. See Sister Jeremy Finnegan, OP, 'Mechtild of Hackeborn: *Nemo Communior*,' in *Peaceweavers*, Medieval Religious Women, 2, edited by John A. Nichols and Lillian Thomas Shank. (Kalamazoo, 1987) 223–239. See also a revised work by the same author, *The Women of Helfta Scholars and Mystics* (Georgia, 1991, rev. ed. of *Scholars and Mystics*, 1962) 44–62. For a new study of Mechtild of Hackeborn, see Caroline Walker Bynum, *Jesus as Mother*, pp. 171–228. Here Bynum discusses both Mechtild and Gertrud the Great.

9. See Elizabeth Alvilda Petroff, ed., *Medieval Women's Visionary Literature* (New York: Oxford University Press, 1986) 207.

10. Cypriano Vagaggini, OSB, *Theological Dimensions of the Liturgy* (Collegeville: Liturgical Press, 1976) p. 740, note 1.

11. On *lectio divina* see Jean Leclercq, OSB, *The Love of Learning and the Desire for God*, translated by Catherine Misrahi (New York: Fordham University Press, 1961); Beryl Smalley, *The Study of the Bible in the Middle Ages* (Oxford: Blackwell-Notre Dame: University of Notre Dame Press, 1964); Jean Leclercq, OSB, 'Lectio Divinia,' *Worship* (May, 1984) 239–249.

12. William of Saint Thierry quoted in Leclercq, *The Love of Learning*, p. 91.

13. See *Heraut*, Book 2 Introduction in *Sources Chretiennes*, p. 54.

14. Leclercq, *Love of Learning*, p. 93.

15. See Jean Leclercq, OSB, 'Liturgy and Mental Prayer in the Life of Saint Gertrude,' in *Sponsa Regis* 31 (1960) 4. What is said here of Gertrud is also true of the transcriptions of Mechtild of Hackeborn's visions in the *Book of Special Grace*, part 1.

16. Leclercq, 'Liturgy and Mental Prayer,' p. 5.

17. From the *Book of Special Grace*, Book One, chapter 4.5: 'Why the Face of the Lord is Compared to the Sun' (*Cur facies domini soli comparetur*) pp. 13–15. All translations are my own.

18. Saint Bernard, *Sermo 5 in adventu Domini 1–3*; *SBOp* (1966) 188–190. This translation is by Henry Ashworth from *A Word in Season Monastic Lectionary for the Divine Office I: Advent-Christmas*, edited by Friends of Henry Ashworth (Saint Bede's Publications & Exordium Books, 1981) 20, 21.

19. See Book One of the *Book of Special Grace*, 'On the vigil of the sweet nativity of the Lord' (*In vigilia nativitatis domini*), pp. 14, 15. The editors of the French edition of the *Book of Special Grace* (*Revelations de Sainte Mechtilde, Le Livre de la Grace Speciale*, p. 16) point out that this text is one of the remarkable passages in which the revelation of Mechtild is confirmed in the Revelation of Gertrud (see Gertrude, *Heraut*, 4.2).

20. *Ibid.*

21. See RB 2.2.

22. In Book One of the *Book of Special Grace*, chapter 9, 'Christ Supplies for the Weakness of the Soul' (*Qauliter Christus defectus animae supplet*), pp. 29–31.

23. In Book One of the *Book of Special Grace*, chapter 13, 'The Mountain with Seven Plateaus and Fountains, and the Throne of God and the Blessed Virgin,' (*De monte et septem gradibus et fontibus, et de throno Dei et Beata Virginis*), pp. 40–45.

24. *Ibid.*, p. 44. The text does not identify the incident or give further explanation. It simply mentions she was to recite three hundered fifty times the antiphon, 'To you all praise, glory and thanksgiving, O Most Holy Trinity'.

25. *Ibid.*

26. *Ibid.* p. 41.

27. *Ibid.*, p. 45.

28. See note 24 above.

29. From Book One of the *Book of Special Grace*, chapter 19, 'Concerning the Resurrection of our Lord Jesus Christ and his Glorification' (*De Christi Resurrectione et ejus Glorificatione*), pp. 60–61.

30. *Ibid.*

31. From Book One of the *Book of Special Grace*, from chapter 19, 'Concerning the Dwelling Place of the Heart' (*De Domo Cordis*), pp. 61–64.

32. *Ibid.*, p. 62.

33. *Ibid.*

34. *Ibid.*, p. 63.

35. From Book One of the *Book of Special Grace*, chapter 22, 'On the Triple Operation of the Holy Spirit in the Apostles and in every soul by desire' (*De Triplici operatione spiritus in apostolis et in qualibet anima diserenante*), pp. 77–79.

36. Psalm 82:6 [Vulgate Ps 81:6: *Ego dixi: Dii estis, et filii Excelsi omnes*].

37. From Book One, chapter 22 of the *Book of Special Grace*, 'On the Vineyard of the Lord, which is the Soul of the Just One' (*De Vinea domini, scilicet anima justi*), pp. 79–80.

38. From Book One of the *Book of Special Grace*, chapter 25: 'Concerning the Wounds of Saint Mary Magdelene' (*De vulneribus sanctae Maria Magdalene*), pp. 86–87.

39. Quoted in Book One of the *Book of Special Grace*, chapter 25, p. 86, '*Incorruptio proximum facit esse Deo*' (Sap. vi. 20) [Vulgate reads *incorruptio autem facit esse proximum Deo*].

40. From Book One of the *Book of Special Grace*, chapter 36: 'How God Dwells with the Soul, and the Banquet of the Lord' (*Qualiter Deus cum anima maneat, et de convivio Domini*), pp. 68–70.

41. From Book One of the *Book of Special Grace*, chapter 19.36 'How God Dwells with the Soul; On the Banquet of the Lord (*Comment Dieu demeure avec l'ame; du banquet du Seigneur*), pp. 81–83, see especially p. 81.

42. See Book One of the *Book of Special Grace*, chapter 19.36, pp. 81–82 (Fr); and chapter 19, p. 68 (La).

43. *Ibid.*, p. 82 (Fr); p. 69 (La).

44. *Ibid.*

45. Cypriano Vagaggini, *Theological Dimensions of the Liturgy*, (Collegeville: The Liturgical Press) 745.

The Spirituality of
Cistercian Nuns:
A Methodological
Approach[1]

† *Edmund Mikkers* ocso

CAN WE REALLY SPEAK of a spirituality of cistercian nuns, as distinguished from the spirituality of the cistercian monks? This distinction is a small one, because the same cistercian life was lived by monks and by nuns. We often understand spirituality as a kind of doctrinal system which represents the theological, spiritual background of the life of the Cistercian Order. But the spirituality of any Order, including that of the Cistercians, includes the daily way of life, the exterior features, the observances, and the laws within which doctrine is lived. So both elements—the theological background and the exterior shape of cistercian monastic life—make it possible to speak of a specifically cistercian way of monastic life, a cistercian way of holiness and of union, in charity, with God. In this sense, both the doctrinal system and the exterior elements belong to the spirituality of the Order, in different ways and with varying importance, and with as many different expressions of it as there are people who follow this spirituality.

Precisely for this reason, the sources of the spirituality of cistercian monks and nuns are extremely varied, and a methodological study of cistercian spirituality must consider the different elements, not only in texts, but also in historical events. As with history in general, these elements should be approached with a critical mind capable of understanding and interpreting texts and data, but, still more, with a kind of inner feeling and understanding that cannot always be demonstrated clearly. Sometimes this can be done only as a result of sharing the same way of life.

The following notes will chiefly try to open some aspects of cistercian spirituality, indicating ways of getting a more complete and therefore clearer view of it than is immediately apparent.

Some main lines of the more doctrinal aspect of cistercian spirituality can be stated in a few words. First of all, cistercian spirituality presents a realistic, but at the same time optimistic, view of human nature before God. The human soul, the human mind, even if it is wounded and weakened by original and personal sin, remains open to God, capable of the desire for God and, with the aid of his grace, capable of returning to God by conversion. The human soul can never lose the image of God within it, but by its nature longs for restoration to full likeness. By accepting the monastic life, the monk and nun are, through their conversion, in a continuous search for God by the *ascesis* of the monastic life, by the penance of renunciation, by the acquisition of christian and monastic virtues under the guidance of the Rule of Saint Benedict, with the aid of the whole of Scripture and the writings of the Desert Fathers recommended by the Rule. The way back to God is through Christ, the universal and unique mediator between God and man; therefore this complete return to God is to be realized by a full conformity to Christ, by imitation of his life and sufferings, by participation in his resurrection. Through Christ, the Word incarnate, man reaches God himself and is absorbed in the mystery of his love, in the Holy Spirit. The human soul, the human mind, can truly experience this union with God in joy and jubilation, in tranquility of spirit and peace, in stability and purity. Union with God is the special grace and the special end of the monastic life, and is nothing other than the fullness of charity.

This spiritual doctrine is present in the writings of the Cistercians of the twelfth, thirteenth, and even the fourteenth centuries, with a great richness and variety of expression. As time passed, it came to be influenced by scholasticism and new trends in theology, yet even in those later centuries, as the exterior shape of cistercian life, rooted in the observances, was changed by historical events, the evolution of the monasteries, and cultural surroundings, something still did not change: the spirit and predominance of charity, the spirit of simplicity and penance, and the search for God alone. So cistercian spirituality is a complexity composed of various elements, influenced by many things, and in turn influencing the lives of monks and nuns in their monasteries.

With regard to cistercian spirituality in general, the Order possesses many sources, published and unpublished, which specifically focus on the doctrinal aspect. In most cases, the study of cistercian spirituality has been limited to this kind of source. But certainly, if we are to study the spirituality of cistercian nuns, we must also take into account the sources which provide information about the life of these nuns. By comparison with the written sources for the monks' spirituality, the sources for the nuns are limited and poor, which is why we are trying, in this paper, to present a general overview of the kinds of materials that would be helpful for further studies.

There is still another problem concerning the sources: very little has been published about the history of cistercian nuns in Italy and Spain,[2] and little even about those in France, despite their comparatively great number. Only recently have some general studies been published about the nuns in England.[3] This present paper was inspired mainly by the publications on cistercian nuns in the Low Countries and Germany. A more thorough, though not exhaustive, bibliography is available for these areas.

COMMON SOURCES WITH THE MONKS

The first and most important source for the spirituality of the nuns was certainly the Rule of Saint Benedict as it was interpreted within the Cistercian Order by their *Usages*, the first and most authentic commentary on the Rule and its adaptation to daily life. There Cistercians found the basic principles of their spirituality—humility, obedience, love for Christ, and charity—together with the exterior observances of silence, solitude, austerity, renunciation, and the exigencies of common life. There, too, they could find the monastic experience of personal and common liturgical prayer. Probably for the nuns, who devotedly followed the daily rhythm of liturgical prayer, singing the psalms, and listening to the readings and to the prayers provided the common and normal way to receive spiritual nourishment. The center of that prayer was, without any doubt, the celebration of the Eucharist, though in the first centuries at least, participation in it by holy communion was limited to a few days.

Here a question arises about the nuns' knowledge of Latin, the liturgical language of the time. In the Middle Ages and even up to the French Revolution, many convents of nuns, especially noble abbeys, held a certain number of young girls who were to be educated by the nuns. At least some instruction in liturgical texts and for this reason an elementary knowledge of Latin by a number of nuns may be presupposed. This knowledge was enough to let them follow the general meaning of the texts according to the liturgical year, particularly because these texts were often repeated. The copying of books also may have increased their knowledge of Latin.[4]

We may suppose that life according to the Rule, under the austere cistercian interpretation, provided for them a great force of purification and helped their spiritual aspirations reach a deep love of God and of others. This fidelity to a life regulated by the *Usages* can be traced even in difficult periods of reformation and renewal, and it sometimes saved some monasteries, for instance, during the Reformation and the French Revolution, when they had no other means of maintaining the original spirit of the Order.[5]

Another very important element in their formation in an authentic cistercian spirituality was certainly the chaplains, called *confessores*. In most cases, they were cistercian monks, delegated by the Father Abbot to hear the confessions of the nuns and to preach. Sometimes if there was not another monk or laybrother who acted as *procurator*,[6] they had to occupy themselves with temporal affairs. *Capellani*, being only clerics and not Cistercians, could say Masses, but in the beginning did not have permission to hear the nuns' confessions; this was granted only much later by the General Chapter.[7] The chaplains could share the spiritual experience they had as Cistercian monks with the nuns. However, the nuns probably did not learn a theoretical approach to cistercian spirituality from them, but their openness to grace, their simplicity, charity, poverty, fidelity and their direct, feminine intuitions enabled them to respond with great receptivity. They were more open to an immense and devoted love for Christ than to christological doctrine, and their zeal to be conformed to the humanity of Christ in its humility and sufferings found concrete expression in various devotions to Christ.[8]

Devotion to the Eucharist, which arose at the end of the twelfth century, was actively spread by the Cistercians, in part by their protection of Juliana of Mont-Cornillon.[9] It was fervently followed in cistercian convents of nuns, as were devotions to the Sacred Heart, the wounds of Christ, his passion and resurrection;[10] they formed an essential part of their monastic life. This was true not only for the thirteenth century and the later Middle Ages, but for nearly the whole cistercian movement in the sixteenth and later centuries. These devotions should be considered not merely exterior practices, but more signs of an inner conviction.

The influence of the chaplains is not easy to trace, mostly because this topic has not been sufficiently studied, because of scarcity of sources. In some places we can follow that influence, as in the case of the Catholic cistercian chaplains who maintained the Catholic faith in several convents of nuns in Brandenburg against the intrusion of Protestant ministers under the protection of the prince-elect of Brandenburg.[11] Another example is the activity of the chaplain, appointed by the abbot of Marienfeld, in the restoration of cistercian life at the abbey of Bersenbrück, in the beginning of the seventeenth century.[12] In this context too, we might already speak about the reformation of Port-Royal. There they not only accepted the exterior regulations of an austere cistercian life, but they also intended to return to the spirit of Saint Benedict, the true spirit of Cîteaux and Saint Bernard, and through them to the Fathers and Scripture. Very soon this reform movement came under the influence of 'French spirituality' and later, as we know, under that of the Jansenists.[13] In these reform movements of the sixteenth and seventeenth centuries many cistercian monasteries disassociated themselves from the government and spiritual direction of the Order. Other currents of spirituality entered the convents: in Spain, that of the Jesuits and Carmelites. The influence of Saint Francis de Sales was very great in the reform movement of Louise de Ballon and others.

Perhaps, in more recent times, during the restoration of the Order after the French Revolution, the influence of the chaplains on the inner life of the nuns' communities continued to increase; in this new situation their function was limited only to spiritual direction in confession, celebration of the Mass, and preaching or spiritual instruction.

The legislation of the Order, its general laws, and its special applications to the nuns, given over the centuries by the General Chapter, provide a remote, but very important source for the nuns' spirituality. There can be found several instructions having to do with poverty, common life, enclosure, confession, profession, faults, reformation, economics—all of which directly have to do with spirituality. In later times, when the authority of the General Chapter declined, there are many examples of constitutions or regulations given by the nuns for a reformed congregation or a group of monasteries, or even for a single abbey.[14]

Included in these kinds of sources are visitation cards, records of visitations made by the authorities of the Order, sometimes by outsiders. They provide material very helpful in understanding the spirituality of a convent. Sometimes parts of them are published in the monographies of an abbey; sometimes they are published separately.[15] Next to visitation cards come the protocols of elections; these allow a look at the real situations in abbeys of nuns, although this material dates only from the sixteenth century.

SPECIAL SOURCES FOR THE NUNS' SPIRITUALITY

All the sources mentioned in the section above belong to the monks as well as the nuns. The following sources deal more explicitly with nuns. For the sake of clarity we can divide them into several sections.

The Biographies of Cistercian Nuns

These are the most important and the most comprehensive sources, but perhaps they have not yet been sufficiently explored from the point of view of spirituality. Three chronological divisions are to be made:[16]

(i) The medieval *Vitae*. The best known group is that of the *Vitae* of the cistercian nuns in Belgium proper, covering the old bishopric of Liège. The best known of these are the lives of Saint Lutgard, Beatrice of Nazareth, the three Idas, Elizabeth of Herkenrode and some others.[17] Other *Vitae* of the same period are those of Lukardis of Oberweimar, Saint Franca, and Ascelina. Another group tells of portuguese nuns, for instance, Mafalda, Sancia, Theresia, Uraca. The problem here is not only the historical authenticity and value of the texts, but also the right interpretation of these *Vitae* in their historical context.

(ii) The biographies of more recent times, from Trent to about the French Revolution. From this period we know Veronica Laparelli and Louise de Ballon, but so many others, such as the promoters of the reform of the nuns' houses in France, about whom biographies were published at the time, are virtually unknown, and it would be interesting to find out how they preserved the original spirituality of Cîteaux in their reformation.[18]

(iii) The biographies of cistercian and trappist nuns of the nineteenth and the first half of the twentieth centuries. Most of them are published in books, pamphlets, or smaller publications, as sometimes in the chronicles of the monasteries in the *Cistercienser Chronik* and the *Collectanea*.

However, an important remark, applicable not only to the biographies of the Middle Ages, but also to those of later times, should be made about these biographies. The biographers of the Middle Ages did not care much about historical accuracy. Rather than relate an historical account about a saintly person, they preferred to convey a message, though often that message was more of a statement of their own beliefs than anything else. Therefore, speaking in a very general way, a distinction should always be made between the cistercian ideal proposed by the biographer and the reality of the human and monastic life of the saint. By their actual monastic life, not by any theory, they attained a high degree of charity and love and union with God. Something like a demythologizing should be done to understand the privileged way of life of the person concerned. So it is very clear that in the numerous biographies published between the two World Wars about cistercian monks and nuns, the distinction between the historical secular-bound ideal and its realization by a monk or nun makes judgment sometimes difficult, but also more acceptable and sincere; the real and authentic values may be more easily detected from an outside point of view.

Autobiographies of Cistercian Nuns

The number of autobiographies within the Cistercian Order is small, but the existing ones are surely of great value. This may be especially true of the work of Beatrice of Nazareth, even though in the extant copies much of the autobiographical character is lost.[19] In the same sense, the works of Gerturd and Mechtild of Helfta contain a great deal of autobiographical material that cannot be distinguished clearly in the text itself.[20] From later centuries we have the autobiographical work of the spanish cistercian mystic, Maria Vela y Cueto,[21] and the no less important life of Mother Louise de Ballon (1591-1668).[22] Another autobiography is that of Antonia Jacinta de Navarra (1602-1656), nun of Las Huelgas.[23]

In this kind of literature we must also include the biographical letter collections of Jeanne de Boubais (+1553), abbess of Flines, and Gertudis Anglesola, nun of La Zaidia in Valencia, Spain (1641-1724). Among these, too, the writings of several nuns of Port-Royal, and their correspondence, could find a place.[24]

Spiritual Works of Cistercian Nuns

Hardly any text by cistercian nuns of the twelfth century is known; their juridical connection with the Order was still uncertain at the time.

The autobiography of Beatrice of Nazareth contains at least the summaries of spiritual treatises of which she was the author.[25] Originally, they were written in Old Dutch or 'thiois', then adapted, and translated into Latin by the editor of her notes, the confessor of Nazareth.[26] These treatises concerning the spiritual life of a cistercian nun are put together in the second book of her *Vita*. The titles of these treatises show their symbolical character: The Triple Exercise of Affections (II.3); The Two Cells of the Heart (II.5); The Five Mirrors of the Heart (II.6); The Spiritual Monastery (II.7); The Two Guards of the Monastery: Humility and Obedience (II.8); The Fruitful Garden of the Heart (II.9).[27] The most famous of these treatises is the 'Seven Manners of Love' (III.14), a summary of the ascent of the soul to God by ever deeper experiences of his presence in the soul. Only this text is preserved in the original Dutch, and there one can feel the strength of her expressions. This work is also a masterpiece of dutch literature.[28]

Chronologically, after Beatrice, we must mention an old text, the Collection of Prayers of Saint Thomas-an-der-Kyll, from the monastery of that name founded for cistercian nuns, in honour of Thomas of Canterbury. The prayers date from the thirteenth century and clearly reveal the spirituality of the nuns. The style is rather simple, with many references to scriptural, liturgical, and even patristic texts; these texts reveal the nuns' devotion to the Holy Trinity, to Christ, the Eucharist, Our Lady, and the saints.[29]

Not less important are the works of Gertrud and Mechtild of Helfta, in which the autobiographical element, their experience of spiritual life, is interwoven with expositions about these experiences. Gertrud is the author of the *Spiritual Exercises*,[30] and *The Herald of Divine Love*,[31] and Mechtild of *The Book of Special Grace*. Both authors present an excellent doctrine of cistercian monastic life, insisting especially on personal, common, and liturgical prayer and on the experiences of an authentic union with God through charity and love. The place of the humanity of Christ in their spirituality is very near to the concept of Saint Bernard.[32]

Surely, these texts are the most important of the cistercian nuns' movement of the thirteenth century. In the history of spirituality little attention has been paid until now to the great cistercian mystical movement centered in the german abbeys of Heilsbronn and Kaisheim, under their well-known abbots, Conrad of Brundelsheim and Ulrich of Kaishem, and in the works of the unknown 'monk of Heilsbronn', perhaps the same Conrad. They had a great influence on monasteries of nuns. Further investigation would probably uncover writings by cistercian nuns in this period and region. Whether an extant commentary on the Book of the Apocalypse from the nuns' abbey of Bersenbrück should be considered an original work of a nun, a translation from a latin original, or perhaps simply a copy written in the monastery, is not yet clear.[33]

That example brings us to a problem that has never been studied sufficiently: that so little is left of the libraries of nuns from the Middle Ages and even from later times. Most of the extant manuscripts from nuns' libraries are liturgical books, texts of the Bible, and sometimes copies of patristic texts. In the case of the manuscripts of the nunnery of Kirchein-am-Ries, currently in the library of Harburg, it is not clear whether they really belonged originally to the nuns; on the other hand they contain a number of spiritual texts and collections of prayers.[34]

For recent times an inventory of works written by cistercian nuns could eventually be made with the help of modern bibliographies.[35]

Spiritual Works Written by Cistercian Monks for Nuns

Here we will give only a few examples, probably others could be found among spiritual literature of later times.

The *Regula inclusarum* written by Aelred of Rievaulx for his sister could be seen as an example of how a twelfth-century abbot would have given instructions to nuns, even if they were not Cistercians. Immediately one can see in these ascetical exhortations to a nun a great similarity to the teaching given the monks, only in simpler and more direct style.[36] Another example from the same period are a number of sermons on the Canticles delivered by Gilbert of Hoyland to nuns. These nuns too, were surely not Cistercian, and belonged probably to the gilbertine congregation of Savigny.[37] The work of Adam of Perseigne *De mutuo amore ad sacras virgines*, was written, not for cistercian nuns but for the nuns of Fontevrault, at the end of the twelfth century.[38] Here again, we can only guess that the spiritual direction given to cistercian nuns at the moment of their integration into the Cistercian Order, in the first thirty years of the thirteenth century, would not have been very different.

From the same first part of the thirteenth century, we have the extremely important text, entitled the *Visions of Saint Thomas an der Kyll*, evidently written by a cistercian monk for the nuns of that abbey.[39] The visions are ascribed to Elisabeth, the first abbess of Saint Thomas, who died before 1205, so the text may have been written in the first decades of the thirteenth century by a monk of Himmerod. The text is a collection of ascetical counsels concerning the monastic life and fidelity to the Rule. Silence, modesty, mutual love, prayer, community life, the divine office, struggle against vices, joy, simplicity, and humility are all mentioned. at the conclusion of the text is a plea from the author to the abbess, asking her intercession for himself and for the community. The question is whether these texts grew out of spiritual direction given by a monk to this community of nuns. The direct inspiration for this work is not clear; some thoughts of Saint Bernard could be found, but so too, can the influence of the *Speculum Virginum*, a work of the eleventh century, present in several cistercian abbeys of monks.[40]

Engelhard, monk of Langheim and later abbot of Ebrach, also wrote, in the first half of the thirteenth century, a *Liber miraculorum*, which he dedicated to the abbess and nuns of Wechterswinkel. It contains miracles of various saintly persons of the Order and others in connection with the veneration of the Eucharist.[41]

We know that the famous abbey of Villers, in Brabant, was interested in the foundation of monasteries for nuns, and that many of these houses were under its paternity.[42] A monk there, Thomas of Villers, wrote two letters to his sister, who was a cistercian nun in Parc-aux-Dames; the second letter, especially, is a collection of spiritual advice about devotion to Our Lady, about interiority, the love of Christ, the liturgical life, and the singing of the psalms. Brother and sister lived in the same spiritual climate.[43]

In the unedited collections of sermons of the later Middle Ages there are sermons most likely delivered by Cistercians to nuns. We have at least one example of such a collection: two manuscripts which belonged to the cistercian nuns' abbey of Heggbach. The sermons were written by the confessor, a cistercian monk of Salem, by a priest Henry Jaedk, and a dominican friar, Felix of Ulm.[44]

In the seventeenth century the writings of abbot de Rancé on behalf of the nuns of Les Clairets and others can also be studied from the viewpoint of spirituality.[45]

In later centuries non-cistercians often took charge of the spiritual direction of cistercian nuns, and their writings, too, have a certain importance in assessing the non-cistercian influence on the spiritual life in the abbeys. One very fine example of such a work is the commentary on the seventh chapter of the Rule of Saint Benedict by the Jesuit Ghirlain Perduyn for the nuns of La Cambre at Brussels.[46]

Monumental Sources

Under this label we would list as a real, though indirect source for our knowledge of the spirituality of the nuns, the architecture, the churches, and other monastic buildings that still exist in great number. In their simplicity, poverty, and purity, they bear witness to a living spirituality.[47] Under this heading could also be listed all kinds of furniture coming from the nuns' monasteries—statues, showing a special devotion to Christ, his mother, and Saint Bernard, especially in the later Middle Ages and after the Reformation in baroque times;[48] here is evinced as well the devotion to the mystery of the resurrection as it was represented in Wienhausen[49] and in La Maigrauge. All kinds of devotional objects from those periods tell something about the spirituality of the nuns. Many of the old cistercian abbeys of nuns which were never suppressed contain within their walls treasures of art which illustrate a spirituality lived without interruption through the centuries. The still-existing abbeys of Seligenthal, Lichtenthal, and La Maigrauge provide examples of these kinds of sources, as do many other abbeys in Germany, Belgium, Italy, and Spain.

We said earlier that we do not know much about the nuns' libraries in the Middle Ages and later.[50] Certainly, liturgical manuscripts were sometimes written by nuns and some fine copies of books have been preserved,[51] as, for instance, a very fine illuminated manuscript containing a collection of prayers and meditations from the abbey of Medingen.[52] But this activity of the nuns should be further investigated. In the same way, other artifacts in the nuns' abbeys, such as weaving and embroidery, of which fine examples exist,[53] could be studied more systematically. We should not forget why the nuns paid so much attention to these objects for daily or conventual use, and should see them in connection with their spirituality.

In a certain sense, the external activity of a monastery, including the economic activity, can reveal much to us about the inner, spiritual life of a community. Equally important are the administration of the possessions and the exercise of their rights. One example is the account books, often preserved; a detailed study of the account-books of the nuns' abbey of Leeuwenhorst in Holland, dating from the end of fifteenth century to the middle of the sixteenth century, shows clearly the ups and downs of the monastic life in the last century before the Protestant Reformation.[54]

A simple survey of the historical development of an abbey of nuns, as is found in many monographies, reveals also a great deal about the spirituality lived there. The inner life took shape within the exterior history, and so every well-done monography, economic study, or biography can tell us a great deal about the spirituality of the community.

CONCLUSION

It is clear in the whole field of the cistercian spirituality that much more study of details has still to be done before a synthesis can be proposed. This is even more true for cistercian nuns, where the written sources are less numerous, than for monks. Only by putting together all the pieces as a mosaic, will we be able to get a clear idea about the spirituality of cistercian nuns in the past as well as in the present, and we will discover an ideal corresponding to the reality.

NOTES

1. Given the present state of the knowledge about the history of cistercian nuns and its sources, we have to limit ourselves to general methodological remarks which may instigate further study.
2. Some exception should be made for a certain number of articles published in the periodical *Cistercium*.
3. See D. H. Williams, 'Cistercian Nunneries in Medieval Wales' in *Cîteaux* 26 (1975) 155-175; J. A. Nichols, 'The Internal Organisation of English Cistercian Nunneries', in *Cîteaux* 30 (1979) 23-40; C. V. Graves, 'English Cistercian Nuns in Lincolnshire', in *Speculum* 54 (1979) 492-499.
4. See the end of this study for what is said about the illumination of manuscripts by nuns, and notes 47 and 48.
5. Here we could mention the various editions of the *consuetudines* of the Order, and the special constitutions of congregations of nuns which juridically withdrew from the jurisdiction of the Order; as, for instance, the Bernardines of Savoie, Louise de Ballon, Louise de Ponconas, or Port-Royal. For example, see Colette Friedlander, *ocso* 'Les plus anciennes Constitutions des moniales de la Trappe' in *Cîteaux* 22 (1981) 321-351. For a fine example of such constitutions for a single house, see J. Hau, 'Statuten aus einem neiderdeutschen Cistercienserinnen-Kloster' in *Cistercienser Chronik* [hereafter *Chronik*] 47 (1935) 129-138, 213-222.
6. This was a condition for the full incorporation of convents of nuns into the Order.
7. See I.-M. Canivez, *Capitulorum Generalium* 1265, 2 (Louvain, 1939) vol. 3: p. 32.
8. Important is the conclusion of S. Roisin, *L'hagiographie cistercienne dans le diocèse de Liège au XIIᵉ siècle* (Louvain, 1947), p. 279: 'L'idee de perfection ... s'appuie sur les vertus fondamentales d'humilité et de depouillement pour tendre, par le Christ-homme, a l'union avec la Trinité dans la charité parfaite. Les mystiques aspirent a gouter des cette vie un prélude de la vision béatifique et des extases qui les arrachent un instant a tout le crée pour les plonger en Dieu; les religieux moins favorisés se contentent d'une exactitude absolue a toutes les éxigences de la Règle; tous étayent leurs efforts sur les devotions eucharistiques et mariales. Leur spiritualité encore très affective accuse déja des tendances speculatives qui annoncent les grands courants du XIVᵉ siècle.'
9. See C. Hontoir, 'La devotion au Saint Sacrement chez les prémiers cisterciens, XIIᵉ et XIIᵉ siècles' in *Studia Eucharistica* (Antwerpen, 1946) 132-156.
10. See further, notes 50 and 51.
11. See F. Schrader, 'Die Zisterzienserklöster in den mittelalterlichen Diözesen Magdeburg und Halberstadt' in *Cîteaux* 21 (1970) 265-278; *Idem, Ringen, Untergang un Uberleben der Katholischen Klöster in den Hochstiften Magdeburg und Halberstadt von der Reformation bis zum Westfalischen Frieden* (Munster, 1977).

12. See O. zu Hoene, *Kloster Bersenbrück* (Osnabrück, 1978), s. v. Raeckmann (p. 392).

13. See F. Ellen Weaver, *The Evolution of the Reform of Port-Royal, from the Rule of Cîteaux to Jansenism* (Paris, 1978) with abundant bibliography.

14. See Roger De Ganck, 'De reformatiebeweging bij de Zuid-nederlandse cistercienserinnen in de 15e eeuw' in *Cîteaux* 32 (1981) 75-86.

15. See Roger De Ganck, 'De Abt van Morimond op visiet in de Brabantsche Vrouwenabdijen c. 1570', in *Collectanea OCR* 7 (1945) 95-109; 8 (1946) 293-301. For the use of such Protocols, see the work of O. zu Hoene, cited above, note 12, and O. Beck, *Die Reichsabtei Heggbach* (Sigmaringen, 1980) pp. 503-510.

16. A very important work for tracing the biographies of cistercian monks and nuns is S. Lenssen, *Hagiologium Cisterciense*, I-III (Tilburg, 1948-1951), published in a very limited run. See also the work of A. M. Zimmerman, *Kalendarium benedictinum*, I-IV (Metten, 1933-1938).

17. The best work in this field is the already cited dissertation of S. Roisin, *L'hagiographie cistercienne*. The author studies the literary genre and the sources of biographical works on Cistercians as well as the methods applied and the conclusions which may be drawn from them. Sometimes these conclusions seem rather negative.

18. To name a few: Francoise de Nerestang, Jeanne de Pourcelle de Pourlan, Anne-Louise de Crevant d'Humieres, Louise-Cecile de Ponçonas.

19. *Vita Beatricis, De autobiographie van de Z. Beatrijs van Tienen. O. Cist. 1200-1268*, door L. Reypens (Antwerpen, 1964) Latin text, with Dutch introduction and summaries in Latin. A translation into English, with the same Latin text, is available as *The Life of Beatrice of Nazareth*, CF50 (Kalamazoo, 1992).

20. See the excellent introductions of Jacques Hourlier to the french translation of the *Exercices*, in Sch 127, and of P. Doyère to the french translation of the *Herald* in Sch 139, 143, 255.

21. See Frances Parkinson-Keyes, *The Third Mystic* (London, 1960); O. G. Hernandez, *Una Mistica Abulense, Dona Maria Vela y Cueto, 1561-1617* (Avila, 1961); D. Maria Vela y Cueto, *Autobiografia y Libro de las Mercedes*, Introd. edicion de O. G. Hernandez (Barcelona, 1961).

22. Louise de Ballon, *Écrits spirituels*, reimpression anastatique des '*oeuvres de piete*', introduction by Edm. Mikkers (Sierre, Geronde, 1979), with bibliography.

23. J. Saracho, *Vida de la Ven. Senora Dona Antonia Jacinta de Navarra* (Salamanca, 1678).

24. See Weaver (note 13).

25. See *Vita Beatricis* (above note 19), especially pp. 56*-60*.

26. See Roger De Ganck, *The Life of Beatrice of Nazareth*, CF 50 (Kalamazoo, 1992), *Introduction*.

27. *Ibid.*

28. See J. Van der Kun, *Beatrijs van Nazareth, Seven Manieren van Minnen* (Antwerpen, 1928); Betrijs van Nazareth, *Van Seuen Manieren van Heileger Minnen*, ing. en uitgeg. door H. Vekeman en J. Tersteeg (Zutphen, 1970); for a french translation, see Hadewijch, *Lettres spirituelles* - Beatrice de Nazareth, *Sept degres d'amour*, french translation by J. B. Porion (Geneva, 1972). English translation of Hadewicjk by Columba Hart, osb, *Hadewijch. The Complete Works* (New York, 1980). For a translation of the *Seven Manieren*, see *The Life of Beatrice of Nazareth* (note 19 above).

29. A german translation of these prayers has been published: *Gebete aus St. Thomas. Geistliche Texte aus eine mittel-alterlichen zisterzienserinnenabtei des Trieres Landes*, übersetzt und zusammengestellt von A. Heinz (St. Thomas a.d. Kyll, 1980) 196 pp.

30. Translated by Gertrud Jaron Lewis, *The Spiritual Exercises*, CF 49 (Kalamazoo, 1989).

31. Translated by Alexandra Barratt (Kalamazoo, 1992).

32. See note 20.

33. See O. zu Hoene, *Die Apokalypse aus dem Kloster Bersenbruck* (San Francisco, 1970).

34. One example of such a collection is the manuscript of the abbey of Medingen, Wolfenbüttel, Codex Guelferbytanus 300.1 Extrav. See Kaspar Elm, *Die Zisterzienser. Ordensleben zwischen Ideal und Wirklichkeit* (1980) 592, 593.

35. Several works by cistercian nuns are listed in *Dictionnaire des auteurs cisterciens* (Rochefort, 1975-1977). Many of them are biographies and chronicles of monasteries, which often contain material for the history of the spirituality. Examples are H. Appuhn, *Chronik des Klosters Wienhausen* (Celle, 1956); see also the same text in A. Schneider, *Die Cistercienser. Geschichte, Kunst, Geist* (Cologne, 1974) pp. 355-362. Th. v. Liebenau, 'Zwei Denkschriften der Äbtissin Ratzenhofer von Rathausen', in *Chronik* 5 (1893) 257-269, 289-293.

36. See *The Works of Aelred of Rievaulx*, Vol. 1: *Treatises, The Pastoral Prayer*, CF 2 (1971) 41-102.

37. As such may be considered sermons 17, 18, 19, 45: english translation by Lawrence C. Braceland SJ, CF 14, 20, 26, 34.

38. G. Raciti, '*Un Opuscule inedit d'Adam de Perseigne, le "Livre de l'amour mutuel"*, in *Cîteaux* 31 (1980) 297-341. [Translation projected—ed.]

39. See the German translation of this text: H. Rissel, 'Ein Zeugnis vom geistlichen Leben in der Frühzeit. Die sogenannten Visionen von St. Thomas' in *St. Thomas an der Kyll. Beitrage zu der Geschichte des ehemaligen Zisterzienserinnenabtei* (St. Thomas, 1980) 55-84.

40. M. Bernards, *Speculum Virginum. Geistigkeit und Seelenleben der Frau im Hochmittelalter* (Cologne-Graz, 1955).

41. B. Griesser, 'Engelhard von Langheim und sein Exempelbuch für die Nonnen von Wechterswinkel', in *Chronik* 70 (1963) 55-73.

42. See E. de Moreau, *L'abbaye de Villers-en-Brabant, au XIIe et XIIIe siècle, Étude d'histoire religieuse et economique* (Brussels, 1909).

43. Edmund Mikkers, 'Deux lettres inedites de Thomas, chantre de Villers' in *Collectanea OCR* 10 (1948) 161-173.

44. O. Beck, *Die Reichsabtei Heggbach* (Sigmaringen, 1980) 451-452. The manuscripts are in Berlin, Staatsbibliothek, SPK Mgf 1056 and Mgq 1241.

45. See A. J. Krailsheimer, *Armand-Jean de Rancé, Abbot of La Trappe* (Oxford, 1974) chapter 9: 'Woman in Religion', pp. 176-210. See also, C. Waddell, 'Armand-Jean de Rancé and Françoise Angelique d'Etampes Valencay: Reformers of Les Clairets; below pp. 591ff.

46. See A. V. D. Zeyden, 'Gislenus Perduyn S.J., predikant te Ter Kameren' in *Cîteaux* 32 (1981) 237-251.

47. See E. Coester, 'Die Cistercienserinnenkirchen des 12. bis 14. Jahrhunderts" in A. Schneider, *Die Zisterzienser. Geschichte, Geist, Kunst* (Cologne, 1974) 363-428; and Anselme Dimier, 'L'architecture des églises des moniales cisterciennes' in *Cîteaux* 25 (1974) 8-23.

48. See, for example, the illustrations in the above-cited books by O. Beck on *Heggbach*, zu Hoene on *Bersenbrück*, and nearly every modern monograph about a cistercian abbey of nuns.

49. A fine example of such a decoration, which illustrates the spirituality of the time, is H. Appuhn, *Kloster Wienhausen. Einführung und Beschreibung* (Hamburg, 1955). For the painting of the church and the Holy Sepulchre, see illustrations 14, 15, 20, 26, 29, 31; the high altar, illustrations 16-18. Appuhn has published several other books and articles on Wienhausen.

50. For a study of the library of Woltingerode, see A. Schneider, *Die Zisterzienzer*, 468-470.

51. In Schneider's *Die Zisterzienzer*, several fine minatures are reproduced: from Woltingerode, p. 487; from Selingenthal, p. 489; from Wonnenthal, p. 494; from Mariastern, p. 500.

52. See note 36.

53. See *Kloster Wienhausen*, pp. 46-59.

54. Geertruida de Moor's study *Prosperity in Holland? An inquiry into the level of prosperity in the county of Holland between 1410 and 1553 mainly based on the accounts of the Cistercian nunnery Leeuwenhorst (1261-1574) by Noordwijkerhout and the village-accounts of Noordwijk,* has not yet been published in English translation.

Part Three:

Continuing *the* Tradition

Introduction

Chrysogonus Waddell OCSO

'BETWEEN THE YEARS 1570 AND 1670 France witnessed the birth, supremacy and death of many splendid Abbesses, who in less than thirty years had re-established in every quarter of the kingdom the nearly vanished prestige of. . . .' It would be comforting indeed to be able to conclude this sentence with a reference to the Cistercian Order. Many readers, however, will have recognized this incomplete quotation as the opening sentence in the chapter on 'The Great Abbesses' in Henri Bremond's *A Literary History of Religious Thought in France*;[1] and those same readers will also know that the Order to whose prestige those splendid abbesses contributed so much was, not the Cistercian Order, but the Order of Saint Benedict. It is doubtful that any historian of religious thought or of monastic spirituality and institutions will ever be able to write a book of any great length on 'The Great Cistercian Abbesses' for the period between Renaissance and Revolution, whether in France or elsewhere. It is equally unlikely that a historian of the caliber of Dom Yves Chaussy, OSB, will ever be able to find enough suitably convincing material to justify a cistercian equivalent of his two-volume *The Benedictine Nuns and the Catholic Reform in Seventeenth-century France*.[2]

By no means, however, does this somewhat negative assessment mean to suggest that, for the period under discussion, cistercian communities of women offer little of note for the historian or for the reader interested in things monastic. The case is quite the opposite. We most certainly need monographs, and more monographs, on great abbesses. But for every great abbess, there are dozens upon dozens of other abbesses who, in our estimation, may fall short of the category of 'greatness', but whose influence for good or for bad was decisive for the life of their communities.

Further, feminine monasticism is not reducible to the category of abbesses. In any religious community, as in any community at large, individual members, no less than superiors, are bearers of tradition and contributors to its enrichment. They too deserve our interest and our gratitude.

Again, it is quite necessary to study, as Dom Chaussy does so admirably, the contribution of benedictine abbesses to the remarkable phenomenon of the Catholic Reform in seventeenth-century France. But we should not overlook another category of contributors to reform movements such as that one—I mean the category of those who benefit from the reforming work of others of a more creative and charismatic stamp than themselves. Their own contribution may be less dramatic, but it is no less essential: they implement and concretize and give living expression to the programs of reform and renewal inaugurated through the initiative of others of a more ostensibly heroic stamp.

There is something quite remarkable about what happened in so many communities of cistercian women religious in the few centuries prior to the Revolution—and France was not the only country that had its 'revolution'. Writing about monasteries of cistercian nuns in France on the eve of the Revolution, Mother Marie de la Trinité Kervignart, ocso, has this to say in the opening page of her contribution to the present volume:

> In the monasteries of nuns the life was generally regular, peaceful, observant of enclosure and fervent. Evidence on this point is abundant, even if in several cases there were exceptions. The nuns had been less affected than the monks by the cultural evolution of the world around them . . . [The] trial which was approaching and would affect everyone would bring out in a significant way that the women's faithfulness to their commitment would be almost universal.

We are light-years removed from the situation prevailing in most cistercian communities of women in late sixteenth-century France, where life was generally irregular, turmoil was the order of the day, enclosure was little more than a word, and fervor was conspicuous chiefly by its absence.

Even if the reader wishes to tone down both this negative description of the average community of cistercian nuns in sixteenth-century France, and wishes also to tone down Mother Marie de la Trinité's very positive description of feminine cistercian conventual life on the eve of the Revolution, it remains indisputably true that, even as the storm clouds of revolution were gathering, the average community of cistercian nuns in France was at a far distant remove from its thirteenth-century antecedents. What had taken place?

A great deal had taken place, but imperceptibly—so imperceptibly that it is difficult to put one's finger on precisely what was happening. It was hardly a matter of 'great abbesses' who energetically took the initiative. There were no significant institutional changes; and serious abuses such as the royal nomination of abbesses remained current. Further, the General Chapter of the Order continued on as resolutely ineffectual in matters touching on the life of cistercian nuns as it was, generally speaking, ineffectual in matters touching on the life of cistercian monks. One may indeed call attention to the provisions for nuns in the Articles of Paris (1494), or the parallel provisions formulated by the 'Grand Chapitre' of 1601. But the sad lesson to be learned from all the many projects for reform drawn up and approved by sixteenth- and seventeenth-century General Chapters is that drawing up projects for reform can turn into a substitute for reform itself.

'The kingdom of God cometh not by observation' (Lk 17:20). 'Great' cistercian abbesses may have been in short supply; but there were still abbesses inspired for the governance of their own communities by the examples of the sister-abbesses of the various benedictine congregations studied by Dom Yves Chaussy. There were the rank and file cistercian nuns, too, the quality of whose spiritual life was influenced for the better by the flood of counter-reformation spiritual writings. Slowly, unobtrusively, and with no dramatic fanfare, the bread was rising. The fidelity and quiet earnestness of this or that individual encouraged in her sisters a like fidelity and earnestness. But who can chronicle an evolution such as this with precise dates and with references to precise individuals and to precise historical events? At what point does irregularity of monastic observance become demonstrably regular? Is there a precise moment when what had been a state of turmoil can be verifiably demonstrated to be 'peaceful'? And are the stages in the passage from rampant mediocrity to general fervor really all that discernible?

For myself, I very much wish that Father Yves Chaussy would complement his first monumental survey of feminine benedictine monasticism in the context of the French Catholic Reform with a further survey of feminine benedictine monasticism on the eve of the Revolution. Tentatively, very tentatively, I would like to suggest, by way of an hypothesis to be verified or disproved, that, as the eighteenth century progressed, the average benedictine nuns in communities reformed at an earlier date by a Marie de Beauvillier or a Françoise de La Châtre or an Antoinette d'Orléans was not very much different from her counterpart in communities of cistercian nuns where renewal had come as a less directly observable phenomenon.

Indeed, there is something rather problematic about some of those cistercian communities where reform came in circumstances of more dramatic sort. The Cistercians, too, had their modest share of abbesses who could be identified in some sense as 'great'. One thinks straightaway of the incomparable Mère Angélique Arnauld. But we know what, despite her best intentions and despite all her valor, happened at Port-Royal. We may, of course, think that Port-Royal and its history subsequent to its break with the government of Cîteaux, is infinitely more admirable and exciting than would have been the case had it remained juridically attached to the Order. But, seen from the perspectives of the Cistercian Order, the fervor and creativity which might have made for a more effective leaven of reform within the Order were lost to us, and resulted ultimately in tragedy for a movement that, for a few brief years seemed destined to enrich the life of the Order and of the Church at large. Or take the case of the first of all cistercian abbeys of women, Tart, just a few kilometers down the road from Cîteaux itself. When the young franciscan religious, Madame de Courcelle de Pourlan, arrived there as abbess designate in 1617, she found the place in squalor. Neither the proximity of Cîteaux nor the very real reforming ardor of the abbot of Cîteaux, Nicholas II Boucherat (1605-1625), contributed then or later to the betterment of that pathetic assembly of poorly motivated women drawn chiefly from the ranks of smart society. Revealing herself as an energetic and potentially 'great' reforming abbess Madame de Pourlan, now become Mère Jeanne de Saint Joseph, under the guidance of the bishop of Langres, Sébastien Zamet, managed to reform Tart right out of the Order and into a mutually unhelpful alliance with Port Royal. The cistercian identity of Tart had long since been lost in the decades before Madame de Courcelle's reform; and the reform, when it finally came, drew its inspiration chiefly from the institutions and spirituality of the enormously popular Carmelites, Visitandines, and Oratorians. It is much the same story with the great and holy savoyard reformer and kinswoman of Saint Francis de Sales (1567-1622), Mère Louise de Ballon, whose 'Bernardines of Divine Providence', with some sixteen communities to their credit (and with twenty-five at the time of the French Revolution), adopted constitutions mostly drawn verbatim from those of the Visitandines. Mother Louise de Ponçanas, another Savoyard and an early collaborator of Mère Louise de Ballon, soon went her own energetic reforming way—a way which led, eventually, to the foundation of the small congregation of 'Bernardines of the Precious Blood'. At their Paris house, the usages were said to be modelled on early cistercian sources, but provided nonetheless for two one-hour periods for daily recreation, two hours for mental prayer, a whole fifteen minutes for spiritual reading, and enjoined the use of the roman rather than the cistercian breviary. Though this reform enjoyed the backing of Jean Jouaud, vicar general of the Strict Observance, its cistercian dimension remains subject to discussion.

What does *not* remain subject to discussion is, of course, the holiness and determination of these 'great' or near-great abbesses. Still, one can regret that the more energetic the 'reforms' and the more creative the 'reformers', the more often the result was a loss to the Order of a badly needed leaven of renewal, and, with respect to the reformed communities, a lessening of the possibility for recovering their cistercian heritage.

The great tragedy is that, whether in the case of those reformed communities which felt constrained to the exigencies of renewal, or in the case of those communities which remained within the Order, the Order, as institution, had little to offer by way of positive help. The exceptions only serve to confirm the generally bleak picture.

In this context, no one should make the mistake of opposing institution to spirit or reforming impulse. So often as institutions are healthy, they raise up the spirit. And so often as the spirit is authentic, it leads to concrete forms and institutions that support and enrich and foster the life of the spirit. Just as the Incarnation ('... the Word was made flesh') is ordered to Pentecost ('... the Holy Spirit, whom the Father will send in my name'), so also Pentecost (diffusion of the Spirit) is ordered to incarnation (birth and spread of the Church). The Spirit acts in function of raising up various forms of Christ present and acting; just as Christ is present and acts in function of the transformation of created being by the Spirit. In the early days of the Order, the spirit of reform and renewal had led to the creation of those institutions necessary to provide a space within which the life of the spirit could flourish and grow creatively; and this life of the spirit led in turn to the further refinement of the life-supporting institutions of the Order such as ensured the vitality of individual monks and nuns and of the Order as a whole. The Cistercian Order at its best marked a period when institution and spirit were bonded in a vital mutual relationship. When spirit waned, so did institution; and the converse was no less true.

H. W. C. Davis has an especially perceptive paragraph in his book, *Medieval Europe*:

> In the development of single communities and groups of communities there occurs now and again a moment of equilibrium, when institutions are stable and adapted to the needs of those who live under them; when the minds of men are filled with ideas which they find completely satisfying; when the statesman, the artist, and the poet feel that they are best fulfilling their several missions if they express in deed and work and language the aspirations common to the whole society . . . Then the prevailing temper is one of reasoned optimism, of noble exaltation, of content allied with hope.[3]

The early days of the Order marked indeed an all too brief moment of equilibrium when cistercian institutions were stable and adapted to the needs of those who lived under them. To the minds of cistercian monks and nuns, ideals of monastic living were completely satisfying, and—*pace* the present day revisionists of early cistercian history—ideals formed a single continuum with reality. In those days the cistercian monks or nuns expressed in deed and work and language an aspiration common to the whole of society.

Given the historical evolution of seventeenth- and eighteenth-century Europe, it would be fanciful to speak of a form of religious life that expressed the aspirations common to the whole of so highly fragmented and diversified a society. It would also be fanciful to suggest that cistercian institutions were stable and adapted to the needs of monks and nuns living under them. Within the Order there was no general consensus as to ideals, and no consensus as to the practical shape and form of those institutions which were meant to serve the needs of the monks and nuns living under them.

All the preceding observations concerning cistercian life in France should have made the perceptive reader aware of the extremely parochial nature of the present discussion. France hardly represents for the whole of pre-Revolution cistercian feminine monasticism. What about communities of cistercian nuns in the Low Lands? in Italy? in Spain? and in countries east of the Rhine? Cistercian nuns in these and other regions are, in fact, the center of focus in the first part of the present volume. But it should be clear that, even where national and regional archives offer an abundance of statistical information about this or that community, much too little is known about the individual nuns and about the life actually lived in their communities from century to century. An enormous and exciting field of research is beckoning. Take, for instance the magnificent series of studies by Father Jean de la Croix Bouton, ocso, *Les Moniales Cisterciennes*: these four volumes serve not only to provide us with a vast fund of new information, but to point out the need for monographs and book-length studies about individual monastics and their communities. We are only at the beginning of a study of cistercian monastic women.

Do we really appreciate our debt to the now unknown cistercian nuns of those problematic past centuries, when ideals were so diffuse, when institutions were so unstable and so poorly adapted to the needs of monks and nuns, and when there was no longer a society with a single shared vision of reality? That there were communities where life was generally regular, peaceful, observant of cloister and fervent, is indeed a witness to the vigor of the hidden springs that still ran deep and strong under the surface of a society in turmoil.

One of the most finely drawn characterizations in the whole of english literature is that of George Eliot's Dorothea Brook in *Middlemarch*—Dorothea, who, to the casual onlooker, falls short of the measure of heroism which could have been hers even in the circumscribed provincial world of Middlemarch. 'Certainly,' writes Eliot,

> those determining acts of her life were not ideally beautiful. They were the mixed result of young and noble impulse struggling amidst the conditions of an imperfect social state, in which great feelings will often take the aspect of error, and great faith the aspect of illusion. For there is no creature whose inward being is so strong that it is not greatly determined by what lies outside it. A new Theresa will hardly have the opportunity of reforming a conventual life . . . : the medium in which their ardent deeds took shape is forever gone.

But Eliot concludes, in the final lines of her book, with these insightful words:

> Her finely touched spirit had still its fine tissues . . . and the effect of her being on those around her was incalculably diffusive, for the growing good of the world is partly dependent on unhistoric acts, and that things are not so ill with you and me as they might have been is half owing to the number who lived faithfully a hidden life and rest in unvisited tombs.

Those cistercian religious who lived in a world growing progressively more absurd, and in an Order where the institutions had become ill adapted to their purpose, and where the personalities one could call truly 'great' were pathetically few, are, in their own way, just as inspiring as those abbesses whom Bremond rightly recognizes as 'great'. From time to time we do catch a glimpse of the true greatness of those who faithfully lived that hidden life. There was, for instance, nothing remarkably heroic about life at the aristocratic cistercian abbey of Saint Antoine des Champs in Paris; but when the moment of truth came, it was their youngest nun, Soeur Rosalie Augustin de Chabannes who, in an odyssey that took her through Switzerland, Russia, and Poland, brought trappistine life to England. Nor was life at Sainte-Catherine-d'Avignon cast in the heroic mould—but this did not stop the two Justamond sisters, Marguérite-Elénore and Madeleine-Françoise, from going to the guillotine at Orange with a song on their lips—literally. Almost every community had its Madame de Chabannes and its Justamond sisters, and also countless individuals whose names we know not. Their life was hidden, and their tombs may be nowadays unvisited and unknown. But if today the life of Trappistine-Cistercians is thriving as it is, and if it is yearly being implanted in new regions and distant climes, this is in part due to the incalculably diffusive effect of the unhistoric acts and the hidden lives of individuals who have left no great name on the earth, but to whom we owe an eternal debt of love and gratitude.

NOTES

1. Henri Bremond, *A Literary History of Religious Thought in France from the Wars of Religion down to Our Own Times* 2, trans. K. L. Montgomery (London: SPCK, 1930) p. 292.
2. Dom Yves Chaussy, *Les Bénédictines et la Réforme Catholique en France au XVIIᵉsiècle*, 2 vols. (Paris: Éditions de la Source, 1975).
3. *Medieval Europe* (London: Oxford University Press, 1960²) p. 7.

The 'Fire Nun' from Cortona Veronica Laparelli 1537–1620

Chrysogonus Waddell OCSO

'WE ARE OFTEN so solemn about love,' writes one modern author,[1] 'that we forget love is a joy, a thing to wonder at and to laugh about.'

In the Counter-Reformation centuries, God's love was celebrated with all the total commitment and absoluteness of any other christian century—but oh, so *solemnly*! We somewhat wearily thumb our way through tome after tome of Counter-Reformation hagiography; and the high jinx of a Philip Neri, the mirth of a Madre Teresa, or even the quiet humor of a Francis de Sales are all the more welcome for their being so unconscionably rare. True, the post-Reformation scene provided scant matter for holy mirth. In the first half of the sixteenth century a Thomas More could still jest with his head already on the block. Is it possible to imagine, a hundred years later, an Archbishop Laud or deposed King Charles I doing so? Only with difficulty. England in the intervening century had grown considerably less merry; and what was true of England was true of the commonwealth of christian nations as a whole. After all, the decomposition of Christendom did not make for a particularly buoyant, light-hearted spirituality; and those who took their Christianity seriously—as millions did—often confused seriousness of commitment with seriousness of mien. Monasteries were no exception. Piety in the cloister—when there *was* piety in the cloister—tended to be of a practical, sober, earnest sort. Though a chasm ought by rights to yawn between sobriety and dullness,

The Fire Nun. Photo courtesy of the Institute of Cistercian Studies.

between earnestness and tight-lipped grimness, for many a sober-minded earnest monk or nun it was but a step, and a short step at that. Perhaps we, more than Swinburne himself, are to blame for that poet's sad blasphemy, 'Thou hast conquered, O pale Galilean; the world has grown grey from Thy breath.'[2]

And on this note of blasphemy I introduce Suor Veronica Laparelli. Laughter and tears have bent her almost double—laughter at the pomposity of so silly a blasphemy, tears for poor old Swinburne, the *poveretto:* such a gloomy fellow, and such feeble verse! It's the business about the 'pale Galilean' which really sends her. For Veronica has been on quite intimate terms with that 'pale Galilean' for the better part of her long life, one uninterrupted celebration of his love for us, our love for him: a love that means sheer joy, a thing to wonder at and to laugh about. No one knows better than Veronica that grief and pain are often an essential part of that love, and that deep sorrow and pure joy somehow have a way of going hand in hand. But the final word of love, Veronica is here to tell us, is that joy, that wonder and laughter which stay with us multiplied a hundredfold in heaven when tears and sorrow have long since been wiped away.

They called her the *Monaca di Fuoco.*[3] 'The Fiery Nun', 'The Ardent Nun', would probably do by way of an idiomatic rendering; but these adjectives suggest rather the Italian *infiammata* or *ardente* or *focosa* or even *infocata*, whereas *fuoco* is a strongly concrete substantive: FIRE! 'Nun of Fire' or 'Fire Nun' sound, I admit, a bit clumsy, but they ring true.

Ever since Veronica's favorite cistercian patron, Bernard of Clairvaux, preached his great sermon on John the Baptist as a 'light shining and burning', it has been a commonplace that the monk or nun or Christian at large should not merely shine outwardly, but burn inwardly with fervor. 'Merely to shine is vain,' Bernard had written, 'merely to burn is little; but to burn and shine at once— that is perfection.'[4] Still, if it is not possible for the wise man to have both heat and light together, he should choose, Bernard says, to burn: and this has always been the consistent choice of the men and women we meet in the pages of the cistercian Menology. They have, most of them, a special knack of fading into the background by their very plainness and unpretentiousness. They tend to be less like the first abbot of Clairvaux, Saint Bernard, who burned and shone in the Church with bright splendor, and more like the eighth abbot of Clairvaux, Peter the 'One Eye', who—to quote his benedictine biographer, Thomas of Reuil—'was like a burning coal covered with the ashes of his own poverty: not much light, but, for all that, plenty of heat'.[5]

If Veronica was not more like Peter and less like Bernard, this was for no lack of effort on her part. No Cistercian has ever tried harder to fade into the background: few Cistercians have so utterly failed in the attempt. Through no fault of her own, Suor Veronica, whom I am now introducing, is an extremely atypical Cistercian. Levitations, locutions, visions, prophecies, miracles are extremely interesting, but not much help for someone with a yen for the unpretentious. For such phenomena in the life of *la Venerabile*, however, we should blame, not Veronica, but God; and he knew, presumably, what he was about. Veronica Laparellis make their appearance from time to time in the annals of monastic history, and generally in the context of a situation where routine and dry rot have taken over, and where the quality of religious life can be reversed only by some intervention of a rather extraordinary sort. The French Revolution provided just such a happy solution to the problem of chronic and generalized mediocrity in cistercian communities in France. But at the more local level, it is enough, usually, for God to enter into the life of a particular religious in so obvious and irrefutable a manner that that monk or nun serves as a sign for others to God's presence and action in the community: a sign of hope, a sign of encouragement, a sign of condemnation for all that is petty and selfish and lethargic in the quality of our own religious commitment. If Veronica's community is today a happy, fervent community—which it very much is—this, in God's providence, may very well be because, more than four hundred years ago, God began intervening somewhat dramatically in the life of a young tuscan nun from Cortona.

In a sense, Veronica's desire to 'disappear' has been more or less realized. How many of us have even heard of her? Still, she remains very much a living presence in her monastery of the Holy Trinity at Cortona, as is clear to anyone with enough Italian to be able to read the occasional monastery report in the *Relationes Monasteriorum* section of *Cistercienser-Chronik*;[6] and in 1962 her monastery published a short biographical notice by S. Lucarini, *Una mistica poco conosciuta: la Venerabile Veronica Laparelli*. There is also a short presentation in one of the issues of *Notizie cisterciensi* for 1977, 'Cisterciensi di ieri e di oggi: La Ven. Veronica Laparelli,'[7] by one of the editors of the revue, Father Vittorino Zanni—four brief pages long on rhetoric, short on facts, with 'Nacque nel 1537' counting as an entire paragraph, and 'Morì nel 1620' as yet another. For those of us with a smattering of Latin, there is the two-page *curriculum vitae* in Father Seraphin Lennsen's *Hagiologium Cisterciense* of 1948.[8] For the reader of German, there is the minuscule notice in Zimmermann's *Kalendarium Benedictinum*;[9] as well as Father Robert Klopfer's brief account published in the March 1939 issue of *Cistercienser-Chronik*, 'Heilige Frauengestalten unseres Ordens: 3. Die ehrwürdige Veronika Laparelli von Cortona,'[10]—just a trifle more than two pages long. Most of this material shares in common the note of brevity and a dependence, direct or indirect, on a common source: Filippo Maria Salvatori's *Vita della venerabile Veronica Laparelli di Cortona, monaca cisterciense nel Monistero della SS. Trinità*, printed at Rome in 1774. The book is rare, and I suspect that most of the twentieth-century notices depend on the french translation published in 1875 by the monks of Lérins in the series *Bibliothèque cistercienne*.[11]

One of the rare surviving copies of Salvatori's *Vita* is in the Gethsemani Obrecht Collection now housed in the Institute of Cistercian Studies Library at Kalamazoo, Michigan. This *Vita* claims to be the first account of Veronica's life to be based on the material collected with a view to her eventual beatification and canonization. '*Scritta e cavata ora per la prima volta da' Processi formati per la sua Beatificazione e Canonizzazione,*' boasts the title-page, mendaciously. For sixty years earlier, in 1714, there had already appeared, printed at Naples, an *Istoria della santa Vita, e Virtu eroiche della Ven. Serva di Dio Veronica Laparelli*, written by the Jesuit Anton Maria Bonucci, and dedicated to the Grand Duke of Tuscany. This book had been commissioned by the 'Abate Onofrio Baldelli', Patrician of Cortona and Postulator for the beatification process appointed at the instance of the heads of the clan Laparelli. Bonucci's *Istoria* is much more rare but far superior to the *Vita* by Salvatori. Not only does it quote directly and extensively from the depositions of eye witnesses, it even indicates the sources in marginal references, down to the precise folio-numbers. The material includes copies of the beatification requests addressed to the Holy Father from the Grand Duke of Tuscany, several bishops, and other eminent dignitaries (including representatives of the Laparelli family, who were funding the whole process). Best of all, however, is a twenty-eight page supplement bound with the *Istoria* but printed separately and with its own independent pagination. This is the *Relazione della Vita della . . . Suor Veronica*, written during Veronica's own lifetime by her then abbess, Margarita Cortonesi. This abbess died a number of years before Veronica; so her *Relazione* is followed by sworn attestations dated 27 October, 1629, in which Sisters Romana dei Pecci and Argentina dei

Mancini identify the manuscript as being in the familiar handwriting of their deceased abbess, Madre Margarita Cortonesi. I presume that the editor, in transcribing the text of the *Relazione* for the printer, has touched up the spelling and the grammar; but even so the verve and vigor of Mother Margarita's tuscan diction rings bright and gloriously clear. We groan when we compare her earthy descriptions with the flowery counterparts in Bonucci and Salvatori, and those two-dozen pages of the *Relazione* became doubly precious. As for the dependence of Salvatori on Bonucci, I think that the evidence is quite affirmative, despite Salvatori's apparent disclaimer to the contrary. The same two engravings which appear in the Bonucci *Istoria* appear also in the later Salvatori *Vita*—an aerial view of Cortona and a *vera effigies* of Veronica herself. The general plan of both books is also the same. What is proper to Salvatori is chiefly an abundance of pious verbiage which even in the eighteenth century must have seemed somewhat excessive. Like the Salvatori *Vita*, so also the Bonucci *Istoria* is part of the Gethsemani *fonds* in the Cistercian Institute Library.

So much, then, for the printed primary and secondary sources. The manuscript sources, or at least the more important manuscript sources, are not in Vatican City but in Paris, at the Bibliothèque Nationale. During the napoleonic takeover of Rome, major portions of the Vatican archives were sequestered and carted off to France. A huge collection of canonization and beatification material was housed first at the Hôtel de Soubize, and then transferred to its present location.[12] Since Veronica's cause for beatification was only interrupted and never terminated, I presume that the dossier has been reconstituted, and that copies of the more pertinent documents are to be had in the Cortona chancery office, in the Generalate of the Cistercian Order at Rome, and in the Sacred Congregation for the Causes of Saints.

All this adds up to a rather formidable collection of source materials, but material *almost* wholly inaccessible to most of us, and *wholly* inaccessible to those of us who know only English. This present effort to introduce Veronica to the English-reading public can do no more than to call attention to an absolutely lovable woman who deserves a much better introduction. But since the extraordinary graces granted Veronica were less for her than for her community, I wish also to call attention to her much loved community. So I shall simply page my way through the antique folios of Salvatori's *Vita* and Bonucci's *Istoria* and, best of all, Madre Margarita Cortonesi's *Relazione*, pausing from time to time to excerpt from among many others some incident which I think, rightly or wrongly, helps us to become acquainted with Veronica and her sisters.

Few cities in modern Italy have a history older than that of Cortona. Etruscanologists hold it especially dear for its having been one of the Twelve Cities in the Etruscan League. Walled and sprawling on a massive hill, like nearby Perugia and Assisi, Cortona is even now a bit difficult of access for the train traveller, who can get no nearer than Terontola, five miles away, or, with the help of a Toonerville Trolley local, the somewhat closer Camucia. Family tradition holds that the Laparellis have been in Cortona ever since the arrival there in 1255 of Monsieur de Laparelli, who had been in the service of King Saint Louis IX. By the time of Veronica's birth on 10 November 1537, the family had long since become one of the principal families of Cortona, distinguished for its galaxy of judges, lawyers, magistrates, military men, poets, and literati.[13]

Perhaps the most decisive single event in Veronica's childhood was the death of her pet chick. The delicate creature doubtless succumbed beneath too much energetic loving. Knowing as yet nothing of death and the more gruesome biological effects of death, the four-year-old girl tucked the strangely quiet chick into a hollow scooped out in the garden, covered it with a bit of slate, and came back two days later to see how the pet was doing. Worms and maggots gave the youngster a shocking lesson in mortality. With the intuitive wisdom sometimes enjoyed by the very young and the very old, Veronica realized that our hearts are meant to be set on treasures in the place where neither moth nor rust consumes. By the age of five, she was already launched on a program of asceticism such as would daunt even the most stout-hearted adult. We can hardly blame the puzzled parents, Antonio Laparelli and Maddalena Rustichelli, for their somewhat jaundiced view of their daughter's precocious piety. Few parents would know what to do with a five-year old who wants to fast, to scourge herself to the point of blood, and to interrupt her sleep for the sake of night-vigils, and who prefers some quiet out of the way nook to active participation in the boisterous life of a large family with many other children and servants. Salvatori, cognizant of the fact that his author's fee was being paid by the heads of the clan Laparelli, provides a somewhat detailed rationale for parental opposition to Veronica's problematic devotions, the main point being that a palazzo is not a cloister. Mother Margarita, in her *Relazione*, beats around the bush much less, and speaks of anger and threats, and the conviction that the girl was, if not quite off her rocker, at least too stubborn an independent thinker: *i quali spesso verso di lei si turbavano e minacciandola, parendoli, che essa fusse di sua testa* . . . .[14] Stubborn she was, and stubborn she remained.

Though we can sympathize with the parental opposition to Veronica's devotional exuberance during her early childhood, we begin to side with Veronica herself as she approached young womanhood, still resolute in her intention to give herself wholly to the Lord in the religious life. The battle of wills lasted much longer than we should reasonably expect. When Veronica was finally allowed to enter the recently founded cistercian convent of the Most Holy Trinity[15] the day after her twenty-third birthday, 11 November 1560, she was, so far as marriageability was concerned, already an old crone. We think of Lady Capulet's words to Juliet, still more than two weeks short of her fourteenth birthday:

> Well, think of marriage now. Younger than you,
> Here in Verona, ladies of esteem,
> Are made already mothers. By my count,
> I was your mother much upon these years
> That you are now a maid.[16]

Clearly, if Veronica can be described as being *di sua testa*, much the same can be said of her parents; and her long, long wait to enter into the seclusion of the cloister is a tribute to her patience and to the seriousness of her intent.

We should not call Veronica 'patient', however, without any qualification whatsoever. Her impatience attained, at times, monumental proportions. Veronica's reception into the community of the Santissima Trinità provides us with a characteristic (and typically cistercian) example of such impatience. Family and friends were in the nave of the church, the community in the choir behind the grille, and Veronica on her knees before the officiating priest, who had just asked the ritual question about her intention to renounce the world and its pomps. The ritual response suddenly erupted in a most unritual performance as Veronica began tearing off earrings, ripping off necklaces, hurling the gewgaws dear to any renaissance lady to the floor of the sanctuary, tearing her lace-frilled garments to shreds. Does she renounce the world? Silly question! The biographer, Filippo Salvatori, who sometimes strikes us as a bit of a pompous ass, should not be blamed for the attempt of the french translator to dignify the episode. 'L'assistance fut profondément touchée',[17] 'The assembly was profoundly moved'. More faithful to Salvatori, the translator thereupon admits that there were 'some, who, not knowing what spirit impelled her, made fun of her'. Actually, Salvatori refers to 'more than one', *piú d'uno*,[18] which is, strictly speaking, correct. More than one person *did* break out laughing. In fact, as our honest Abadessa Margarita Cortonesi tells us, *everyone*, nuns included, broke out laughing. And even though most of the readers may not understand Italian, still less Tuscan-Italian, Madre Margarita Cortonesi's description deserves to be quoted in full:

> Ella diceva quelle parole di rinunziare alle vanità,
> pigliava le perle, pigliava la collana,
> i vezzi, che ella haveva al collo,
> e le gettava come se fossero state fango,
> gettava gl'ornamenti della testa,
> gattava (*for* gettava?) le vesti, quali haveva indosso,
> e per dir meglio straventava di sorte,
> che tutti i circonstanti furon commossi a ridere,
> non sapendo la causa di tal novità,
> le Moniche anco non si potevano contenere di ridere,
> perche fin quì di lei non si era vista cosa d'importanza,
> e nessuno sapeva il segreto del cuor suo.[19]

What a splendid final line! All that laughter, because 'no one knew the secret of her heart'. In a few moments Veronica had acted out in prophetic symbol what it had taken our Cistercian Fathers years to spell out in detail. God had been at work within their hearts, drawing them to a type of inward experience of such simplicity and absoluteness that it made mandatory a change in their outward style of life and environment. The directness and simplicity of their architecture, their unpretentiously austere but noble manner of celebrating the liturgy, their refusal of involvement in the complexities of feudal society—all these simply reflected in the outward order their interior stance before the Lord. The exterior had to be in continuity with, had to be in harmony with the interior. So too with Veronica. All the frippery of her outward attire suddenly seemed too outrageous a contradiction to *il segreto del cuor suo*, to 'the secret of her heart'. In the ordinary course of the vestition rite, Veronica would have retired briefly to a private place to exchange her secular finery for the cistercian habit; but the few minutes required for this must have seemed an eternity—so, off *now* with the earrings! off *now* with the necklaces! off *now* with all the other ornamental finery! For the next sixty years, Veronica was to follow through consistently on the strength of this parabolic action: her love for what was poorest and humblest and simplest was only an expression and an imperious exigency of *il segreto del cuor suo*.

Not that it was always easy for Veronica to realize her ideal of absolute renunciation. The chief, though quite an innocent, obstacle, was the community itself. The poverty of individual resources was always extreme—for there *were* individual resources; and in this the Monastery of the Most Blessed Trinity was in no way different from many another convent of the period which had not yet been touched by the reform movement begun by Dom Luigi Barbo (+1443) and his wonderfully flourishing Congregation of Santa Justina. Upon entering the community, the young women brought with them not only their dowry, but their *donamento*—a lifelong supply of linens, bedding, clothes, furniture; in brief, everything needed to set up housekeeping in their own private apartment. The goods were stored away and handed out to the nun according to need, real or fanciful. Personal income came in part from family and friends, in part from the sale of the fine needlework in which girls from upper-class families so often excelled. All this was covered, of course, under the conveniently flexible vow of obedience. There was next to nothing which could not receive, indeed, did not receive the blessing of obedience.

This, then, provides the setting for the immediate aftermath of Veronica's reception of the habit. Madre Margarita had doled out to Veronica a part of her *donamento*, all according to customary procedure: *come si suol concedere à tutte l'altre*. Veronica had accepted everything with good enough grace, *benignamente*—at least initially. It was not long before she started having second thoughts. She was much too comfortable; she had more than what she really needed. 'She kept pestering me day and night,' writes Mother Margarita, *Mi molestava giorno e notte*. She thought that 'I ought to take these goods (*robbe*) for the monastery,' that is to say, to put them at the common disposition of the entire community. 'She wanted to observe her Rule in its *entirety*, and she did not want anything, not so much as a needle, to be hers to dispose of freely': *che Ella desiderava osservare la sua Regola intieramente, e non voleva cosa nessuna, non pure un'ago in sua libertà*. It must have been a new experience for the good abbess, who continues: 'She became such a nuisance (*tanto mi fù molesta*), and she knew how to make such a reasoned appeal based on her vow [of poverty], that I was forced to consent' (*io fui forzata consentirle*). Mother Margarita gave in, but, I fear, without much good grace, for she goes on to add how she warned the stubborn Veronica that she was going to suffer from the monastery's poverty—as in fact she did; and that what Veronica was saying was just words, words, words (*furono tutte parole*). It must have been quite a shouting match. But the divinely stubborn Vernoica got her way (which also happened to be God's way), and deprived herself of everything she had, 'committing herself wholly to God, under the obedience of the one who governed her'. A few days later she came to Mother Margarita with two pennies she had overlooked; and the abbess concludes that the foundation of Veronica's exemplary life is the fact that she never, and I mean *never* (*mai mai*), wanted anything of her own. This, however, is not quite the proper point of emphasis. In Mother Margarita's own terms, she wanted nothing of her own, *niente di proprio*, but in order to be wholly God's, *tutto in Dio*. Radical self-dispossession was an important concern, but it was secondary to Veronica's main focus of attention, which was the possession of God, or better, her being possessed by God.

This episode tells us almost as much about the tenor of observance in the monastery as it does about Veronica herself. In case of institutionalized mediocrity, the novice had to fight with the abbess simply to be allowed to take seriously the renunciation which everyone had promised. In no way is this meant as a censure of Madre Margarita or of any of the other members of the community who still speak to us through the pages of Veronica's biographies. A Boccaccio would look to them in vain to provide him with even the slightest incident flavorsome enough to be served up in the pages of the *Decameron*. They were good women, devout women. But their standard of religious life was determined by economic factors, by sociological conditioning, by practical considerations. The level of observance left little room for community enthusiasm, for communal generosity beyond a certain common measure; and it left next to no room for real joy. Laughter there certainly was, laughter at the funny over-aged postulant who turned her vestition rite into a circus. But that sort of laughter is not the same thing as joy.

One of the drawbacks about all the early printed sources is the arrangement of the material. Madre Margarita could well be the mother of stream of consciousness writing as she tosses out her reminiscences without much regard—without *any* regard—for chronology. Bonucci and Salvatori, on the other hand, are overly structured in that they present their material with a view to the beatification process, in which it must be proved in systematic order that the Servant of God practiced, in a heroic degree, faith, hope and charity, as well as prudence, justice, fortitude and temperance. Impossible, then, on the basis of present sources to trace any evolution in Veronica's spiritual life, to discern any process of development and maturation from the first day to the last. We can take for granted that she really did grow; but the nature of that growth is part of the *segreto del cuor suo*, the secret of her heart.

What surfaced in Madre Margarita's consciousness immediately after Veronica's initial spirit of renunciation, was her extraordinary zest for mortification: disciplines with spiked cords, beatings of the breast *à la* Saint Jerome, a metal cincture that ate into the flesh, hair-shirts of the roughest, thorn-like herbs draped around the shoulders. 'To want to recount all those penances in detail would be really difficult, and not without annoyance for the listener,'[20] writes Madre Margarita—though whether *fastidio* here means annoyance, trouble, boredom, disgust, or all four together, I am not prepared to say. Some of this litany of bloody macerations the abbess admits to having learned from Veronica's confessor, who here as elsewhere in the account seems to have been surprisingly loose-tongued. I might add, however, that this is the first and last really gory paragraph in Mother Margarita's narrative; and, given the subject-matter and renaissance popular tastes in hagiography, it is surprisingly and mercifully brief. This paragraph tells us, however, rather more than the abbess probably intended: Margarita Cortonesi may have been the abbess, but it was the confessor, not herself, who was privy in the first instance to Veronica's extraordinary practices. She also mentions from time to time details learned from the confessor rather than from Veronica herself. It was possible, then, for Margarita to be abbess without being spiritual mother and spiritual guide in the deep things of the spirit. Her characteristic stance *vis à vis* Veronica is that of a shrewd, loving, admiring, but also sometimes distant observer. Only rarely did she take the initiative, as in one instance when Veronica had fallen desperately ill. The other nuns, well aware that their moribund sister was a saint, suggested as much by making off prematurely with various objects which, as things then looked, would soon be relics of a *bona fide* saint. Veronica flew into a rage, and such a rage! The frightened confessor had to call the abbess and ask that all the pious thefts be brought back. Veronica was not so moribund as to be beyond insisting that, after her death, whatever she left behind should not be given away, but sold as alms for the poor. 'Sister Veronica,' roared the abbess, magnificently, 'that is none of your business: I'm boss here!' *Suor Veronica, non tocca a voi a pigliarvi cotesti pensieri, perchè IO SONO LA PADRONA.*[21] It is also a matter of record that when Veronica learned that her abbess had started writing the *Realazione*, she fell into 'a holy rage', *se ne sdegnò santamente.*[22] The fuming Veronica went so far as to threaten Mother Abbess with the wrath of heaven; but in this instance— probably unique—heaven proved uncooperative, and Madre Margarita wrote on.

The next point taken up by Mother Margarita is rather extraordinary. She refers to Veronica's practice of fasting, which was only slightly less remarkable than that of Saint Lutgard with her several series of seven-year fasts. Veronica's preference was for a cycle of forty-day fasts coordinated with the various liturgical seasons; no sooner would one *quadragesima* end than, after a short respite, she was off on another. What interested Mother Margarita, however, was not the fasting itself, but the *result* of Veronica's fasting and habitual practice of virtue: it all led to a deepening of *la Venerabile's* desire to receive the Eucharist with increasing frequency. This connection between fasting and longing for the Eucharist is a point noted by the canny Abbess, but by-passed by the professional theologians Bonucci and Salvatori. And, as usual, once Veronica had her mind set on a thing, the outcome was a foregone conclusion. 'The confessor,' explains Mother Margarita, needlessly, 'was forced to satisfy her'; *onde il Confessore fù forzato di contentarla.*[23] Habituated as we are to daily communion, we are doubtless aghast to read that Veronica's 'frequent communion' meant, at first, only every other week. But this was at a time, we should remember, when even fervent nuns received communion only on the principal solemnities, or, at most, once a month. Twice monthly, however, was just the start. Soon the rhythm was increased to include every Sunday, and before long feasts of the apostles were thrown in for good measure. Little by little the frequency was left up to the confessor; and at last Veronica ended as a daily communicant, or an *almost* daily communicant; for there were times—and this also throws light on life in the community—when a priest was unavailable for Mass or confession because of business connected with lawsuits and litigation in court. Veronica's thirteenth-century flemish sister-Cistercians, so celebrated for their eucharistic piety, were doubtless looking down from heaven and applauding their renaissance sister. But even they must have been astonished on occasion when—and we have Mother Margarita's word for this—Veronica was seen going through all the ritual actions for the reception of a communion, including the wiping of her lips with a purificator: but there was no visible host, no visible chalice, no visible purificator.[24] Communion from the hand of an angel is, however, a hagiographical commonplace; and Veronica is here, as in so many other respects, in a great tradition.

Mother Margarita next tells about the time when Veronica rang the bells for the customary evening Angelus, and then proceeded, also in keeping with custom, to ring in the feast of the following day. This was the feast of the *Poverello*, and Veronica's baptismal name was, in fact, Veronica Francesca. The prescribed measure was *un bel doppio di Campane*, which I take to mean that both bells were to be rung, or perhaps rung twice as long as on ordinary days. But Veronica went on and on. And on . . . *Suona, suona*, writes Mother Margarita. The nuns had long since retired for the night, and still the ringing of the bells went on, went on, horrible to relate, for more than three hours—*di sorte, che ci parve un gran disordine*, 'with the result that things were in a turmoil'. The townsmen began converging on the monastery. Was it fire? robbery? armed assault? *Chiama, chiama*; shouting, and more shouting. Not even Easter rated such a drawn-out pealing of the bells, notes Mother Margarita. Finally the abbess and her nightgowned nuns grabbed their candles and poured into the church. There was Veronica, rapt in ecstasy, tugging away at the bell-ropes for dear life. 'It would have gone on all night', writes Mother Margarita, 'if we hadn't cut the bell-ropes.' It is a fine point that the strands left in Veronica's hands remained stretched taut and upright until hours later when *la Venerabile* finally emerged from her rapture. 'We never saw the like of it,' the Abbess concludes; *mai più havevemo visto tali cose*—and never wanted, I dare say, to see the like again.[25] There were, however, similar episodes. Once Veronica pealed the bells loud and long to accompany the lengthy procession which she saw escorting Our Lady into heaven on the eve of her Assumption;[26] at other times it seemed as though only the music of the bells pealing over the rooftops and towers of Cortona could express the joy she felt. Veronica probably had no idea that for her sisters of an earlier age, the bells, finely crafted to sound forth precise musical proportions, were meant to make explicit something of the music of the spheres, something of the beauty and harmony of the universe which had been created good by God, and which even now was joyfully and majestically moving in a great cosmic dance in which Veronica herself, bell-ropes in hand, was tripping the light fantastic.[27]

One of the features of Veronica's spirituality most disconcerting for us is a feature prominent, even predominant, in the lives of our early flemish nuns. I know of no precise english term capable of suggesting all the nuances of the greek term *parrhesia*,[28] but it is the very touchstone for our understanding of Veronica's life in the Lord. In the non-christian context *parrhesia* had to do with the open and free right of speech enjoyed by citizen-members of the town assembly; in the christian context it has to do with the uninhibited and un-selfconscious attitude of the child who loves and reveres the father, and who can speak up on the strength of that love with so much directness and spontaneity and simplicity that we, who are less experienced in the ways of love and reverence, find it disconcerting. It is *parrhesia*, then, which features in almost every episode of a new section of the *Relazione*, in which Veronica's experiences are coordinated with the cycle of feasts and fasts of the liturgical year.

After the Night Office on the feast of the Immaculate Conception, Veronica, like her sisters, was still in church, deep in prayer on behalf of those sisters and still others. *Il suo dolce Sposo*, 'her sweet Spouse' Jesus, was not in a particularly giving mood, and explained why he was unwilling to grant some of the graces asked for. When Veronica realized she was not getting the answer she was expecting (*le riposte non erano à modo suo*) she turned on the tears. Tears failing, she tried shouting, shouting for the Lord to stretch out his arms of mercy to the people for whom she was praying. It only got the Lord angry: *il Signor era irato, perchè ella non cessava di piangere, e gridare misericordia*. Veronica stretched out her arms, sprawled on the floor, and started shouting all the louder. The nuns were scared out of their wits, thinking that Veronica was trying to ward off the end of the world which was just about to crash down upon them all. Suddenly the shrieking stopped. Veronica was now all smiles. She knelt upright and, joyful, launched into a *Te Deum*. Veronica had scored her point. As usual.[29]

That is not the way I am used to praying for myself or for others. I would be much consoled, however, to think that there was someone praying for me and my loved ones with something of Veronica's sincerity and intensity. These are the days of anti-nuclear demonstrations and signed petitions and mass marches; and all this is mightily important. Public manifestos of this kind might be still more effective, nonetheless, if backed up by an intercessory prayer as insistent and confident as Veronica's.

And though it means a rupture with the order of Mother Margarita's *exposé*, perhaps now would be a good place to speak of Veronica's compassionate concern and love for the whole world. So long as it was a question of only herself, no one was better at the practice of 'holy indifference' than Suor Veronica. In the midst of keen sufferings, and even when immobilized by pain and debility, she had a single answer for everyone who asked how she was doing: *Come piace à Gesù*, 'Just the way Jesus wants it'—spoken with a smile, *con volto ilare*, and with high good humor, *tutta gioviale*.[30] But if it was a question of someone else, then Veronica was ready to do battle with the Lord himself for the sake of that person. She was remarkably well equipped for such a ministry of mercy.

Her gift of prophecy, while quasi-habitual, was exercised only to forestall situations which would otherwise have redounded to the harm of individuals. Hers was also the gift of reading hearts, and the self-righteous or the hypocrite or the secret sinner were well advised to keep a safe distance from this unpredictable woman with an unfortunate tendency to tell it like it was. But for the 'honest' sinner, the *Surora Santa* was all love and understanding. A steady stream of sufferers poured into the parlor of the monastery; and no one left without receiving through the sympathetic nun behind the grille healing of body, healing of soul. She did what she could, though unsuccessfully, to minimize her own role in the miraculous cures attested by the hundreds. 'All through the intercession of Saint James,' she would marvel; and she doubtless meant it. For she took seriously the 'Saint James water' she doled out, and the pious texts written in her own hand and applied to the ailing members and organs. Prelates and peasants, monks and merchants, oldsters in second childhood and babes in arms, heads of state and common criminals—there was room in her heart for everyone.[31] Indeed, part of the 'secret of her heart' was that it had grown big enough, behind the cloister wall, to take in the whole world.

The universality of the concerns carried in Veronicas's heart was doubtless due to the fact that that heart was fixed in so paradoxically exclusive a fashion on a single center: Christ Jesus. We return now to the order of Mother Margarita's narrative, who spends several pages of her brief *Relazione* showing us how Veronica participated in the mysteries of Christ according to the unfolding of the liturgical year. Christmastide was one long celebration of the infancy of Christ, with Veronica lavishing her maternal attentions on the newborn Babe, whom she would carry around the cloister wrapped in her scapular. No one saw the Babe, but they did see the shape of the Babe by the contours taken by Veronica's scapular. I frankly have a hard time relating to the scenes of Veronica playing the equivalent of 'Patty Cake, Patty Cake' with the incarnate Son of God. But just when *parrhesia* seems almost to have gotten out of hand, something is said to suffuse the whole episode with a theological insight that strikes the reader as too profound not to be authentic.

Take, for instance, this Christmastime scene. Our Lady had told Veronica that it was time to give her back her Bambino. Veronica was as free and easy with the Mother of God as she was with the Son. No, she wanted to have him a bit longer. And wouldn't it be all right to let some of her sisters hold the Babe? The nuns who were listening to what seemed to them to be a one-sided conversation understood, by Veronica's reply, that Mary must have said No, the nuns couldn't have her boy to hold; they didn't love him enough. To which Veronica responds: 'Well, if they don't love him, it's because they haven't *seen* him. But no, they don't really know him . . . But if they *saw* him, they'd taste him, they'd know him, they'd love him', *Se lor non l'amano, perchè non l'hanno visto, però non lo cognoscono, però se lo vederanno, l o gusteranno, lo cognosceranno, et amaranno.*[32] The vocabulary here is the traditional vocabulary of contemplation dear to Saint Bernard and the Fathers: *gustare—cognoscere—amare*, to taste or savour, to know, to love; and we are smack at the heart of the theology of the Incarnation: *ut dum visibiliter Deum cognoscimus, per hunc in invisibilium amorem rapiamur*, as the Christmas Preface sums it up: 'through him whom we recognize as God made visible we are carried away in love of things invisible'. Veronica had seen God at his most lovable, and had been swept away in the torrent of love for all the realities still accessible only by faith. This, however, was not enough for her. She wanted her much loved sisters to know and experience what she had known and experienced.

But Veronica was not always cuddling Baby Jesus. With the help of the lenten liturgy she would enter into a fuller participation in the redemptive mystery. As in the case of so many other mystics, she followed moment by moment the chronology of the Passion from the Holy Thursday upper room—and here there is something which, so far as I know, is quite unique. She *saw* the agony in the garden, the judas-kiss, the flagellation, the crowning with thorns, the carrying of the cross: and then it stopped. So intense was her response to the horror of it all that she would never have survived the sight of the actual crucifixion. 'She didn't see him nailed [to the cross],' writes Madre Margarita; 'She would have died of grief': *Non lo vidde conficcare, che sarebbe crepata dal dolore.*[33]

Veronica in ecstasy and Veronica in rapture were too common a sight to be much of a problem for the community. If it was just a case of run-of-the-mill ecstasy, but of a somewhat protracted sort, her sisters knew what to do. They simply carried her to her cell, stretched her out on her bed, and left her there until, a day or two later, she came to herself. Rapture had to be handled somewhat differently, since one of its concomitant phenomena is usually immobility and rigidity of the members. There was the time, for instance, when Veronica had gone to the garden to cut a sprig of rue. She ducked into the tiny oratory there, for just a quick word with the Lord. The other nuns, who had been taking their evening recreation in the garden, returned to the monastery, having, as usual, carefully locked the garden gate. It was some time before they realized that Veronica was not in the house. Night had fallen. A search was made. The worried nuns finally found their missing sister in the garden oratory, plunged deep in rapture and utterly unresponsive to all attempts to rouse her. 'It just wasn't right to leave her there,' writes Mother Margarita, 'and we ourselves couldn't very well stay outside [the cloister] at night.' The only thing left to do was to pick her up, stiff as a marble statue and still kneeling, and process with her to church, where they plopped her down for the night in front of the altar.[34] Living with Veronica was better than a course in applied mystical theology.

More problematic than ecstasy or rapture was levitation. Here Veronica had to insist on her right to privacy, and the Lord finally had to agree after the embarrassed nun had several times been made a spectacle of in public. Especially rankling was the time Sister Plautilla Semboli came across her levitating in the nuns' sacristy. Unfortunately the sacristy could be looked into from the grating near the altar; and before long quite a crowd of admiring spectators had gathered, Suor Plautilla's father among them. He asked his daughter to pass some object beneath the levitating nun, so that everyone could be sure at that distance that she was really without physical support. So Sister Plautilla swished a rod beneath her airborne sister. Everyone was convinced; everyone was edified.[35] And Veronica, when she learned of it, was—well, better to pass on to a new paragraph.

Though Veronica insisted on absolute poverty for herself, she was lavish when it came to providing for the Lord in her capacity as sacristan. Many of the alms and donations which came her way went towards the purchase of suitable altar linens, vestments, sacred vessels, and church furnishings in general. Indicative of the poverty of the monsatery is the fact that when the bishop asked the community to take its turn at celebrating the Forty Hours devotion, they almost had to say No; there wasn't enough oil for the lamps, and no money to buy more. At Veronica's insistence, the invitation was accepted, and there was to be no skimping with the lights and candles. It was hardly coincidence when, on the opening day of Forty Hours, a farmer from one of the Papal States, otherwise unidentified, knocked on the door and delivered a barrel of the finest oil.[36]

Veronica also knew how to take care of the material needs of the community. It would take as much as eighty *scudi* to pave the humid cellar and to run a pipe-line to the courtyard and to the kitchen, which was without so much as a water-spigot. Veronica asked to be put in charge of the project. Funds on hand rose to a grand total of nine whole *grosetti*. But this was enough, she assured the convent administrator, Signor Orazio Rigoni, to start with. The sisters, some of them, were more than critical of the whole operation. There was next to nothing in the larder, and the problem, as they saw it, was not how to ensure a convenient water supply in courtyard and kitchen, but how to find enough food to keep from starving. Veronica and the Lord managed to see both that the building projects were completed and that the larder was replenished, and bountifully.[37] Veronica was also a good one to have around in case of fire. Twice the *Monaca di Fuoco* fought fire with fire—the fire of conflagrations which threatened to burn down the monastery with the fire of her faith and prayer.

It would be wrong to make the totality of Veronica's monastic life one uninterrupted extraordinary event. When not plunged into ecstasy or rapture, she prayed quite simply according to the grace given her. She said her vocal prayers, she murmured her ejaculatory prayers. She loved the Office, and even as an old, old woman she came to choir, though she had to hobble there, leaning on two younger sisters for support. Her preference was always for the dirtiest chores, even though we know from stray remarks made by the biographers that there were servants on hand to do such things.[38] In spite of the extraordinarily vivid nature of her many visions, she never lost her taste for quite ordinary spiritual reading. Though during the Sacred Triduum she might actually *see* Our Lord on his way to Calvary, this in no way made Saint Bonaventure's meditations on the Passion less worthy of her own constant perusal and study. She loved, too, the *Imitation*; and the Lives of the saints provided her with reading matter.

One of my favorite scenes is that of Veronica, old and soon to die, sprawling on the infirmary floor next to the arm-chair from which, as old folks sometimes do, she had fallen. Too weak to move from her painful position, and unwilling to bother her sisters by calling for help, she just lies there murmuring the name of Jesus, weeping copiously and laughing for sheer joy: not one or the other, and not one and then the other, but the two together, simultaneously. Tears with laughter. We can tell something of the nature of that laughter by this, that when the two infirmarians finally found her, they could not pick the feeble old lady off the floor without having first joined with her in a round of holy laughter. Later, in the depositions for the inquiry into Veronica's cause, the two nuns reproached themselves for having just stood there and laughed.[39] But that is just the way

Veronica would have had it. It was something within herself that had passed to them; and this, I think, is one of the most important aspects of Veronica's vocation.

It was not just good advice and healing that Veronica dispensed; not just monstrances for the chapel and paving for the cellar and a water faucet in the kitchen that she provided. Something of the quality of her own inner life suffused itself throughout the whole community simply by her presence there. At Christmas time she had wanted to pass the Bambino round to all her sisters, so that they too could hold him and grow to love him even as she did. In this, I think she ultimately, in a quiet, hidden way, succeeded wonderfully well. She had entered a community of good-living, devout religious, but still, a community in which one had to fight the system in order to live to the full the monastic life. It is clear from the depositions of many of her sisters that by the time of Veronica's death, the whole community was the more joyful and the more generous and the more loving for her sixty years with them. Something of Veronica had passed into their very selves. One of the most characteristic scenes is that of Veronica running around the monastery shouting *Amore, amore!* There must have been times—especially during the Grand Silence—when the nuns wished Veronica would tune her piety to a somewhat lower pitch.[40] But it was difficult to be around Veronica for any length of time without beginning to realize that, though love means pain and suffering, it is also a joy, a thing to wonder at and to laugh about.

The death of Veronica on 3 March 1620, plunged Cortona and the surrounding region into sorrow. She remained more, however, than simply a living memory. She was buried in the sacristy; and ten years later, when the nuns wished to move the casket to a place less exposed to dampness, they found that, though the casket had caved in under the pressure of mud and dirt, Veronica's body had been preserved whole and intact. In 1682, Bishop Oliva found, for a second time, the body still incorrupt; and in 1731, the judges delegated by the Sacred Congregation of Rites, Mgr Gherardi of Cortona and Mgr Vantini of Montepulciano, repeated the same experience. The official investigation into Veronica's holiness began as early as 1629, at Cortona itself; and a second official inquiry followed in 1679. By the late seventeenth century, the Laparelli family had secured funds sufficient to have the process of inquiry transferred to Rome. Then followed the lengthy investigation into Veronica's virtues and miracles, first *in genere*, then *in specie*; and this led to the official decree signed by Clement XIV on 24 April 1774, declaring the heroicity of Veronica's practice of the virtues.[41] And then came the chaos of revolution and the Pope in captivity in parts abroad.

To get to Veronica's monastery today we have to leave the bus behind and walk. Even cars have to be careful as we enter the twisting streets and narrow lanes of the old section of Cortona; and the honking of automobile horns and the shrieking of Vespas have faded to a distant murmur by the time we reach the Via San Nicoló, Number 2. Over the past few years a number of building and restoration projects have been undertaken and completed. In 1955, the garden oratory where Veronica used to pray was restored, as was the nuns' choir where the community attends Mass. Kitchen facilities have been modernized, but the old kitchen in which Veronica used to warm the Bambino on cold Christmas nights is still carefully preserved. An altar is there, and the nuns gather to pray every Christmas for love of Veronica and the Babe.

On 10 November 1960, ceremonies to inaugurate the four-hundredth anniversary of Veronica's clothing in the habit were celebrated. The anniversary date was, of course, November 11—the day when a very determined, no-nonsense woman raised great gusts of laughter as she tossed earrings and frills and necklaces around the sanctuary. The opening conference of the celebration was followed by the canonical recognition of the body of *la Venerabile*. The double casket locked with the three keys kept at the episcopal chancery was opened. The assembly saw the body of a woman dead since 1620, but a body preserved perfectly incorrupt. The account published in *Cistercienser-Chronik* notes that everyone was struck by admiration and emotion, *Tutti siamo rimasti ammirati e commossi*.[42] It all sounds a bit solemn and awesome. Was there no one there who laughed? No one to chuckle and remind us, in the tuscan inflections of Cortona, of the day when a four-year old tyke exhumed her pet chick and learned her first lesson in mortality? And now just look at her! At which point I suspect that the 'Fire Nun' would start spewing flames. Corrupt or incorrupt! bodily preservation or a fist full of dust and ashes! What difference does it make, *cari stupidi*! The one thing to remember, the only thing that really counts is *amore, amore!!!*

As one modern author writes, 'We are often so solemn about love that we forget love is a joy, a thing to wonder at and to laugh about. . . .'

NOTES

1. David P. Neil, *About Loving*, as quoted in Louis Savary and Thomas O'Connor, *Finding God* (New York: Newman Press, 1971) p. 140.

2. From one of the poet's more often quoted efforts, his *Hymn to Proserpine*.

3. Fr Vittorino Zanni, O.Cist., reminds us of this in his short article, 'Cisterciensi di ieri e di oggi: La Ven. Veronica Laparelli,' in *Notizie cistercensi* 10 (1977) pp. 43 (119)–46 (122), with special reference to p. 45 (121).

4. *Sermo in Nativitate S. Ioannis Baptistae, 3: Est enim tantum lucere vanum, tantum ardere parum: ardere et lucere perfectum.*

5. As quoted in Fr Chrysogonus Waddell, ocso, 'Simplicity and Ordinariness: The Climate of Early Cistercian Hagiography,' in *Simplicity and Ordinariness*, CS 61 (Kalamazoo: Cistercian Publications, 1980) p. 38.

6. During the last few decades notices have appeared in *Cistercienser-Chronik* 63 (1956) pp. LXII–LXIV; 66 (1959) pp. LXVI–LXVII; 69 (1962) pp. XXXV–XXXVII.

7. See above, note 3.

8. Dactylographed at Tilburg, Holland; the brief notice is in Vol. I, pp. 177–178.

9. Vol. 1 (Metten, 1932) p. 274.

10. *Cistercienser-Chronik* 51 (1939) pp. 86–89.

11. Translated under the title, *Vie de la Vénérable Véronique Laparelli de Cortone, Religieuse cistercienne du Couvent de la T.-S. Trinité . . . Composé d'après less documents des procès de béatification et de canonisation par Philippe-Marie Salvatori, Prêtre romain* (N.-D. de Lérins, 1875).

12. For a listing of the contents of this collection, and notes on history of the material after it left Rome, see Amedeus Comes de Bourmont, 'Index Processum authenticorum beatificationis et canonizationis qui asservantur in Bibliotheca Nationali Parisiensi,' in *Analecta Bollandiana* 5 (1886) pp. 147–161.

13. Salvatori's introductory letter to his Laparelli patrons, *Vita . . .*, pp. (V)–(XI), offer abundant though fulsomely expressed notes on the family background. All this material was omitted in the French translation of 1875.

14. *Relazione . . .*, pp. 3–4. Here as elsewhere I follow the orthography (including accentuation or lack of it) and punctuation of the printed text.

15. Founded in 1540. There is no satisfactory history of the monastery in its early days. According to the latest official statistics kindly given me by the Right Rev. Blaise J. Fuez, O. Cist., the present community is composed of fifteen nuns including the abbess, two novices, one lay sister, and one lay oblate.

16. *Romeo and Juliet*, Act I, Scene III, 73–77.

17. *Vie . . .*, p. 24.

18. *Vita . . .*, p. 13.

19. *Relazione . . .*, p. 5. The whole episode is described magnificently in pp. 5–6 of the *Relazione*. Comparison with the parallel accounts in Bonucci and Salvatori does little to bolster our confidence in these biographers. What saves Bonucci is his practice of quoting eye-witness reports *verbatim*, rather than paraphrasing them in flowery language, as does Salvatori. Even Bonucci, however, is loath to cite Mother Margarita textually, probably because what delights us as strong and vigorous and typically Tuscan struck the eighteenth-century literati as crude and semi-literate.

20. *Relazione . . .*, pp. 6–7. Mother Margarita's word for 'penances' is *astinenze*.

21. Salvatori, *Vita . . .*, Lib. I, Cap. V, p. 31.

22. Salvatori, *ibid.*

23. *Relazione . . .*, p. 7.

24. *Relazione . . .*, p. 7. References to the chalice and purificator do not point to communion under two kinds. After receiving the host, the communicant drank an ablution of wine before re-entering the choir stalls.

25. *Relazione . . .*, p. 8.

26. *Relazione . . .*, p. 18. Yet another bell-ringing episode is recounted, p. 20.

27. Should Veronica ever be canonized, she ought to be declared patron saint of bell-ringers—though, on second thought, this might be a bit dangerous.
28. See Heinrich Schlier's detailed article under this word in Kittel-Friedrich (eds.), *Theological Dictionary of the New Testament* 5 (Grand Rapids: W. B. Eerdman, 1968) 871–886.
29. *Relazione* . . . , p. 9.
30. Salvatori, *Vita* . . . , p. 35.
31. The hundreds of instances of Veronica's 'pastoral ministry' are by no means limited to the sections of the various Lives dealing with Veronica's charity towards her neighbors. In general, her extraordinary spiritual gifts were on behalf of others rather than of herself.
32. *Relazione* . . . , pp. 10–11. The Italian text is punctuated with the lack of logic characteristic of Mother Margarita's written style. Salvatori re-tells this episode in such a way that Veronica's sisters are said to love the Babe, but to be able to love him still *more* if only they could see him. He is, however, citing the version deposed by Ortensia de'Ghini, who had spent nine years at the monastery as a young girl. (Like many other convents, this one provided for a girls' school. The girls has a quasi-oblate status, and were known as *Educanda*.) See Salvatori, *Vita* . . . , Lib. III, Cap. I, pp. 106–107.
33. *Relazione* . . . , p. 14.
34. *Relazione* . . . , pp. 17–18.
35. Salvatori, *Vita* . . . , Lib. III, Cap. I, pp. 96–97. It was probably a mistake to follow the considerably more detailed account by Salvatori. Bonucci, *Istoria* . . . , p. 94, quotes Plautilla Semboli's deposition (*V. Testis fol. 80*), which is rather more low-geared. Her father, Averardo, was at the grille, and there saw Veronica kneeling at prayer. She struck him as being taller than usual. On her own initiative, Suor Plautilla passed her hand beneath Veronica's knees, and found that Veronica was indeed raised above the ground. In this version, there is no crowd, no paternal directive to the daughter, no rod passed beneath the levitating Veronica.
36. The episode is told by Salvatori, *Vita* . . . , Lib. II, Cap. III, pp. 60–61. The initiative for the celebration came, actually, from the Grand Duke of Tuscany. In this instance, Salvatori is more faithful than usual to Bonucci's version, *Istoria* . . . , pp. 54–55.
37. Salvatori, *Vita* . . . , Lib. II, Cap. III, pp. 61–63; Bonucci, *Istoria* . . . , pp. 53–54.
38. Mother Margarita, for instance, refers to the place where the monastery servants (*Serve*) used to kneel in church on days of general communion. This is in her account of Veronica's Holy Thursday participation in the Lord's Supper, *Relazione*, p. 13.
39. The account is given by Salvatori, *Vita* . . . , Lib. I, Cap. VI, pp. 35–36.
40. Mother Margarita speaks about the whole community being kept awake by Veronica roaming around the house in a state of ecstasy, and shouting *Amore, amore, amore* in an excess of fervor for her *dolcissimo Sposo Gesù*. I know of no present day Cistercian monastery in which this sort of thing could happen more than once, but Mother Margarita speaks of many similar incidents, by night and by day; see the *Relazione*, p. 20.
41. Copious details, and in this instance, reliable details, about the various stages of the investigations are in Salvatori, *Vita* . . . , Lib. III, Capp. IX-X, pp. 167–179.
42. See *Cistercienser-Chronik* 69 (1962), pp. xxxv–xxxvi, for a summary of the events connected with the anniversary celebration.

Simplicity as a Principle of Reform in the Writings of Mère Louise de Ballon

Charles Dumont OCSO

SOME THIRTY YEARS after the death of Mother Louise de Ballon in 1668, her *Spiritual Works*—her *Oeuvres de Piété* —were assembled and published by Jean Grossi, priest of the Oratory. At the end of the volume, in his 'Advice to the Reader', he suggested that the texts be arranged according to related subject matter:

> For example, everything that is said in this work on charity, humility, and simplicity could be gathered together, and placed under the same heading. [In this way] a summary of the whole spiritual doctrine of this very learned and enlightened disciple of the Holy Spirit could be composed.[1]

Not only are charity, humility, and simplicity connected, as Father Grossi understood, but the title 'simplicity' should be given to the whole doctrine of Mother de Ballon. We hope that a synthesis of this type will someday be made. Because of the great number of texts which have to do with simplicity, in these pages we will simply give a sketch of their content. From a statistical point of view, the frequency with which the word 'simplicity' recurs indicates already how dear this theme was to the seventeenth-century reforming nun, just as it had been to the Cistercian Fathers. In this not unimportant respect she showed that she was a faithful follower of the authentic tradition of the Order of Cîteaux.

The Congregation of Religious of Saint Bernard, or Bernardines, dates from 1622, some fifty years before reform was introduced at la Trappe and Tamié. The bernardine reform, of which Louise de

Ballon was the soul and first superior, began, with the full consent of the abbots of Cîteaux and Tamié, at Rumilly, in Savoy, in a dwelling placed at the sisters' disposal by the Montfalcon family. Thirty years later the congregation counted more than thirty monasteries in France, as well as one in Valais, Switzerland. Of these houses, only Collombey and its foundation at Géronde (1935), also in Valais, exist today.

The study of the history of Mother de Ballon's reform is of interest to us because it speaks to our times on more than one point. Unfortunately, this history is not very well known and has sometimes been judged in a summary fashion. And yet Father Grossi's account of it reads like a novel, in spite of its six-hundred pages.[2] Simplicity—the form of the monastic life and the characteristic trait of cistercian life—is the only aspect of the doctrine underlying the reform which will be dealt with in this article. Mother de Ballon grasped it with admirable intuition, for she gave it both an evangelical meaning and a mystical meaning in the ancient sense of the term just as the first Cistercians had done.

Louise Blanche Thérèse de Ballon was born 5 June 1591, at the châteaux of Vanchy, near Bellegarde in the Département of Ain, France. She was the fifth child of Charles Emmanuel Perrucard de Ballon and Jeanne de Chevron. Her two younger sisters, Gasparde and Jeanne, would also pursue a monastic vocation. The family was one of the most prominent of the region, and Louise was a cousin of Saint Francis de Sales, bishop of Geneva and Annecy. Louise entered the cistercian monastery of Sainte Catherine, near Annecy in Savoy, when she was seven years old, and made profession in 1607, at the age of sixteen. It was during the twenty-four years she spent at Sainte Catherine's that she received her formation in simplicity.

In 1608 Saint Francis de Sales was approached by the abbots of Cîteaux and Tamié and asked to accept the mission of reforming the monastery of Sainte Catherine. Saint Francis applied himself with zeal to this task, but without success, because these ladies, whose abbess was also his cousin, manifested stubborn resistance.

As for Louise de Ballon, it was only in 1617 that her first desires for reform made themselves felt. For five years *Monsieur de Genève* (as Saint Francis was commonly called), secretly helped Louise and the several other young sisters who were eager to initiate reform. When the abbess was notified of the young sisters' desires she asked them to explain their position freely and with confidence. It would perhaps be interesting to note the three points they considered particularly in need of reform:

Their reply was that they desired enclosure to be established in the monastery in order to prevent the religious from going to spend the greater part of the year with their parents, where they did nothing but pass their time in diversions; in addition, secular domestic servants of the abbey should be lodged outside the enclosure, so that a stop might be put to all communication with them; finally, whatever the religious had kept as their private property ought to be put in common, since this is what the Rule prescribes.[3]

The older nuns were opposed to having the course of their life changed, and advised the abbess not 'to consult the ones who were stirring things up' or 'listen to these young girls whose heads are merely full of vain thoughts and imaginings'.[4]

And yet, as *Monsieur de Genève* told Mother Jeanne de Chantal and several of the Visitation nuns at Annecy, it was the simplicity of these young sisters that had won him over:

This morning these good girls at Saint Catherine's let me know about their plan to undertake a reform. They have had it for a long time. The simplicity which I have remarked in them has obliged me not to make them wait any longer. Yes, they are going about it so simply that I can no longer resist them.[5]

Later on, Mother de Ballon liked to call to mind these words of Saint Francis. She also said that they took great care to act with sincerity and simplicity, and that this did not prevent either prudence or secrecy.[6]

In 1622 Francis permitted them to begin to lead a regular life at Rumilly, near Annecy. During her last meal in the refectory at Sainte Catherine's, Louise de Ballon wept bitterly at the thought of leaving the sisters 'with whom she has so long shared such particular customs and such close-knit relationships'.[7]

SIMPLICITY: THE HEART OF THE REFORM

The Simplicity of God and the Angels

If our reforming nun gave unique importance to simplicity as the form of the cistercian soul and life, it is because the attribute of God which most attracted her, as it had Saint Bernard, was simplicity. Simplicity is a quality which God requires in a person who wishes to attain conformity with him. Louise de Ballon was a mystic, but her scant interest in what she called 'particular leanings', and her discretion with regard to them, was exceptional enough at that time to be considered a sign of authenticity and fidelity to the ancient mystical tradition. The following passage is an account of a rapture which she had on 2 June 1624. What she most retained from it was her experience of the divine simplicity:

> They were reading something to us in the refectory about this mystery of the Holy Trinity. I was so strongly drawn out of myself that they had to carry me to my bed. I spent several hours there in the fullness of such intimate union with God that it seemed to me I was in the very union of the Father, Son and Holy Spirit. There one hears things which it is impossible to explain about this Trinity in unity. Since that time I have been more strongly attracted to simplicity, because of the knowledge which remained in me; that is, that in this unity of God there is simplicity which is the beauty and perfection of unity, and in this same beauty of the simplicity of unity there is a name which no one would know how to explain . . . O triune God! O one God, what beautiful and charming simplicity is in you! For it is, as it were, the beauty of your unity.[8]

This rapture, the nature of which is not for us here to determine (and which is, furthermore, of only secondary interest), should be seen as related to another one which occurred much earlier, when Louise was still sacristan at Sainte Catherine's:

> While I was working one day at some task in the sacristy of Sainte Catherine's, I had the sentiment of the presence of an angel (whose name I do not know). I have heard that when God commands these blessed spirits to do something they accomplish it while remaining in his presence, since they return to him as to their center, being occupied not with what they have done but solely with the one who ordered them to do it. In a certain way, I saw the plain and pure simplicity with which they go about this. This simplicity has an air of heaven more than of earth. By it, God is at the same time both in the action and the person who acts; and after the person has accomplished the action, he turns aside from it to direct himself wholly towards God who is in him.[9]

Simplicity—Fruit of the Cross

Simplicity has 'an air of heaven' because it is divine, as the quotation above states. Thus the whole work of grace appears as a simplification; only the infinite complications of the passions, pride, and self-love present obstacles to it. Mother de Ballon would become a worthy rival of the Desert Fathers in this struggle against the passions, which she ferreted out in spite of their very subtle disguises.

This work would be a work of truth, by the way of humility and radical self-stripping. It was when she situated moral combat in the way of the Gospel and of the cross of Christ that Louise de Ballon showed herself truly 'Bernardine'—a true disciple of Saint Bernard and also of Aelred of Rievaulx: *Ordo noster crux Christi*.[10]

The first chapter of the second treatise in Louise's *Oeuvres de Piété*, which is consecrated to the principal means of interior 're-formation', is entitled 'De la Victoire des Passions' ('On Victory over the Passions'). It begins:

> What is the meaning of the fact that so many years go by before we mortify our passions? We devote ourselves to mental prayer, we frequent the sacraments, we practice the virtues; finally, we lead a life which is exteriorly well-ordered and exemplary. And yet, as soon as someone touches something which concerns us, look at how our passions come forth and make themselves felt. What is the cause of this, except that we have not yet put into practice this lesson of our divine Master: If anyone wishes to come after me, let him deny himself, take up his cross, and follow me. To carry one's cross means to die to oneself. Oh, how important it is to understand this truth correctly and still more, put it into practice.
>
> And so, as concerns virtue, we would be very mistaken if we thought only of our exterior appearance and applied ourselves to improving it alone, while scorning and neglecting the interior. For although the one can scarcely exist without the other, we should give our attention principally to the latter. We must be attached to it and work principally on its formation. This consists particularly in mortification of our passions.[11]

Predominance of the interior over the exterior by no means implies that the exterior is given no attention. Rather, the interior makes use of the exterior and keeps it ordered to its own ends. This priority of interiority was a characteristic of the Catholic Reformation, just as it had been of the Protestant Reformation. Mother de Ballon affirmed it in a clear way and at the same time rediscovered the finely balanced doctrine of Saint Bernard, as it is found, for example, in the *Apology*.[12] We might ask ourselves if greater interiority is not a requirement of every reform, at least of every monastic reform.

For Mother de Ballon, the 'interior' was the world of thoughts and movements of the heart. This comes out clearly in the continuation of the passage which we have just quoted:

> It is not only because of their gross and too human aspect that we must mortify them [the passions], but still more because of their

spiritual and less perceptible aspect: for example, the thoughts
which they suggest to us, the plans which they prompt us to make,
the desires which they inspire in us, the judgments which they
cause us to form, and so on. For alas, if the christian soul is not
particularly careful to watch over and observe the movements of
this heart which cannot be seen, how many and how serious are
not the faults to which it can succumb and cultivate?[13]

Watchfulness over the heart and mastery of thoughts have a place
of great importance in cistercian monastic teaching, but a person
can find many ways to escape from assuming the responsibility of
practicing this *ascesis*. One way to escape it is knowledge:

Because of the same lack of care, how many great minds filled
with knowledge have been lost! That is, because they did not
learn, and consequently did not practice, the important science of
death to self. They became puffed up with their vain knowledge;
they took pride in the lofty things they knew; they gloried in
their excellent discourses; they were dazzled by their extraordinary
talents, and they neglected true science. . . . [Jesus Christ] takes
such great pleasure in seeing this mystical death in us, and he is
so strongly attracted by it, that as soon as we enter into it he
enters into us, not only to act by himself but also by us, as he was
pleased to make me understand by a special light.[14]

We do not find the word simplicity in this passage, but it seems
to me that these lines give a very clear description of the basis of
the spiritual life in Mother Louise's doctrine, a doctrine modelled
on that of Saint Bernard. In fact, the 'mystical death' about which
she speaks is closely connected with the moral struggle against the
subtlest aspects of the passions. As soon as we undertake this struggle
by consenting to grace, Christ enters into us and causes us to act.
In Saint Bernard this is at the same time both *ascesis* and mystical
life. If we re-read his *Sermon Twenty on the Song of Songs*, we will see
that the devotion to the humanity of Christ introduces us into the
mystery of the Word, not by intellectual contemplation but by moral
conformity. This conformity of the will is love, which is itself vision.
Like Bernard, Louise de Ballon was on the path of the mystical life
as it was understood in ancient monasticism. It has been described
in this same way in the writings of Dom Anselm Stolz, where *ascesis*
and mystical life form one single spiritual entity, and no attention is
given to the psychological aspect of mysticism.[15] This doctrine of the
spiritual life is essentially sacramental, just as it is in Saint Bernard
where the focus is on the evangelical 'mysteries', and particularly

on the mystery of the passion and cross. Mother de Ballon quotes Saint Bernard often, as does Saint Francis de Sales, by repeating a few of the more significant words. Her citations lack precision. In one such passage, when speaking of the instruments of the passion, she mentions the image of the bouquet of myrrh which Bernard pressed upon his heart.[16] With reference to this image, let us quote Louise de Ballon on the subject of her most famous vision, the one she had at Annecy in 1617, when she had just concluded her retreat with a confession to her director, *Monsieur de Genève*.

> When I had knelt down in the choir before the Blessed Sacrament and had begun my penance, I suddenly saw myself spiritually stripped before God, as it were, and in the complete nothingness of creatureliness. I shuddered with fright at this. Then, raising my eyes, I saw above me at about the height of a person a large cross which appeared very heavy. It was completely inlaid with precious stones which concealed their brilliance on the outside and confined it to the inside. Curious to know what supported this cross I saw suspended before me, I cast my regard still higher and saw that it was the Son of God himself. He made me understand that he was presenting it to me. And yet I did not feel prompted to take it. Furthermore, I could not have done so; it was too high.[17]

This vision, which she had at the moment when the thought of a reform was taking shape in her mind with some clarity, profoundly marked both her life and her whole work of reform. The simplicity which is the predominant note of her whole spirituality has none of the aesthetic elegance that can be admired in modesty and reserve. For her, simplicity meant the cross of Christ and the narrow door of renunciation and sacrifice. Uniting these two considerations, she said of her reform that the passion of the Saviour was its principal founder, and that the religious were to have it unceasingly before their eyes. Still more specifically she declared:

> I believe with great certainty that this way of holocaust is *the* way for the daughters of the congregation. No other way keeps us in such a state of surrender to the spirit of our institute, which is the spirit of simplicity, as the one by which we remain united to the holocaust of Jesus by the holocaust of ourselves. Mortification, which is crucifixion of the soul, is inseparable from simplicity; and anyone who wishes to abide in simplicity should be in [a state of] continual sacrifice of herself . . . This spirit of simplicity is the true spirit of the reform . . . Nothing keeps our soul more clean and pure than this virtue. It brings unexplainable treasures with it. It desires nothing but God. Superiors, especially, should love

and practice it, because their subjects will willingly walk along the same road they do if they see that they esteem this holy simplicity. For then they also form a lofty idea of it.[18]

The Simplicity of the Religious Life

Three treatises of Mother de Ballon, comprising one hundred twenty-five pages, develop her doctrine of simplicity in all its aspects. These are: the *Entretien spirituel: sur la simplicité religieuse*, written in 1630, when Mother de Ballon was superior of the monastery of Seyssel; the *Traité de la Simplicité religieuse*, written in 1655; and the first *Retraite de dix jours*, of May 1656, which is an appendix to the *Traité*. The fundamental principle of simplicity was to have a penetrating influence not only on the interior life of her religious, but on the way in which the whole exterior life of the monasteries was regulated.

Simplicity is identical with the very name 'monk'. It has always characterized the monk, but almost without his knowing it, because he cannot 'practice simplicity' without deflecting from it. A person does not make himself simple. Newman pointed this out: 'Simplicity, which characterizes the child and the poet, also gives the monk his temper. From the monks of Egypt to the Trappists of our day, unity and simplicity characterize the monk'.[19] As the ultimate perfection of man—in Zen buddhism, for example—simplicity excludes in advance all self-seeking and all cleavage between the spirit and one's idea of self. The man who worries about his identity, seeking his own image as if in a mirror, finds himself paralyzed by his reflection, because it cannot possibly keep pace with and correspond to his life of thought and action. The spirit stiffens as soon as it tries to focus on and cling to a consciousness of itself. No definition of simplicity can exist independent of a person's experience of it, just as no one can know what it is to love except by loving. Phenomenology alone offers us some chance of success in discerning what simplicity is, and anyone who has the courage to try this approach will find a good many precious, subtle, and profound observations on monastic simplicity in the writings Mother de Ballon consecrated to it.[20]

Simplicity is so simple that it seems in some way to elude all grasp and all comprehension. Since it does not enter into composition with anything else (for if it did, it would no longer be simple), simplicity remains inexplicable. It is not the contrary of anything, for multiplicity exists only outside it, and begins with duality, dialectic, or duplicity.[21] According to its etymology, as Heidegger found,[22] simplicity envelops and joins in a single fold both explicitness and implicitness, the inside and outside. Within its hiddenness, as Blondel said when speaking of Saint Bernard's doctrine, 'the most ordinary acts and thoughts are espoused to the divine Spirit'.[23] Simplicity creates a favorable milieu for 'mystical moralism'—a better term, we feel, than 'christian socratism'—which Mother de Ballon practised with the same ease as had Saint Bernard himself. Like love, simplicity has no source and no other end other than itself; it is therefore situated in the beginning-less and endless circle of the infinite and indefinable, which brings to mind the divine. Like love, it is over and above everything. 'God loves', says Saint Bernard, 'and loves with his whole being, because the whole Trinity loves, if the word *whole* can be said of what is infinite and incomprehensible, or even of what is simple'.[24] This is why Saint Bernard accumulated superlatives to denote the transcendence of the divine Unity and Simplicity: '*Tam simplex Deus . . . si dici potest, unissimus est*',[25] '*simplicissima unitas*';[26] '*purissimum simplex.*[27] And yet man is the image of this extreme divine simplicity, and it is thus that we must understand Saint Bernard's beautiful expression: '*Simplex natura simplicitatem cordis exquirit*' (A simple nature requires simplicity of heart).[28] It is indeed the heart that must be freed from all alloy. For man's original simplicity is his likeness to God which, as Saint Bernard taught, was not lost but covered over and completely deformed by falsehood and duplicity, which mask and obstruct it. The heart must reject the mendacious illusions to which it is attached. It must renounce the superfluous things which disfigure its beauty; it must have the courage that comes from humility and simplicity, so that it may be just what it is and nothing more, just as God created it. He made it simple and it has complicated itself with passions.[29] This 'renunciation' does not take anything away and does not despoil anyone of anything; rather, it gives, and gives the inexhaustible strength that comes from what is simple'.[30] To rediscover this simplicity of intention is to find God, because the experience is its own fruit.

When Mother de Ballon was asked by the sisters of the community at Annecy to write a treatise on simplicity, she wanted to find a way of escape, like the Zen monk about whom the following story is told. A novice asked him one day: 'What is simplicity?' He replied that at the very moment he was being asked the question he lost all clear and distinct idea of it. Mother Louise's sisters had given her a large notebook so that she could write about simplicity for them. She sent it back to them without a word written on its white pages, and explained:

This virtue is itself so simple that I had to return this book to them, and inform them that they could see it in the very whiteness of its paper.

Both her gesture and her answer would have been highly commended by the Zen master!

And beyond any doubt this concerns the restoration of the image of God, because she continued:

They were not content with this advice. They are set on my giving them some practical pointers to help them to be simple and thus return to the original innocence which has been completely ravaged in us by original sin, or rather, by the sin of Adam.[31]

Openness of Heart

One of the most direct and important applications of simplicity, in Mother de Ballon's opinion, is openness of conscience, the fifth degree of humility in the *Rule of St Benedict*. She describes all the forms of humility and all the difficulties connected with it, and she extends its practice in community life both to the relations of the sisters with their superiors and the relations of the sisters among themselves. This aspect of simplicity is nothing but a spontaneous frame of mind which permits acts and words to flow forth naturally, and makes apparent that it is more useful to insist on interior dispositions than on practical details.

We are perhaps surprised to notice in Mother de Ballon's long, almost too-detailed developments on openness of heart that both the attitude and the practice of openness are totally gratuitous, that is to say, they are not done at all in view of receiving direction by advice or counsel. Rather, they are exclusively means of setting oneself free and of acquiring a pure heart and simple regard.

I assure you that one of our greatest evils is a lack of openness of heart, which some persons may maintain on pretext that it is good. It is in such an attitude that self-love, with all its subtleness and shrewdness, arranges its affairs very well, and it is by such an attitude that it impedes our perfection in a strange way. So without sorrow and without reserve let us disclose everything which harms our soul, even if it should cost our life itself. Let us go headlong, so to speak, to unveil ourselves, without seeking so many long ways around or so many pretexts for exempting ourselves from it. It is so important for the daughters of Saint Bernard not to have a heart which will not open up willingly and freely.[32]

Be as simple as doves . . .

In the *Constitutions*, simplicity is found among the principal religious virtues. Who would find this astonishing? Under the heading: *De la simplicité et naïveté*, we find this: 'The sisters should love the dovelike simplicity which the Saviour recommended, and avoid all kinds of subtleness, pretense, and duplicity. . . .'[33] The following passage, which occurs at the beginning of the *Traité de la simplicité religieuse*, gives an idea of Mother Louise's tone and way of speaking:

> Simplicity knows neither disguise, nor pretext, nor human respect, nor concern for self, nor fear of losing favor when a reprimand is received. What will they say if I do this? What will they think of me if I say that? Simplicity does not let itself stray after superfluous subjects of curiosity such as these: Why do they order us to do such a thing? Why do they forbid this other thing? Simplicity is the adornment and, as it were, the enamel of truth. The more we are possessed by simplicity, the more prudence will lead us. Be as prudent as serpents, the Saviour tells us, but at the same time be as simple as doves.[34]

And at the beginning of the *Entretien spirituel*, she describes this *columbina simplicitas* (dovelike simplicity):

> [Simplicity] is even so agreeable to the divine Majesty that one may say that the Holy Spirit reposes and makes his abode in the soul of a person who has true simplicity. Saint Scholastica, the worthy sister of our great patriarch Saint Benedict, recognized very well that spiritual perfection consists principally in being simple; for, as visible proof of the excellence of the christian simplicity that she had practiced all her life, at the moment of her death God transformed her soul into a dove, so to speak, and let her dear brother see it as it flew to heaven in the form of this innocent bird. Why did he use this way of representing her, except to signify and intimate that while this illustrious virgin lived here below she had become a spiritual dove by letting herself be led by grace at all times without the least opposition.[35]

Since simplicity is union with God and consequently the expression of grace itself, it is also strength in our weakness.

> It is therefore in the sight of their fragility that they [the sisters] should make true simplicity walk. It has such a mild and peaceful air that it never troubles the soul, for its character is to keep the soul united with God. And God is a God of peace . . . There is very much and, at the same time, very little to do in order to be

simple. This is because all this 'very much' reduces itself to little. This simplicity is in fact such a little thing that the soul which has undertaken to practice it finds that it has nothing to do on its own. It has its regard fixed on God; and this regard causes it to go on its way in everything with the greatest truth.[36]

We find here the same identification of simplicity and truth that we find in Saint Bernard. The following text shows this quite well:

My daughter, God is simple in himself, and he is of a simplicity which we will never be able to understand. And because true simplicity depends on God who is Truth itself, those who really wish to serve him and make themselves perfectly pleasing to him seek only to walk in the truth. Now to be really truthful one must have a liking for being simple and apply oneself to being so. Simplicity takes away everything which could disguise or hide the truth even the slightest bit.[37]

Since simplicity has only one eye, it makes a person see nothing but the truth, provided that this eye is the truth. And what is perfectly marvelous is that, although in this mystical eye a person sees herself to be of so little worth, it is in it and by it that she learns the greatest things about eternity.[38]

Conversion and Spiritual Childhood

At the end of the *Entretien spirituel* there is a long, charming meditation on the spirit of childhood. Here we can only summarize it. Mother Louise speaks of novices who do not like to be treated as children, and who show by their facial expressions that they do not easily tolerate others having little respect for their age and their intelligence:

'Really', she says to herself, 'I'm thirty years old and I'm a grown-up woman; what do they think I am, and what are they trying to make of me! I want them to know that I am no longer a child'. Well, my poor sister, if you are not, you have to become a child. You would have to do so even if you were twice as old as you are.[39]

Then, after giving the example of the Gospel scene where the Lord puts a child before the Apostles, she continues: 'And so, ladies of thirty, forty, or sixty years, or still older, you who live in monasteries of Saint Bernard, resolve to become one-year old children, if you will'. But Mother de Ballon makes clear to her sisters the meaning of true spiritual childhood, and insists on it. This attitude cannot be identified with a type of infantilism which is nothing but stratagem and disguise, because the heart is not in conformity with the childish face, and the interior lies to the exterior. In a word, infantilism lacks simplicity.

Mother de Ballon stresses the importance of experiencing our dependence and our need of being saved by the grace of Christ, and in this she is once again like Saint Bernard. Such an experience is indispensable for conversion of heart and must not be fled in an endless quest for advice and encouragement. To do this would merely be a means of evading the decision to cry out to the Lord and wait for his coming, as the patriarchs and prophets did.[40] The following colorful lines about nuns and their spiritual directors illustrate this point:

> To how many spiritual fathers does a sister wish to speak? How many conferences does she want to have with them? How much advice does she want to receive from them? And when she comes back from talking with them, how many times does she repeat these words of vain joy and self-love: This Father is really fine! He is so clever! He expresses himself so well! What he says is so right! He is so enlightened and intelligent! He told me everything I wanted to hear! But if anyone so much as lays a finger on this sister, so to speak, alas! there she is, the same as ever. And if she would consult a hundred fathers among the most capable ones, she would not draw any more profit from it. What is needed, I repeat, what is needed is practice. She can converse as much as she likes with different directors, seek as many excuses as she wishes, or make up as many pretexts as she desires to justify her itching to talk all the time about her difficulties, her doubts, her scruples, and her troubles, most of which are imaginary. If she does not put her hand to the work she will find that she always remains the same, even if fifty years go by. She must pray a great deal and must experience her own need before God, as did the good patriarchs of the Old Testament. She will make more progress that way than by all those conversations with other people, whoever they may be.[41]

Simplicity of Observance and Community Life

Mother de Ballon not only left us a doctrine of simplicity, she practiced it herself. If, as the saying goes, the style *is* the person, by her writings we can see that she was a person of charming simplicity. And this simplicity, combined with good sense and wisdom, was put to excellent advantage in her government of monasteries.

The two most important points of the reform, the ones which were also the most difficult to interpret intelligently, were enclosure

and abstinence. The latter was a subject of particular dispute at the
time, when the war of cistercian observances was at its height and
completely absorbed with the question: meat or no meat! Let us state
clearly that Mother de Ballon's interest in the questions of enclosure and abstinence stemmed principally from their importance for
community life and spirit. In this respect she was a true disciple of
the early Cistercians and their spirituality of the common life. She,
just like Saint Bernard and Saint Aelred, who elaborated at length
on the subject, realized that the community was indispensable to
the *schola caritatis*.

Near the beginning of this paper we saw that the young nuns
who wished to introduce reform considered enclosure one of the
most important monastic observances. The reason for this was its
value for community life. As they were about to leave Sainte Catherine's, the young nuns told the abbot of Tamié, in the presence of
their abbess:

> Monsieur, we are leaving this monastery because of an inspiration
> which we have long had. By making us see that enclosure is the
> principal means of forming true community, this inspiration has
> constantly until now urged us to adopt the type which is in accor-
> dance with the decree of the holy Council of Trent . . . Because
> of the opposition to enclosure which exists here, and which you
> see well enough, Monsieur, we could not do anything like that in
> this monastery.[42]

The same concern for community life finally led Mother Louise
to decide not to adopt abstinence from meat. The matter was settled
only after a great deal of discussion and conflict of opinions. She
had set about drawing up new constitutions as early as 1624, while
she was at Grenoble, where the first foundation of the congregation had been made. Sensing that opinions in the community were
divided, she first consulted the strictly-reformed men religious of
Grenoble, and then asked her religious for their views. The most
fervent among them wanted the strictest abstinence. But during
these debates something happened which was useful to Mother
Louise, who herself was inclined toward moderation. A sister of
Rumilly, strongly bent on austerity

> . . . toward the end of November 1625, became afflicted with very
> great infirmities which were not less harmful to her mind than
> to her body. Her blood, burned by her extreme abstinence, made
> melancholy vapors rise to her brain, and caused her to commit
> excesses which occasioned trouble in the whole monastery.[43]

Mother Louise told the community about this during a conference in which she enumerated the reasons for permitting the use of meat. Its use, she explained, would be very limited, since the constitutions would require abstinence on Mondays, Wednesdays, and Saturdays throughout the year. The first reason she gave was merely a kind of compensation: enclosure is a harder penance than abstinence, although it is not even mentioned in the *Rule of Saint Benedict*. The second argument is of interest to us: a rule that is too strict brings in its wake dispensations and privileges which end by annulling the rule itself, because they take away its seriousness. And thirdly:

> I made them understand that they had seen very well that those among them who were the most inclined to austerity had been the least submissive as regards obedience, that they had shown themselves to be subject to vexation, that they were ill-tempered toward others, less cordial, and more attached to their own opinions in many things.[44]

But the final argument is exclusion of singularity by the simplicity of the common life:

> Besides, see what inequality that [abstinence] causes in a community. There have to be three or four kinds of meals on the same table: one for the sisters who are infirm, boiled meat for this one, roast for that one, fried for another one, ground for another, while there are only a few thin little fishes for those who are healthy. Who can fail to see how reluctant we should be to permit such variety in a refectory? These things are very dangerous and disadvantageous for communities, where partialities which are tolerated under the guise of necessity make the religious fall into I do not know how many faults . . . Tell me, my poor daughters, what more do you think you will have when you eat meat? Most of the time it will be only a bad-tasting, cheap piece of beef which, since it will simply be boiled, will be much less tasty than eggs which have been well prepared. But at least there will be the same thing for everyone. No singularity will be seen among us, no difference in food any more than in everything else. And believe me, this uniformity in the refectory is not a thing of small importance or of little advantage in a community.[45]

This concern for the common life, in the two-fold sense of life in common and a perfectly ordinary life, is constant in Mother de Ballon's teaching; and it is simplicity which guided her in the measures she took to keep it intact. Simplicity is, furthermore, identical with humility, the servant of charity. Let us quote the following text where the reforming nun revealed a sure grasp of the benedictine and cistercian monastic tradition:

> One of the effects of humility is the rejection of all singularity . . .
> so that after it has stripped us of the tatters of ourselves, so to
> speak, it may clothe us with the robe of charity, which it is then
> careful to keep clean just as a faithful and vigilant servant is careful
> to keep the clothes of her mistress clean. Because I then learned
> that humility is truly the servant of charity . . . I have often noticed
> that it is in this community spirit that the holiness of the spirit
> of our institute consists; and the excellence of this same spirit is
> simplicity. . . .[46]

Both by her life and writings, Mother de Ballon showed that she had a perfect grasp of the, we may say, active spirituality, which was so important to the first Cistercians. By this I mean the struggle against disordered passions and emotions, and also against uncontrolled thoughts and everything else which hinders the free action of the Spirit in the heart of the monk who has not yet got free from sins and vices. This struggle leads to simplicity and a certain ease which permits him to live in union with God quite naturally, without effort, and by love.[47] There is, in fact, a field of interior activities between the exterior observances of the monastic life and application of the spirit to contemplation, which is the monk's principal concern during his whole life. Aelred of Rievaulx clearly indicated in the conclusion of the treatise he sent to his sister, a recluse, that in the program of the school of charity there are:

> 1) rules for bodily observances by which a recluse may govern the
> behavior of the outward self;
> 2) directions for cleansing the interior self from vices and adorning
> it with virtues;
> 3) a threefold meditation to enable you to stir up the love of God
> in yourself, feed it, and keep it burning.[48]

Mother de Ballon gives us many precious pointers on this second category: the reforming of the interior self. We might almost say that, in her mind, the word 'reform' meant principally this particular aspect of cistercian monastic formation. For her, the practice of monastic exercises meant 'putting life into our actions spiritually'. This is how she understood—very correctly, we believe—Saint Bernard's famous remark, written either to Henry Murdach or Aelred of Rievaulx, that he was able to be open to grace more easily while working in the woods than amidst books in the libraries:[49]

If I am not mistaken, this is what our father Saint Bernard wanted us to understand when he said that he had learned what he knew while cutting and carrying wood for the needs and use of his brothers. He meant by this that it was especially by his actions done with the right intention—that is to say, accompanied by holy interior dispositions—that he had acquired holy doctrine and the true science of the saints. For many persons are learned, but they are not saints because they go no further than their doctrine and in their actions do not apply themselves to interior recollection, even though this is so very necessary in all exterior occupations. O good Jesus, how badly things go in religious houses when the best practices are done by custom or routine, with nonchalance and I do not know what kind of insensitivity. Because of this they are done without savor, without affection, and often even without the least attention of the soul.[50]

Anyone who knows Saint Bernard even a little will easily be able to annotate these lines with numerous references. As an example of the way in which Mother de Ballon practiced what she taught, here is a very clear passage:

In a little while I am going to strip hemp, because in our houses we do a little of everything . . . I am going to do this, Lord, as someone who belongs to you, and I will keep my attention on you during this little action. This will preserve me from the unprofitableness of thoughts. . . .[51]

A comparison of Mother de Ballon's reform with, for example, that of Mother Angélique Arnaud, her contemporary, or with the benedictine reforms of the seventeenth century, would no doubt lead us to say that this principle of simplicity preserved the religious of Saint Bernard from tendencies and practices incompatible with the monastic life. We have seen this in Mother Louise's disapproval of sisters who continually run to directors. She also escaped what Bremond called 'mystical invasion' (*l'invasion mystique*), in the same way as the twelfth-century Cistercians escaped the manifestations of thirteenth-century mysticism, that is, by the same concern for simplicity. It is because of this lack of glitter, no doubt, that Bremond abandoned his reading of the life of Mother de Ballon.[52]

Her prayer life was not very 'mental', and she seems to have received her greatest graces everywhere but in church: at manual work, in the refectory, in the parlor, or even in bed. One morning before the rising bell, while she was still half asleep, she heard these words spoken in the softest kind of voice: '*Benignitas et humanitas apparuit*

Salvatoris nostri, with all the rest that is said in the Little Chapter at Vespers on Christmas Eve'.[53] She understood these words as clearly as if they had been said in French. There was no question of the gift of tongues, because Father Grossi tells us that Louise had learned Latin during her sojourns at her parents' château instead of wasting her time at home on diversions as other religious did.[54]

We who are seeking how to live in our day according to tradition could learn from Mother de Ballon how to keep our balance on many other points of cistercian discipline. In the delicate problem of silence and the use of speech, charity in the community was once again her prime concern, and simplicity was the principle by which she judged. She could not find words sufficiently severe for talkativeness and back-biting, the bane of monasteries.

> As for me, I confess frankly that I have never been able to un-understand how anyone can talk so much, especially in malicious tale-bearing, quarreling, speaking ill of persons, murmuring, and so on. I have never had friends (men or women) for those things, and I do not know how anyone in good faith can pass so many hours in chatting, often at the expense of her neighbor . . . I would think that any of our houses where this disorder is in vogue would be very unfortunate, but we know well enough that this sort of thing is all too frequent in monasteries that are not reformed. O miserable kind of friendship, which I have always held in horror![55]

If, on the other hand, she insisted on openness of heart, it was to facilitate what the ancient monks called spiritual friendship, which is at the same time fraternal correction and mutual support. Mother Louise was certainly demanding when it came to sisters disclosing things to the superior, but it was because she did not want the sisters to be tempted to hide things. And she advised superiors to entreat those sisters who could not speak freely with them to speak 'with an open heart' to someone else, 'because we permit it easily in our monasteries'.[56] On this kind of friendship, she wrote:

> Truly, as far as possible, I like this, and I could not approve of the sisters not loving one another. When I see persons with no friendship, it seems to me a great hardship, not to say a very cruel thing. I would like to be able to give affection to those who lack it. I certainly believe that God wants us to love one another, even tenderly, but without flattery, and not to the point where we conceal our imperfections from one another . . . O what true and perfect friendship that is! Divine grace is its source and cause. It makes us point out our faults to one another by a

motion of charity, and without bad temper or bitterness . . . thus I have learned to prize these friendships wherein persons love one another, and love one another for eternity.[57]

Simplicity and Generosity

One of the finest and most useful distinctions made by Mother de Ballon is found in her comparison of simplicity and generosity, and the contrast she draws between the two. Her remarks are like a warning against a danger that exists in cistercian austerity, and which has posed a threat to its value and liberating efficacity during the whole history of the Order, from the very beginning until our day. We do not need to speak here of the temptation to 'voluntarism', which leads to a type of harshness that makes the heart hard, haughty, and scornful, and causes it to fail lamentably in the school of charity. The three following passages, taken from the *Entretien spirituel*, express Mother de Ballon's thought perfectly:

Here, my daughter, is something new and, at the same time, altogether contrary to simplicity; consequently you should be very careful, and very much on guard against it. That is, there are souls who take devotion to such extremes that they think they must do everything for God with extraordinary fervor and generosity . . . Their attention is so strongly centered on this, it is so deeply plunged into it, so to speak, that they entirely forget the tenderness that they should have for their neighbor, and for their sisters in particular . . .

My daughter, we must therefore be on guard against this deceptive generosity, and allow in ourselves only that type which is in harmony with simplicity. Simplicity wants us to be generous, but it also wants us to conquer ourselves, to humble ourselves, to accuse ourselves, to desire to be held in contempt; and it wants all this to be effortless and without violence, because otherwise we would be crushed instead of strengthened. Simplicity likewise does away with all bitterness, all disdain, all partiality. It does away with them, I say, banishing them from the generous love we ought to have for each other, and it leaves us with only tender love exempt from all imperfection. Or if there is some imperfection, the simple eye gets rid of it first . . .

[The superiors and novice mistresses] . . . will make all those who are under their authority or guidance understand that although they wish to be generous they should not stop being very simple. I do not mean, of course, a naïve kind of simplicity or one which comes from stupidity, but an innocent simplicity which is born of spiritual childhood . . . So beyond all comparison, our

sisters should shine more because of their simplicity than their
generosity.[58]

CONCLUSION

We must conclude, and we shall do so briefly, because we have
purposely let Mother de Ballon herself tell us her thoughts on simplicity. Bergson recognized in christian mystics 'the taste for action,
the capacity to adapt oneself to circumstances, firmness joined to
flexibility, prophetic discernment of what is possible and what is not
possible, a spirit of *simplicity which triumphs over complications*, briefly,
superior good sense'.[59] He also said: 'Most of all, she [the mystical
soul] sees *simply*, and this *simplicity*, which strikes us in her words
as well as in her conduct, guides her through complications which
she does not even seem to see'.[60] In our day, when complications
and problems accumulate to the point of paralyzing the energies of
many, which of us would not like to meet some of these mystics who
triumph over their problems while giving the impression that they
do not even see them? Both in her activity and in her prayer life,
Mother Louise knew how to let herself be guided by simplicity,
which was basically nothing but the form which grace and God
himself took in her. It gave her a fearlessness which can be compared
to that of Teresa of Avila when she was making her foundations.

> May simplicity cut multiplicity out of our minds [Mother Louise
> said]! It is like an abyss into which everything within us that does
> not come from God falls and is annihilated. We need only to
> surrender ourselves to it and hold fast; then we can let God act,
> because he will change that abyss into an abyss of grace for us.[61]

In the bull *Parvus Fons*, addressed to the Cistercians, Pope Clement
VI commended them for having preserved in its integral purity the
great simplicity which existed at the origin of the Order: *Et quia
praefatus ordo in multa simplicitatis puritate fundatus, profecit laudabiliter
in eadem . . . .*[62] We can see, and say with admiration, that during
the course of the Order's long history there have always been men
and women who recognized that evangelical simplicity was the main
characteristic of the cistercian reform. Through it they rediscovered
the original intuition of our founders and made it live again in their
times, in one century after another, so as to transmit it to our times,
purely and simply.

Translated by Elizabeth Connor, OCSO

NOTES

1. *Les Oeuvres de Piété de la Vénérable Mère Louise Blanche Thérèse de Ballon, Fondatrice et première supérieure des Religieuses Bernardines Réformées de Savoye et de France, recueillies de ses propres Ecrits, par le Révérend Père Jean Grossi* of the Oratory (Paris, 1700). Containing: *Les Oeuvres de Piété, Entretien spirituel, Traité de la simplicité religieuse, Première retraite de dix jours, Seconde, Troisième et Quatrième Retraites, Lettres*. A facsimile of this orignal edition was published by the monastery of Géronde [CH–3960 Sierre, Switzerland] in 1979.

2. *La vie de la Vénérable Mère Louise-Blanche-Thérèse de Ballon*, by Père Jean Grossi of the Oratory (Annecy, 1695) 592 pages.

3. Grossi, *La Vie*, p. 134.

4. *Ibid.*, p. 135.

5. *Ibid.*, p. 178.

6. *Ibid.*, p. 180.

7. *Ibid.*, p. 250.

8. *Les Oeuvres*, p. 191.

9. *Ibid.*, p. 70.

10. Aelred, *In ramis palmarum*, PL 195: 263D; CCCM 2A (Sermo 10.31).

11. *Les Oeuvres*, p. 40.

12. Apologia to Abbot William, SBOp 3 (Rome, 1963). Translation by Michael Casey, ocso, *St Bernard's Apologia to Abbot William*, CF 1A.

13. *Les Oeuvres*, p. 41.

14. Idem.

15. A. Stolz, *Théologie de la mystique* (Chevetogne, 1947). 'Once this unilateral psychological interpretation is rejected, we are led to say that ascesis is not at all a prelude to the mystical life but an essential element of it, the progressive death of the sinful life of the body. *Ascesis* and mystical life are therefore two factors of a single and same supernatural process'. pp. 122–123. 'When the Christian listens to what God inspires within him, avoids distractions of the exterior world, applies himself to the divine life which he bears within himself and deepens it to the point of experience, he is a mystic'. p. 260.

16. Grossi, *La Vie*, p. 305: 'The true and characteristic happiness of the daughters of Saint Bernard is attached to the sacrifice of ourselves to the cross. This saint is commonly represented with the instruments of the Passion, which he clasped to his breast. He himself said that he had made of them a bundle of myrrh which he bore on his heart . . . What also distinguishes us is that it is principally our spirit that we must crucify, since God asks principally for our heart, that is to say, what is interior'.

17. *Ibid.*, p. 67.

18. *Ibid.*, pp. 307–308.

19. J. H. Newman, *Historical Sketches* (London, 1876) III, 2: 'The Mission of Saint Benedict', p. 405.

20. Grossi, *La Vie*, pp. 548–549: 'Having had the desire to reside in one of the monasteries (Cavaillon) by concern for her health and in order to be far from her home and parents, she heard an interior reproach which made her see, she said, that she was "straying from the state of interior and exterior despoilment in which he had placed me before I entered the reform . . . [But] by this reproach which passed very softly through my mind in less than three words, I heard: Neither health nor sickness; neither air nor place; neither life nor death; neither any other creature nor oneself; neither desire to be known nor desire not to be known; neither fleeing nor stopping."' Some readers will perhaps think of the hindu principle of non-duality, but here it is quite simply a question of the mystery of the cross to which the soul completely surrenders.

21. Saint Bernard also plays upon the pejorative moral sense of the word *duplicitas* when he opposes every kind of duplicity to simplicity: '*Et simplicitas candor est.*

Probamus e contrario, nam naevus duplicitas. Parum dixi: macula est. Quid duplicitas nisi dolus?' SC 71.3.
22. See below, note 30.
23. M. Blondel, *La Pensée* II (Paris, 1934) p. 372. And also: 'True contemplation is not abolition of knowledge of individual realities; it consists of giving each one its place and loving it in the total plan, where no being is without its use and none is inconsequential . . . This is why the center of our intellect always implies a state which, because of its indistinctly known virtualities and the ways of access it opens to the divine touch and grasp, merits the name of 'mysticism' (*Ibid.*, pp. 363–364).
24. *De Diligendo Deo*, IV, 13.
25. *De Consideratione*, V, vii, 17.
26. *Ibid.*, V. xiii, 29.
27. *Sermo super Cantica canticorum* (SC), 81, 2.
28. *Sermo in labore mensis*, 3.9.
29. *Sermo* 82.2–3 *super Cantica Canticorum*.
30. M. Heidegger, *Le chemin de campagne*, in *Questions III* (Paris: NRF, 1966) p. 15; and p. 12: 'For someone who is dissipated, what is simple appears to be monotonous. Monotony repels. Those who are repelled no longer see anything but uniformity around them. The simple has vanished. Its silent power is drained.'
31. *Première retraite de dix jours*, pp. 81–82.
32. *Entretien spirituel*, pp. 25–26. Also pp. 22–23: 'I implore you again, my daughter, to completely banish from your mind this belief that people want to know everything that goes on inside us, when we are so strongly urged to disclose our interior life. I am very glad that this thought came to me here; because this temptation could easily attack some of you. Right here I say this to them: It is neither the Mother nor the Directress [of novices] who wants to question you. It is Saint Benedict himself, the author of our *Rule*, who tells you by the mouth of the superior: My child, reveal your thoughts, especially your bad thoughts, to your superior'.
33. *Règles, Constitutions et Exercices spirituels des Religieuses de la Congrégation de saint Bernard, Ordre de Cîteaux* (Turin, 1901) p. 49.
34. *Traité de la simplicité religieuse*, pp. 52–53.
35. *Entretien*, pp. 1–2.
36. *Ibid.*, pp. 9–10.
37. *Ibid.*, pp. 10–11.
38. *Ibid.*, p. 16.
39. *Ibid.*, p. 49.
40. Cf. Saint Bernard, *SC*, 2.
41. *Première Retraite*, pp. 85–86.
42. Grossi, *La Vie*, p. 211.
43. *Ibid.*, p. 407.
44. *Ibid.*, p. 411.
45. *Ibid.*, pp. 412–415.
46. *Les Oeuvres*, pp. 176–177.
47. *bis.* Cf. A. Stolz, pp. 225–226. 'The benedictine Rule also shows us the unity of ascesis and the mystical life . . . At the end of the chapter [Seven of the rule], after the twelfth degree of humility . . . [the monk] will practice monastic observances, let us say the ascetical life in a completely natural way and without difficulty 'as the Holy Spirit will deign to reveal in him'. Here we should see a direct allusion to the mystical life of grace, which will be able to manifest itself in flesh that is mortified'. Dom Stolz also refers to the commentary on the *Rule* by Dom Albert L'Huillier, who wrote: 'Chapter Seven, on humility, becomes for us also the Chapter about *Theoria*, in the ancient sense of the word, that is to say, contemplation'. *Explication ascétique et historique de la Règle de saint Benoît*, par un Bénédictin, Tome I (Paris, 1901) pp. 270–271.

48. *A Rule of Life for a Recluse*, translated by Mary Paul Macpherson, ocso, *Aelred of Rievaulx, Treatises and Pastoral Prayer*, CF 2 (1971) p. 102.

49. Bernard, *Ep* 106; *SBOp* 7:266; see also Aelred of Rievaulx, Prefatory Letter to the *Mirror of Charity*, translated by Elizabeth Connor, ocso, CF 17 (Kalamazoo, 1990) pp. 70–71.

50. *Les Oeuvres*, p. 102.

51. *Ibid.*, p. 120. We also read in the *Vie*: 'It is all this reasoning that God wants us to get rid of. I mean these superfluous and unnecessary reflexions that we make about happenings which concern us in a particular way and which either our vain curiosity or self-love cause us to make. He does not want us to amuse ourselves at all with "Why this?" "Why that?" For once, let us leave our reason, just as our soul, entirely submissive to his guidance and to that of the persons who govern us in his place. To live without rationalizing is to live in continual prayer'. p. 534.

52. 'Although I do not succeed in getting interested in this pious nun, whether by my fault, which is probable, or the fault of her formidable biographer (six hundred pages, and eloquent ones), I point her out to the curious, who will find in her *Vie* a great number of details about the religious history of that period'. Henri Bremond, *Histoire littéraire du sentiment religieux en France, 6, La Conquête mystique* (Paris, 1922) pp. 417–418. Bremond does not cite *Les Oeuvres de Piété*.

53. Grossi, *La Vie*, p. 400.

54. *Ibid.*, p. 29.

55. *Les Oeuvres*, p. 172. See also pp. 171–172: 'In addition, I have received from God a good inclination which I hardly dare to reveal . . . it is the inclination not to speak much. Our sex is commonly accused of the contrary vice. So, being a woman as I am, one would have trouble believing me, if God were so partial in bestowing his graces as to reserve them all for men alone.'

56. *Entretien*, p. 21. And further on (p. 30): 'But it is not only during the novitiate that we must be faithful to this discovery. We must be faithful all our life, right up until our last breath. If then for our last words, my dear daughter, we could humbly accuse ourselves of some fault, how happy we would be to expire in an act of humility!'

57. *Les Oeuvres*, pp. 58–60.

58. *Entretien*, pp. 39, 41 and 47.

59. H. Bergson, *Les deux sources de la morale et de la religion* (Paris, 1932) p. 244.

60. *Ibid.*, p. 245.

61. *Traité*, p. 55. Elsewhere she also advised: 'Thus, one should speak simply, write simply, confess simply, reveal one's interior to one's superior simply. As for me, I feel so full of this simplicity that it is all I have in mind. It is simplicity which writes by my hand what I say about it'. *Retraite*, p. 98.

62. This is the reason mentioned by the Pope for dispensing the Cistercians from solemn ceremonies foreseen by the Lateran Council for election of abbots. *Statuta Capitulorum Generalium Ordinis Cisterciensis* 3, ed. J. Canivez (Louvain, 1935) p. 25.

598

Courtesy of Gethsemani Abbey Archives.

Armand-Jean de Rancé and Françoise-Angélique D'Étampes Valençay: Reformers of Les Clairets

Chrysogonus Waddell OCSO

THE IMPERATIVES OF CONTEMPORARY monastic renewal have done a great deal to stimulate interest in those past movements of renewal which are the inevitable concomitant to the longevity of any long-lived religious institute. Like all other institutions, religious institutions are necessarily and deeply affected by the vicissitudes of human history, and a world in constant change and evolution throws out a permanent challenge to a religious family to enter into the course of sacred history by becoming more and more what it already is in all that touches on its deepest identity and its institutional charism. Roots firmly sunk into bed-rock of the past, total involvement and incarnation in the present, inner direction and forward movement that carries it towards eschatological fullness— eliminate any one of these three, and the mission of a religious institute in the Church and in the world becomes seriously, perhaps fatally, compromised.

The cistercian family has been challenged as often if not more often than most of the older monastic institutes. Her long history is one of bewildering complexity, in which signs of an astonishing vitality sometimes coexist with symptoms of institutional sclerosis and dry-rot of the extremist sort. My own interest bears in a special way on reform-tendencies and reform-projects in seventeenth century cistercian France, and—most particularly—on the reform at la Trappe carried out under the aegis of Armand-Jean de Rancé (1626–1700). In spite of the abundant literature dealing with la Trappe and its illustrious reformer, no comprehensive study of the Rancéan ideas about monastic reform has ever been attempted. Indeed, the time for this is probably not ripe, since such a study presupposes the existence of preliminary monographs dealing with particular topics. When consulted about matters touching on monastic renewal, Rancé could be lavish with advice and encouragement. But his own efforts were concentrated chiefly on his community at la Trappe, and his direct involvement in the reforming activity of other communities was limited in the extreme. There was one great exception: the royal abbey of les Clairets. The present article, then, will simply examine briefly some of the more salient aspects of the contribution made by the abbot of la Trappe to the reform of these nuns.

PROLEGOMENA

The Cistercian Milieu in Seventeenth Century France

> Man's chief difference from the brutes lies in the exuberant excess
> of his subjective propensities. Prune his extravagance, sober him,
> and you undo him.
>
> William James[1]

By the end of the sixteenth century, the exuberant excesses of the Golden Age Cistercians were no longer much in evidence in their descendants. Devout extravagances of an earlier, more enthusiastic, age had been pruned away by force of circumstances and the horrors of troubled times. In France, the periodic ravages of plague and famine, the commendatory system, and the sempiternal series of wars that began in 1337—the Hundred Years War (1337–1453), the wars connected with the annexation of Burgundy to France (1470–1478), and the Wars of Religion (from 1562 onwards)—had all left the Cistercian Order nothing if not sober. There are some who would say, sober and undone.

Recent historians of the seventeenth-century cistercian scene have rightly pointed out that, grim though the general picture was, it was by no means uniformly black. These historians are surely right. But the glimmers of light pointed out by Polycarp Zakar[2] or Louis Lekai[3] only serve to make the vast canvas as a whole all the more darksome. Given the historical setting, we should not expect to find much by way of exuberant excess of piety; the immediate problem was bare survival.

This is not to say that exuberant excess and unpruned extravagance were wholly lacking to the cistercian enterprise as the Renaissance drew to its close. What extravagance and enthusiasm there was, was generally concentrated in isolated individuals who held their own in a monastic milieu less than ideal, or in groups of enthusiasts whose reform tendencies often propelled them straight out of the cistercian orbit. Admittedly, of the many national or regional Cistercian Congregations to arise in the course of the fifteenth, sixteenth, and seventeenth centuries, a good number managed to retain their cistercian identity as well as formal membership within the much-ailing cistercian body politic: the Congregations of Upper Germany, of Calabria and Lucania, of Rome, of Aragon, of SS Bernard and Malachy. Other Congregations cared little or not at all for their juridical affiliation with Cîteaux, mother of them all; and although a number of these splinter-groups proved remarkably successful—the Feuillants, and the Congregations of Castille, of Saint Bernard in Italy, of Lombardy and Tuscany, and of Alcobaça—they were nonetheless schismatic to varying degrees, and all too careless, some historians opine, of their cistercian heritage.[4]

As Congregation after Congregation arose within the Order or split off from it, sincere but ineffectual attempts were made in the direction of Order-wide reform. Yet between Jean de Cirey's *Articuli Parisienses* of 1494[5] and the detailed program of general reform presented to the General Chapter of 1601,[6] reform at the level of the entire Order was never more than a pious velleity. Indeed, even after the Chapter of 1601, reform at the level of the entire Order fared little better than before.

There was a brief period attendant on the beginnings of what was to emerge as the Strict Observance, when it looked as though the reform-tendency then manifesting itself in a number of communities might well spread peacefully on the strength of its own inner momentum. It turned out to be a false spring that heralded decades of internecine warfare between Abstinents and Ancients.[7] The miracle is that, given the battle-prone cistercian milieu, there were still communities and superiors with the spiritual resources and energy needed for serious renewal at the level of local communities. The general scene was none too brilliant, and in 1675, after a decade of intense involvement in the affairs of the Strict Observance, the disillusioned abbot of la Trappe looked back dejectedly over the preceding sixty-year period, and complained that, if the Strict Observance had lost out all round, it was probably their own fault. 'They were interested more in getting control of monasteries,' he wrote, 'than in forming religious.'[8]

The long, convoluted history of the rise of the Cistercian Strict Observance in seventeenth-century France[9] has its pages of grandeur, but on the whole, it makes for rather dreary reading. It would seem, in retrospect, that Rome had little choice but to preconize the *modus agendi* crystallized in the papal constitution *In suprema* of 1666.[10] The provisions of this document envisaged a sincerely intended program of general reform, in which objective grounds for real grievances between the two opposing cistercian camps would be either eliminated or considerably minimized. The constitution ensured for the Strict Observance the possibility of continued existence, but also protected non-adherents of the Abstinent platform from the danger of an eventual take-over by Strict Observance partisans.

A monastic reformer of Rancé's stamp could be admired with sincerity in papal chancery and in royal court, and both Pope and Grand Monarch were pleased and proud that the phenomenon of la Trappe existed in the Church and in the realm of France. But the Pope at Rome and the Sun King at Versailles both understood well enough that monks are only men, and that to make the exuberant excess of la Trappe normative for the ordinary monk in the choir-stall would be to court disaster. More prudent, then, to allow the possibility of exuberant excess at the local level, while demanding from the Order at large a standard of excellence realistically within the purview of sincere monks less extravagant than the denizens of la Trappe.

Reference to History in the Rancéan Program of Reform, or A Practical Program for Monks: *du Premier Esprit de L'Ordre de Cisteaux*

The shrill, tendentious polemicist, Armand-François Gervaise, tells in his chronicle of the fortunes and misfortunes of the Strict Observance, a story that probably (like so many of Gervaise's stories)[11] improved with the telling. Already as a simple novice at Perseigne, Rancé, Gervaise claims, had plans for a particular reform of the abbey of which he would soon be regular abbot—a particular reform stricter than what was envisaged by the Strict Observance platform. Indeed, if we are to believe Dom Gervaise (always a bit risky), Rancé made his solemn profession in 1664 conditional on his receiving permission from the Vicar General of the Reform (Jean Jouaud, Abbot of Prières, in Normandy) to initiate at la Trappe his own program for reformed cistercian monks. What did this particular reform envisage? Greater fidelity to the spirit of early Cîteaux. For, notes Gervaise, Rancé 'saw nothing in the Reform

(=standard Strict Observance) close enough to the first spirit of our Fathers and Founders'—*rien dans la Réforme qui approchât du* premier esprit *de nos Pères et de nos Fondateurs*. . . .[12]
Premier esprit, first spirit, early spirit. Implicit in this is a reference to the book which was to become Rancé's *vade mecum* of cistercian reform: the thrice-printed tome by the learned Julien Paris, Abstinent Abbot of the monastery of Foucarmont (1645–1671):

DV PREMIER

E S P R I T

DE L'ORDRE

D E   C I S T E A U X

OV

SONT TRAITEES PLVSIEVRS CHOSES
necessaires pour la connois-
sance & le retablissement du
gouvernement & des moeurs des
Instituteurs de cét Ordre;

ET POVR   L ' I N T E L L I G E N C E
de la Regle de sainct Benoist[13]

It was this book which served as Rancé's introduction to the history of the Cistercian Order, and which provided him with the background material incorporated in his later writings touching on matters of monastic reform and cistercian tradition.

Early proof of Rancé's dependence on Julien Paris is to be found in an important pamphlet-length memorandum submitted in mid-December, 1664, to Prospero Fagnani, jurist-member of the special Congregation appointed by Alexander VII earlier the same month to settle the war between the two Observances.[14] The memorandum was drawn up in Rome and submitted, in the name of the abbots of the Reform in France, by the two delegates of the Strict Observance, Dominique Georges, abbot of Val-Richer, and Armand-Jean de Rancé, who had made his solemn profession and had been blessed as abbot of la Trappe barely six months earlier in the year. Thomas Nguyên-Dình-Tuyên, whose *Histoire des controverses à Rome entre la Commune et l'Étroite Observance de 1662 à 1666* is indispensable for our understanding of the peripteries of these years in the fortunes of the Strict Observance, writes that 'We can easily conclude that this long memorandum was drawn up on the basis of the book by Julien Paris, *Du premier esprit de l'Ordre de Cisteaux*. This extremely dense résumé of two-hundred and thirty-nine pages of the book remains quite faithful to the *abbé* Paris, apart from a few details'.[15] And Father Thomas adds: 'We shall find the same spirit later on, in the writings of the reformer of la Trappe'.[16] The same spirit and, we might add, even the same basic ideas.

In his great work, *The Rise of the Cistercian Strict Observance in Seventeenth Century France*, Father Louis Lekai called attention to the importance of Paris' tome.[17] There are, however, two points in Father Lekai's description of the work to which I would take friendly but firm exception.

'In spite of its title and impressive bulk,' Father Louis writes, 'Paris' work is not a systematic treatise on the indicated subject but rather an oversized pamphlet, an apology for the Strict Observance. . . .'[18] This observation would hold good were we to take as the title simply *The Early Spirit of Cîteaux*. We could then say that the title sins by excess and defect: by excess, since major portions of the book treat of post-twelfth century developments, and offer a concrete proposal for Order-wide reform; by defect, since in the first sections which do indeed treat of the early spirit of the Order, the sources drawn upon are too limited, at least for modern standards of scholarship. We have to remember, however, that seventeenth-century titles were often page-long affairs, and that the full purport of many a book is to be found, not just in the opening words, but in the full-length title. If we take the full title—*On the Early Spirit of the Cistercian Order: With a Discussion of a Number of Things Necessary for the Understanding and Re-establishment of the Government and Way of Life of the Founders of This Order*—we perforce conclude that the actual contents of the book correspond wonderfully well with the title, and the whole arrangement is, indeed, systematic and carefully reasoned. Given the importance of the book for Rancé's program of monastic reform, and given also the unfamiliarity of the book to almost all modern readers, it might be well to outline the main divisions of this practical program for reform-prone Cistercians, based on historical sources.

The plan of the work admits of four major parts.

PART ONE deals with the early Cistercian Order, and attempts to discover the spirit of the Order by a survey of her early history, key-legislation, and early practices. Chapter One describes the foundation of Cîteaux and the consequent growth of the community into a great Order. Chapters Two-Three are devoted to an analysis of the Charter of Charity, and Chapter Four to the pivotal principle that is the heart of the book: the integral observance of the Holy Rule as the expression of the true cistercian spirit. Chapters Five through Thirteen then pass in review concrete cistercian usages, showing how these faithfully harmonize with the prescriptions of the Holy Rule: norms for the foundation of monasteries (Five), the cistercian habit (Six), vows and profession (Seven), the Divine Office (Eight), confession, Communion and Mass (Nine), fasts and abstinence (Ten), solitude and silence (Eleven), manual labor, reading, mental prayer (Twelve), hospitality and alms-giving (Thirteen).

PART TWO studies the administrative machinery of the Order and the role of Superiors: exemption from episcopal control (One), the form of government called for by the Charter of Charity (Two), the General Chapter (Three), the system of filiations (Four), local abbots (Five), a sort of 'Mirror of Abbots' composed of texts from cistercian sources and Saint John Climacus (Six), priors and other officials (Seven), the penitential code (Eight), and, finally, a general summary about the excellence of cistercian observance for the first three centuries of the history of the Order.

PART THREE makes for gloomy reading. Here Paris traces the decline of the Order. Basing himself on Bernardine texts, his prefatory Chapter One assigns as the causes of monastic decline: 1) vanity and ambition, 2) disenchantment with an austere, penitential way of life, and 3) infidelity to the religious vocation. By way of illustrating the first cause of decline, he reproduces *in extenso* a General Chapter discourse by the fourteenth century cistercian abbot Justus (Two). The easy-going life alleged as the second cause of decline is dealt with in the context of Benedict XII's Constitution for the reform of the Cistercian Order, *Fulgens sicut stella matutina* of 1335, and also with much material taken from General Chapters of the period (Three). Lack of fidelity—the third cause of decline—is laid chiefly at the door of overly indulgent Superiors with little real understanding of the nature of their pastoral ministry to the community (Four). Efforts on the part of Popes Eugenius IV, Nicholas V, and Innocent VIII to recall superiors to a sense of duty are passed in review (Five), but these papal directives fell on deaf ears, as did also the articles of reform drawn up at the insistence of King Charles VIII (Six).

With PART FOUR we arrive at the climax of the bulky tome, which here discusses at length the proper and necessary means for the Order's renewal in its early spirit. Chapter One presents an ideal (perhaps idealized) picture of the early days back then, drawn from coeval sources, both cistercian and non-cistercian. Is such a renewal a matter of obligation? Chapter Two answers the question in no uncertain terms. But how are we to revive this spirit? The shortest, easiest way of doing this, Paris tells us, is simply to re-establish the integral observance of the Holy Rule: *rétablir l'entier Observance de la Règle de S. Benoist* (Three)—here the author once again draws upon papal pronouncements and cistercian documents already familiar to us from earlier pages of the book. How does one go about re-establishing this integral observance of the Rule? Chapter Four gives us the answer, and with it the second necessary means for a return to the early spirit of the Order: simply implement the early documents that expressed the spirit of the Order in the early days—the Charter of Charity, General Chapter decrees, and the early Cistercian usages. Chapters Five and Six treat of two important corollaries of the preceding program: 1) in the future, all novices have got to be trained in the integral observance of the Rule and of the 'constitutions' of the Order, and all Superiors will themselves have to be committed to the same integral observance, 2) all dispensations—most especially the dispensation from meat-abstinence—have got to be foresworn. A final chapter (Chapter Seven, wrongly numbered as Chapter Eight—at least in the edition of 1670 which I have at hand) deals with the rise of particular Congregations, and of the imperative need for a reform of the french houses, if the particular Congregations were eventually to be reintegrated with the parent body.

This seminal work is indeed systematic, and the contents correspond perfectly to the title of the book (the *complete* title, that is to say).

Here an important observation is in order, touching on the importance of a historical frame of reference in matters concerning monastic reform as conceived by Julien Paris (and Armand-Jean de Rancé). Never was there a question in their minds of a new program for monastic living. The problem, rather, was that of re-establishing a vital link with a living tradition that had long ceased to exist—or so they claimed. Their watchword, implicitly at least, was: Return to tradition. This stance was, of course, wholly coherent with the general climate of the seventeenth-century, when a much beleaguered, enormously evolved Church had to answer the claim of dissident bodies that the Church of Rome was not the Church of the springtide of Christianity. The flowering of patristic and historical studies reflects wonderfully well the preoccupations of serious, history-minded churchmen of the post-Tridentine centuries.

This passion for history can easily degenerate into historicism and archeologicism, and modern-day historians and theologians point to the more articulate of the seventeenth-century Jansenists as examples of how not to reassert or re-establish a living continuity with a tradition rooted in the distant past.

Large numbers of seventeenth-century churchmen were not, however, particularly noteworthy on the score of sensitivity to history, and much of the incredibly rich post-renaissance flowering of christian experience and of new forms of religious life strikes one as being akin to the fruits of spontaneous generation, without much explicit reference to the historical past. Herein lies a certain danger no less harmful than that of exaggerated historicism: the danger of an institutional subjectivism which, when left unchecked, can end in collective lunacy. And even when the final result is not lunacy, we can still regret, in at least certain instances, that what was intended to be a deeply experienced renewal of an ailing tradition ended in an evolution into something different and by no means as deep and noble as the abandoned tradition. It is salutary to pass in review the reform movements initiated in houses of cistercian nuns in the seventeenth century, and to note how quickly what looked like a sudden burst of new life fizzled out or turned into something as moribund as what had preceded. Port-Royal, Tart, the Bernardines of Mère Ponçonas, or of Mère Louyse de Ballon—their late-eighteenth-century history was assuredly no more moribund than that of most Common or Strict Observance monasteries, but this is faint praise indeed.

As for Rancé, it was surely in large measure his historical frame of reference that saved la Trappe from the exuberant excess of the illustrious abbot's subjective propensities. Whether or not Rancé really understood twelfth-century Cîteaux is a question generally (if I think, wrongly) answered in the negative.[19] It remains nonetheless true that Rancé's understanding of the early cistercian tradition proved a providential check on his individualistic tendencies, channeled his subjective propensities in a generally positive direction, and pruned most of what needed pruning without sobering him overmuch or essentially undoing him.

Penance as Discipleship

This brings us to the second point in Father Lekai's description of *du premier esprit*, to which I wish to make a respectful demurrer. 'The author's concept of Cistercian spirituality is clear from the very beginning. In Paris' view the purpose of the Rule, in fact of monasticism in general, was to establish a life of heroic mortifications. . . .'[20] By way of illustrating this, Father Lekai quotes a passage from the Novitiate Directory added to the editions of 1664 and 1670. He writes:

> Toward the end of the book, for the benefit of novices who may have missed his point, Paris condensed once more the essence of monastic life, which was not established and shaped to please by offering satisfaction to the flesh and blood, but, to the contrary, for the mortification of senses or, more specifically, for bringing about the death of all faculties, both of the body and soul. . . . He who is called to this vocation must renounce at the moment of his entrance his own self and to swear enmity (even against) the most innocent pleasures of his body.[21]

Though it would be difficult to overemphasize the importance of mortification and renunciation in the thought of Rancé (or of Saint Bernard, Saint Benedict, Cassian, or the early monastic tradition in general), it is hardly consonant with the spiritual teaching characteristic of Rancé (or of Paris) to make the monastic life a life of 'heroic mortifications' without situating this essential component of monastic life within its proper context. What is this proper context? The following of Christ. If penitence and mortification pertain to the essence of monastic life, this is only because the following of Christ is bound up essentially with the Cross of Christ. Neither Paris nor Rancé were particularly preoccupied with *heroic* mortifications; they sought those mortifications requisite in the life of the disciple of Christ called to follow the Master along the paths traced out by the monastic tradition crystallized in the Holy Rule. If mortification is heroic, this is because the following of Christ calls at times for true heroism. In brief, to take the Strict Observance emphasis on mortification and renunciation outside its evangelical context of the following of Christ is to falsify the perspectives hopelessly.

Indeed, if we are looking for a convenient formula which does, in fact, provide an essential description of monastic life according to Julien Paris, we can find it easily enough in the opening lines of the passage quoted above. Paris is describing the *Attitudes and Resolutions of the Person Entering the Novitiate*,[22] and his opening sentence begins: 'Souls called by God to the religious life should realize that this state is only a renewal (*renovation*) and an imitation of the life of the early Christians. . . .' The author then goes on to state that the maxims on which this life is based were preached by Jesus Christ on the cross. This leads directly into the text quoted by Father Lekai, but only incompletely; for 'the most innocent pleasures of the body' is followed without a break by:

> in order to embrace with the Cross of Jesus Christ everything that it [the Cross] has to teach: in particular, penitence, poverty, humility, chastity, and obedience—and all this unto death.[23]

This life is, says Paris, a 'life of penitence and toil' (*vie pénitente et laborieuse*), but, once again, always within a christocentric context. From the moment the aspirant enters the novitiate, he must

> renounce not only the world and all it contains by way of possessions, honors, and pleasures, but also himself, in order to sacrifice himself to a life of penitence and toil *like unto that of Jesus Christ*.[24]

The christological dimension of this page is all the more evident in that, following the convention of the time, the name JESUS CHRIST is set in capital-type, so that it leaps out at the readers four times within a single page (set in rather large type). The novice is urged to consider that there is no other place in the world than the monastery, 'to which JESUS CHRIST had called him for his salvation'. Novices are to find their consolation in the company of their guardian angels,

> with our Lord JESUS CHRIST, with whom, from now on, they are to hold conversation, for whom they are to do and suffer all things, to whom they are to dedicate all their thoughts and all their affections, and to whom they are to commit all that concerns them.[25]

My own summary of Paris' understanding of the essence of religious or monastic life, based on a reading of the integral text quoted only in part by Father Lekai, would probably run: 'A life of radical renunciation lived in total union with Christ, under the ever-present sign of the Cross'. This formula is still inadequate, because it omits reference to monasticism as the form under which the infant Church is present in these latter times.

We must be careful in reading authors of the stamp of Paris or Rancé. If they are talking about silence, then, obviously, the essence of the religious life is SILENCE. If they are talking about obedience, the essence of the religious life is OBEDIENCE. And so it goes.

Then, too, our modern-day tendency to equate 'heroic mortification' with Rancé's concept of 'penance' (the word he uses is actually 'penitence') is about as insightful as understanding the gospel term *metanoia* to mean taking the discipline unto blood, and only that. In his major work, *On the Sanctity and on the Duties of the Monastic State,* for instance Rancé structures the bulk of his material on a sixteen-point index of means by which all religious, no matter what their particular Order or Congregation, are expected to arrive at true holiness. Items One through Five follow in this order:

1. The love of God, or divine charity.
2. Entire confidence in the superior.
3. Charity and vigilance on the part of superiors.
4. Fraternal charity, or mutual love of the members for one another.
5. Fervent assiduous prayer.[26]

Items Six through Sixteen form the following list:

6. The love and constant practice of humiliations.
7. Frequent meditation on death.
8. Habitual attention to the presence of God, remembering his judgments.
9. The spirit of holy compunction.
10. Exact solitude and retirement.
11. Profound silence.
12. Corporal austerities and mortification of the senses.
13. Manual labor.
14. Night Watching.
15. Evangelical poverty.
16. Patience in sickness and corporal infirmities.

Where is there mention of penance in the above list? In point of fact, Rancé introduces his chapters on items Six through Sixteen by a brief chapter (Chapter XII) on penitence; and he presents the last ten points of his *elenchus* of means towards holiness as being simply so many expressions of penitence: interior penitence (6–9) and exterior penitence (10–16). Evidently, Rancéan penitence is a rich, all embracing concept capable of subsuming many divers practices, interior and exterior. Still this does not give us the core of Rancé's thought of penance/penitence. The key text is this:

> As the penitence of a monk owes its birth, strength and merit to the penitence of Jesus Christ, so ought it to be a continual retracing, a faithful imitation of *his* penitence.[27]

The penitence of Jesus Christ? The idea is foreign to us. We are more at home with soteriological terms such as 'redeeming love', 'redemptive suffering and death', 'the Man for others'. Rancé is formal: 'To know what the penitence of solitaries ought to be, we must consider what the penitence of Jesus Christ was.'[28] And our professional penitent thereupon proceeds to draw up a list of episodes drawn from the *gesta Christ* to demonstrate that items Six through Sixteen in his list of means of sanctification are simply so many means of participating in the Mystery of Christ—or, more specifically, the Mystery of the Cross of Christ.[29]

Is the monastic life essentially a life of penitence/penance, according to Rancé? Absolutely—but hardly in the superficial manner understood by most of us who know Rancé only in caricature. And while we are at it, we might note that, when Rancé provides a systematic treatment of his understanding of monastic life, he begins with a lengthy disquisition on love: God's love for us, and ours for him; our love for our superior, and his for us; and our mutual love of one another: all of which expresses itself in a life of fervent assiduous prayer.

A Passion for the Absolute and the Spirit of the Age

Before passing on to the immediate topic of the reform of les Clairets, we will touch briefly on another factor which needs to be considered in evaluating the fierce asceticism of the program of reform expounded by persons of the ilk of Julien Paris or Armand-Jean de Rancé. It is unfortunate, very unfortunate, that even the well-read student of monastic history almost inevitably knows about Rancé and the Trappist ideal chiefly in the perspective of the famous polemic between Rancé and Mabillon. Rancé, the epitome of the severe Trappist spirit; Mabillon, the incarnation of the gentler, more humane, more Christian Maurist ideal. La Trappe on one side; and on the opposing side, the Congregation of Saint-Maur: and never the twain shall meet.[30]

In point of fact, a good argument could be made out in favor of this hypothesis: The Congregation of Saint-Maur was more Trappist in its spirituality than the Abbey of la Trappe. Not that I really want to defend this hypothesis—but it does serve wonderfully well to draw attention to a rather startling study by a latter-day Mabillon—Dom Jean Hesbert, osb, who contributed an important article on the 'monastic theology' of the Congregation of Saint-Maur to a volume in the series *Archives de la France monastique*, devoted to the theology of monastic life according to great monastic personages of recent times.[31]

Dom Hesbert's synthesis of the theology of the monastic life lived and experienced by the Maurist Congregation is based largely on his detailed analysis of the nine bulky tomes that make up the *Histoire de la Congrégation de Saint-Maur.* Without falling too much victim to the statistical method, Dom Hesbert drew up a list of 'key-words' corresponding to the contents of the material analyzed. At the head of the list comes *Pénitence!* With 'penitence' assigned the coefficient 100, the rest of the list (which excludes those terms with a coefficient less than 25) reads as follows: prayer (72), regularity (71), austerity (50), 'retreat' (retraits) (41), exactitude (39), mortification (38), observance (34), solitude (34), silence (32), duty (27), separation from the world (26).[32] Dom Hesbert then proceeds to group these frequently overlapping terms around three poles: ASCESIS (penitence, austerity, mortification); MONASTIC DISCIPLINE in its constitutive aspect (separation from the world, 'retreat', solitude, silence), as well as under the aspect of fidelity to the exercises of monastic life (regularity, exactitude, observance, duty); and, finally, PRAYER (more the spirit of prayer, and rarely with reference to liturgical prayer as understood nowadays).[33] The author next draws up an interminable series of texts and examples to flesh out the bare bones of his statistical analysis.[34] It would seem that the *Histoire de la Congrégation de Saint-Maur,* Dom Martène's *Vie des Justes,* and the *Relations de la Trappe* are all cut from one and the same fabric. Surely the Maurist Dom Jean Savoureau, slipping into the stables during the summer heat and baring his back to insect bites, belongs, not to the maurist but to the trappist tradition. And what about Dom Martin Le Poitevin, who used to rub his infected leg ulcers with salt and vinegar? Or the great Dom Marc Bastide, salting his food with generous doses of wormwood? In point of fact, a good deal of all this has little counterpart at la Trappe, where restrictive and self-afflictive practices had to be contained within the limits traced by monastic *simplicité* and *régularité.*

But surely Dom Hesbert must be wrong when he draws up a synthetic description of maurist spirituality in terms that would seem to fit the phenomenon of la Trappe equally as well. Where does Dom Hesbert place the famous *études* which are clearly the hall-mark of the maurist experience? Unfortunately, Dom Hesbert cannot find a place for *études,* since these have a coefficient of less than 25 in the author's tabulation! He notes, further, that even in texts alluding to studies, more than half of them refer to studies only in the context of the scholar's zeal for *régularité.*[35]

For myself, I feel a bit uncomfortable with Dom Hesbert's statistical methodology, but I also find it impossible to gainsay the general soundness of his conclusions about the 'monastic theology' of the Maurist Congregation. Clearly, the 'trappist spirit' was not a monopoly of la Trappe. It seems to have been an all-pervasive spirit wherever, in sixteenth- and seventeenth-century France, the traditional monastic Orders launched any kind of really serious program of renewal and reform. What is so striking about the la Trappe of that distant period belongs not only to la Trappe, but to the general spiritual climate of the century. Rancé and his community crystallized in a somewhat absolute form a spirit that was widely diffused, but generally in forms less concrete, less absolute. In no way do I mean to suggest, however, that la Trappe expressed the spirituality of the seventeenth century. The age was one of incredibly rich varieties of religious experience. There was more than enough room for not only a Francis de Sales, but also for a Bérulle, a Vincent de Paul, a Fénelon, a Mabillon, even an Abbé de Rancé.

In the preceding pages I have tried to suggest, then, that Armand-Jean de Rancé's ideas on monastic reform within the Cistercian Order were marked by:

> 1- a strong historical point of reference, such as provided an extremely concrete practical program based on the two-fold principle of integral observance of the Holy Rule as interpreted by the early Cistercians;
> 2- the strongest possible evangelical and ecclesial emphasis: evangelical, since monastic life is unconditional discipleship in a state of penitence that is essentially union with Christ under the sign of the Cross; ecclesial, since the community is the Early Church reactualized;
> 3- a passion for the absolute which corresponded to the aspirations of many in exuberant seventeenth-century France.

LES CLAIRETS: 1202–1687

The story of the royal abbey of les Clairets begins with the death of the Comte de Perche, Geoffroy II.[36] Having entrusted the affairs of state to his noble-born wife, Matilda of Brunswick, a sister of Emperor Otto IV, Geoffroy took up the Crusader's cross in 1202, struck out for the Holy Land, got as far as Soissons, and had to be carried back dying to his castle at Nogent-le-Rotrou. By way of redeeming Geoffroy's unfulfilled crusader's pledge, Matilda undertook the foundation of a religious house in the neighborhood. She found the ideal spot a few miles away in the wooded valley of les Clairets, barely within the north-western uttermost boundary of the diocese of Chartres.[37] Given the cistercian preference for valleys as foundation-sites,[38] it is not surprising that the place was offered to a group of women desirous of living the benedictine life according to the cistercian interpretation of the Rule. The historical problems connected with the beginning years need not concern us here. (The papal bull confirming the foundation dates from before the foundation-charter.)[39] Only in 1221 was the first Lady Abbess installed and blessed by Gautier, bishop of Chartres. Dame Agnes (1221–1232) was the first of a long series of abbesses whose history offers nothing of great interest to the scholar on the look out for *memorabilia*. Lands were acquired, abbess succeeded abbess, life flowed on peacefully, monotonously. Sometime at an early date, however, this abbey of cistercian nuns was placed under the general care of the abbot of la Trappe, in the neighboring diocese of Séez.

The situation changed radically in the time of Abbess Marguerite de Chemens (1442–1473), who had the misfortune to be at the helm of her community at the time of the english incursions in Normandy. The 'godams' were everywhere, pillaging, burning, raping, destroying. For the better part of a quarter-century, the region in which les Clairets was situated passed back and forth from French to English, from English to French. None of this did much to add tone to the monastic observance of les Clairets, which seems at this period to have plunged into a spiralling decline. Things reached such a pass that, when the king appointed Marie de la Croix as Lady Abbess of les Clairets in September 1557, the wilful nuns ignored the royal nomination and proceeded, in March 1558, to the election of Dame Petronille Barbe d'Or (1558–1567). The nuns were adamant. The abbot of la Trappe intervened, but the advice he offered and the threats he fulminated were to no avail.

Then came the Huguenots, and from 1562 onwards, round followed round of violence. The castles of Beaumont and Nogent were sacked; the church of St-Jean was burned; and the nuns of les Clairets had to choose between death or dispersion. They chose dispersion. The abbey church became a center of Huguenot worship, the woods were cut down, and virtually all the buildings of the monastic plant were demolished. In 1567 the Lady Abbess, Dame Petronille, had second thoughts about her election, and graciously abdicated in favor of the royal nominee of 1557. Abbess Marie de la Croix (1567–1576), however, was for almost a decade superior of a phantom community. Her successor, Madeleine des Fiefs (1576–1587), managed to return to the abbey, and set about recalling the scattered members of the community. She was able to get five to return. From all accounts, Lady Abbess Madeleine and her community formed a total of six worldly women living a pretty worldly life in the ruins of the demolished abbey.

The royal nomination of abbots and abbesses had been one of the chief causes of the downfall of monastic France, but in rare instances the choice made by the monarch proved providentially felicitous. This was the case with Madeleine's successor, Marie de Thou (1588–1611). That Marie had been a dominican nun of the convent of Prouilly mattered little. Most convents had reached such a dismal level of non-observance that religious could pass comfortably from house to house without there being all that much distinctive to mark off Dominican from Cistercian. Marie, however, became happily infected with the post-tridentine spirit of reform which at that time was sweeping over France with such splendid results. The abbey of la Trappe had long since fallen, yet another victim of the commendatory system, and so the immediate paternity of les Clairets reverted to the father immediate of la Trappe itself—the abbot of Clairvaux. This was, from 1596 until his death in 1624, the saintly Denis Largentier. Himself a prudent, cautious, but deeply committed reforming abbot, Dom Denis was in a position to second Abbess Marie de Thou in her energetic efforts to raise les Clairets quite literally from the ashes. Discipline returned, community life resumed, abbey buildings rose on a scale larger than before.

The achievement of Marie de Thou is impressive, and we have every reason to admire her sterling character and dedicated reforming activity. Even so, it was Abbess Marie who introduced at les Clairets an element of ambiguity *vis-à-vis* the traditional cistercian understanding of monastic life. Given the madness and the violence of the preceding decades, a break with tradition was virtually inevitable. In re-organizing life at les Clairets, Abbess Marie re-organized it along the lines followed elsewhere in convents where the spiritual life was taken seriously. She set up a boarding-school of the sort connected with most of the abbeys of women at this period, and she drew up plans for a large-scale orphanage—a plan to be realized only by her successor, who as Marie's *coadjutrix* from 1602 till 1611, remained faithful to Abbess Marie's concept of monastic life throughout her own twenty-nine years as abbess of les Clairets (1611–1640). In describing Lady Abbess Marie's activity, the historian of les Clairets, the Vicomte de Souancé, notes that 'Each time there was question of good to be done in the vicinity, this abbess never hesitated to be the first to set the example. Thus, when the Capuchin church at Nogent was dedicated on June 20th, 1601, the Abbess of les Clairets was there, and gave two paintings to the community'.[40] Given the historical context, it would be churlish indeed to fault our Abbess for this sort of extra-mural good-will excursion. Churlish, too, to object to the large-scale *pensionnat*, which provided a source of income and of postulants for most convents of the period. Even a strait-laced community like Port-Royal took it for granted that a boarding-school for girls was not only a necessary, but even a welcome, necessary, adjunct to any abbey of women.

Marie's successor, Cathérine-Charlotte du Prat (1611–1640) carried to completion the good work begun by Marie—but with the same inherent ambiguities. Abbess Marie had built a comfortable, large guesthouse near the enclosure—*l'Hospitalité*—to encourage visits (and benefactions) from relatives of the boarders and from other visitors. Abbess Cathérine-Charlotte carried out her predecessor's plans for an orphanage. It was built a bit more than a half-mile from the abbey. *La Babillerie*, as the orphanage was called, answered a chronic need in the area. Famine in the district of le Perche was a periodic recurrence, and desperate parents frequently left their abandoned infants at the gates of convents. So regular a feature was this in the much ravaged area that les Clairets had adopted a carefully thought-out program for taking care of the poor waifs. The children were boarded singly with nursing mothers of peasant families in the countryside; and at the age of two or three, they were brought back to les Clairets and adopted as abbey orphans. A lay-woman supervised their education at *la Babillerie*.[41] We shall return to this subject later.

Madame Cathérine-Charlotte had been preceded in her office as abbess by a member of the de Thou family, and upon her death in 1640, another member of the same family succeeded her.[42] Louise de Thou (1640–1671) left behind her a reputation for unaffected simplicity: she never let her nuns kneel before her, but she was aggressive enough to battle her way through a lawsuit with the comte d'Orval, Lord of Nogent-le-Rotrou, and come out the winner. She was blessed as abbess by the Archbishop of Tours, Victor le Bouthillier. Archbishop Victor was uncle to Armand-Jean de Rancé, the future abbot of la Trappe, and to Armand-Jean's sister, Thérèse, who entered les Clairets as a young woman sometime before 1647.[43]

Of the many letters Rancé wrote his sister at les Clairets until her death early in 1684,[44] a number have survived. In none of these letters is there any evidence of a critical attitude on Rancé's part as regards the monastic observance in his sister's abbey. On the contrary. In an undated letter written in answer to Thérèse's complaint that she was afraid of death, Rancé replied in lines filled with affection, understanding, and sound advice.[45] He begins by expressing his surprise that Thérèse should be afraid, since God has called her to a life which, by its very nature, should free one from the fear of dying—a life lived 'under a most holy Rule, and in a monastery in which it [the Rule] is observed with every sort of exactness, good example, and edification'.[46] Only twice does he elsewhere have a critical word with respect to monastic observance at les Clairets. In the first incident, Rancé had been consulted by a third party about the advisability of Thérèse, whose health had been giving cause for concern, going to Vichy to take the waters.[47] Rancé, predictably, opposed the idea; besides, he was certain that Thérèse herself has no desire for a jaunt to Vichy.[48] In another incident, Rancé wrote to an unidentified friend about the time that the abbess of les Clairets and Thérèse, her traveling companion, passed within a few miles of la Trappe. 'But I didn't want to see them,' says the intransigent brother: 'there's never any occasion that permits one to authorize something that isn't right'.[49]

Even here, Rancé's critical attitude towards taking the waters and unauthorized visits by cloistered nuns was a criticism of observance at les Clairets only by implication. It is not from Rancé that we learn that not all was well at the royal abbey.

Early in the General Chapter deliberations of May 1686, the Promoter of the Chapter laid before the Definitors an appeal against unspecified prohibitions and *ordinationes* of the abbot of Clairvaux.[50] The appellants were the abbess of les Clairets and a certain number of her nuns (*aliquot monialibus*), whose griefs against their Father Immediate were based on certain unwarranted impositions (*de quibusdam gravaminibus*) forced on the community by Monsieur de Clairvaux, Pierre IV Bouchu.[51] Whatever the nature of the difficulty, it is clear that the appeal failed to rally the suffrages of all the nuns of les Clairets, since it was presented only in the name of Madame de Fiennes and a certain number of her nuns. No immediate settlement of the dispute was attempted. The General Chapter, with the consent of the abbot of Clairvaux, took the unexpected initiative of recognizing the absent abbot of la Trappe as the proper Father Immediate of the ancient abbey of les Clairets. This decision was based, of course, on the historical fact that les Clairets had been under the government of the abbot of la Trappe until la Trappe had lost its regular abbots under the commendatory system. Since Rancé's health was chronically bad and ever worsening, it was only reasonable that the General Chapter should state that the dispute was to be settled by the abbot of la Trappe in person, or else through his own officially appointed delegate.[52] It is also a tribute to the realism of the capitular fathers that they provided further for the possibility that the stay-at-home abbot of la Trappe might resist even so formal a mandate as this one emanating from the General Chapter; for, in the event of Rancé's non-compliance, the difficult situation at les Clairets was to be committed to the Father Visitor of the Province.[53]

The Visitor of the Province of Normandy appointed by the General Chapter of 1686[54] was an old comrade-at-arms of the abbot of la Trappe. He was the same saintly Dom Dominique Georges, abbot of Val-Richer, with whom Rancé had been in close contact ever since 1664–1665, when they had been sent to Rome as official delegates of the Strict Observance. Monsieur de Val-Richer was the right man in the right place at the right time. Soon after his first visit to the divided community, Rancé was writing to his old friend:

> It would have been a real consolation to have you stop by here on your return from les Clairets. I've heard word that you left the community very much united and with everything taken care of. I look on this as a real wonder. It can't be other than God's work.[55]

Perhaps the solution to the difficulties at les Clairets was facilitated by the fact that, at this juncture, Madame l'Abbesse died, on 31 March 1687. The arrival of her successor opened not only a new page, but a new major section of the book in the history of les Clairets.

FRANÇOISE-ANGÉLIQUE D'ÉTAMPES DE VALENÇAY AND HER FIRST YEARS AT LES CLAIRETS

What were the credentials of this new abbess, who received her royal appointment to les Clairets on 15 August 1687?[56] The earliest references to this remarkable woman are to be found in letters by that incomparable correspondent, Madame de Sévigné. In a letter to her daughter, dated from Paris, 18 February 1671, Madame de Sévigné writes: 'You've told me wonderful things about the tomb of

Monsieur de Montmorency and about the beauty of the Valençay girls.'[57] We begin, then, with a tomb and two pretty *demoiselles*.

The two girls were Angélique and Henriettè d'Étampes de Valençay; and the splendid tomb was that of the universally beloved marshal of France, Henri II, duc de Montmorency. In 1632 he had led a revolt against the all-powerful Cardinal Richelieu, and, in spite of the fact that for many years he had stood second in line of succession as heir presumptive of Louis XIII, considerations of royal birth could not save him. His head fell on the scaffold at Toulouse, 30 October 1632. The Duc's widow raised a perpetual memorial to him in the form of an impressive mausoleum in the huge church of the Visitation Convent at Moulins. The convent became the permanent residence of several members of the Montmorency family, and Françoise-Angélique (whose mother was niece to the unfortunate Duc) was raised in the shadow of the noble tomb. A number of Madame Sévigné's letters mention her presence at the Moulins Visitation, where Madame herself—the grand-daughter of Jeanne de Chantal, the great religious foundress and reformer whose heart was enshrined in the convent church at Moulins—was a frequent visitor. Thus, on 17 May 1676, Madame is again writing her daughter from Moulins. It is after Sunday Vespers, and she is in the very room where Grand-mére Chantal died. The Valençay girls are with her. 'The little girls are here, pretty and lovable as always.'[58] A month later Madame is back again, dining at the convent in the company of *les pétites de Valençay:*[59] and the following year she remarks how alert and bright the girls are—*fort éveillées*.[60] Years pass. It is now late November 1692, and Madame is writing from Paris to her friend, the Comtesse de Guitaut. There is quite a stir going on about the recently widowed Madame de Mornay. She had gone to la Trappe in the train of Her Royal Highness, Madame de Guise, Élisabeth d'Orléans. From la Trappe, the young woman had run off to les Clairets, insisting on immediate admission as a postulant. Les Clairets, Madame de Sévigné writes,

> has become a holy place since the reform there under Madame de Valençay. She left the Visitation at Moulins and wandered about from abbey to abbey for three years, until, with the reform of les Clairets, she herself became a holy woman.[61]

Just how much wandering about Françoise-Angélique actually did between the Visitation at Moulins and the cistercian abbey of les Clairets cannot be determined on the strength of the meager documentation at my disposal, apart from the fact that, before coming to les Clairets, she had been a nun at the cistercian convent of Parc-aux-Dames (diocese of Senlis in the seventeenth century, of Beauvais at the present time).[62] Whatever the trajectory of Madame de Valençay's *vie mouvementée* may theretofore have been, it is clear that from her earliest days at les Clairets she was now steering a course towards reform. It is also clear that Françoise-Angélique had every intention of playing Paula to Rancé's Jerome.

Madame l'Abbesse made the first overtures. Rancé was not interested. Not the least bit interested. The General Chapter mandate of 1686 had not succeeded in getting him to reassume responsibility for les Clairets; nor had subsequent letters from his higher superior, Dom Bouchu of Clairvaux, or from the highest superior of all, the Abbot General of Cîteaux.[63] His own position was clear. Besides, Dom Dominque Georges was handling matters at les Clairets, and doing well at it.

It is unfortunate that Rancé's biographers brush so lightly over this important period at les Clairets. In their concern to get the abbot of la Trappe on the scene as soon as possible, they virtually ignore the importance of the ground-work laid by the gentle, self-effacing abbot of Val-Richer. There was at least one, perhaps two, visitations by Dom Dominque.[64] (Rancé was to re-confirm, at a later date, the visitation card drawn up by Dom Dominique.) And, on the basis of the documents to be examined in just a moment, it would seem that by the time Rancé himself became directly involved with the reform of les Clairets, there simply was not much left that needed reforming. But more of this.

On 21 June 1688, three letters were dispatched from les Clairets to la Trappe: one from Madame l'Abbesse; another from the prioress, Madame d'Auvergne; and a third collective letter signed by the members of the community.[65] This epistolary bombardment failed to shake the unshakable abbot of la Trappe. On 13 August, less than two months later, Reverend Mother Françoise-Angélique was giving Monsieur de la Trappe a piece of her mind: 'I just don't see how in God's sight you can find any excuse for yourself,' she writes. ' . . . Everywhere I'm looked on as your daughter.'[66]

Rancé managed to hold out for yet another month. Clearly, he was not one to be pushed into things. In September of 1688 he capitulated.

The nuns of Les Clairets waxed ecstatic. 'Even the sick left the infirmary,' Reverend Mother writes him, 'to take part in the *Te Deum* we sang after reading your letters. Everyone wants copies; and I've been asked to read them from time to time in chapter. Reverend

Father, at long last! Your name is all it takes for a wonderful renewal of fervor.'[67]

The enthusiastic nuns went to ingenious lengths to consolidate their victory. By way of an *ex voto* offering for the health and preservation of the reluctant Father Immediate, the nuns kept a vigil light burning day and night before a picture of Our Lady; and individual nuns went to communion each Saturday (this was in the days of relatively infrequent communion) on Rancé's behalf. These practices were kept up until Rancé's death in 1700.[68]

THE VISITATION OF 1690

Preparations and Arrival

The immediate objective of the nuns' efforts was now to get Rancé to put in a personal appearance as Father Visitor. Prayers rose heavenwards; additional days of General Communion were introduced for this most special intention. Rancé agreed to come. Then, in mid-November, the weather turned unexpectedly bad; the ailing Abbot's rheumatic pains grew worse, and soon deep winter had set in with a vengeance. The visitation would have to be postponed. There is something almost pathological about Dom le Nain's description of the crying, moaning, and groaning that began at les Clairets, but we have to remember that this is the *Grand Siècle*.

Rancé kept his word. In early February a temporary amelioration of his health coincided with a momentary lull in the bitter winter weather. On Tuesday, 14 February Rancé mounted his horse, and, in the company of Father Zozime, who was to be Secretary of the Visitation, headed for les Clairets. It was the first time he had left la Trappe in fifteen years.

The two travellers arrived at their destination late the same day. The abbot had been fearful of the grandiose reception that would surely await him had the nuns been given half a chance to prepare in advance. So he saw to it that news of his coming preceded his actual arrival by only an hour. Reverend Mother had barely time to place a carpet, arm-chair and prie-dieu in the sanctuary of the church, and to post a look-out in the outer court of the monastery enclosure. The party of two was sighted; the tower bells began pealing. The nuns rushed to church, and as Rancé entered the sanctuary and knelt on the cold stone pavement (quite predictably, he ignored the prie-dieu), Mother Françoise-Angélique intoned the *Te Deum*.

It was too late to open the visitation that night, so Rancé withdrew to the guest-quarters for the first encounter between the abbot of la Trappe and the abbess of les Clairets.

The Opening Exhortation

February 15th fell, in 1690, on Ember Wednesday of Lent. The mass readings provided a splendid context for the opening of the visitation—Moses ascending higher and higher on Sinai, and finally entering into the heart of the cloud for forty days and forty nights (Ex 24:12–18); Elijah on his journey to God's own mountain, Horeb (1Kgs 19:3–8); and the sign of Jonas, with the men of Nineveh doing penance, and rising up in judgment of the present deaf generation (Mt 12:38–50). The Father Visitor read his low mass at five in the morning in the abbey church. This was not the conventual mass, which would be celebrated later in the day by Father Jacques de Lanchal, the first of the several confessors sent by Rancé from la Trappe to les Clairets.[69]

The visitation began at the end of Rancé's Mass with the prescribed inspection of the Eucharist in the tabernacle. Meanwhile, the nuns in choir took the initiative of doing something not provided for by the rubrics: they began chanting the First Responsory of the Cistercian Night Office of Saint John the Baptist (June 24):

R. There was a man, one sent from God,
whose name was John [= Armand-JEAN de Rancé].
* This man came as a witness,
to bear witness concerning the light,
to prepare for the Lord a perfect people.
V. There came John in the desert,
preaching a baptism of repentance.   * This man.

A bit overdone, perhaps, but the nuns certainly were sincere enough. The Visitor chanted the prescribed collects—*de Sanctissimo Sacramento, pro Rege,* and *pro Monachis*—and the scene shifted to the chapter room.

At the door to the chapter room, Reverend Mother knelt and handed the keys of the monastery to Father Immediate. Her message was clear: Rancé was in total command. Father Immediate handed the keys right back—but with *beaucoup de douceur et d'honnêteté,* writes le Nain.[70] His message was no less clear. *Qui legit intelligat.*

The chantress asked for the usual blessing, and proceeded to read the prescribed *Forma visitationis*—a lengthy text dating from the twelfth century, giving the norms for carrying out a visitation in a spirit of charity and concord.[71] Then Monsieur de la Trappe began his opening discourse.

For the text of Rancé's two exhortations and visitation card, we have to thank the initiative of the nuns of les Clairets. They were chiefly instrumental in getting the text printed by François Muguet, at Paris, in September 1690.[72] The publication and wide circulation of the visitation card was to be a source of considerable unpleasantness, as we shall see. Writing to M. l'abbé Tétu on 26 October 1690, Rancé assures him that he had nothing to do with the publication of the controversial visitation card. 'I refused those who asked for copies of the visitation card; the nuns were the ones who made it public.'[73]

What, then, was the message of our intransigent, ultra-penitential, reforming abbot, as he began his historic visitation? Rancé begins by remarking how evident it is that the finger of God is very much at work in les Clairets: you have only to look at Mother Abbess and at the nuns of her community. In Madame de Valençay, Rancé sees

> lively sentiments, an energetic will, light, zeal, and good example; and when I consider those destined to live under her in dependence and submission, I perceive pure intentions, ardent desires, and dispositions such as persuade me that they come from God.[74]

First the superior, then the community. The order is intentional. For Rancé, the superior is not someone outside or over and above the community, but rather someone so totally identified with the community that he or she encapsulates or recapitulates in himself or herself the experience and vocation of the community, while at the same time truly acting as the representative of Christ in the monastery. Writing on the charity and duties of superiors, Rancé says, in Chapter Nine of his *Devoirs*:

> It is not sufficient, my brethren, that [the superior] hold the place of Jesus Christ, that he govern in his name, nor that he be invested with his power and authority for that purpose. It is, moreover, necessary that he do everything in the monastery as our Lord would do, if he were there in person; that he should exert himself for the salvation of his brethren, as Jesus Christ did for the sanctification of his disciples; that he ought to evince the purity of his faith and charity in all his works; and that he should, if I may be allowed the expression, so fulfill the duties of his ministry, with such piety and exactitude, that the invisible pastor may in him become visible. And as Jesus Christ, to the end that he should omit nothing that might render his disciples more pleasing to his

heavenly Father, and worthy of the distinction and choice he had
made of them, was pleased to form them not only by his word,
but also by his example; as he watched over their conduct with
unwearied application, and never ceased to sustain their weakness
by the strength of his prayers; so should a true superior labor,
without intermission, to form his brethren; so should he instruct
them in their duties, both by word and work: thus he should apply
himself to regulate the order and state of their lives, with constant
vigilance, and so should he, above all, join fervent prayer to his
labor and solicitude.[75]

And in the preceding chapter of the same work, where he discourses on the need for entire confidence in one's superiors, Rancé
writes:

[The superior] is the head of a body of which all his brethren
are the members and parts; and as the proper function of the
head, in the human body, is to govern and direct, to form all the
motions and actions, and everything that relates to it, all things
must proceed from it as from a source and principle. In like manner, everything should be performed, in a religious community,
according to the order, and in the spirit of an entire submission
to the will of the superior. Let him regulate all things for the
common good, and for the benefit of each individual.[76]

There can be no doubt but that this concept of the community
as dependent in so absolute a sense on a single superior can be
easily challenged in the climate of contemporary theologizing about
the nature of community and obedience and related matters. The
point here, however, is not that Rancé's concept of superior and
community was right or wrong, but simply that this is what it
was. There can be no possibility of community reform without a
community united heart and soul with a superior who sums up, in
his or her own person, the ideals on which the reform in question
is to be structured.

Proof of the God-inspired nature of what was happening at les
Clairets was to be found not only in Mother Abbess and in her
community, but in the very fact, Rancé says, that he is now at les
Clairets, in spite of his sincere intention

never to be responsible for the conduct of outsiders, and to limit
myself solely to the responsibility I have for my brethren . . .[77]

This rings true. Rancé was lavish with his spiritual counsels, but
from 1675 onwards, he steadfastly refused involvement in any official capacity with the internal affairs of other communities. He

would go so far as to lend personnel to other reform-minded communities, or even to train an occasional novice destined for another community.[78] But never did he agree to accept an administrative or juridical responsibility outside the immediate purvue of la Trappe—not until les Clairets. God alone could overcome his repugnances, Rancé bluntly tells the nuns; but it was their unanimity that made him realize that God was speaking to him through them.[79]

As things now stand at les Clairets, then, splendid! But the community cannot remain static. Further fruits of piety must be brought forth, both for the sanctification of the individual nuns, and for the edification (edification in the pauline sense of the term) of the church at large.

An entire page is devoted to the stance of the nun *vis-à-vis* the world. No one looking for a rancéan *contemptus mundi* text will find it here. The cloistered nun owes the world her prayers, but also the example of a christian life of holiness. 'Don't say, "But I'm not responsible for my brothers' salvation". You are!' Rancé insists; and goes on to apply to the religious insensitive to the needs of others Saint Gregory the Great's sobering words: *Non pavisti, occidisti*, Which Rancé renders as: 'You refused your neighbor the spiritual nourishment he needed, and with that you dealt him his death blow.'[80]

As for the sanctification of the individual nun, the religious life is

> a steady progress, a continual going forward. Persons consecrated to Jesus Christ have got to keep on the constant move by their works and actions, uninterruptedly. The saints have it that to call a halt and settle down means to look backwards—and according to the word of Jesus Christ, such a person is unfit for the Kingdom, and not destined for it.[81]

But how does one go about fulfilling the obligation always to go forward, doing God's will with the unremitting generosity this demands? Saint Paul has the answer. *Sectamini pacem et sanctimoniam, sine qua nemo videbit Deum.* (cf. Heb 12:14). 'Follow peace and holiness, without which no one can see God.' But Rancé has slightly distorted the text to bend it to his pastoral purpose. Where the author of the *Letter to the Hebrews* had written, 'Follow peace with all men,' Rancé eliminates 'with all men', and thus gives 'peace' a more general point of reference: peace of every sort, at every level of life and experience, peace within and peace without. With the same disconcerting casualness, Rancé translates *sanctimoniam* by the French term *chasteté*. 'Seek with care, with eagerness, with solicitude, that peace and chastity (*chasteté*), without which no man can see God.'[82] Peace, then, and chastity.

Peace. Rancé's reflections fill five entire pages. Peace, he says, is essential to the religious; for God's Spirit is not to be found in souls filled with disorder and confusion. *Non in commotione Dominus* (1 Kgs 19:11). How are we to obtain this peace of God? Rancé quotes the Psalmist: 'Much peace have they that love thy law' (Ps 118: 165 Vulg.). We come now to a typically Rancéan passage:

> [The Psalmist] did not say simply, 'they that OBEY God's law,' but rather, 'they that LOVE it'. For you cannot carry out the precept unless you *love* it.[83]

Peace—God's will—love. The *nexus* is of essential importance. All christian spiritual writers stress the interior dispositions from which thought and action ought to spring, but with Rancé, this constant preoccupation with interiority becomes, at times, a veritable obsession.

> Whoever carries out the precept without loving it, that is to say, without his love, will carry it out in a dry, sterile manner; and it will bring forth for him anything but the advantages, and blessings for which he had hoped. The religious, for example, who fasts, keeps vigil, chants, and takes part in choir, yet who does all this without the principal disposition of dilection, charity, and love, does no more than satisfy the letter of the precept. His *regularity*, which is not the principle of merit, will be without fruit for him; because God, who looks into the heart of the one giving, does not see in the heart of that religious what ought to be there: I mean love and charity.[84]

The question of observance as necessarily rooted in love is then approached from a somewhat different angle. Building up a sustained crescendo of the *dura et aspera* essentially bound up with the monastic life as codified by Saint Benedict, Rancé suggests that the *Rule* presents an absolutely impossible challenge—impossible, that is, unless one loves. And he quotes the latin psalm-text, *Volui legem tuam in medio cordis mei* (Ps 39:9 Vulg)—though only after first paraphrasing it in an untranslatable french phrase of incomparable beauty: 'Ah, Lord, how I have longed to fulfill your law, with all the feeling and all the tenderness of my heart.'[85] Heart-tenderness. This is the true source of Rancé's fierce asceticism.

Having discoursed at length on that peace to be had only by carrying out God's will through love, Rancé returns to his original text: 'Follow peace and *chastity*'. Is 'chastity' really convertible with the latin term *sanctimonia*? Yes, if we understand the term within the space of a few lines *chasteté, pureté,* and *sainteté*. His reflections on this 'chastity' make clear, however, what a rich, all-embracing term it is. For chastity is two-fold: *Ut sit sancta corpore et spiritu* (1 Cor 7:34)—'That [the bride of Christ] may be chaste in body and in spirit', writes Rancé, once again substituting chastity for holiness. For chastity of body Rancé barely mentions. As usual, his attention is focussed on integrity of heart and spirit. He goes so far as to say that, for souls consecrated to Jesus Christ,

> exterior integrity [of body] will only serve to render them all the more culpable, unless physical integrity is accompanied by integrity of heart and spirit.[86]

The religious, then, cannot be content with an ordinary sort of piety (*pieté ordinaire*), for God wills nothing less for her than absolute perfection. And now our Man of the Absolute touches on a point essential for a proper understanding of his ascetical program. 'I don't say that you have to be perfect in order to be saved,' he says; 'but I do say that you can't be saved unless you work at becoming perfect. This obligation is bound up with your state of life, and is essential to it.'[87] Please note. Rancé is not here referring implicitly to the monastic vow of conversion of manners, traditionally understood in terms of an uninterrupted, on-going *metanoia*. Rather, he is envisaging the life of perfection essential to every institutional form of religious life in the Church. Rancé is persuaded that, radical though his stance is, it reflects the common teaching of the Church. Without giving explicit references, he invokes the authority of theologians of distant times (Saints Basil and John Chrysostom, Cassian) and of times less distant (Saints Bernard, Thomas Aquinas, Francis de Sales, as well as the Jesuit masters of the spiritual life, Fathers Rodriguez and Saint-Jure).[88]

Then comes a reflection, surprising, some might think, in the most notorious of the protagonists of Strict Observance rigorism. Yet what Monsieur de la Trappe here says is to be found frequently in his letters and other writings touching on monastic observance:

> Austerity can be lessened; penitence toned down; exterior practices changed. This the Church has done, and she can still do it. But as for piety and the obligation [of tending towards perfection], this the Church has never touched and never will.[89]

We should take care to read these lines in the concrete situation which obtained at les Clairets. This abbey did not belong to the Strict Observance—neither in the form already adopted in a good number of cistercian houses nor in the form proper to la Trappe. But for Rancé, it made little difference that, with the blessing of the Holy See, the nuns had daily recreation and ate meat a few times weekly—so long as the life of the spirit was thriving, so long as the nuns were tending toward perfection. Because, insists Rancé in the final pages of his first exhortation, the bride of Christ can never be beautiful enough for her Bridegroom. Hers must be a beauty proportioned to the beauty of Jesus Christ himself.[90]

Rancé rose, bowed to the crucifix, and turned to leave the chapter room. But Mother Françoise-Angélique's propensity to fling herself in Father Visitor's path was once again exercised. She knelt, and pronounced the formula: 'Reverend Father, I promise you and your successors obedience unto death.'[91] All were suitably impressed.

The Second Exhortation

After the official opening of the visitation on 15 February, Rancé began the official inspection of the monastery buildings and accounts. Members of the community were seen individually, and there were no doubt long private conversations with Mother Abbess. But the Visitor was anxious to be off on his return journey. It is a tribute to the good order he found at les Clairets that he was able to bring the whirlwind visitation to an end as early as the next day, Thursday, 16 February.

Once again the community gathered in chapter, and Rancé began the second and last of his *ferverinos*.[92] After a brief expression of regret over his early departure—an apology not wholly sincere, one suspects—the Visitor expressed his deep happiness. The last two days had served to confirm him in his first highly positive impressions. What then is to be the proper response to what God has wrought in this community? Praise. And here Rancé renders his latin quotation of Tobit 12:6 with a felicitous french paraphrase: 'Praise the God of heaven before the face of the whole universe, and confess his holy Name; for he has looked upon you in his mercy'.[93] This praise is to be more than the mere mouthing of words, for it has got to rise and well up from the very depths of the sisters' hearts, and from there, as from its source, break forth into actions and deeds. In brief, the life of the nun at les Clairets must be a life of continual gratitude expressing itself in an ever deepening fidelity to the carrying out of God's holy will.[94] But this is merely a preamble to the heart of Rancé's message:

> The most important advice I have to give you, my sisters . . . is that you preserve among you an inviolable charity, and that you live lives of such modesty and circumspection towards one another that charity suffers not even the least attenuation or slight. *Ambulate in dilectione sicut Christus dilexit nos* [Eph 5:2]. This is what the Apostle tells us. Let charity guide your every step; let charity be the norm for your every action. For it is through charity that you imitate Jesus Christ, who in every circumstance gave us, and still gives us, so many marks of his love. Keep watch, I tell you, sisters, keep watch over this charity with such care of devotion that you protect it from the slightest thing capable of impairing it. For charity it is that forms and preserves holy communities. Charity is their foundation, charity their bond of union; charity the source of all their strength, beauty and permanence. Communities subsist and grow only so long as charity abides in them and reigns supreme. Let charity cease, and souls that had once been at one in this holy bond become straightway divided, disunited. Then God, who is the principle of charity—no, say rather, God, who is very charity—God, I say, leaves those souls and abandons them to the passions and cravings that cause division. So preserve this charity, my Sisters, I repeat: preserve this charity! And always be mindful of whatever can keep this treasure of inestimable price and value from being snatched away from you.[95]

But this long citation is merely the beginning of Rancé's long hymn to charity as the essence of community life. He turns first to Mother Abbess as to the head of this 'holy flock of Jesus Christ'. Her sole function is to lead Christ's flock, and her whole concern is for its welfare. Her charity must extend to each and every need of her sisters, needs material and spiritual. Jesus Christ has placed them in her hands, and she must place them back in his. On their sanctification depends her own salvation.[96]

Rancé next turns to the sisters. If the abbess is as instrumental in their salvation as he has just suggested she is, then their attitude towards her should be one of total docility.[97] But love for the Abbess is not enough. The sisters have got to love each other—not with a studied affectation, but with a love that springs from their deepest selves and brings about a communion so close and so chaste that each nun regards the good or bad experienced by the least of her sisters as good or bad happening to herself. Rancé devotes a long paragraph to spinning out the implications of this communion of love, and concludes with the exhortation:

> All of you should have but one soul, one heart, one will, one sentiment, even as you have, all of you, but one and the same faith, one and the same hope. For only thus can you obtain from God those blessings that he never refuses to those who come together in his Name, and who serve him in community.[98]

As though he still had not discoursed at sufficient length on love, our rigorist now tells the nuns that they must love not only the abbess and each other, but themselves as well—and this love for self, he says, is the most important love of all! He raises the objection: Jesus says that we should hate ourselves (an implicit reference to John 12:25: He that loves his life shall lose it; and he that hates his life in this world, keeps it unto life eternal). This love for self, Rancé explains, is perfectly compatible with the self-hatred that our Lord commands, and is, indeed, a necessary part of it. 'Have pity on your own soul, by pleasing God,' (Sir 30:24), he quotes, and then exegetes this sapiential text in a long passage about mortification and abnegation as the means essential for removing the obstacles to our perfect following of Christ. Quoting Saint Bernard, he asserts that this 'cruelty to self' is full of charity and mercy towards oneself:

> Thus it is that you will satisfy this two-fold precept both to love yourself and hate yourself: a precept two-fold in appearance only, but really one in truth. For the hatred we have for ourselves is no more than the effect of our love, since its only purpose is to remove from our path all that could possibly be a cause or occasion of fall or of stumbling: and [the unobstructed following of Christ] is what makes us perfect disciples of Jesus Christ.[99]

There is yet another long paragraph on love as the essence of the religious life. What makes the true religious? Charity. Rancé goes so far as to state that all the exterior practices of the monastic life, unless they are rooted and grounded in love, can do no more than offend God.[100]

In the final pages of this second exhortation, we return to the opening theme: gratitude. 'The hope of the unthankful shall melt away as the winter's ice,' (Wis 16:29) Rancé quotes. An ungrateful religious, he says, is like water frozen solid and hard by the winter cold. It looks solid enough, and has a certain hardness and transparency, and even a certain beauty and bright quality. But let the rays of the sun strike the ice: it melts, turns back to water, and loses whatever it had of beauty, solidity, brightness. Without gratitude, the religious is pure sham. She might look good, as others see her. But as soon as the Sun of Justice, Jesus Christ, rises and sheds his rays upon her, that will be the end of her! Devoid of charity, she has no real substance; she is without foundations, without solidity. This is the moment of truth. The mask will be snatched away, and there she will be: exposed in all her error, illusion, deceit.[101] Rancé's final words are a prayer that

> Jesus Christ, and he alone, may possess the hearts of every one of you, and that, as chaste, faithful brides, you may have no glory, no pleasure, no happiness other than the glory, pleasure and happiness of belonging wholly to Jesus Christ, and of serving him and pleasing him.[102]

The Visitation Card

'Frére Armand-Jean, Abbot of la Maison-Dieu Notre-Dame de la Trappe, of the Strict Observance of the Cistercian Order, in the diocese of Séez, superior and Father Immediate of the Abbey of Notre-Dame des Clairets of the same Order, in the diocese of Chartres', begins his remarks with high praise for the tenor of observance and regularity he has found at les Clairets. This happy state of affairs is due mostly, he says, to the efforts, zeal, and example of Mother Angélique-Françoise, as well as to the fidelity and devotion (*réligion*) with which the community, composed of twenty-nine choir-nuns, four novices, and ten lay-sisters, has responded to her efforts, and has entered into her *sentiments*.[103]

Human nature being what it is, however, we need rules in order to protect ourselves against our weakness, and to ensure the permanency of our enterprise. Saint Bernard had the right attitude: he would have liked to have had a hundred superiors watching over him, and not just one. The humble, obedient religious, then, is only too happy to submit to authority in a spirit of total openness.

The purpose of the following regulations, then, is either to preserve the good already wrought by God, or to foster its growth, because

> the life of persons consecrated to Jesus Christ has got to be one of continual progress. They must keep rising incessantly to higher and higher degrees of piety; and those who are charged with their direction should omit nothing that can assist them in fulfilling so essential and obligation.[104]

Communication with Persons From Outside

> One of the first and most important points is that the sisters shall
> have no communication with people from outside, no matter what
> their rank or profession, unless they are obliged to do so by real
> necessity.[105]

Visits to the parlor featured large in every relaxed convent in seventeenth-century France, and were a problem even in more observant
houses. In many of the nobler but less affluent families, providing
the elder daughter with a suitably large dowry often meant that
the younger sisters had to be packed off to a convent. Angélique
Arnauld's account of her own entry into religious life is well known:

> I was only seven years old when my grandfather, observing that
> my father had five daughters . . . resolved to make some of them
> nuns, and chose me . . . to be first . . .[106]

Angélique's experience was by no means unique. Most convents
had their share of spinsters and unwanted daughters—not all of
whom were remarkable for their dedication to the nicer points of
traditional monastic observance. Little wonder, then, that it was the
parlor rather than church or cell that often became the focal point
of convent life. At les Clairets, there was the added problem of the
girl's *pensionnat*, with the large adjacent *Hospitalité*, built precisely in
order to attract families and other visitors. Then, too, not far away
was Bellême, a much frequented spa to which many went to take
the waters—often with a side trip to near-by les Clairets.[107]
Rancé is careful to spell out the reasons for his jaundiced attitude towards the parlor, with all the proper nuances. Such contacts
can become 'occasions of danger, capable of drying up the heart
and leaving the religious dissipated, thereby distracting them from
God'. When, however, it is God's *ordre* (one of Rancé's favorite
words) that takes them to the parlor, no need to worry; if it is
restlessness and curiosity, look out! Following the strict conventions
of convent etiquette—a convention still followed in some cloistered communities—the nun is always to have another nun with
her during parlor visits, Mother Abbess and Mother Prior alone
excepted. On an almost apologetic note, the Visitor says that no
one will find this prescription really burdensome or painful, if one
but realizes that some of the worst conventual disorders began in
the best of houses with seemingly the most innocent conversations.
The intimacy with Jesus Christ enjoyed by brides of Christ means
that they cannot be too careful about all that touches on purity
of senses and purity of heart. The reader will be minded, perhaps,

of that abbess who found her *gallant* nephew, a member of the Guards, whispering sweet nothings to a nun at the parlor grille. *Je t'apprendrai de faire cocu le bon Seigneur*, she shrieked as she chased him out.[108] But Rancés focus of concern is directed less to anything so gross and extreme than to the ideal of uninterrupted attention to God at the deepest possible level.

Silence and Proper Speaking

At la Trappe, the practice of silence was virtually absolute. At les Clairets, Monsieur de la Trappe is a bit less demanding. 'As much as possible, the Sisters will try to preserve the silence so strictly prescribed by the Rule.' Characteristically, however, Rancé harps on the need of proper motivation. The nuns are to think often of the reasons which led Saint Benedict to prescribe silence in so exact a manner. Community discipline and piety require a spirit of silence, but silence is, above all else, for the sake of that charity which makes the community one. This charity can be compromised by the sort of talking that leads to murmuring, divisions, and particular friendships.

Places and times for a more absolute practice of silence are specified. Then the subject changes to a community exercise in which talking was central: the daily recreation, when the nuns gathered (often with their sewing or with vegetables that need preparing) and the ban on speaking was lifted. Certain topics of conversation obviously have to be avoided—news of the world, and anything that might start a quarrel or disagreement, or anything that could impair or wound charity. The talking has to be done, however, *sans gesne et sans contrainte, mais avec une sainte liberté*, without embarrassment, without constraint, but with a holy liberty. Mother Abbess may be excused from recreation only if impeded for a serious reason. Our great Rigorist concludes his remarks about recreation with the observation that such conversations can be of real profit (*ces sortes de conversations peuvent avoir de l'utilité*) provided one observes the rules and exercises the requisite discretion.[109]

Poverty

On the point of poverty, Rancé is brief and uncompromising. Any and every practice incompatible with an integral observance of poverty must be banished. Two specific points are mentioned. The nuns are to have in their cells nothing contrary to the 'simplicity' of the monastic state. (One catches a glimpse of a cell cluttered with knickknacks and pious objects.) Gifts of any kind are to be regarded as the common property of the entire monastery, and in the case of money, this is to pass into the community chest, and the nun through whom it was received is to have nothing to say directly or indirectly about how it is to be spent.[110]

We might do well to remember that the problem of private ownership was especially acute in those tumultuous times, when religious were often left to fend for themselves in matters of food and clothing, and the desperate poverty of many houses forced individual members to depend on friends or relatives for the bare essentials of physical subsistence. Reform programs often began with a return to the practice of religious poverty—as happened at Port-Royal on the feast of Saint Benedict, 21 March 1609, when the nuns carted their private linens, flower vases, and souvenirs to the chapter room, and laid them before their very determined young Lady Abbess, Mère Angélique Arnauld.[111] But even in the more affluent houses, and in periods of relative calm, religious frequently had their own spending money, as well as private hoards of food and clothing.

Calefactories

The calefactory in the traditional cistercian monastery was the room with the fireplace to which freezing monks repaired in wintertime to get thawed out. Conditioned as most of us are nowadays to central-heating and climate-control systems, few of us could have survived even a mild winter at early Clairvaux. Later on, the introduction of heat in private rooms was generally regarded as a symptom of decay and of the ascendancy of an effete generation of monks. (Wood stoves found their way into carthusian cells only in the nineteenth century.) One would expect our ascetic-minded Visitor to approach the question of winter-heating at les Clairets from this angle. He does not. The problem with calefactories, he notes, is that they too easily become the places for small gatherings and private chats—*réduita tout propres pour s'assembler*. Accordingly, there should be only two calefactories for the community at large, one in the dormitory and another outside; a third calefactory, in the infirmary, is to be reserved for the sick. Private rooms are not to be heated for the same reason.[112]

Contact with Novices and Junior Professed

In the seventeenth century, final vows were pronounced at the end of a year-long novitiate. The general practice was to leave the newly professed in the novitiate for a longer period. Rancé reminds the nuns that there should be no talking with the novices or with the young professed still in the novitiate. He fails to spell out the reason, saying only that this is the practice followed in all really observant communities *où l'on vit avec exactitude*, and that the contrary practice exposes both novices and senior professed to *inconvéniens considérables.*[113]

Separation of novices from professed was a practice based on the prescriptions of the Rule of Saint Benedict, which assigned the novices their own *cella*, where they ate, slept, and did their spiritual reading.[114] This relative isolation ensured for the newcomer a certain intensity of supervision and formation, and protected him from that occasional middle-aged religious who was all too prone to exercise an unwanted spiritual paternity over the hapless youngster.

The Parlor after Compline

No visits were to be made to the parlor after Compline, even— as much as possible—by Mother Abbess. If this particular point was not included in the earlier remarks about communication with outsiders, it is probably because it posed something of a special problem. Rancé justifies this prohibition by an appeal to the mind of the early Cistercians, so clearly expressed in the Usages of the Order. Here he is referring to Chapter 82 of the ancient *Officia ecclesiastica*, 'Qualiter se agant fratres post completorium'.[115] This is the time of the 'great silence'—the period of silence throughout the entire night, from evening Compline till morning Prime.[116]

Spiritual Reading

The subject of spiritual reading elicits the longest series of comments by the Visitor. It also provides ammunition for the anti-Rancé camp that had been marshalling strength ever since the publication of *On the Sanctity and on the Duties of the Monastic State* back in 1683. Spiritual reading was one of the preferred themes of Monsieur de la Trappe. 'Nothing,' he writes, 'so contributes to warm hearts and to purify them, and to fill minds with holy maxims and truth, as reading.'[117]

Be it noted in passing that Rancé's alleged anti-intellectualism rests largely on our failure to grasp the terms of his all too famous polemic with the learned and saintly Dom Jean Mabillon. For Rancé, *lecture* is a slow, meditative, prayerful reading aimed at the interiorization of the realities of faith, and the subject matter, directly or indirectly, is rooted in the word of God from which it springs and to which it leads. *Étude* is more of a scientific study focussed, as often as not, on objects peripheral to the things that should absorb the monk's whole attention. Rancé's quarrel was not with *études*. The theologian has to be a man of study, for his office in the Church demands that he be a man of comprehensive knowledge, with the right answer for every possible question. Church history, canon law, theology—all are of supreme importance in the Church. Rancé's quarrel was with monks who devoted themselves to *études* instead of to *lecture*. Each vocation in the Church has its proper end and proper means; and, for the abbot of la Trappe, *études* were not a means proper to the monastic life (although he readily admitted that, in individual cases, they could be). Each to his trade, then: the monk to his *lectio divina*, and the theologian and scholar to his *études*.

Accordingly, the question for Rancé is not: should the monk use his intellect? Obviously, the monk has to use his intellect, no differently than the theologian or scholar. The question is, rather: what is the proper object of the intellect, so far as the monk is concerned?

We can, of course, deplore the narrowness of Rancé's views as to the proper scope of the monk's intellectual endeavors, and we rightly feel uncomfortable about his evident distrust of 'theology'. But even here, we have to remember the theological climate of seventeenth-century France. In time, Rancé developed a genuine appreciation of Saint Thomas Aquinas, whose authority he frequently invoked. But 'theology', in his own personal experience—and do not forget, he was a doctor of the Sorbonne—was a sadly fallen *fin de siècle* scholasticism. Theological enquiry was based, moreover, on the disputed-question method, in which scoring a point over the opponent too easily became more important than the serene contemplation of truth. Then, too, the theology of Rancé's France was virtually identical with a perverse kind of *Kontroverstheologie*. To study theology meant to dive into the maelstrom of the war waged between Protestant and Catholic, Jansenist and Jesuit, Gallican and Romanist.

The sisters, then, are to apply themselves to reading, and this with a great seriousness of purpose. Not every book will be equally helpful for everyone. The choice of books and discernment of individual needs pertains to the functions of Mother Abbess. Religious should avoid books beyond the scope of their understanding, as well as books that merely arouse curiosity, lead to distractions, and dry up the heart.[118]

It is difficult to take exception to these principles. Who, after all, would be so rash as to suggest that nuns should pore over tomes beyond their understanding, or spend time on books that arouse curiosity, leave them distracted, and dry up the heart? But are these somewhat negative norms not a bit dangerous in the application? Do they not lend themselves to the encouragement of a steady diet of pious drivel? The danger is there, perhaps, but we can understand what Rancé means if we glance at the books he offers by way of example. These books fall into two main groups: books that instruct us in the truths and duties of our way of life; and, above all, the Bible pure and simple.

First of all, there is the *Imitation of Christ*. *The Ascetical Writings of Saint Basil* come next. The translation Rancé had in mind was the one by his friend, Godefroy Hermant, doctor of the Sorbonne and canon of Beauvais. The presentation copy he received upon its publication in 1673 had sparked a letter of sincere and enthusiastic gratitude. The chief portion of the tome is devoted to the *Long Rules* and the *Short Rules* of the Cappodocian Doctor.[119]

Next, Cassian's *Conferences* and *Institutions*.

Patristic homilies on the Scriptures are next on the list of suggested reading. 'Homilies' are probably meant to include not only homilies in the strict sense, but all kinds of commentaries on biblical texts. No specific titles are mentioned, but Rancé refers, by way of example, to the homilies of Saint John Chrysostom, Saint Gregory the Great, and Saint Augustine.

Which of the writings of the Last of the Fathers, Saint Bernard, are to be recommended? All of them; and also the *Life* of the Saint— by which Rancé probably meant the *Vita Prima* with its supplement of other twelfth-century biographies of the Abbot of Clairvaux.

From the more modern period, the first author to be mentioned is one of Rancé's favorites, Saint Teresa of Avila, who is here represented by her *Way of Perfection*. Then a global mention of the writings of Father Rodriguez (known chiefly for his bulky *Practice of Christian and Religious Perfection*) and of Father Saint-Jure, whose books fill a sizable shelf. Though the rigorist Rancé had little patience with 'Molinist casuistry', his prejudices in no way affected his esteem of Jesuit spiritual masters: the next three authors, like the preceding two, are members of the Society. Rancé recommends the meditations of 'Père du Pont' (Luis de la Puente), P. Julien Hayneuve, and P. Nouët. The fourth and last name in this group of authors is that of one of the greatest of the Oratorians, P. Bourgoing.

The list is far from closed; but in the next section, titles are given without designation of the author.

The first in this series of recommended reading was to involve Rancé in a bit of unpleasantness. *The Interior Christian*, by Jean de Bernières-Louvigny (d. 1659), was a posthumous work of the celebrated norman mystic, whose position as Grand Treasurer of France, strange to say, seems not to have affected adversely his spiritual life, or his marked influence on the many ecclesiastical and lay *dévots* who gravitated in his circle of followers. *The Interior Christian* zoomed through thirteen editions in twelve years.[120] Pierre Nicole, who, so far as Henri Bremond is concerned, represents the quintessence of the french anti-mystical tradition, lamented the appearance of more than forty editions within sixteen years.[121] Of all the Port-Royalists, Nicole was probably one of the least aggressive, but he shared the general tendency of the *Parti* to hold suspect anything written after Saint Bernard (the writings of the Port-Royalists excepted, of course). The list of recommended books included in the visitation card became public knowledge months before the publication of the text—without Rancé's authorization—in the fall of 1690. One can imagine the shock experienced by the pious Jansenists: no less than *five* Jesuits rubbing shoulders with the Fathers, to say nothing of the deluded lay-mystic, Bernières-Louvigny! Relations between Pierre Nicole and Rancé had always been cordial, as their exchange of letters demonstrates.[122] Unwilling to attack openly the man he still sincerely admired, Nicole circulated under the cloak of anonymity two letters bearing on the books recommended by Rancé. *The Interior Christian*, he says in accents of shock and indignation, has been recommended to the poor nuns of les Clairets in the wake of its official condemnation by Rome.

In a letter written soon afterwards to the *abbé* Nicaise, Rancé protests that, till now, no book had ever met with so general an approbation as *The Interior Christian*. Having no roman contacts, he had heard nothing about the book being placed on the Index. But if this proves to be the case, he will inform the nuns of their obligation to condemn all the books condemned by Rome, without themselves examining them or reading them.[123]

In point of fact, it was not *Le Chrétien intérieur* that had been placed on the Index in 1689, but an unsatisfactory italian translation.[124] Rancé's readiness to condemn without examination whatever Rome condemned is, in the historical context, a bit more edifying than might at first appear. In gallican France, the Roman Index was not 'received'. Nor should the irony of Nicole's offended piety escape us. Neither Nicole nor any of the other Port-Royalists had ever been conspicuous for their delicacy of conscience *vis-à-vis* decisions emanating from Rome.

It is especially gratifying, then, that the very next book recommended is Nicole's own splendid *Moral Essays on the Epistles and Gospels.*

The next title is given in too abbreviated a fashion for us to be sure of the author. Does *Instructions chrétiennes* refer to P. Hercule Audiffret's popular *Ouvrages de piété: Instructions chrétiennes et religieuses* (1675)[125] or—less likely—to Antoine Godeau's *Instructions et Prières chrétiennes* (1646)[126] or to yet another similarly-titled devotional book of the period?

Also a bit uncertain is the next recommended book, *La religieuse parfaite et imparfaite*. It sounds suspiciously like Mother Agnès Arnauld's *L'image d'une religieuse parfaite et d'une imparfaite.*[127]

Rancé recommends his own *Sainteté et devoirs de la vie monastique,* as well as the *Explication de la Règle de saint Benoist* 'by the same author', himself.

Finally, hagiographical literature of every kind: the lives and actions of holy monks, of ancient solitaries, and of all the saints.

This closes the first large group of recommended books. Only one book comprises the second part of Rancé's list—the Bible, which Father Visitor recommends first and foremost (*par dessus tout*) as the source and principle of everything to which we are committed in virtue of the monastic state.

Had Rancé stopped at this point, all would have been well, and Nicole might have been magnanimous enough to overlook Monsieur de la Trappe's offending reference to his own *bête noire,* Bernières-Louvigny. Unfortunately, Rancé proceeds to restrict his recommendation of Holy Scripture to the New Testament ('which, containing, as it does, the word of Jesus Christ, thus comprises the whole of evangelical perfection'), and to two Old Testament books, Psalms and Proverbs. 'The reading of the Old Testament,' he explains, 'is not really suitable for nuns—all those different episodes, all those events and narratives that have nothing to do with the simplicity which nuns profess.'[128]

We are appalled. Nicole and company were outraged. In his anonymous letter of 3 September 1690,[129] Nicole took Rancé to task in the name of Saint Paul, Saint Jerome, and Saint Benedict. In the long letter to Nicaise already referred to above,[130] Rancé asks, defensively, what the commotion is all about. If the Church condemns his position, he will condemn it, too. But what about the authority of Saint Basil, who once wrote to the monk Chilon, a monk of *consummate* virtue, that the reading of the Old Testament was not only unsuitable for him, but might actually hurt him?[131] And what about Saint Nilus, who wrote that the Old Testament is not suitable for solitaries?[132] With his back to the wall, Rancé invokes the authority of his friend, Godefroy Hermant, who, he says, is even more restrictive than himself.[133] There follows a list of Old Testament *loci* deemed unsuitable for the ears of women obliged by their state of life to a consummate chastity: the Song of Songs, the story of Susanna, that of Judah and Tamar, Judith, the account of what happened to the Levite's wife in the episode at Gabaon, Leviticus, Ruth, certain passages from Sirach.

Rancé's apparent pastoral prudery will doubtless draw a smile from some of us, if not an outright laugh. Yet it would be foolish of us to forget the distance that separates us from seventeenth-century France. It could be argued that the century was not only a time of unbridled moral licence, but also a time of affected and rather silly delicacy. In his discussion of female education in the Splendid Century, W. H. Lewis passes on with particular relish the two characteristic examples often put forward by Louis XIV's wife, Madame de Maintenon, when denouncing—as she was wont to do—the silliness of society girls raised in the hot-house atmosphere of convents. We are told about 'the convent-bred girl who nearly fainted with horror at the gross indecency of her father in using the word *breeches* in her presence; and another . . . who, when asked by Madame de Maintenon to give a list of the Sacraments, stopped short at marriage. At being prompted, she giggled and said that all references to that sacrament had been forbidden in her convent.'[134]

Personally, I do not believe that Rancé tended to encourage silliness of this sort. In his conferences on the reading of Scripture given to his own monks, Rancé places no restrictions on the reading of the Old Testament.[135] Even in his *Conduite Chrétienne*, written for Her Royal Highness, Madame de Guise, he speaks about the Old Testament under the same title as of the New.[136] But monks, being men, are made of grosser stuff than women; and even so exemplary and dedicated a woman as the widowed Madame de Guise is situated differently than the bride of Christ who is dedicated by a life of consecrated virginity to the attainment of an ideal too lofty for most of us to contemplate.

Probably feeling the need for moral support, Rancé turned to his lifelong friend since their student days at the Sorbonne, Bishop Bossuet of Meaux. In a letter which is a masterpiece of conciliatory art, the bishop of Meaux managed to reassure Rancé of the basic rightness of his position, while at the same time nuancing it where nuancing was needed. 'The real solution to this difficulty, is to give permission for the reading of the Old Testament with discretion, according to the capacity of the subjects.'[137] Later in the same letter, Bossuet summarizes his own position:

> In the final analysis, I agree that we cannot allow the Old Testament [to be read] indiscriminately, but only after testing the spirits. This is my own practice; and I told Monsieur Nicole [who had delated to him his grievance against Rancé] that experience has taught me that the Old Testament, when authorized without discretion, does nuns more harm than good.[138]

In his *Instruction sur la lecture de l'Écriture Sainte qu'il composa pour les religieuses et les communautés des filles du diocèse de Meaux*, Bossuet is a bit more generous, but still cautious. 'There are, in Job, depths which not everyone can penetrate.' 'Genesis will be helpful only for religious with more of a background in Sacred Scripture, and who are steeped in real piety.' 'Ceremonial precepts are to be passed over more lightly.' 'One can dispense with the reading of Leviticus.' And in the case of a good number of religious, it will be best if they pass over lightly certain passages of even the books which are otherwise recommended to them.[139]

As for Rancé, who rarely had difficulty in allowing exceptions to the general principles he tended to overstate with such absoluteness, he had written to Nicaise, in his letter of 11 September 1690:

> I have no doubt but that there are nuns capable of this reading [of the Old Testament]. But that doesn't keep one from being able, and even being obliged to say that, in general, it [i.e., the Old Testament] is unsuitable for nuns—though permission can certainly be given to nuns for whom this reading might be helpful.[140]

In spite of its obvious limitations, Rancé's program of recommended reading covers a wide range and offers a real challenge. Still, there is a certain element of contemplative disinterestedness that is missing. Even in the case of Scripture, the abbot of la Trappe is more concerned with finding a practical expression of the will of God than with quietly and serenely contemplating the whole panorama of salvation history. Everything is to be aimed at our better understanding of our duties and of our state of life. Admirable—so long as it does not result in an unbalanced egocentric moralism.

Manual Labor

Manual labor, we are told, is in line with the spirit of Saint Benedict, with the mind of Saint Bernard, and with the prescriptions of the Rule. As much as possible, it is to have a community or public character, and Mother Abbess should take part unless hindered by real necessity. One suspects that this 'manual labor' consisted in large measure of sewing and mending clothes, since the Visitor warns that the work engaged in ought not to serve the interests of worldly luxury or vanity.[141]

Letter-writing

Letters are to be written as rarely as possible. This is a bit thick, coming as it does from one of the most prolific letter writers of his century. (Though Rancé was no doubt thinking that his own prodigious correspondence would be much reduced, if only so many nuns did not keep him busy answering their queries and requests for counsels.) Letters going out of the monastery were to be subject to control by Mother Abbess, whose responsibility for the monastery extends to the least detail.[142]

Workmen Within the Monastery

The material needs of the house require that certain jobs be done by workmen from outside. These artisans are not to have free access to the monastery, however, but are to be accompanied to the place of work. Contact with outsiders within the abbey is to be avoided when possible, in the spirit of the Church's norms governing enclosure. (Rancé here refers obliquely to the canons of the Council of Trent.) Persons coming to the abbey for reasons of *piété* and *édification* are likewise to be avoided. Rancé reserves to himself, as Father Immediate, the authorization of any derogation to the general norms of enclosure, in keeping with common law and the decrees of the Church.[143]

The Porter at the Enclosure Gate

The traditional monastery was surrounded by an enclosure wall that left a considerable area in the fore-court of the abbey. Here there was much coming and going of guests, workmen, and beggars. A faithful, dependable porter was to be stationed at the outer enclosure gate to control the flow of visitors when the sisters had work to do in the front court, outside the cloister in the strict sense.[144]

Presence at Refectory Reading

Rancé gave a high order of priority to the reading that takes place at community meals. So that the Sisters assigned to the portress' room leading to the cloister proper will not have to miss the reading, Rancé directs that the monastery be closed during dinner-time, and the keys deposited on Mother Abbess' table in refectory.[145]

Reading at Meals in the Infirmary

Even the sick nuns in the infirmary are not to escape some form of reading at meals. Their repast is to begin with the reading of a few lines from the *Imitation of Christ*. This reading is meant to keep the ailing Sisters in the presence of God, and to provide a few holy thoughts as a caution against the 'useless or bad thoughts that sick people can sometimes fall into'.[146]

Holy Water in the Guest-rooms

Mother Abbess is to see to it that there are holy water stoups in the guest-chambers.[147]

Confirmation of the Last Visitation Card of Dom Dominique

Finally, Father Visitor confirms everything contained in the visitation card left by his predecessor, Dom Dominique Georges, Abbot of Val-Richer.[148]

He reminds the nuns once again that theirs is an incomparable glory, and that their dignity as brides of Christ obliges them to nothing less than perfection. He prays that they may enjoy even here and now the blessings and consolations prepared in the next life for persons whose happiness it is to be consecrated to Christ, and who are faithful to their plighted troth.[149]

The present visitation card is to be read in chapter on Fridays or Saturdays of the Ember Weeks throughout the year. It was signed and sealed by Frère Armand Jean, Abbot of la Trappe, and by his secretary, Frère Zozime.[150]

The prescriptions touched on are, of course, of unequal importance. Roughly speaking, they can be grouped around a few main headings: separation from the world; reading; silence. Poverty and manual labor come in for special consideration, too. The prescription about holy water stoups in the guest quarters hardly figures in importance with the preceding. The above grouping, however, is inadequate, since there is a great deal of overlapping, and since such a *schema* fails to suggest the underlying concern for charity and community that runs throughout these *règlements*. It can also be said that separation from the world, silence, and reading find their place within an overriding preoccupation with preserving and deepening the maximum of interiority and conscious absorption in God and the things of God.

Perhaps what Rancé does *not* stress in his two exhortations and in the visitation card is worth adverting to. Anyone searching for purple passages on penance and mortification as the essence of monastic life according to Rancé will have to exercise a high degree of creativity to find them here.

It would probably be in better taste not to touch on the leave-taking scene as described by the man who best knew and loved Rancé, Dom Pierre le Nain. In another of Mother Françoise-Angélique's dramatic gestures that triggered the semi-hysteria that swept over the community, everyone knelt at the end of the reading of the visitation card to receive the Holy Man's blessing. Emotions were running high—so high that the chaplain had to answer the responses in the weeping nuns' stead. Rancé bowed to the crucifix and started to withdraw. Mother Abbess went into her wonted routine, but this time the whole community followed her example, and the hapless abbot found himself hemmed in by a mob of weeping and overwrought nuns. Rancé had to grab a chair and sit down to avoid being knocked down.[151] Oldsters will be reminded of similar scenes in the early career of a Frank Sinatra in the days of the Bobby-sox Generation. Younger readers will probably think of the phenomenon of Beatlemania in the days of the Rock Generation. There must have been something extraordinarily attractive about this stern monastic reformer to generate such excitement and enthusiasm. This is a Rancé quite different from the one we generally picture. Rancé was, of course, a man of many moods. But if we want a really balanced portrait of him, let us not forget the close of the visitation at les Clairets, 16 February 1690.

LA TRAPPE AND LES CLAIRETS 1690–1695

The Abbatial Blessing of Madame de Valençay

1690 to 1695. These were to be the halcyon days of les Clairets. Under the leadership of an energetic Abbess, the deeply united community gave itself enthusiastically to the joy that comes from living the monastic life generously, in a spirit of concord, and without cutting corners. From his retreat at la Trappe, Rancé continued to give encouragement and counsel, but at a distance, by letter only. No sooner had he returned home after the February visitation of 1690, than Madame de Clairets began taking steps to ensure another visit in the not too distant future. Though abbess since 1687, she had not yet received the abbatial blessing. She would be blessed, not by the Bishop of Chartres or by his delegate, not by the Abbot of Cîteaux, but by Monsieur de la Trappe. Prevailing on the Princess of Mecklenburg (her aunt) and the Maréchal de Luxembourg (her uncle) to use their powerful influence with the abbot of Cîteaux, she managed to get Rancé delegated, against his protests, to carry out the rite.[152]

Determined to avoid at all costs the pomp and circumstance and worldly fuss inevitably attendant on such occasions, Rancé gave Mother Françoise-Angélique only two days advance notice of his coming. He arrived early in the afternoon of 3 July 1690. But he was a sick man, who had already pushed himself too far. The next morning found him totally exhausted. As usual, he forced himself, and though it seemed highly doubtful that he would be able to get through the long ceremony, once he had started, he actually began gathering strength. His exhortation to Reverend Mother took the form, for the most part, of a line-by-line commentary on the prayer appointed for the blessing of an abbess, *Vere dignum . . . affluentem spiritum benedictionis.*[153] Once again the thrust of Rancé's message travelled in the direction of interiority:

> All the glory and beauty of the King's daughter is wholly interior and comes from within. *Omnis gloria filiae Regis ab intus* (Ps 44:14). *You* are that King's daughter, for yours is the honor of being bride of Jesus Christ, son of the King of kings. Therefore there can be for you no longer any glory, any beauty, save that which can come to you from the depths of your conscience, from the purity of your heart, from the integrity and uprightness of your life . . .[154]

Rancé's *ferverino* laid particular stress, in its final paragraphs, on the special care the newly blessed abbess must take in avoiding all worldly influences that could compromise the simplicity and poverty of the monastic state. Was Rancé afraid, perhaps, that, for all her evident sincerity, and notwithstanding her somewhat dramatic posturing in attitudes of humility and obedience, Madame de Valençay still had about her too much of the *grande dame*?

As on the occasion of his earlier visit, the abbot of la Trappe insisted on returning home at the earliest possible moment. Like latter-day Scholasticas, the nuns prayed up a torrential downpour. But God was on Rancé's side, and the weather took a turn for the better in time for Monsieur de la Trappe to take his leave early in the morning of the day after the abbatial blessing.[155]

The Publication of the Carte de Visite

Rather many of Rancé's published writings were first printed without his knowledge or cooperation; and of these, a number were the occasion for subsequent unpleasantness. This was the case with the Visitation Card. It appeared in print, along with the two visitation exhortations, in September 1690.[156] Under the same cover, but with separate pagination and as a separate publication, appeared Rancé's *Instruction sur la mort de Dom Muce*—an edifying account of the conversion of one of the more lurid penitents of la Trappe.

Inevitably, Rancé was accused of being a publicity-hound. But writing to his friend of long-standing, the academician Têtu, *abbé* of Belval, Rancé defended himself.

> As for the Life of Dom Muce and the les Clairets Visitation, I've learned rather much of what has been said. But I'm not the one who had these two writings printed. I refused to give the visitation card to people asking for copies. It was the nuns who gave it to the public.[157]

Indeed, this is what was already implied in the unsigned *Avis du Libraire au Lecteur* that prefaces the printed *Carte de Visite*. The publisher explains that various versions of the visitation had been circulating, but in accounts filled with mistakes and *très-peu conformés à la verité*. The Publisher, then, is doing the public a favor by making available an exact, faithful text of the visitation card and the two exhortations.[158]

We have already seen something of the reactions evoked by Rancé's recommendation of *Le Chrétien intérieur*, and by his position concerning the unsuitability of most of the Old Testament for nuns. Painful as was this episode in his relationship with les Clairets, it was easily compensated for by Rancé's deep satisfaction with the community and with their able abbess.

Les Clairets Adopts the Reform: 1692

At this point the reader needs to be reminded that les Clairets was not a house of the Strict Observance. How could an extremist like

Rancé tolerate in a community under his direction *relâchements* as incompatible with the early cistercian tradition as meat-eating and daily recreation? The fact is that he did, and without the slightest difficulty. One suspects that the abbot of la Trappe must have been gratified when signs of a desire to embrace a more ascetical program began manifesting themselves in the royal abbey of women. His pastoral procedure was just the opposite of precipitous or imprudent. He himself offers us the best possible insight into his own mind in a letter he wrote at this juncture to the archbishop of Paris, François Harlay de Champvallon.[159] Why did Rancé ask Harlay's advice on the matter of les Clairets and the Strict Observance? The archbishop had the moral fiber of a jellyfish. Indeed, when he died unexpectedly in 1695, P. de Gaillard, SJ, who had to preach the funeral eulogy, was hard put to find anything positive to say about the poor man. 'Two teeny trifles made this difficult,' wrote Madame Sévigné, "but only two: his life and his death.'[160] Harlay, however, was metropolitan of the region where les Clairets was situated. In his (undated) letter, Rancé writes:

> Please allow me, Monseigneur, to have recourse to you in a current difficulty. Three years ago I was obliged to assume responsibility for the abbey of les Clairets . . . I found it following the common observance of the Rule; and when the nuns asked me if they could follow the mitigated observance and still have a clean conscience, I told them not to have the slightest doubt, since they have the Church's authorization and approval; and that, though exterior practices of penance can be extremely helpful, the Church dispenses from them when she things best to do so; and that they could become great saints just by practicing all the interior piety called for by St Benedict, and by observing exactly all the interior virtues that shape one's conduct, such as charity, humility, obedience, self-forgetfulness, and religious poverty. Although I never spoke to them either directly or indirectly about their embracing the strict observance of the Rule, a number of them told me, more than a year ago, that they felt impelled by a strong desire to practise abstinence and to adopt the Reform. I didn't listen to them, and gave them to understand that, provided they did what they did with all due devotion and purity, they were doing enough. Since that time, some of them have written me about this, indicating that they feel the same as before.
>
> Around a month ago I went to visit this monastery. Out of thirty-three or thirty-four choir nuns, there were as many as twenty-seven or twenty-eight, with their abbess first and foremost, who pressed me insistently to allow them to adopt the Reform.

They said that God was asking this of them, that they felt strongly about it, and that it all depended on me, since according to the Brief of Alexander VII [Rancé is here referring to the Constitution of 1666, *In suprema*] all that's needed is the permission of the Father Immediate. Which is precisely what I didn't want to give. So all I told them was that they have to be patient, take their time, and examine the thing with greater deliberation.

Since then they've written again—a collective letter—with considerable enthusiasm and insistence. The letter was signed by all the religious with the exception of five.

I thought, Monseigneur, that I couldn't do better than to explain to you my present situation, and to follow whatever advice you'll be so kind as to give me. Had they been under any obligation to live in the Reform, or had they decided to do so before I had anything to do with the direction of their monastery, it would be a different situation. But this isn't the case, and I didn't want to agree to it and have them run the risk, if things don't work out, of having to give up something that they've undertaken to do. Which won't happen, Monseigneur, if you think that I really ought to say Yes, and if I do so on the strength of your advice. It's certain that the undertaking would be a source of edification and good example, if only it is seen through to the end. But there's nothing I'd like less than to see it begun, only to turn out badly and have to be abandoned.[161]

Rancé's reference to the Constitution *In suprema* as a norm of approved observance may come as a surprise to readers familiar with cistercian history of this period. For him and his Strict Observance colleagues, the promulgation of the text and its acceptance by the General Chapter of 1667 were mortal blows struck against all the Strict Observance stood for. There was no real question of the Strict Observance *not* accepting the unwelcome document, and the Abstinent abbots knelt with non-Abstinent abbots for the ritual acceptance of *In suprema*. Whereupon Monsieur de la Trappe rose, received permission to speak in virtue of his position as a Definitor, and lodged a formal statement of reservations shared by himself and the Strict Observance abbots whom he was representing.[162] The official protest was badly received at Rome. Pope Alexander VII, moribund for many months, had finally died on 22 May, less than a week after the General Chapter of 1667 had concluded. The new Roman Pontiff, Clement IX (1667–1669), was none other than his predecessor's Secretary of State, Cardinal Rospigliosi, whose sympathies had been consistently with the abbot of Cîteaux and his Common Observance. In a brief of the new pope, dated from

Rome, 26 January 1669, formal endorsement was given the General Chapter of 1667; and the collective protest made by the Abstinents came in for special mention:

> As regards the protestations made at the aforesaid Chapter by the abbot of la Trappe and his adherents, asking for a new appeal to the Holy See with respect to the documents of Our predecessor, Alexander VII, under pretext that there had been introduced therein things obscure, doubtful, opposed to the Rule and early statutes of the Order, and against the intentions of that Pontiff, to whom almost nothing would have been communicated because of his declining health—all this we reject, following the advice and counsel of the Cardinals and Prelates of the Congregation, and declare it temerarious.[163]

Disappointed as Rancé must have been, his own line of conduct was consistently loyal to the Apostolic Constitution of 1666. When the abbess of the easy-going Common Observance Abbey of Leyme, near Cahors, wrote Rancé for advice about raising the tone of observance, the abbot of la Trappe replied in a letter of 10 May 1674:

> Since you want me to tell you what I think, Reverend Mother, my opinion is this: I think that you're bound in conscience to have your monastery observe the Brief given under Alexander VII . . . Although the Brief weakens the austerity of the Rule, it can't be said that you can't follow the Brief and still be saved, provided that your observance is accompanied by the right spirit and piety essential to the religious, and from which no one has the power to dispense.[164]

His advice continues in the same vein. His complaint against a mitigated observance is that interior perfection is difficult to acquire if the exterior practices are not 'perfect'. Accordingly, the ideal would be to use observance of the Apostolic Constitution of 1666 as the necessary minimum, but with the hope that the nuns of Leyme would eventually spontaneously desire to embrace a more integral observance of the Rule.[165]

The abbess, Madame Anne d'Orviré de la Vieuville, acted with rather too much energy. The nuns became alarmed, the abbey confessor sided with them against the abbess, and an appeal was made to the Father Visitor for deliverance from so tyrannical a superior. It was in this context that Rancé again wrote the imprudent abbess, lamenting the fact that those chiefly responsible for implementing the Rule (confessors and Fathers Immediate) are the ones who most contravene the exigencies of regular observance. His main point is that reform at Leyme has got to begin with herself. She has got to become a 'living book' in which instruction is given to the nuns, not by what she says, but by what she is and does. He also tells her that she is right in giving up the exterior signs of her aristocratic condition, for these are opposed to the simplicity of her state of life.[166]

Help from higher superiors was not forthcoming. The Visitor's position was that the Apostolic Constitution of 1666 was binding only on cistercian houses founded or affiliated to the Order *after* 1666. He also forbade the reading of the book so highly commended by Rancé—*Le premier esprit de Cisteaux*, by Julien Paris—under the ridiculous claim that the dangerous tome had been condemned by the General Chapter. Reverend Mother refused to let the wolf into her sheepfold, and sent the Visitor packing—but not before he had fulminated an excommunication against the abbess and her followers. The abbot of Cîteaux lifted the excommunication. But Mother Abbess was badly shaken. Should she withdraw from the Order and place Leyme under the jurisdiction of the bishop of Cahors (who at that time was the saintly prelate, Nicolas Sevin)? Rancé replied that such a drastic measure could be adopted only if the superiors of the Order, given by God as fathers, physicians, and shepherds, ruined and destroyed the souls committed to them instead of giving them spiritual birth, healing their maladies, and nourishing them on divine truths. But since things have come to this pass in the case of Leyme, Mother Abbess would be justified in proceeding to really drastic action.[167] The abbot of Cîteaux finally got the message, gave in to the abbess, and provided new confessors and a different Father Visitor. Madame de Leyme and a few of her nuns adopted the stricter regime of the Abstinents, but the house survived as a Common Observance house, faithful to the norms established in the Papal Constitution of 1666.[168]

Rancé's mentality was evidently conditioned by a careful study of Saint Bernard's *De precepto et dispensatione*, where the abbot of Clairvaux addressed himself to the problem of the co-existence of different forms of observance of one and the same Rule. Writing to the sub-prioress of the cistercian Abbey of Maubuisson, in a much copied and widely circulated letter of 14 November 1680,[169] Rancé adopts as the principle from which all else follows the axiomatic truth that 'the purpose and end of the Rule . . . is to raise [us] to the perfection of the Gospel through the practice of the precepts, counsels, instructions and examples given us by Jesus Christ'. But where does the Rule come in? 'Saint Benedict . . . our first father, has prescribed for that [purpose of evangelical perfection] ways and means.' Following Saint Bernard (though with certain commendable simplifications), Rancé distinguishes between the two kinds of precepts in the Rule. The first deal directly with things interior and spiritual, and, being immutable, admit of no exception or dispensation; no one can be dispensed from being charitable, humble, poor in spirit. The second kind of precept is exterior; and here we must distinguish between those exterior observances so bound up with the interior spirit that they can hardly be dispensed from (poverty, external obedience, for instance); and those exterior observances which can be dispensed from so long as the dispensation is in the spirit of the Rule, corresponds to a real need, is justified by good reasons, and does not lead to anything wrong in itself. Rancé also admits that there are some points of observance which have been 'changed or abolished by the decisions of Superiors, by contrary customs, and one is no longer obliged to practice these [points of observance], or take them up again.'[170]

The horrible truth is that, even at la Trappe, exterior observances were not quite 'perfect'. Writing to an overly energetic and somewhat reckless reforming abbot, Rancé tells him about his own experience at la Trappe:

> We took up [the fasts prescribed by the Rule] and observed them with great exactitude for two years. There were fifty religious who had asked me for this with all possible insistence; they had but one heart, one spirit, one will, on this point as on all others. But there were only ten or twelve capable enough, and healthy enough to keep it up. . . .[171]

The hours for mealtime were accordingly adjusted, and the fasts rendered a bit less extreme. Rancé expresses his fear that his correspondent is asking too much of his monks, and that their health will suffer. God won't mind it, he says, if our fasts aren't identical with those of our Fathers, so long as we don't otherwise differ from them. And then, in an admirable formula:

> Discretion, when exempt from all laxity and carnal condescension, is a greater virtue than penitence. And you can even think of it as humility, if there's a certain distance between your own exterior practices and those of our Fathers. *They* were saints, and were animated by a spirit no longer found in the same degree and the same plenitude in those who have come after them. . . .[172]

It is against the background of this mentality that we should understand Monsieur de la Trappe's readiness to be satisfied with the mitigated regime of les Clairets. The manifestation of a spontaneous desire to follow a stricter observance was surely what Rancé had been hoping for. In answer to the evolving situation at les Clairets, he made his third visit to the royal abbey, arriving on 24 March 1692, in time for First Vespers of the Feast of the Annunciation. According to the habitually well-informed Dom le Nain, he expressed his joy at finding so much enthusiasm for the Reform; but God was no less admirable in those of the Sisters unable to go along with the others. What touched him most deeply was the fact that their former charity, concord, union, and mutual understanding, far from being compromised, had grown. There was discernible a deeper degree of mutual submission, respect, deference, and esteem. Such a profound community spirit could come only from the Spirit of God. Rancé also alluded to the experience of some of the sisters who, not initially in favor of the idea of a stricter observance, had nevertheless spontaneously, and without pressure adopted a more severe regime since the preceding Easter, by way of seeing whether their health permitted them to fall in line with the more robust enthusiasts. The experiment had been positive. Then there was Rancé's own policy. Far from encouraging Strict Observance aspirations, he had adopted a policy of being 'difficult', even 'opposed'—though he honestly admits that, in his heart, he felt quite differently.[173]

Mother Abbess accordingly asked the Father Immediate for his official approbation of their adoption of the Reform. Still he held off. At this juncture he wrote the archbishop of Paris, asking his advice. In the meantime, he told the community of les Clairets to spend the next twelve months as a sort of novitiate in the Reform, for one final testing of the spirits before making a final, unqualified decision. Actually, however, he made them wait only another half-year. He returned to les Clairets early in October of the same year; and the entire community embraced the Reform 'of one accord, and in a spirit of perfect unanimity' on 4 October 1692.[174]

Dom le Nain adds an edifying tale by way of a postscript. One of the older nuns fell seriously ill, and her sickness was accompanied by a painful malady of the throat. Through her confessor she got the abbot of la Trappe to pray for her, and her recovery verged on the miraculous. Having considered herself too old and too feeble to embrace the Reform, she now had second thoughts. If the holy abbot's prayers could bring her back from the brink of the grave as they had, perhaps he could obtain the further gift of sufficient health for her to embrace the Reform. Needless to say, this is precisely what happened, except that her throat condition remained such that she was unable to chant in choir. When the Visitor came for his third visit to les Clairets, in March 1692, she took him to task for the fact that she still could not chant in choir. 'You're asking for too much at a time,' he told be. 'You should be satisfied with the grace the Lord has already given you.' Not her. 'Que je chante, je vous prie, mon Révérend Père, que je chante; demandez, demandez. . .' The reader will not be surprised to learn that Mother X went to Vespers that very day, took her turn at intoning the antiphons, and was able to keep up her chanting in choir till the end of her days.[175]

The abbot of la Trappe paid four visits in all to les Clairets. After the official inauguration of the Reform there in early October, 1692, Rancé returned to la Trappe. He was never to see the community again.

LA TRAPPE AND LES CLAIRETS, 1695–1700

For years Rancé had been talking about resigning his abbatial authority. When old age and shattered health finally forced him to take up permanent residence in the infirmary towards the end of 1694, he at last carried into effect his earlier intention. His own choice as successor, Dom Zozime Foisil, was installed on 28 December 1695, but Dom Zozime survived his installation as abbot by only two months. He died as the result of sudden illness on 3 March 1696.

Rancé's second successor was likewise a man of his own choosing. But the resigned Abbot was not particularly remarkable as a judge of character. His confidence in others was all too often misplaced, and his predilection for Dom Armand-François Gervaise, a former Carmelite, and the last choir monk professed by Rancé in 1695, had disastrous results. Gervaise was installed as abbot of la Trappe on 18 October 1696. By the end of 1698, he was out of office. And the intervening two years were sheer madness. Rancé's excellent biographer, A. J. Krailsheimer, suggests that Gervaise's worst crime was imprudence;[176] and this is, it seems to me, an honest and accurate appraisal—though mention should also be made, surely, of some of the morbid character traits that became more evident as Gervaise's personality degenerated in his old age: his defensiveness, his vindictiveness, his carelessness of truth.[177] But here we are concerned only for Abbot Armand-François as Father Immediate of les Clairets.

From the very first, Gervaise and Madame de Valençay seem to have conceived for each other a deep, sincere, mutual detestation. Initially, the chief fault of poor Gervaise was simply that he was not Rancé. Truth to tell, whatever her protestations to the contrary, Madame l'Abbesse remained beneath her monastic weeds the aristrocratic *grande dame* who, as abbess reformer, gave new luster to the name d'Etampes Valençay. And Gervaise? Very much a commoner, and a somewhat uncouth commoner at that—a commoner intent on exercising his juridical right to call the signals at les Clairets. A further complication was the hostility of Rancé's private secretary of many years, Charles Maisne. Though a layman, and in no way a member of the community, he had gained a Svengali-like ascendancy over the feeble Rancé in his capacity as secretary in charge of all correspondence. (Both Rancé's hands were too ulcerated and paralyzed to allow him to write his own letters.) On at least one occasion, Maisne had accompanied Rancé to les Clairets, for in a letter addressed to his friend, Jean Gerbais, Doctor of the Sorbonne, and Provisor of the College de Reims, and dated 12 September 1694, Rancé denies categorically the rumor that he had introduced his secular secretary into the cloister at les Clairets. He had used him as a travelling companion, he explains, to avoid having to take one of the brethren away from la Trappe; also, Madame des Clairets needed to consult Maisne concerning some particulars of a building project in progress at the abbey, for the secretary was knowledgeable in such matters. But Maisne had never gone into the cloister.[178]

As Dom Gervaise himself tells it, the nuns of les Clairets had been asking for a visitation from their new Father Immediate. Mother Abbess had been insistent, too. But he himself had put it off for more than a half-year, knowing, he says, 'that this abbess was of an extraordinary haughtiness and pride'. Her treatment of Dom Zozime had forewarned him. Dom Zozime was the son of a mere bourgeois from nearby Bellême; our aristocratic Abbess stated publicly that the low-born abbot 'barely deserved to be her lackey'. But this, remember, is being told us by Gervaise, and in a book published only in 1742, after he had brooded for decades over his long life of persecution and misery.[179] Gervaise paid his first visit to les Clairets in August, 1696, on the occasion of the solemn profession of one of the nuns. 'The entire community was apparently extremely satisfied with his style (*de se manières*) and his exhortations,' he humbly tells us.[180] When taking leave of Mother Abbess, however, he made his first major blunder. He told her—'charitably'—to be more prudent about the letters Maisne was sending her frequently. Some of the nuns had been disturbed by their contents, and had complained to the new Father Immediate. Which nuns? demanded Madame l'Abbesse. Monsieur l'Abbé refused to say. The war had begun.

Gervaise's visit was followed by a letter from the Abbess to her la Trappe correspondent, Maisne. The letter 'fell into the hands of the new Abbot', Gervaise demurely tells us. (One wonders just how it happened to fall into the hands of the new abbot . . .) The letter was an invitation to Maisne to leave those 'sneaks' (*ces moines cafards*) at la Trappe, and take up residence at les Clairets. Rancé advised Gervaise to resign his official responsibility for les Clairets at the first opportunity[181]—quoth Gervaise.

The next clash was more serious. Madame l'Abbesse had written Gervaise asking for permission to allow one of the nuns to leave the enclosure and take the waters at a health resort. Rancé's position on nuns' taking the waters was notorious. Gervaise refused permission. The abbess addressed herself to Maisne, asking him to wrangle permission from the resigned abbot, Rancé. The permission was desperately needed, since she had already told the nun's family that the ailing woman could go to the spa. Rancé insisted on referring the matter to the present incumbent in the abbatial office. Like another Nicholas of Clairvaux, the secretary drew up the needed document, signed and sealed it with Rancé's private seal, and dispatched it on its clandestine way to les Clairets.[182] Knowing Gervaise, we are hard-pressed to determine how much credence to put in this sort of tale.

At Rancé's urging, Gervaise returned to les Clairets for an official visitation. He arrived on 27 March 1697. Mother Abbess was indisposed with a bad cold. Could the Visitor please hold the chapter in the infirmary? Gervaise agreed.

The community had grown considerably since Rancé's first visit in 1690. It now numbered some sixty-three persons, including forty-three choir nuns, five novices, ten lay sisters, and five *soeurs données*. The private interviews began on 28 March and lasted two full days. The visitation was to close on the third day. But Mother Abbess asked that the closing be postponed a day, since a lay sister had just finished her year of novitiate preparation, and wanted to make her profession in the presence of Father Immediate. Gervaise agreed, and spent most of the next day preparing his profession exhortation. On the following day, he communicated the text of the visitation card to Mother Abbess before initially presenting it to the community. Mother Abbess replied that the visitation had lasted longer than the prescribed three days, so that now she no longer acknowledged him as Visitor. Doubtless she remembered Rancé's refusal to prolong his own visits to les Clairets, and he must have appealed to the ancient legislation touching on a three-day limit. There are, in fact, such prescriptions to be found—in the *Institutiones Capituli Generalis*, Dist. VII, cap. 9;[183] in the *Libellus Antiquarum Definitionum*, n. 20;[184] in the Papal Constitution of Benedict XII, *Fulgens sicut stella matutina*, n. 13.[185] In vain Gervaise pleaded with Mother Françoise-Angélique. Les Clairets was a larger community than those envisaged by the earlier legislation; he had had to spend time on things other than the visitation; earlier visitations (probably under Dom Dominique Georges) had lasted two weeks. The Abbess was adamant. Gervaise felt within his rights to fulminate the excommunication the situation called for. Instead, he asked the strong woman to think over what she was doing, and to let him know just what it was in the visitation card that had displeased her. He would gladly drop anything she found offensive. 'The whole thing is offensive, from beginning to end', she answered, and closed the parlor grille in Father Visitor's face. Thus far, Gervaise.[186] Once again, it is difficult to know to what extent this narrative needs demythologization.

Not yet discouraged, the gentle, long-suffering abbot invoked the help of the abbey chaplain, who tried to reason with the abbess till four o'clock in the afternoon. Meeting with no response, Gervaise had the bell rung for chapter, gave his final exhortation, charitably urged the nuns to take good care of Mother Abbess' health, and promised that he would return to provide them with a visitation card when Mother Abbess was feeling better. When Gervaise returned to la Trappe with his tale of woe, Rancé once again advised him to break his ties with les Clairets. But for the moment, they agreed on a policy of silence.[187]

For the next week there was an uninterrupted exchange of mail between abbess and Charles Maisne. Then, three months later, Gervaise was graciously invited by the aristocratic Lady Prioress of les Clairets, Madame Auvergne (niece of both Turenne and Cardinal Bouillon) to return to les Clairets to preside at the solemn translating of a coffer of relics recently sent the abbey by her uncle in Rome. Once again, Gervaise modestly tells us that everyone was favorably impressed with him during his three days there, during which he admits he received every token of christian charity and good will.[188]

At the end of the year, Mother Abbess wrote in person, urging him to return to give a directed ten-day retreat to a number of the nuns on whose behalf she was writing. Gervaise was too busy, but would send the Prior, he promised. No, it had to be Gervaise himself; no one else would do. 'Go,' Rancé told him; 'perhaps this is the means God wants to use for you two to come to a perfect understanding with each other.' Gervaise went. The retreat, given to a dozen nuns, was wonderfully well received. Even Mother Abbess assisted at the daily general conference. Surely the unpleasantness of the preceding (attempted) visitation had been but a temporary lapse on the abbess' part, due to her excessive *vivacité*. Clearly, Mother Françoise-Angélique was trying to make amends. As for Gervaise, he intended to be noble and forgiving.[189]

The blow fell soon thereafter. Gervaise had been delated to as high a personage as His Most Christian Majesty himself. Louis XIV had received complaints abut the oppressive visitation card. He was not pleased. The Grand Monarch told his all-powerful confessor, Père de la Chaise, to call Gervaise to order. Père de la Chaise wrote Gervaise a strongly worded letter, accusing him of contrarying His Majesty's intentions by failing to act in concert with his benefactor and predecessor, the resigned abbot. His conduct at les Clairets was offered as a case in point.

> . . . The interest that I've always taken in supporting the Reform established in so holy a manner and with so much approbation, obliges me to tell you that, if you change its spirit, and adopt a policy that differs from the ideas of your former abbot, you are going to undermine the esteem your house has acquired, and you will diminish considerably the consideration His Majesty has for it.[190]

In the Splendid Century, the quickest, most direct form of suicide was to do something that struck the Great Monarch as *fort mauvais*. Rancé dictated a letter witnessed officially by a number of the brethren, and in attestation to the perfect harmony between resigned Abbot and his successor. Unable to sign his own name, Rancé managed to scrawl his initials in huge, shaky lines. Gervaise chose a discreet way of refuting the charge of misgovernment of les Clairets. He simply sent Père de la Chaise a copy of the offending visitation card. A few days later a reply came from Versailles. The King was overjoyed to learn that all was well between the abbot of la Trappe and his holy predecessor. As for the affair of les Clairets,

His Majesty could not see what the abbess had to complain about; Gervaise's directives were quite moderate.[191]

As a matter of fact, the famous visitation card is relatively moderate. It breathes a spirit quite different from Rancé's earlier *carte de visite*, nonetheless. 'Fussiness' might be the adjective to describe its provisions—or at least some of them. Where Rancé had said that visits to the parlor are to be made in the company of another religious, Gervaise adds that two *young* nuns must not be together in the parlor. An obvious exception to Rancé's prescription had not been specified by him: the case of nuns who want to speak to their confessor or director, without the presence of a third party. But this must be done in the confessional, says Gervaise. And he reminds the nuns that the confessional has to have a small grille covered with cloth. There are further prescriptions about the choir grille, which must be kept closed during all liturgical functions apart from a few exceptions (during which times the nuns are to have their veils modestly lowered). And then there is the problem of nuns' fashions. At les Clairets, robes and cowls are too ample; they trail after the nuns like the robes of fashionable women in the world. Hemlines should merely touch the floor. In the same spirit, the nuns must forswear bodices, petticoats, and all over-size whalebone stays. Another abuse to be eliminated: guests are being served meat and meat bouillon. Time was when General Chapters excommunicated superiors for allowing such flagrant abuses. As for the sick nuns who take advantage of the prescription of the Rule that allows sick or decrepit religious the use of flesh-meat, they should remember that, in order to qualify, they should be *really* sick. A further caution: there are too many visitors coming to les Clairets from the nearby spa, Bellême. Reverend Mother and the nuns could take more seriously the Church's legislation touching on *sorties* outside the enclosure. In particular, Mother Abbess should not make visits to the abbey farm or to property outside the enclosure. By way of concession, however, Gervaise concedes an occasional outside excursion, so long as it conforms to his seven-point guideline: 1) during her absence, no outsider may be present in the abbey; 2) all the outer gates of the abbey must be closed; 3) the abbess must be accompanied by two senior nuns and one of the confessors or the cellarer; 4) the prioress has to remain in the abbey, in case the nuns need her in the abbess' absence; 5) the outside visit must take place in broad daylight; 6) no more than twice a year; 7) for no longer than two hours. Then there is the problem of breakfast, which is not prescribed in the Rule, but only permitted by the Order for those who need it. Therefore the bell for breakfast ought to be suppressed, for fear that breakfast might be invested with an 'official' character. Dispensations from particular points of observance are come by much too easily: infirmities have got to be *real, actual*. Also, though the Rule allows the abbot to dispense from the fasts during the summer heat so often as heavy work has to be done, Saint Benedict really had Italy in mind, where summer is hotter than in France; also, the work done nowadays is not anywhere nearly as hard as the work done by the first disciples of that Great Saint. There is also a problem with respect to the nun in charge of the clock. Apparently she has been setting it back a bit during the night, in order to give the Sisters a little extra sleep. Obviously this is misplaced and misguided charity. Think of the foolish virgins who were caught still slumbering when the Bridegroom came! Also, everything smacking of 'magnificence' must go—particularly in the case of the meals served outsiders. By way of silverware, only forks and spoons are to be permitted.[192]

Poor Gervaise! But he meant well.

As regards the matter of his delation to Versailles, Gervaise knew very well that the mischief had been the work of the abbess and her henchman, Charles Maisne. But he kept his silence. Letters from les Clairets he answered in a few words.[193]

Then Madame Françoise-Angélique went too far. Gervaise discovered that she had gone visiting 'persons of quality', taking two nuns with her, without having obtained prior permission. Gervaise wrote her not to do it again. Otherwise, he might have to advise her that she had incurred the excommunication aimed at nuns who leave the enclosure without the written permission of their superior. To make his point clearer, Gervaise was rash enough to send Madame's chaplain an authorization to absolve her from the censure *ad cautelam*, but for this time only. Madame was furious.[194]

The next episode in the battle was no more than a minor skirmish. At the beginning of the new year Gervaise wrote a pastoral letter addressed to the entire community—a letter of the sort generally read publicly to the nuns assembled in chapter. Mother Abbess had the letter read only in refectory, and at a meal from which she remained absent.[195]

It was early spring. Gervaise received a nicely worded request from Madame Françoise-Angélique. The papal bulls confirming her in office, and expedited from Rome ages ago, had been lost on the way. The question of the validity of all her official acts as abbess had arisen. Could she please come in person to la Trappe to discuss the problem with the holy former superior, Rancé? Gervaise replied Yes. Madame arrived, garbed, Gervaise tells us, in the world's most 'reformed' religious habit. The material was like the roughest homespun; the length was such that, far from sweeping the ground, the robe barely came down to her shins. Madame's footwear was no less rustic—over-size clogs of the sort worn by peasants. Her wimple was cut from a bolt of cloth generally used for towels and her veil was made of cloth no less thick. All done just to impress her former Father Immediate, snarls Gervaise, careful to add that Madame's religious habit was like a wedding gown, meant to be worn only once in a lifetime. It is, however, characteristic of Gervaise's carelessness with facts that, when he tells us it had been a long time since Rancé had seen the aristocratic Abbess, he specifies 'eight or ten years'. But we are only in the spring of 1698, and Rancé's last visit to the royal abbey had been in October of 1692. Gervaise's penchant for distortion descends even to matters of petty detail.[196] The real reason for this visit from the abbess of les Clairets, Gervaise suggests, was contact with his nemesis, Charles Maisne.

It was time for a second visitation of les Clairets. For obvious reasons Gervaise was reluctant to go in person. He delegated the prior of la Trappe. The abbess took the substitution badly, considered it an affront to receive as Visitor a mere prior, and refused to allow him to go about the business of visitation.[197]

Worse was to follow. Five or six weeks later Gervaise received word from the abbot of Tamié, in Savoy, that Madame l'Abbesse was using her influence with Cardinal de Bouillon (uncle of the prioress) to obtain a papal brief making les Clairets independent of la Trappe. Rancé is alleged to have remarked, 'Please God, I hope she gets it. . . .'[198] Two days later a letter from the cardinal arrived, dated from Rome, 12 May 1698. The cardinal asked that the abbess and prioress of les Clairets be allowed to choose confessors from elsewhere than la Trappe.[199] This was the last straw. Gervaise assembled the brethren in chapter, exposed his griefs against the abbess, and asked their advice as to the best course of action to adopt. Of more than seventy religious present, only one (a former chaplain at les Clairets) was not in favor of Gervaise renouncing jurisdiction over les Clairets. An official statement was drawn up and was signed by all, including Rancé (who tried to use his left hand to do so). Maisne sent the abbess news of this development by special messenger. Gervaise still hoped that the initiative taken at la Trappe would bring the abbess to her senses. He was mistaken. He thereupon sent two of his monks to les Clairets, charged with the delivery of three letters. One was addressed to the community, expressing his satisfaction with their 'holy dispositions', and regretting that their abbess' behavior obliged him to abandon them. The second letter was to the abbess, brief and to the point. Gervaise was handing her and her monastery over to the abbot of Clairvaux to whom she was now to address herself for whatever was needed. The third letter recalled the la Trappe religious at les Clairets back to their abbey. Gervaise also wrote to the cardinal. The cardinal's wishes were his commands. The la Trappe confessors and other religious had been recalled from les Clairets; and the abbess, the prioress, and the entire community were now at liberty to choose not only suitable confessors, but a suitable superior as well. The letter was expedited from la Trappe, 20 July 1698.[200]

The foolish abbess was now faced with the consequence of her anti-Gervaise campaign. Juridical separation from la Trappe would do nothing to improve public esteem for les Clairets; and now she complained to all who would listen that the abbot of la Trappe, in an attempt to heap opprobrium on the royal abbey, had renounced responsibility for les Clairets. Once again, Louis XIV found the situation *fort mauvais*. Père de la Chaise arranged for the matter to be arbitrated by Paul Godet des Marets, bishop of Chartres, and Mathurin Savary, bishop of Séez (les Clairets was in the diocese of Chartres; la Trappe in the diocese of Séez). The prelates drew up their terms of settlement. The abbess would sign, Madame des Clairets stated, just as soon as Monsieur de la Trappe had signed. Gervaise signed. But then Madame l'Abbesse decided she could not sign in conscience, since her nuns were unwilling to be once again dependent on la Trappe—a patent lie, according to Gervaise. The handwriting had long since been on the wall, and Gervaise's days as abbot were numbered. By the end of the year he was out of office. His successor, Dom Jacques de la Cour, at the urging of mutual friends of la Trappe and of les Clairets, re-assumed responsibility for the troublesome abbey. He lived to regret it, says Gervaise in one final snarl.[201]

Who, not knowing the depressing history of the war between the abbess and the abbot, would ever be able to read between the lines of statute 43, formulated during the seventh session of the General Chapter of 1699? This statute more or less spelled *finis* to the problem of les Clairets. It confirmed the incorporation of les Clairets into the Strict Observance, already ratified by the abbot of Cîteaux on 20 July 1697; it maintained the abbot of la Trappe as the Father Immediate; but it assigned as Visitor, not Monsieur de la Trappe, but the Vicar General of the Strict Observance for the regions of Brittany and Perche.[202] The opening lines of the statute make it clear that the General Chapter was well aware of the whole recent shabby history:

> Moved by the zeal and extraordinary fervor of the Venerable Abbess and nuns of the monastery of les Clairets, the General Chapter exhorts them, for the honor of God and the glory of the Order, to be zealous in the Lord, in the future, for the better gifts.[203]

Given the implicit reference to 1 Corinthians 12:30, the General Chapter is saying: however much zeal there has been at les Clairets, there has been all too little charity. This, too, is the overall impression of A. J. Krailsheimer, who quotes one of the Trappist chaplains at les Clairets as saying about the Abbess: 'She needs a superior more to moderate her zeal than to keep her from falling into laxity.' And, Professor Krailsheimer adds, for his own part: 'Moderation and charity seem to have been the two qualities in which she was conspicuously lacking.'[204]

And what was the attitude of the decrepit old ex-abbot who lay dying in the infirmary?

It was 26 October 1700, late in the evening of the day before his death. Dom Jacques de la Cour was with him, and Rancé asked his Father Abbot to offer his excuses to the king of England. He had begun a letter to his royal friend a few days earlier, but had not the strength to finish it. He thought, too, of a number of his close friends, and asked Dom le Cour to write them, telling them that Rancé had loved them and remembered them to the end. This is the letter he dictated for Madame l'Abbesse des Clairets:

> I feel certain, Reverend Mother, that you in particular and your whole community received with real sorrow the news of the various ailments that have attacked me for such a long time, and that have finally brought me to the point of death. God knows, Reverend Mother, that I would have liked to have given you a last token of the esteem I've always had for you; but I was much too sick, helpless and unable to do anything. Still, I die praising God for the protection that he has given your monastery; and I'm convinced that, should you ever have to suffer such extreme afflictions (and, please God, you won't), he will sustain you with the same protection, so long as you remain faithful in his service.
> I haven't been as helpful for you as I would have liked; but I trust that, if God takes pity on me, I'll soon have ways of making

you realize with how much sincerity, tenderness, and respect I've always been, for you and your dear daughters, your most humble and obedient servant.

And below, the added lines:

Please tell Madame d'Auvergne [the prioress] that I'll remember her before the Lord.[205]

Armand-Jean de Rancé died at half-past one in the afternoon of 27 October 1700.

LES CLAIRETS, 1700–1792

Madame Françoise-Angélique d'Éstampes de Valençay survived by seven years the reformer of la Trappe. Two days before Christmas of 1707, she died; and the following year, on 7 September, M. Gontier, Doctor of the Sorbonne and Canon of the Cathedral of Chartres, preached at les Clairets his splendid *oraison funèbre* in praise of the deceased abbess, who had ever been a paragon of every virtue.[206]

The new abbess, Marguerite-Élisabeth Bouthillier de Chavigny (1708–1729), was closely related to Rancé through his uncle Claude de Chavigny. Having been Prioress at Sainte-Cathérine, near Angers, she arrived as a total stranger when she came as abbess to les Clairets. She was a practical woman, and undertook major building projects much needed as a result of the neglect of her predecessors in office. The girls' *pensionnat* took on a new lease of life. The trees within the enclosure were cut down and sold to help pay off the large debt incurred by the building program. It was also Madame de Chavigny who got the archives of the abbey into some semblance of order, and had the abbey chartulary drawn up in 1720.[207]

Marie-Adélaide de Merbouton (1729–1765) continued the material amelioration of the abbey at a time when the economy was in a precarious situation. As for the inner life of the abbey, the momentum generated at the turn of the century had spent itself. The nuns found their abbess overly exigent in her demands, and when Marguerite-Hélène de Portebise (1766–1782) assumed the role of superior in 1766, conditions were ripe for outright rebellion. The new abbess intended to fall in line with the spirit of la Trappe. Not so, her daughters. Unfortunately, Madame de Portebise was both energetic and irresolute. At the insistence of the nuns, she asked the abbot of la Trappe to replace his chaplains, and he complied.

But the nuns continued in their discomfirture *vis-à-vis* la Trappe. The abbess finally turned to the abbey of Perseigne as a source of spiritual directors and confessors. The result was disastrous. The religious finally sent was a militant Jansenist—not quite what the easy-going community had expected. Once more, les Clairets was restored to the jurisdiction of Monsieur de la Trappe; and once more Monsieur de la Trappe recalled his religious and renounced his jurisdiction. A clique within the abbey made a clandestine appeal against their abbess to the abbot of Cîteaux. In the civil war which then broke out in full fury, two of the rebel nuns had to be sent to another abbey. To avoid further scandal, the abbess closed the *pensionnat*, and then transferred to the unoccupied buildings within the enclosure the children from the abbey-supported orphanage, *La Babillerie*. The nuns reacted badly to the good abbess' concern for the orphans. They accused her to higher authority of 'spoiling the poor children, dressing them in magnificence, and making them her little jewels'. The abbess admitted that the life style of the orphans was now somewhat better than it had been, but that it cost less to support them inside the enclosure wall than outside. And she adds, magnificently:

> And if I give them some token of my affection, is that so strange a thing? These are children being raised under my very eyes. Is a father, a mother to be blamed for showing tenderness to their children?[208]

An official enquiry vindicated the abbess. Once again the abbey was under the jurisdiction of la Trappe. Discipline returned—at least to some degree. But the nuns had their own modest victory, too. The *pensionnat* was reopened and the orphans returned to their less pretentious quarters well outside the enclosure.[209]

Julie de Galard de Brassac de Béarn (1782–1784) died after only two years in office. It is with Thérèse-Gabrielle de Villeneuve de Trans (1784–1790) that the monastic history of les Clairets comes to an end; and this, not with a burst of glory, but with something of a whimper. In 1789 the *Ancien Régime* came to an end. There was no place in the new order of things for a royal abbey—or an abbey of any sort, for that matter. On 28 February 1790, almost exactly a century after the first visit of Rancé to les Clairets, the municipal officials arrived at the abbey to make an inventory of its goods. A sad little episode took place on the following June 15. The nuns drew up a formal petition touching on a member of the community, Madame Felicité. For some twelve or fifteen years, the good woman had been insane. Now she had taken a turn for the worse. She was found throwing stones and breaking the windows of the abbess' suite. The demented nun had been ordered to leave the abbey along with the other nuns. But the community asks that she be kept safe in a separate room, and under medical attention, until her family can come and get her.[210]

Twenty-nine choir religious, eight lay sisters, three *soeurs données*, two chaplains. The abbess declared publicly to the municipal officials that it was the desire of the nuns to remain at les Clairets, and to live and die there in keeping their vows. But Marie-Louise-Gélasie de Fourchais left the abbey on 18 June 1790. Françoise-Thérèse Landry slipped away three days later. On 18 October, Marie-Louise Gélasie de Fourchais, in an act of heroism, returned to the doomed abbey. But the departures continued, singly and in groups, till only the abbess and a few brave souls were left. The municipal officials were once more at the abbey on 17 October 1792. The public auction of the abbey goods and property was to be held the next day. They had a passport to Toulon for the *ci-devant abbesse*. On the next day, Madame l'Abbesse saw the last of her nuns depart. And then she too took her leave.[211]

ABBREVIATIONS OF FREQUENTLY CITED WORKS

Bre   Henri Bremond, *Histoire littéraire du sentiment religieux en France depuis la fin des Guerres de Religion jusqu'à nos jours*, 13 vol. (Paris: Bloud et Gay, 1916–1933).

Car   A.-J. Rancé, *Carte de visite faite à l'abbaye de N.-Dame des Clairets par le révérend père abbé de la Trappe, Le seiziéme Février 1690* (Paris: Muguet, 1690).

Dub   L. DuBois, *Histoire de l'abbé de Rancé et de sa réforme*, 2 vol. (Paris: Ambroise Bray, 1866).

Ger   A.-F. Gervaise, *Jugement critique mais équitable des vies de feu M. l'abbé de Rancé* (London [=Troyes], 1742).

Gon   B. Gonod, *Lettres de Armand-Jean le Bouthillier de Rancé, Abbé et Réformateur de la Trappe (Paris: Librarie d'Amyot, 1846).*

Kra   A. J. Krailsheimer, *Armand-Jean de Rancé, Abbot of la Trappe. His Influence in the Cloister and the World* (Oxford: Clarendon, 1974).

Lek   L. J. Lekai, *The Rise of the Cistercian Strict Observance in Seventeenth Century France* (Washington, DC: Catholic University Press, 1968).

Len   P. Le Nain, *La vie du révérend père Dom Armand Jean le Boutillier de Rancé*, 3 vol. ([Rouen], 1715); a 2nd, much revised version, 2 vol. (Paris: Florentin Delaune, 1719). Unless otherwise indicated, references are to Vol. 2 of the Paris edition, 1719.

Let   *Lettres de piété écrites a différentes personnes, Par le R. P. Dom Armand Jean Bouthillier de Rancé*, 2 vols. (Paris: Muguet, 1701–1702).

Lew   W. H. Lewis, *The Splendid Century. Life in the France of Louis XIV* (Garden City, N.Y.: Doubleday Anchor, s.d.).

Sou   Vicomte de Souancé, *Abbaye Royale de Notre-Dame Des Clairets. Histoire et Cartulaire* (Nogent-le-Rotrou: Hamard, 1894).

Tou   Henri Tounoüer, *Bibliographie et iconographie de la Maison-Dieu Notre-Dame de la Trappe au Diocèse de Sées: Deuxième Partie. Livres liturgiques, documents manuscrits.* Documents sur la Province du Perche, 4e Série, N° 2 (Mortagne: L. Fournier, 1905).

NOTES

1. As quoted without further reference in W. H. Auden and L. Kronenberger, *The Faber Book of Aphorisms: A Personal Selection* (London: Faber and Faber, 1970) p. 4.

2. P. Zakar, *Histoire de la Stricte Observance de l'Ordre Cistercien depuis ses debuts jusqu'au générelat du Cardinal de Richelieu (1606–1635)*, Bibliotheca Cisterciensis 3 (Rome: Éditiones Cistercienses, 1966) pp. 42–49.

3. Lek, p. 26, final paragraph for a summary statement.

4. For a brief treatment of the Cistercian Congregations of this period, see Jean de la Croix Bouton, *Histoire de l'Ordre de Cîteaux*, Tirage à-part des Fiches 'Cisterciennes', 2 (Westmalle, 1964) pp. 313–316, 325–328, 329–332. At the time of writing, Fr Louis Lekai's *The Cistercians. Ideals and Reality* (Kent, Ohio: Kent State University Press, 1977) was not yet available for reference. Chapter X is devoted to 'The Rise of the Congregations'.

5. Text in *Nomasticon Cisterciense seu antiquiores Ordinis Cisterciensis Constitutiones*, ed. nova a R. P. H. Séjalon (Solesmes: E Typographeo Sancti Petri, 1892) pp. 548–557. Summary analysis in Bouton, *Histoire* 2; 319–320.

6. J.-M. Canivez, *Statuta Capitulorum Generalium Ordinis Cisterciensis ab anno 1116 ad annum 1786*, vol. 7 (Louvain: Bureux de la Revue, 1939) pp. 197–249.

7. Lek covers in detail the entire period; Zakar, *Histoire* (Note 2, above) treats of only the first decades of the controversy, but reproduces much of the more important documentation *in extenso*. Chapter XII of Lekai, *The Cistercians* (note 4, above) gives a succinct recapitulation of the *summa capita* of the controversy.

8. Unedited letter to Pierre Bouchu, newly elected abbot of Clairvaux, in Troyes, Bibliothèque municipale, MS 2183, f. 43r; dated October, 1675 on f. 43r, but November 1675 no f. 43v.

9. One area that still remains to be explored is the effect of the reform in cistercian abbeys of women.

10. The indispensable study for an understanding of this essential document is Thomas Nyguên-Dình-Tuyên, 'Histoire des controverses à Rome entre le Commune et l'Etroite Observance de 1662 à 1666' in *ASOC* 26 (1970) 3–247. The author edits the key documents, many of which are here published for the first time.

11. For a better understanding of Gervaise's 'historical method', see P. Zakar, 'Inquisitio de methodo ab abbate Gervaise in prima parte operis sui *Histoire générale de la réforme de l'Ordre de Cîteaux en France* adhibita,' in *ASOC* 20 (1964) 237–264.

12. Ger, 275–277; passage cited *in extenso* in [H. Séjalon], *Annales de L'Abbaye d'Aiguebelle* (Valence: Jules Céas et Fils, 1863) 2: 562–564; and also in A. Mensáros, *L'abbé de Rancé et la Règle bénédictine*, in *ASOC* 22 (1966) 168–169, note 39.

13. First printed in 1653, with two subsequent augmented editions appearing in 1664 and 1670. Title here reproduced from the edition of 1670—the only one currently accessible to me.

14. Edited as Document 14, pp. 101–113 of the work described above, note 10.

15. *Ibid.*, p. 31.

16. *Ibid.*

17. Lek, 184.

18. *Ibid.*

19. Among many others, see A. Presse, 'L'Abbé de Rancé a-t-il voulu fonder une nouvelle observance particulière?', in *Revue Mabillon* 21 (1931) 49–60; or V. Hermans, *Spiritualité monastique* (Rome, 1954, *pro manuscripto*) pp. 324–325.

20. Lek, 184.

21. Lek, 184–185.

22. Paris, *Du premier esprit*, p. 7 of 'Directoire Pour la Conduite & l'Instruction des Novices', added at the end of the edition of 1670 as a supplement with separate pagination.

23. *Ibid.*, p. 8.

24. *Ibid.*
25. *Ibid.*
26. Chapter 6, 'Principal Means by Which Religious Persons May Attain to the Perfection of Their State', vol. 7: 77 of the lovely (but occasionally inaccurate) english translation, *Treatise on the Sanctity and on the Duties of the Monastic State*, translated by an anonymous 'Religious of the Abbey of Melleray, la Trappe' [Father Vincent, founder of Mount Melleray, Ireland] (Dublin: Richard Grace, 1830).
27. *Ibid.*, p. 214 (translation slightly emended).
28. *Ibid.*
29. *Ibid.*, pp. 214–216.
30. Though there is an abundant literature on this particular subject, the subject still deserves further study. H. Didio, *La querelle de Mabillon et de l'abbé de Rancé* (Amiens: Imprimerie Générale, Rousseau-Leroy, 1892) is still useful; still more useful as a brief introduction to the question is F. Vandenbroucke, 'L'esprit des études monastiques d'après L'abbé de Rance', in *Coll.* 25 (1963) 224–249.
31. *Théologie de la vie monastique d'après quelques grands moines des époques moderne et contemporain.* Archives de la France monastique, vol. 50 [re-printed from *Revue Mabillon*, 1961, fascicules 204–205] (Ligugé: Abbaye Saint-Martin, 1961). Dom Hesbert's contribution, 'La Congrégation de Saint-Maur' is found on pp. 19–66.
32. Hesbert, 'La Congrégation', p. 20.
33. *Ibid.*, p. 21.
34. *Ibid.*, pp. 22–62.
35. *Ibid.*, p. 66.
36. Sou, 1 writes 'Geoffroy IV'.
37. Sou, 1–2. The ruins of les Clairets are now in the diocese of Séez.
38. See M. Aubert, *L'architecture cistercienne en France*, 2nd ed. (Paris: Vanoest, 1947) pp. 89–91.
39. Sou, 67–70. The summary early history of les Clairets in the following paragraphs is based on Sou, 23–48.
40. Sou, 41.
41. For a brief history of the institution from foundation till suppression, see Sou 42–44.
42. The office of abbess frequently remained the prerequisite of a single family for generations, with the dignity passing from aunt to niece.
43. For details on Thérèse, see Kra, 177–179.
44. The year of Thérèse's death is one of the many heretofore unknown details about Rancé's family brought to light by A. J. Krailsheimer's patient study of Monsieur de la Trappe's unedited correspondence. See Kra, 178.
45. Edited in Gon, 412–418.
46. *Ibid.*, 412.
47. A. J. Krailsheimer identifies this 'third party' as the abbot of Clairvaux; Kra, 178. The letter was printed in Let 2: 194–196, but without a date. The copy at la Trappe, as described in Tou, 265, n. 1218, is dated 26 May 1679.
48. Let 2, 194: *Je ne crois pas qu'elle ait eu cette vüé là, ni qu'elle se soit portée d'elle-mesme à une chose si contraire à son état . . .*
49. French citation in Kra, 179.
50. Canivez, *Statuta* 7, 587.
51. *Ibid.*, p. 592, n. 58.
52. *Ibid.*
53. *Ibid.*
54. *Ibid.*, p. 608, n. 170.
55. P. Buffier, *La vie de M. l'abbé du Val-Richer, Restaurateur de la Discipline regulière de ce Monastère* (Paris: Jean Boudot, 1696) p. 145.
56. Sou, 48.
57. Citations from Madame de Sévigné's *Lettres* based on the French text edited

by Gérard-Gailly, Bibliothèque de la Pléiade, 3 vols (Paris: Gallimard, 1953, 1957 and 1957). The first citation, from Letter 84, is in Vol. 1: p. 201.
  58. Vol. 2: 95 (Letter 424, to Madame de Grignan).
  59. Vol. 2: 125 (Letter 435, to Madame de Grignan).
  60. Vol. 2: 361 (Letter 531, to Madame de Grignan).
  61. Vol. 3: 817–818 (Letter 1099).
  62. Biographical notice and bibliography by A. Dimier, 'Étampes de Valençay (Françoise-Angélique), in *DHGE* 15 (1963) 1104–1105; a similar notice, also by the same author, in *Dictionnaire de biographie française* 13 (Paris: Librarie Letouzey et Ané, 1971) p. 173.
  63. M. l'abbé de Marsollier, *La vie de Dom Armand-Jean le Bouthillier de Rancé. Seconde Partie.* (Paris: Jean de Nully, 1703) p. 161; Len 2, 203 (ed. of 1715).
  64. The sequence of events, the nature of the community divisions, and other related questions could possibly be settled had I access to the article by H. Le Court, 'Un monastère au Perche à la fin du XVIIe siècle; Visite de l'abbé du Val-Richer à l'abbaye des Clairets en 1688: Quatre documents inédits', in *Archives historiques du diocèse de Chartres* 3 (1899) 389–401.
  65. Len 2: 204 (ed. of 1715).
  66. French citation in Kra, 179.
  67. Len 2: 205–206 (ed. of 1715).
  68. Len 2: 206 (ed. of 1715).
  69. Kra, 180.
  70. Len 2: 212 (ed. of 1715).
  71. See the *Instituta Generalis Capituli apud Cistercium*, xxiiii 'De forma visitationis', in P. Guignard, *Les monuments primitifs de la Règle cistercienne* (Dijon: Imprimerie Darantière, 1878), pp. 259–260. The text is found in even earlier redactions of the Order's legislation.
  72. The text was re-printed by Muguet in 1715; but it was also frequently inserted into other publications, such as the *Réglemens de l'abbaye de Notre-Dame de la Trappe en forme de constitutions avec des réflexions, et la carte de visite faite a N.-D. des Clairets, par le R.P. abbé de la Trappe* (Paris: Florentin Delaulne, 1718) (text p. 150 ff.); or the *Nouveau recueil des vies et mort de plusieurs religieux de l'abbaye de la Trappe et les réglemens d'icelle avec la carte de visite faite par le R. P. vicaire général et celle faite a l'abbaye de N.-D. des Clairets* (Trévoux, 1697), etc.
  73. Extracts cited in the description of the letter given in Tou, 376, n. 2015.
  74. Car, 21.
  75. Translation described above, Note 26; vol. 1: 136.
  76. *Ibid.*, p. 108.
  77. Car, 22.
  78. Many details in Chapter 7 'Religious of the Cistercian Order', and Chapter 9 'Women in Religion', Kra, pp. 123–151, 176–210, *passim*.
  79. Car, 23.
  80. Car, 24–25.
  81. Car, 25.
  82. Car, 26.
  83. Car, 26.
  84. Car, 27–28.
  85. Car, 31.
  86. Car, 32.
  87. Car, 32.
  88. Car, 34–35.
  89. Car, 35.
  90. Car, 35–38.
  91. Len 2, p. 212 (ed. of 1715).
  92. Car, 39–53.

93. Car, 40. The latin text reads: *Benedicite Deum caeli, et coram omnibus viventibus confitemini ei: quia fecit vobiscum misericordiam suam.*
94. Car, 40–41.
95. Car, 41.
96. Car, 43–44.
97. Car, 44–45.
98. Car, 46.
99. Car, 48–49.
100. Car, 49–50.
101. Car, 50–52.
102. Car, 53.
103. Car, 3–4.
104. Car, 5.
105. Car, 5–6.
106. See *Mémoires historiques et chronologiques sur l'Abbaye de Port-Royal-des-Champs* (Utrecht, 1758) 1: 247–249. Translation adapted from Lew, 115.
107. Ger, 565–566.
108. Lew, 118.
109. Car, 7–10.
110. Car, 10–11. On problems of religious poverty, see Lek, 17–18.
111. *Mémoires historiques* 1, pp. 333–335.
112. Car, 11.
113. Car, 12.
114. *Holy Rule*, Chapter 58, 5.
115. Guignard, *Monuments primitifs*, pp. 186–187; and in parallel versions of earlier redactions.
116. *Holy Rule*, 42 'That No One May Speak after Compline'.
117. Car, 12.
118. Car, 13.
119. Tou, 241, n. 1060, dated 28 January 1673. In an earlier letter of 22 September 1672, edited in Let 1, 231–235, Rancé expresses his enthusiasm for the work of translation still in progress: 'I praise God for his having inspired you to give us the Ascetical Treatises of Saint Basil. I've wanted them, ardently, for a long, long time, having always looked on them as sources of monastic truths and maxims.'
120. Bre 6, 230.
121. Bre 4, 477.
122. Five of Rancé's letters to Nicole are to be found in Paris, Bibliothèque nationale, MS franç. 17755. Nicole often sent the abbot presentation copies of his newest publications.
123. Gon, 187.
124. Details in an extremely long footnote, Bre 6, 233–234.
125. Bre 7, 166, Note 1.
126. Bre 10, 239.
127. Bre 12, 351–352.
128. Car, 14–15.
129. According to P. M.-L. Serrant, *L'Abbé de Rancé et Bossuet* (Paris: P. Téqui, 1903) p. 316, note, Nicole wrote two anonymous letters against Rancé's position; both letters were in the private collection of the la Trappe bibliographer, H. Tournoüer.
130. Printed in Gon, 184–188.
131. Letter 42, 3, in Y. Courtonne, *Saint Basile. Lettres* (Paris: Société d'Édition 'Les Belles Lettres', 1957) 1: 103.
132. Gon, 184.
133. *Ibid.*
134. Lew, 240–241.
135. Detailed discussion in Serrant, *L'abbe de Rance*, pp. 323–326.

136. *Conduite chrétienne adressée à son Altesse Royalle Madame de Guise* (Paris: Delaulne, 1703) pp. 84–87.

137. Letter 161 of the series of *Lettres diverses*, in *Oeuvres complètes de Bossuet* 17 (Besançon and Paris: Outhenin-Chalandre Fils) p. 252.

138. *Ibid.*

139. Excerpts quoted in Serrant, *L'abbé*, pp. 322–323.

140. Gon, 187.

141. Car, 15–16.

142. Car, 16.

143. Car, 16–17.

144. Car, 17.

145. *Ibid.*

146. Car, 18.

147. *Ibid.*

148. *Ibid.*

149. Car, 18–19.

150. Car, 19–20.

151. Len 2; 213–214 (ed. of 1715).

152. Len 2; 222–223 (ed. of 1715); Dub 2: 212–213.

153. *Rituale cisterciense*, Lib. VIII, cap. 6—pp. 333–334 of the Westmalle edition of 1949, which is essentially a re-edition of the normative edition of 1689.

154. The text of the entire exhortation is included in the *varia* assembled by le Nain for Book VIII of his biography of Rancé (1719 edition). For the *Discours que fit le révérend père à l'Abbesse des Clairets, dans la Cérémonie de sa Bénédiction*, see Len 2: 685–691.

155. Len 2, 225–226 (ed. of 1715).

156. For full title, see under list of Abbreviations, Car.

157. As cited in Tou, 376, n. 2015, in the letter to M. l'Abbé Têtu, of 26 October 1690.

158. Car, (1)-(2), *Avis du Libraire au Lecteur*.

159. As printed in Let 1: 500–504, the letter is addressed simply to an 'Archevêque de ses amis'; but, in the circumstances, the archbishop can hardly be other than the archbishop of Paris. The diocese of Chartres was a suffragan see of Paris, and les Clairets was therefore ultimately the responsibililty of the archbishop. It was moreover, a royal abbey, with abbesses nominated by the king. The introduction of the Reform into the royal abbey might well have considerable repercussions; and it was just as well that the archbishop of Paris be fully aware of the state of the union at les Clairets.

160. Madame Sévigné's *bon mot* seems to have summed up general opinion about the poor archbishop, suggests H.-H. Fisquet, *Notre-Dame de Paris*, La France Pontificale (Paris, s.d.) 428–444.

161. Let 1: 500–504.

162. Canivez, *Statuta* 7, p. 444: General Chapter of 1667, n. 11. Detailed description of the proceedings in Dub 1: 338–339.

163. Dub 1: 341.

164. Quoted *in extenso* in A.-F. Gervaise, *Histoire générale*, pp. 401–402, and repeated in Dub 1: 479.

165. *Ibid.*

166. Gervaise, *Histoire générale*, pp. 403–404. For the question of Rancé's interest in Leyme, see Kra, 185–188.

167. Gervaise, *Histoire générale*, pp. 405–407. See all Let 2: 412–418.

168. E. Albe, 'L'abbaye cistercienne de Leyme au diocèse de Cahors', in *Revue Mabillon*, 2e série, 23 (1926) 201. In the course of this long study (pp. 143–165, 192–217, 314–330), most of the material relative to Abbess Anne de la Vieuville is borrowed from Gervaise and Dubois.

169. Gon, 371–383.
170. Gon, 372–375.
171. Let 2: 90.
172. Let 2: 93–94.
173. Len 2: 310–311 (ed. of 1715).
174. Len 2: 312–313 (ed. of 1715).
175. Len 2: 313–315 (ed. of 1715).
176. Kra, 56.
177. See L. Lekai, 'The Unpublished Second Volume of Gervaise's *Histoire générale de la réforme de l'Ordre de Cîteaux en France*', in *ASOC* 17 (1961) 278–283.
178. Paris, Bibliothèque de l'Arsénal, MS 5172 Réserve, f. 104v.
179. Ger, 414–415.
180. Ger, 415.
181. Ger, 416–417.
182. Ger, 422–423.
183. Séjalon, *Nomasticon Cisterciense*, p. 326.
184. *Ibid.*, p. 375.
185. *Ibid.*, p. 479.
186. Ger, 424–427.
187. *Ibid.*, 427–429.
188. *Ibid.*, 429–430.
189. *Ibid.*, 430–432.
190. *Ibid.*, 432–435. Gervaise cites the entire letter.
191. *Ibid.*, 437–438. Gervaise cites the entire letter.
192. *Ibid.*, 559–574. Gervaise reproduces the entire *Carte de visite* as an edifying Appendix to his book.
193. Ger, 439.
194. *Ibid.*, 439–440.
195. *Ibid.*, 440.
196. *Ibid.*, 440–442.
197. *Ibid.*, 442–444.
198. *Ibid.*, 444.
199. *Ibid.*, 445–446. Gervaise cites the entire letter.
200. *Ibid.*, 447–451. Gervaise gives the complete text of his reply to the Cardinal, pp. 450–451.
201. *Ibid.*, 452–454.
202. Canivez, *Statuta* 7, p. 628: General Chapter of 1699, n. 43.
203. *Ibid.*
204. Kra, 180.
205. The letter is printed as an Appendix to M. de Maupeou, *Éloge funèbre du très-révérend père Dom Armand Jean Bouthillier de Rancé* (Paris: Muguet, 1701) 131–132. Maupeou had close contact with les Clairets through his close friend, Charles Maisne, who had supplied him with the bulk of the material used in his biography of Rancé (1702). Also, Maupeou's brother, a former Dominican before his entry at la Trappe, was for several years one of the chaplains of les Clairets. In his *Au Lecteur* preface, Maupeou states that he began his *éloge funèbre* on 11 November, at the request of Madame l'Abbesse des Clairets, and that he finished it in early December of the same year, 1700. In the initial rubric to Rancé's death-bed letter to les Clairets, Maupeou claims that the letter was written two hours before Rancé's death; and he makes the same claim towards the end of his eulogy, p. 119. Here, however, he inserts in the margin the date 26 October—which is the day preceding Rancé's death. Le Nain, who is generally reliable even for points of detail, notes that Rancé tied up the final loose ends of his correspondence sometime after Compline, 26 October (Len 2: 385–386). It seems likely, then, that the letter was dictated by the dying man in these circumstances.

206. A. I. Gontier, *Oraison funèbre de très-illustre et trés-vertueuse Dame Françoise-Angélique d'Estampes de Vallançay, abbesse des Clairets* (Paris: Louis Guérin, 1709).

207. Sou, 54–55.

208. Sou, 43–44.

209. Sou, 57–60.

210. Official memorandum signed by community and municipal officials, in Sou, 289.

211. Sou, 62–63. Statistics and diary of departees during the final months, in Sou, 289–294.

Madame de Maintenon. Photo courtesy of the Bibliothèque Nationale, Paris.

The Sun King's
Wife and the Abbess

Elizabeth Connor OCSO

'MY DEAR ABBESS, let us both think of our sanctification; you to build the world and life in the convent, I to appear before God when it will please him' [Letter 21].[1]

These lines were written by an elderly woman seated in a splendid though chilly room of the palace of Versailles. The time was early January 1707, and this greeting brought the New Year's wish of Madame de Maintenon, wife of the Sun King, Louis XIV, to Dame Marie Anne de la Viesville, young abbess of the cistercian monastery of Gomerfontaine.[2]

The Marquise de Maintenon had had an eventful life. Born Françoise d'Aubigné in 1635, she first saw the light of day in the quarters of the custodian of Niort prison, where her father was being held for conspiring with the English. Baptized a Catholic, Françoise was raised in early childhood in the Calvinist faith. It was only after her return from Martinique, where she had accompanied her father, that she embraced Catholicism again. She was still a little girl, just eleven, and about to enter the Ursulines' boarding school in Paris. When she finished her studies she went to live with her mother on Rue d'Enfer, and soon married a neighbor, the comic poet Scarron, who was infirm. The young girl from a convent school quickly became a familiar figure in literary circles, but in a few years Scarron died, leaving a twenty-five year old widow. Some time later, Françoise was engaged as governess for the children of Mme de Montespan, including the young Duke of Maine. Louis XIV took a liking to her, and in 1675 gave her the domain of Maintenon. Then, when Marie Thérèse of Austria died, Louis XIV and Madame de Maintenon were secretly married by the archbishop of Paris.

Three years later, in 1686, they undertook the establishment near Versailles of the Ecole de Saint Cyr for girls of impoverished noble families.[3] During the first years of the school the atmosphere was rather worldly, but Madame de Maintenon reacted and set about giving the girls a serious program of life. Among the pupils she preferred, one whom she looked upon and loved as a daughter, was Marie-Anne de la Viesville, daughter of an old family of Flanders and a relative of Cardinal de Noailles.[4] Marie-Anne was active, intelligent, and had the incomparable strength characteristic of persons who patiently and slowly direct all their efforts toward a single goal.[5] After school, she entered the cistercian monastery of Argensole in the diocese of Soissons, and there she lived the simple life of a young nun seeking God.

By 1705 Madame de Maintenon was seeking a place to set up a 'branch' of Saint Cyr for the education not only of poor girls of the nobility, but for daughters of the bourgeoisie. As it happened, Gomerfontaine was without an abbess at the time, and it was toward this cistercian abbey that she turned her interest. The abbey of Gomerfontaine was situated northwest of Paris, in the part of the diocese of Beauvais which had in the past belonged to Rouen. In a pleasant valley, midway between the castles at Trie and Chaumont, it had sheltered the cistercian life since the thirteenth century, and would continue to do so until the French Revolution.

Data about the origin of Gomerfontaine is meager. The nuns claimed Henry I as the founder of the monastery,[6] which enjoyed the status of a royal abbey and received official approval as such in 1256 from Louis IX.[7] The first document mentioning Gomerfontaine, however, is a charter dating from 1209, by which 'Hugh Lord of Chaumont, and Petronilla his wife, ceded to the religious of the Order of Cîteaux' various donations, among which were a house and garden at Gomerfontaine and the revenues from eels from the ponds of Gomerfontaine and Natinville. By reason of their generosity, the lords of Chaumont subsequently claimed rights as founders of the monastery and were often a source of considerable trouble to the nuns. In time, the lords of Trie-Château also made claims against the nuns. Their pleasant valley sometimes became the ground for a tug of war between their neighbors.

Though little is known of the early days of the abbey, two important thirteenth-century dates are certain: 1) In 1226 the monastery, hitherto a priory, was erected into an abbey. Guillemette, the first abbess, died in 1248. 2) On 13 October 1266, the abbey church was consecrated, in the tenure of the fourth abbess, Agnes. The history of the monastery from the thirteenth to eighteenth century followed the vicissitudes of the times and reveals a pattern similar to that of numerous other monasteries of nuns.

Although the monastery prospered during the thirteenth and fourteenth centuries, it was not outstanding at the time either for its material importance or for its abbesses, who were selected by the king from the aristocracy. Gomerfontaine was simply a fervent community living the Rule of Saint Benedict in the cistercian way. Like other monasteries, the abbey suffered during the Hundred Years' War and the Wars of Religion which brought in their wake a decline of vocations and dearth of donations. In 1434 the monastery was pillaged by the English. During these hard times the nuns eked out a meager and precarious existence by the work of their hands. Reform entered in the seventeenth century as it did in many other monasteries. For a century and a year Gomerfontaine would have at its head daughters of the House of Médavy.[8] The first, Judith de Rouxel de Médavy (1604–1614), administratrix, began restoration of the monastery which since the wars had been in a stage of neglect. The second, Abbess Madeleine (1614–1638), known as the 'second foundress', continued the material restoration and introduced a spiritual reform. It was then that Gomerfontaine entered the Strict Observance.[9] The third superior of the Médavy family was Marguerite (1638–1705), who had perhaps only one fault; she lived to be more than a hundred years old. In the early years of her government she continued the work of reform begun by her predecessor, but afflicted by senility in old age she could no longer fulfill her duties and the house fell into a period of monastic decadence. The buildings were in ruins, the fields overgrown; the abbey had once again lost its splendor. When Dame Marguerite died, in 1705, Madame de Maintenon looked upon Gomerfontaine as a means of realizing her hopes for another school.

As abbess for the monastery she selected the former Saint Cyr pupil, Marie-Anne de la Viesville, whom the king summoned from Argensole at her request and installed at the head of the ancient abbey. Madame de Maintenon was to assume a very active role in the formation of the new abbess, aiding her in numerous ways both in the education of the girls she entrusted to her and, more important, in the spiritual and temporal reform of her monastery.

Thanks to a series of thirty-nine letters written by Madame de Maintenon from September 1705 until April 1713 (to which have been added a letter to Mlle d'Aumale [Letter 26], one from the community [Letter 31], and one from the young abbess [Letter 42] to their benefactress), we are able to see how this reform was carried out. The letters show that Madame de Maintenon was willing to be all things to her protégée: advisor to the abbess, mother, spiritual directress, financial aid, doctor, and confessor (!), as circumstances might require [Letters 8, 18, 26, 25]. 'There is no role I would not willingly fulfill toward you, if it could be useful to you' [Letter 25). The advice found in the letters could as easily serve as a directory for a young abbess today, as for one of the eighteenth century. Almost every aspect of the monastic life is touched upon. Madame de Maintenon's extraordinary good sense, human warmth, and insightful knowledge of human nature are joined to a down-to-earth approach to life and, at the same time, to a high spiritual ideal. One can well understand, when reading these letters, why Louis XIV consulted her on all important matters, frequently asking: 'What does Your Solidity think about this?'

Although our attention in this article is focused principally on the monastic life of the Cistercians of Gomerfontaine, a few words should be said about the girls sent to the abbey from Saint Cyr. The custom of taking girls into monasteries to educate them, as a means of supplementing the revenues of the community, was quite common. The board Madame de Maintenon would pay for the pupils would be welcome. Six girls were sent to Gomerfontaine to begin with, then in December 1705, three others arrived [Letter 10]. Still more were foreseen for following years. 'Take good care of the girls I send you. Be a mother to them, even though you yourself are young' [Letter 1], the Lady Abbess was told.

Madame de Maintenon also promised to send to Gomerfontaine 'any girls here [at Saint Cyr] who are ready to become religious. I will pay their board during the time of their novitiate . . .[10] but perhaps you think it would be best to see your community about this before having anyone come' [Letter 1]. Assurance was given that she was not going to fill Gomerfontaine with cast-offs from Saint Cyr: 'You will never find yourself at a disadvantage because of the girls I will give you, because I will send them back here when they do not please you' [Letter 1]. Better a half-empty house than dangerous subjects.

Not least among the persons to be sent from Saint Cyr was Mlle d'Aumale, one of Madame de Maintenon's most trusted aids, who was to be an assistant to the Lady Abbess. 'Aumale', as she was called, lent a hand everywhere: working in the fields, helping the young abbess build beds for the boarders, and, as the abbess's secretary, seeing to the delicate task of correcting her spelling, which Madame de Maintenon found very poor. It was principally for this, it seems, that 'Aumale' was sent to Gomerfontaine. The abbess grew to count on her to such an extent that the directress of Saint Cyr was obliged to ask repeatedly, and even finally to insist, that she return.

To what extent did Madame de Maintenon see Gomerfontaine as a second Saint Cyr? References throughout the letters show that her desire to see her own work propagated was tempered by respect for the type of life at Gomerfontaine, and also by her innate sense of reality. On the one hand, she says, 'I would give my blood to communicate the Saint Cyr education to all religious houses' [Letter 40], and 'We are forming Gomerfontaine into a second Saint Cyr, and perhaps something better' [Letter 37]. On the other hand, she admits: 'you cannot do in your monastery what is done at Saint Cyr . . . but you can take what is essential' [Letter 41]. 'You have your constitutions, your rules, and your customs, from which you must not depart. Do not put the spirit of Saint Cyr into your novitiate. Its obligations are completely different' [Letter 5]. 'Each house has its own way of doing things' [Letter 3]. This advice was given soon after Dame Marie-Anne became abbess, and before the year was out Madame de Maintenon stressed once again: 'Profit from my experience, and do not let yourself follow all the tastes of Saint Cyr' [Letter 12].

One aspect of life at Saint Cyr which she could, and would, recommend, and which Dame de la Viesville could adopt without fear was this one: 'The maxim of Saint Cyr is always to begin with gentleness' [Letter 9]. One other point was made very clear: the king was not to be involved in any of the activities at Gomerfontaine. 'I do not want your name heard in the court' [Letter 23].

Advice to the Abbess

In the eighteenth century, as today, abbesses often found themselves overburdened by their daily tasks. Although Madame de Maintenon was adamant in her insistence on devotion to duty, her maternal solicitude pin-pointed dangers and indicated a way to maintain the endurance needed for long term governing. Dame Marie-Anne had all the talents necessary for doing a great deal of good; all she needed was a little experience [Letter 30]. She was to put her resolutions into practice: 'Work with moderation so that you will be able to work for a long time [Letter 4]. 'If our days were two hours longer, we could not make them yet still longer' [Letter 4]. Then, as if to temper her reproach: 'It seems to me that in spite of your duties you *do* take a little diversion, and you do very well to do so' [Letter 9].

During her second year as abbess, Dame de la Viesville fell ill. With this illness came discouragement, and the young abbess was thinking of ceding her place to someone else. In a letter to Mlle d'Aumale, the directress of Saint Cyr wrote:

> I am quite discontented with our abbess, in learning that she has been sick so long, and that she is tired of being abbess. . . . Should a person become tired when she has just begun to run? What will it be like after I die? Rouse her courage . . . this despondency is a consequence of her illness [Letter 26].

And to the abbess there is some straight-from-the-shoulder advice, once the worst of the illness was past:

> You caused me anxiety, my dear daughter, and thank God for having preserved you. It seems to me that you are not yet good enough to die, and you need to have many more trials and accomplish a greater abundance of good works. Profit from your own experience, since you did not profit from mine. Your vivacity brought you to death's door . . . Monsieur Fagon [the doctor] prescribes above all, tranquility. . . . It is absolutely necessary for your soul and for your body' [Letter 28]. In God's name, Lady Abbess, do not be precipitous. Here [at Saint Cyr] I have seen girls of such character. They wear everyone out, and they also wear themselves out. I am lively and active by nature. I have had a great many troubles in this house, and I have made much more progress since I have become more moderate. You have a good mind; your intentions are upright; believe in my experience and friendship. Do not rush, and do not rush others. Relax a bit, have some diversion, and work joyfully. Little by little everything will work out [Letter 27].

After chiding her for having tried to do in two years what had taken twenty-three to do at Saint Cyr, Madame de Maintenon turned to the serious question of the temptation to resign.

> I am not persuaded that you should leave your post. I look upon this proposal as something that should be driven out of your mind. Did you think that you were going to occupy a post that would give you pleasure? Consider this: at the age of twenty-eight you took over the government of a convent in both spiritual and temporal ruin, filled with women used to doing their own will. They esteem you, they respect you, and they let you do what you

want. This is good fortune that you could hardly have expected [Letter 28].

But she does not avoid the important question of the possibility of her resigning in the future: 'I have a very good opinion of Sister Champlebon. I believe that you have, in her, a good subject. Form her to succeed you, and after that we will permit you to become a simple religious again' [Letter 28].

Spiritual Government

Madame de Maintenon's advice about spiritual government of the monastery is of value for all times. The happiness of both the abbess and the community depends on solid and upright piety, and only submission can give piety this character of authenticity. 'No one will ever obey you unless you obey' [Letter 37]. Discharge of duty, straightforwardness, and rectitude were her bywords [Letters 7, 5, 19]. The abbess is to have no illusions, anyone in a position of authority will be criticized. Saint Benedict knew this well. 'Scorn murmuring. Has anyone ever governed with everyone's approval? To get angry with those who find fault with you is the best way to increase their numbers' [Letter 34].

> Do your duty and do not pay attention to the stories one tells you! Oh, who is not subject to calumny? Have you never heard the king and his ministers blamed? And if you knew what they say about me! If I were to show you all that has been written about me [Letter 27].
>
> Go straight ahead, my dear Abbess . . . and then suffer in peace the evil which will be said of you. The truth will not be stifled for long [Letter 19].

Two letters deal at length with the qualities of disinterestedness and dependence on God so important for an abbess:

> What do you mean to say, my dear daughter, when you complain about yours sisters' ingratitude? Is it that when you work for them you work for their love? You will never be satisfied if you do not rise above this. . . . In your letters . . . I have more than once read: 'She is not on my side'. A superior having a 'side'! Everyone should be the same to you. Are you not the mother of them all? Should any of them notice that one sister is dearer to you than another? [Letter 35].
>
> . . . God destines another reward for you. Work for him; work with him, work as he does. If you work for him, you will be

indifferent to the approval of your nuns; if you work with him, you will have a center of peace which cannot be troubled by any disappointment; if you work as he does, it will be with strength and mildness, without haste, without anxiety, and without grief [Letter 27].

Summarizing her thought tersely, she wrote:

A man once told me that our griefs come more from the intrigues in which we become involved than from our faults. And since that time I have seen a hundred times that he spoke the truth. Be vigilant and patient . . . nothing is more important for someone who governs, or for someone who obeys [Letter 35].

Not wanting to impose her own ways on Dame Marie-Anne, [Letter 11] Madame de Maintenon suggested that she consult other people about the way to govern; the abbess of Jouarre, for example:

I found her to be simple, humble, and zealous. She told me that her time does not belong to her, and that there is no moment during the day when her nuns cannot speak to her if they wish. She said that it is a great mortification to see her own will upset so often, but that she believes that it is her duty. . . . There you are, my dear daughter, that is how I would like you to be . . . and you will be, if you yourself want it strongly enough [Letter 30].

Spiritual authors were likewise recommended for guidance in governing, notably Saint Francis de Sales. The directress of Saint Cyr promised to send the Lady Abbess his works, on condition that she promise 'to accept his spirit, and not be put off by his old-fashioned language [Letter 20]. Dame de la Viesville was apparently more proficient in reading that in writing, unless of course Mlle d'Aumale's dexterous tutoring had begun to produce its effect. This, however, is not certain. There is a dry remark at the end of the letter of 28 November 1705: 'I see nothing to reply to your letter of the 24th, except that your spelling is better . . . but not as good as you think it is' [Letter 9].

Running like a leitmotif through a piece of music, this fundamental counsel keeps recurring: 'Make yourself loved, and you will have done everything' [Letter 2]. This is the only way to accomplish good in the community, and what cannot be done by mildness cannot be done by harshness [Letter 24]. It is the way to overcome lack of sincerity, which is a fault peculiar to convents [Letter 21], and to establish 'the spirit of liberty: this spirit of children which puts to flight that of hirelings who always want to hide everything from their master' [Letter 32].[11] To correct a certain lack of order which she found at Gomerfontaine, she recommends 'extreme regularity' [Letter 19], and if the abbess wants to instill rectitude, the nuns should be able to see it in their abbess' conduct: 'Never let them see the wretched craftiness which some religious take for cleverness' [Letter 29]. Still, she adds, it is not improper for a superior to be a 'little suspicious, provided that she is conscious that she is, and that others never notice it' [Letter 19].

As Mme de Maintenon mentioned in describing the abbess of Jouarre, the availability of the abbess is important for the spiritual atmosphere of the community. This availability concerns both time and attitude. She must be close to her nuns. 'Take away those airs of grandeur which cause everyone to make fun of abbesses. There is one abbess who wanted to have the throne of the king of Siam, because none of the thrones of kings and bishops she had seen were high enough for her! This is not a story I have made up—I was told her name' [Letter 24]. If the nuns are to be of use to the abbess, she needs to instruct them in their duties, not by long, vague, and useless sermons, but by telling them things with practical details [Letter 37]. Another way of gaining their aid and support is to consult them in council, as the rule prescribes.

> Do you not have a council for the little matters of the house? Always reserve the liberty of deciding to yourself. Even less capable sisters, however, may open the way to good advice. When people help each other to see clearly, those with whom one has deliberated feel committed to give their support to what one wishes to do. But the council should help you, and not constrain you [Letter 4].

Could there be any more timely advice?

Direction and correction

The need for nuns to have utmost liberty in their personal conversations with the abbess is brought out forcefully. Great discretion is needed on the part of the abbess with regard to their interior life. Their confidence will increase in proportion to the feeling of liberty they have when speaking with her:

> You will lead them to God only by the confidence they have in you. And you will establish regularity in your house only by the friendship you have for them. How can that be if you do not know them? How can you get to know them if you never see

them alone? How will they love you if you do not persuade them
that you love them? How will you persuade them of this if you do
not console the afflicted, or have compassion for the nun who is
ill; if you do not instruct the scrupulous, if you do not give some
joy to someone who is melancholy? All that seems difficult to you,
and you are right. But it is the only reliable way of governing. I
agree with you that it is a very hard practice. You have to do a
great deal of talking which seems useless, you have to put up with
capriciousness, grossness, and the guile of certain persons . . . and
you have to do all that with mildness [Letter 21].

As we can see, Madame de Maintenon did not paint a gilded
picture of the abbatial task. She is demanding, but through this *ascesis*
of direction the abbess will eventually be able to see that her labors
bear fruit. But patience is necessary, and when she glimpses even
the slightest progress in her nuns she should rejoice. It is already a
great deal that they do not oppose the good she desires for them
[Letter 7]. While waiting for further progress, she can help them by
praying for them, providing them a good example, and being kind
to them. After that, she should expect the rest from God [Letter 9].

In spite of this painstaking work of guidance, there are inevitably
times when correction is needed. Public correction is discouraged
[Letter 34], and if faults occur which must be mentioned openly
in chapter, 'the sister should be prepared ahead of time'. Serious
reprimands are better *tête-à-tête*. 'The goal should be to correct,
and one does not correct when one embitters another person. A
reprimand is vexatious enough in itself, without the abbess adding
embarrassment for the sister' [Letter 32].

Yet reprimand she must, if she is to help the sisters to overcome
their faults and make progress in the spiritual life.

Tell them frankly what you find wrong in them, beginning with
what is most urgent. Do not tell them everything at once, and
do not seem astonished by their failings. Show them friendliness,
persuade them that you must answer to God for their souls, that
it pains you to correct them, that you want to help them save
their souls. And say a hundred nice, caressing things to them . . .
It is not authority which touches the heart, and the gentleness
of a friend is not incompatible with the firmness of an abbess
[Letter 20].

You must see the sister's virtues as well as her faults [Letter 32],
and you must know the character of the person you wish to
reprimand [Letter 9].

The young abbess must have replied: Fine! But when my efforts bear no fruit? What then? The answer came straight as an arrow: 'You say that you have spoken to the religious in question, and that you will speak to her again. You will be fortunate if you can win her over after speaking to her twenty times. Arm yourself with patience if you want to do God's work [Letter 21]'.

Patience, patience, always patience!

It is not only the sisters who commit faults seen by the whole community; the abbess can do so too, and Dame Marie-Anne failed in some way which she felt called for public satisfaction. When Madame de Maintenon learned of this she commended her for the 'heroic' act of humbling herself before her daughters, and encouraged her by assuring her that nothing was more likely to draw blessings upon her work. But with her laconic and practical good sense she added: 'You must not repeat that type of thing very often; you would cheapen authority. One must keep these acts of humility for times of great need' [Letter 32].

Madame de Maintenon herself did not hesitate to reprimand the young abbess when she felt she should. Among the postulants who had come from Saint Cyr, Dame Marie-Anne found one more pleasing than the others, to the point that the girl came to be known as her 'little favorite'. This situation evoked a severe reproach. 'Forget that title if you want to make her a good Bernardine' [Letter 37]. 'Bring her up like the others. For a girl to be the favorite or the niece of the abbess makes for the worst possible type of formation' [Letter 24].

Recreation

Madame de Maintenon considered daily recreation one of the principal ways of maintaining the good spirit and unity of a community. In the houses of the Strict Observance during the eighteenth century recreation did have a place,[12] but whether it was among the customs of Gomerfontaine when Dame de la Viesville took over is not certain. The letter of 23 February 1706, would lead us to suppose that it was not:

> When I spoke to you about recreations, I thought that your daughters had them in common. You must not force them to come, but realize that they are an excellent thing. . . . It is there that an abbess can gain the sisters' love by her good-naturedness. It is there that she can get to know them, and it is there that she can make them happy. There she can casually mention in

> passing certain maxims which make more impression on them than
> what is said in prepared exhortations . . . [Recreations] do away
> with partialities, individual conversations, dangerous sharing of
> confidences of the heart, and—still more dangerous—murmuring.
> When the sisters can let their hair down for two hours a day they
> are not eager to seek for other diversion. And how many virtues
> does a superior not practise there . . . ? [Letter 17; see also Letters
> 2, 29, 34].

Here, as occasionally elsewhere in the letters, we find views which
do not harmonize completely with cistercian doctrine and spirituality. The teaching of Aelred of Rievaulx on spiritual friendship, for
example, is too well-known for us to deny that sharing confidences
of the heart can be beneficial, or that individual conversations of a
serious nature may be encouraged. Madame de Maintenon's insight,
that the sisters would have less inclination to indulge in unprofitable
chatting if they could speak freely and informally at fixed times
however, retains a certain value.

Observances

Numerous references are made in the letters to the manner in
which various monastic observances should be lived. Only a rapid
summary will be given here. The accent is on duty, just as it was in
the advice given to the abbess for accomplishing her charge. The
reader will perhaps find this overemphasized at times.

Prayer and Divine Office

> It is not the taste which one finds in devotion which constitutes
> its solidity [Letter 17].
> We would all be very unfortunate if our salvation depended on
> emotional fervor, which does not depend on us. . . . As long as you
> do what you should, you will certainly be very pleasing to God
> [Letter 17].

Here Madame de Maintenon is in perfect harmony with cistercian
spirituality. The teaching of Saint Bernard and Saint Aelred is faithfully reflected in her viewpoint: love of God consists in conformity
of one's will to God's will. Purity of intention, services of others,
walking in God's presence—these are the criteria for pure prayer
[Letter 22].
She is also in accord with the Cistercian Fathers[13] when she insists
that participation at the Divine Office is not a question of emotional

enjoyment. If a sister has a real reason for missing Office, it is one thing, but she 'must not push it too far . . . because we are dealing with a Master whom one cannot trick' [Letter 38]. Fully aware that she may be considered inhuman, she caricatures those nuns who lose their voice when it is time to sing the Office, but marvelously find it again when they can sing songs they like [Letter 7].

Spiritual Reading

There is no mention of real *lectio divina* in the letters, at least not as we understand it today. Madame de Maintenon's attitude reflects a rather general distrust of 'book learning' for women, and can be traced no doubt to her experience in the court of Louis XIV. Then too, Molière's *Les Femmes Savantes* and *Les précieuses ridicules* had not faded from memory. As a woman of her times Madame de Maintenon thought that the New Testament, the *Imitation of Christ*, Grenada, Rodriguez, Saint Francis de Sales, and the books of the Order sufficed for the nuns' sanctification [Letter 12]. 'Let [the nuns] read little, and speak little about what they have noted. My dear abbess, do not make of your daughters people who give spiritual discourses. Nothing is more dangerous and more unprofitable' [Letter 22].

Work

Though there are numerous passages in the letters concerning the precarious economic situation at Gomerfontaine (as we shall see in more detail later), references to the actual work of the sisters are rather rare. The practical necessity of work was, of course, recognized. To make ends meet the sisters had to make their own candles and weave their own habits [Letter 4]. They also made garments to sell, and to help the community organize its workshop Madame de Maintenon furnished part of the funds needed for the purchase of looms [Letter 23]. The work, however, was time consuming. Some years later, in 1732, steps were taken to introduce new work methods at Gomerfontaine. A mechanical loom was procured for making the stockings sold by the community, and one of the sisters, Apollina Quentier, went out to serve an apprenticeship to learn how to operate this loom. With this mechanization, one sister could do the work of several, but the increase in production did not come up to the nuns' hopes.[14]

In May 1737, Gomerfontaine found itself in trouble because of its weaving. The inspectors from the Drapers' and Serge makers'

Guild at Beauvais found a piece of material made at the abbey
and registered a complaint that it did not bear the mark of the
place where it had been made. Dame Marie-Anne, who already
had obtained authorization to make the sisters' tunics, was obliged
to obtain a new permit, and all garments were henceforth to be
marked 'Abbaye de Gomerfontaine'. Once this was taken care of,
the nuns worked 'without fear of impinging on the serge Makers'
Guild, which was just as suspicious as all the other trade guilds of
the *Ancien Régime*'.[15]
In summer the sisters, dressed in these rough, heavy, homemade
garments, worked in the vegetable gardens and in the fields. 'On the
golden plains of Vexin, beneath the blazing summer sun, girls from
the noble families of Gouffier, Ségur, Sarcus, and d'Espies could be
seen gathering up the hay and bringing it into the barns'.[16]

Poverty—Simplicity—Fasting

These three aspects of monastic life must be taken together. The
advice given by Madame de Maintenon for putting them into practice, while varying according to varied circumstances, shows that
she was not intransigent, especially when the good of persons was
at stake. There are many ways of practising poverty, and often
these are ways that a person does not choose herself. When choice
was possible for Dame Marie-Anne, as for example when she was
restoring her monastery, poverty was seen as an aspect of cistercian
simplicity:

> Whether in the church, in the cloisters, in the gardens, in the
> matter of furnishings, everything should have the aspect of the
> poverty which you have vowed. Is God honored by a little more
> or a little less gilt, or by beautiful vestments? All that is needed
> is that everything everywhere should be clean. . . . Simplicity, and
> not magnificence, honors God. I have seen convents where half
> the sisters pray only for fifteen minutes on the great feastdays of
> the year. They adorn the altar and then forget God [Letter 29].

The fact that the community included noble girls whose families
possessed great wealth, and others whose families had become poor
after having possessed great wealth, prompted special remarks:

> Is it possible that girls who have enough courage to sacrifice
> themselves by the vows of religion do not have the courage to
> admit before the world that they are poor [Letter 20]?

Is it fitting for religious to be ashamed when their relatives do not have nice clothes, or to draw glory from it when their families come to see them stylishly dressed [Letter 20]?

In the years when these letters were written, a time of relative well-being for the monastery, Madame de Maintenon tended toward indulgence with regard to the sisters' diet. It was to be in keeping with the health and strength of the community, taking into account age and even 'former habits'[Letter 7]. This advice was followed by a word of wisdom:

> They say that the sisters can live on so little. But you must consider that the rule has already taken away from them what is superfluous, and has reduced them to what is necessary. So if you take away still more, after what has already been taken away, they do not have enough to live [Letter 23].

When the economic state of the community had deteriorated because of the ravages of wars and extremely bad weather during several successive summers, special counsel was called for:

> I did not think that foodstuffs were so expensive. Here, people complain only about the cost of bread. . . . Your cows must be very useful to you. Porridge, rice, butter make a good meal. I cannot lament about your not having wine to drink, especially since you have such abundant dairy products. . . . I am in my seventy-second year and I drink nothing but water. Rice has been promised to me. If it arrives, I will send you some [Letter 37].

In this same letter, she looked beyond the material difficulties and urged the abbess to use them for the deepening of the community's spiritual life:

> It is at present [when you lack food] that the religious will be truly poor. Formerly they made poverty consist of having nothing of their own, but they also lacked nothing. That poverty was tolerable, but I doubt that it was real. To be poor, one must suffer something, and now you are in such a position. May God grant you to suffer with the patience and resignation which will make all of you saints [Letter 37].

Enclosure—Silence—Solitude

Madame de Maintenon considered convent parlors a sort of evil. They were, at least, to be avoided as much as possible, and for this reason she told Dame Marie-Anne 'to make them as unpleasant as you can' [Letter 20]. The best way to keep the sisters out of the parlors, and consequently to avoid scandal, was to keep them occupied [Letter 4]. Letters which come into the house or go out were also proposed as a subject for vigilance [Letter 19], because in her opinion silence concerned not only conversations but also correspondence [Letter 9]. 'When there is free access to the parlors, and when letters are permitted, there is as much intrigue [in a monastery] as at Versailles' [Letter 40]. Since enclosure and silence are points of rule, Madame de Maintenon felt that surveillance over them was perfectly normal. But to prevent its becoming a source of bad feelings it should be practised quite openly, and never behind the sisters' backs [Letter 40]. Particular emphasis was placed on curtailing visits with men. Here again, Madame de Maintenon was no doubt giving Dame Marie-Anne the benefit of her experience in the king's court:

> You cannot exercise too much vigilance over your community. I have always seen that the most efficacious way of establishing and maintaining life according to the Rule is entire separation from men, no matter who they are: monks, clergymen, domestics, peasants, young men, old men, handsome men, ugly men, masters or disciples, all of them can be dangerous, and you cannot take too many precautions [Letter 19].
>
> When a girl seeks to please men, one cannot do too much to deprive her of occasions of seeing them. It is only complete separation which can cure this illness [Letter 20].

Amusing as we may find these observations, we must remember that in the eighteenth century some noble girls entered convents unwillingly, with no desire to forego masculine company. Such counsels, therefore, were not excessive.

Recruitment and Formation

When Dame de la Viesville entered the office of abbess, it would seem she intended to act as novice mistress as well [Letter 5], but by December 1705, after several months in charge, she named a nun for this important post. As usual, Madame de Maintenon had advice to give, both about receiving girls into the novitiate and forming them there. 'Your novitiate is your real resource' [Letter 5], and vocations should not be rushed [Letter 18]; no one should be forced [Letter 18], and never under any pretext should mediocre subjects be accepted [Letter 5]. What would she mean by a 'good subject'?

> A girl who is truly given to God, who wishes to devote herself
> to the rule, who renounces the world, who does not keep up
> contacts with it, who loves to obey; a girl who is good-natured and
> has an uncomplicated conscience, who is joyful and courageous
> [Letter 5].

There is a severe warning against accepting girls for purely human
motives: 'Woe to your religious when flesh and blood will make
them accept poor subjects!' [Letter 8]. And, 'I would be very happy
if you had a good organist, but I would prefer that you have no
organ at all than to have a poor subject in your house' [Letter 7].

Once accepted, novices should be introduced to the austerities of
the *Rule* gradually [Letter 5], and should not be allowed too much
contact with the senior nuns [Letter 5]. Novices must be patiently
tolerated during their formation: they laugh at the wrong times and
cry at the wrong times . . . and they need cheer in their young lives
[Letter 35]. Because forming novices is an arduous task, the abbess
should give her full support to the novice mistress and train her to
give herself to the life of the novitiate [Letter 11].

Material Administration

During Dame de la Viesville's entire abbacy, the temporal administration of the monastery was difficult. Since she took over the government of the abbey at a young age, she needed help, and the years
which followed gave proof that she had learned her lessons well.
Instruction began early. In November 1705 (shortly after Dame
Marie-Anne's installation as abbess), Madame de Maintenon wrote:

> Why do you not tell me positively: 'I received the 1670 pounds',
> or 'I have not received them'? Are you a Norman? Don't you
> know how to say 'yes' or 'no'? As for me, I am precise, and I want
> to know the state of my accounts. . . . You will always be obliged
> to concern yourself with temporal affairs . . . [Letter 8].

And understanding quite well that nuns need help from competent
persons outside the community, she counselled: 'Choose someone
from the bourgeoisie of Gisors, a man of confidence. People of
high station are usually less useful' [Letter 6]. Shortly afterwards,
she added: 'Be punctual, I beg you, and clear and precise in your
business affairs . . . I like order. All details should be written in a
book. Let us try to restore your house . . .' [Letter 10]. As we shall
see further on, the accounts of Gomerfontaine were, in fact, kept
with exactitude during the time of Dame de la Viesville. Even the

greatest care, however, was of no avail when calamity struck, and at such times Madame de Maintenon's fundamental attitude of faith in God appeared clearly:

> I am very edified at the way you have accepted this hailstorm which has ruined you. All you have done until now to establish your temporal situation is not as meritorious as the submission with which you have accepted this little setback. Self-love often slips into most of our actions. But there is hardly any of it in our acts of resignation [Letter 28].

No doubt remains that the spiritual aspect of the nuns' life is always what is most important. Administrative concerns should always be subordinate to it, even in little things: 'I would like you to be less afflicted by an expenditure than by an irregularity' [Letter 35].

Not only by advice did Madame de Maintenon help Gomerfontaine's abbess. From the very beginning she did her best to obtain funds for the monastery from her friends [Letter 4]. In 1708, when famine had taken a high toll in the district, she did her utmost to come to the nuns' aid. But at the time she was unable to do as much as she would have liked, because everyone was suffering the same calamity [Letter 33]. It was also understood, of course, that she would pay fees for all the girls she sent to Gomerfontaine.

The Order of Cîteaux

We might wish that there were more references to the Order of Cîteaux in the letters, so that we might learn something of Gomerfontaine's relationship with the Order and with its Father Immediate, the abbot of Lieu-Dieu. Surprisingly, very little is said about Cîteaux, and what is said is so fragmentary that we cannot grasp entirely the situations referred to:

Letter 1 speaks of Dame de la Viesville's abbatial blessing. Cardinal de Noailles had explained to Madame de Maintenon that it was not customary for the abbess to receive a cross at the time of her blessing, but since the nuns of Gomerfontaine seemed to have their hearts set on this, she could write to the abbot of Cîteaux, 'who had already shown great courtesy to [her] in a previous letter' [Letter 1].

In June 1707, some doubt seems to have arisen about the validity of Soeur de Champlebon's profession. The circumstances are not explained, but evidently Dame de la Viesville was quite upset, for she was told 'not to revolt against [her] superior' [Letter 28].

At one time there seems to have been some trouble about jurisdiction.[17] Madame de Maintenon admitted that her own personal preference was that monasteries depend on bishops rather than on religious superiors: 'It seems to me that houses are better governed that way' [Letter 28]. She definitely did not want to become implicated with the Order of Cîteaux. 'You can use my name for your own use, but not to get me involved in problems with the Order of Saint Bernard' [Letter 34]. Yet in a letter dated just a month and a half later, she informed the abbess that she had written to the abbot of Cîteaux about a nun who was causing some difficulty at Gomerfontaine [Letter 35].

One last reference to the Order is found in Letter 37. There is an allusion to Bermont, a monastery which was at the time without an abbess. The abbot of Cîteaux had asked Madame de Maintenon to find a good nun for the post, presuming that the king would accept anyone she proposed. Madame de Maintenon acquiesced, but told Dame Anne-Marie: 'Truthfully, the best ones are always the least known' [Letter 37].

The Confessor

These pages would be incomplete without some mention of the regular confessor, so important in monasteries of nuns, and all the more so because 'there is nothing so difficult as to find as a confessor who is exactly the kind we want' [Letter 6]. Her own experience at Saint Cyr had led Madame de Maintenon to value a confessor's piety more than his intelligence [Letter 6], and to realize that, for religious, confessors who are religious are preferable to secular priests [Letter 33]. 'But monk confessors are not easy to find, because good monks do not like to leave their cells' [Letter 7]. At Saint Cyr, the house had been so ill served by secular priests—confessors that she had thought it would be necessary to close the school. It had reached its present quality only since 'we have confessors from communities, who always refer to the constitutions, the rules, and the superior; who limit themselves to absolving sins; and who never mix in the government of the house either in a general way or as regards particular matters' [Letter 23; cf. Letter 21].

During the period 1705–1713, two or three confessors seem to have succeeded one another at Gomerfontaine. It would appear from Letter 1 that Madame de Maintenon sent the nuns a certain Abbé de la Charmoisé. By Letters 21 and 23 one has the impression that there is a new confessor: 'I have just come from a long conversation with your holy confessor, and am very pleased with him. He was not at all shy with me, nor I with him, and I assure you that we got acquainted with one another'. Madame de Maintenon had spoken with him about the primordial necessity of accord between the abbess and the confessor. 'Without it, things cannot go well in a house' [Letter 23]. The situation at Gomerfontaine does not appear clearly through the letters, but one has the impression that this confessor did not give the satisfaction expected. Nevertheless, Dame de la Viesville was urged to 'have more confidence [in your confessor] and give him the liberty, in your confessions, of pointing out your faults to you and giving you some advice. It is very dry, and does not exercise humility, when we simply recite our faults and receive absolution' [Letter 30], and 'it is very difficult to avoid pride when one commands all the time and never obeys' [Letter 37]. If the confessor is a man of experience, the abbess may also find it profitable to ask his advice, occasionally and in a general way, on her manner of governing the monastery [Letter 23]. As for the sisters' confessions, they should be as brief as possible, so as not to make others wait their turn. 'If someone has something a bit long to discuss, she should put it off until another day' [Letter 23].

Toward the end of 1707, Madame de Maintenon took steps to have a certain Monsieur de Treilh sent to Gomerfontaine, apparently as an occasional confessor [Letter 30]. For this, authorization of the bishop of Rouen was necessary [Letter 36]. The community appears to have been very happy with Monsieur de Treilh, and Letter 31 is a collective thank-you note from the nuns of Gomerfontaine to Madame de Maintenon for having sent him their way. A regular confessor seems to have remained, and in Letter 40 we find this terse remark, so characteristic of Madame de Maintenon: 'I saw your confessor and I was very edified. The judgment I might make about his merit would be imprudent, however, because no one can judge a man at first sight'.[18]

In December 1709, Madame de Maintenon confided to Dame Marie-Anne that she would have to learn to get along without her [Letter 38]. Her strength was failing and her health was not good. She felt that her days were drawing to a close, and sensed that 'it is time for me to write my will' [Letter 38]. In her last letter, there is the simple remark in which all her affection for the abbess can be felt: 'I would like to see you once more before I die' [Letter 41]. Actually, Madame de Maintenon was not yet ready to receive her reward, and would live on until 1719. When the extant correspondence ended, the abbess of Gomerfontaine to whom she had devoted so much of her time and attention was still relatively young. As she matured, Dame de la Viesville would become one of the great cistercian abbesses of the eighteenth century, one on whom Madame de Maintenon could have looked with great satisfaction. Dame de la Viesville was forty-three years old at the time of Madame de Maintenon's death. She was to govern Gomerfontaine for another thirty-one years. But as early as 1722 she spoke of an illness which caused her, on the advice of Cardinal de Noailles, to consult doctors in Paris. She returned uncured, 'with only a gold cross given her by the abbess of Chelles',[19] and would suffer for the rest of her life without complaining.

On the last day of each year Dame de la Viesville presented an annual report to the community. In these reports she gave not only a summary of the most important events in the life of the community during the year, but also related significant occurrences in the Church and the kingdom of France. At the same time, a carefully prepared financial report was given to the community.[20] As we might expect, all of this was put in a spiritual perspective, so that the nuns would be stimulated to live their cistercian life ever more fully by seeking God purely in prayer and by means of their observances. It is chiefly by these annual reports that we know of the many hardships suffered by the community because of political disturbances and crop failures during the eighteenth century.

The report of 1715 begins with the death of Louis XIV: 'Death is a tribute which all men must pay according to the established order, and prescribed from all eternity in God's decrees. Crowned heads cannot be dispensed from it any more than the rest of men'. The 1716 report is truly a remarkable one. In it Dame Marie-Anne explained to her sisters in a masterful way what inflation is, and what effects it was having on the economic state of France at that time. Clearly, inflation was as much an evil in her times as in ours. The same 1716 report mentions that soldiers helped with the harvest at the abbey.

Among the greatest trials for Gomerfontaine while Dame de la Viesville was abbess came from a next-door neighbor at Trie-Château. Until 1710, Louis III, prince of Condé (grandson of '*le Grand Condé*') was lord of the Château. He respected both Louis XIV and the protegée of Madame de Maintenon, and was a good neighbor to the sisters. At his death, however, the property passed to the Count of Charolais (the son of Mme de Nantes and grandson of Louis XIV), a young man of incredible cruelty and rudeness of character. In 1734, real trouble began. The Count of Charolais decided to repopulate the game on his domain. Animals overran the nuns' fields and woods: 'The number of hares, rabbits, and wild

beasts that one sees is already so great! Like flocks of sheep they are!'
(Annual Report, 1734). Since Gomerfontaine's economy, like that
of the peasantry of the region, depended on its arable land, grazing
pastures, and woods, the invasion of creatures who ate everything
in sight constituted a real calamity for the community. Jean-Jacques
Rousseau, who finished his *Confessions* at Trie-Château, later described this 'barbaric audacity' which he himself had witnessed:

> The peasants [and, we might add, the nuns] were forced to suffer
> the damage done to their fields by the game without daring to
> defend themselves except by noise, and had to pass their nights
> among their beans and peas with kettles, drums, and bells, to drive
> off the wild boars.[21]

At the end of the 1736 Report there is a detailed account of the
damage done to the property of the abbey. The complaints the nuns
made to the prince were of no avail: 'It is God whom we must call
upon, he holds the hearts of kings in his hands. After having chas-
tised us, he will have compassion on this house if we have recourse
to him with faith and confidence'. Whenever Dame Marie-Anne
spoke of this trial she did so with mildness, christian resignation,
prudence, and the deference due to 'His Most Serene Highness',
but this did not prevent her from plotting a bit of legitimate long-
term vengeance.

When by error the count of Charolais had trees planted on property belonging to the monastery, the abbess remained silent. But in
this same 1736 Report she pointed out to the community that the
land remained abbey property and 'it will be up to those who come
after us to take possession of the trees when it is time to cut them.
I leave this note to the house so that this will not be forgotten'.
We can almost see her dignified smile of satisfaction at the thought
that the nuns would, in the end, outwit the count. This situation
continued for a number of years, perfecting the sisters in patience;
but when the count's youth vanished, grace seems to have touched
him and he showed real signs of repentance. We may hope that
his new attitude, which inclined him to performing good works,
extended to the nuns of Gomerfontaine. Dame de la Viesville could
apply to her neighbor the age-old adage: when the devil gets old he
becomes a hermit.

Dame Marie-Anne de la Viesville, thirty-first abbess of Gomerfontaine, died in 1751 at the age of seventy-four, leaving a reputation
for holiness and energetic leadership. In a period when it was not
common to weep over abbesses, even the royal court mourned. King

Louis XV named as her successor the virtuous and intelligent Anne-Jeanne du Pouget de Nadaillac, daughter of the Marquis de Nadaillac. Jean-Jacques Rousseau, her friend in spite of their differences in philosophy of life, tells us she was 'young, kind, and amiable'.[22] She continued the work of Dame de la Viesville, but the times were less favorable for monasteries and neither Madame de Maintenon nor Cardinal de Noailles were there to give her aid and counsel. When Dame Anne-Jeanne died in 1781, Elisabeth de Sarcus became abbess. Little is known about her government of Gomerfontaine. Her annual reports are very brief; perhaps she was acting out of prudence, for the situation of the monasteries became more and more precarious as the end of the eighteenth century approached and the rumblings of Revolution drew near. In 1792 the nuns were driven from Gomerfontaine forever.

The community, however, was not completely extinguished. It came to life again at Nesle, then moved to Saint Paul-aux-Bois, where it was to flourish until the turn of the twentieth century. In 1904, once more obliged to flee because of political disturbance, the community sought refuge at Fourbechies in Belgium. There it remained until 1919, when the nuns transferred to Chimay, where the community continues its monastic life today at the abbey of Notre Dame de La Paix.

NOTES

1. Numbers in parentheses refer to the *Lettres* de Madame de Maintenon a Me de la Vieuxville, Abbesse de Gomerfontaine, Tome II des *Lettres de Madame de Maintenon*. Seconde edition (Amsterdam, 1756). Lettres I-XLII, p. 124–210. My gratitude to Soeur Lutgart, Abbaye N.D. de La Paix, Chimay, for making this document from the monastery archives available to me.

2. Though in the 1756 edition of M. de Maintenon's *Letters*, the name of the abbess of Gomerfontaine is written *Vieuxville*, it is more correct to use the spelling *la Viesville*.

3. Saint Cyr, or *L'Institut de St Louis*, had at this time about two hundred fifty pupils and thirty-six teachers. Girls from seven to ten years of age were accepted; they could remain until they were twenty. Madame de Maintenon herself set up the rules and managed the house. Saint Cyr was abandoned during the Revolution and was subsequently used first as a hospital and then as a school for officers' children, before becoming the renowned military academy.

4. Marie Anne was a great-grand-niece of Adolph and Adrian de Vignacourt, Grand Masters of the Order of Malta. Her parents were Louis de la Viesville, Lord of Rouviler, and Marie-Anne de Fayot. Her brother, the Marquis de la Viesville, married into the family of Mailly. Cardinal de Noailles would be a constant source of encouragement and support to Dame Marie-Anne. In 1726 he spent several days at Gomerfontaine, to the great joy of the sisters. Dame Marie-Anne devoted a large part of the 1729 annual report to a eulogy of the cardinal. See Baron de Maricourt

and A. Driard, 'Une Abbaye de Filles au XVIIIe siècle', *Revue des Questions Historiques* 37 (1907) p. 4, 18.

5. *Ibid.*, p. 5.

6. *Ibid.*, p. 2. According to Jeanne de Bouillonné, abbess of Gomerfontaine at the beginning of the sixteenth century.

7. *Idem.*

8. Gomerfontaine was not the only monastery to have daughters of the house of Médavy as abbess. The following could also be mentioned (seventeenth and eighteenth centuries): Louise (1593–1652), abbess of Almenèches and Argentan; Anne (1600–1655), abbess of Vignats; Guyonne (1608–1669), abbess of St Nicolas; Charlotte, abbess of Fontaine; Marie, abbess of Parc aux Dames; another Charlotte, abbess of Bouvières; Françoise (1630–1692), abbess of Vignats; Bernarde (1632–1704), abbess of Vignats; Madeleine (1649–1727), abbess of Almenèches; Anne (1650–1696), abbess of Parc aux Dames; Marguerite (1661–1723), abbess of Parc aux Dames. Another Charlotte was prioress at Gomerfontaine in the late seventeenth century. *Table généalogique* de la Famille de Jean Rouxel, from the Archives of N.D. de La Paix.

9. Baron de Maricourt, 'Une Abbaye', p. 4. The community voted to enter the Strict Observance by 14–11. Only when the eleven opposing nuns died did the abbess, who by then was elderly, see peace restored.

10. In Letter 5 we read: 'The king never pays board (for the pupils). He gives it only for those who become religious, on the day of their profession'.

11. It sometimes happened that certain nuns did, in fact, try to hide things. In Letter 8 Madame de Maintenon related the following incident: 'The king told me two days ago that he paid board for three women in a convent. One of them died five years ago, and the good ladies still receive board for the three of them. And have no doubt about it: they receive communion three times a week!'

12. Chrysogonus Waddell ocso, 'The Reform of LaTrappe', in *Cistercians in the Later Middle Ages*, Studies in Medieval Cistercian History, 6 (Kalamazoo: Cistercian Publications, 1981) p. 117.

13. For example, Aelred of Rievaulx, *The Mirror of Charity* II. xxiii. 69.

14. Baron de Maricourt, 'Une Abbaye', p. 14. 'The apprenticeship and the purchase of the loom cost us four hundred pounds. Sr Apollina Quentier, who learned the trade because of her attachment to the good of the house and also because of her aptitude, took only four months to do so.'

15. *Ibid.*, p. 17.

16. *Ibid.*

17. In 1742 there was more jurisdictional trouble. It caused considerable agitation in the community of Gomerfontaine. The bishops, jealous of their rights, obtained a declaration from the king saying that no novices could be accepted for profession, either in exempt or non-exempt monasteries, without examination by the bishop (10 February 1742). This touched upon the privileges of the Order of Cîteaux. Dom Andoche Pernot, Abbot General of Cîteaux, wrote to Dame de la Viesville: 'If a vicar remits this declaration to you and speaks to you about it, you must take it and without entering into any discussion simply say that you know your obligations which you contracted when you entered religion, and that you are ready to fulfill them. If he tries to make you answer otherwise, change the subject and talk only of rain and nice weather.' De Maricourt, 'Une Abbaye', p. 19.

18. In Letter 42, from Dame de la Viesville to Madame de Maintenon, the abbess had to defend the confessor, it seems, with regard to suspicions of Jansenism.

19. de Maricourt, 'Madame de la Viesville, Abbesse de l'Abbaye de Gomerfontaine, une ami de Madame de Maintenon'. Comité archéologique de Senlis. 4e série, tome VIII. *Comptes-rendus et mémoires.* (Senlis, 1906) 271–272.

20. As today, the accounts of the nuns' monasteries had to be verified by superiors of the order. In 1736, at Gomerfontaine this task was taken care of by the 'abbot of

Barbery, Nicolas Lambelin, Vicar General of the Order of Cîteaux, regular superior of the houses of the Strict Observance in the provinces of Normandy, Maine, Perche, and Anjou, and delegate of the Abbot General of the Order of Cîteaux'. He found that the accounts were kept with wisdom and fidelity, and that the economy was worthy of praise. What is remarkable about this evaluation is that the abbot checked through all the accounts from 1723 to 1736 in twenty-four hours (September 13 and 14, 1736). Though in general the accounts were very well kept, an important error had crept in at the end of 1727 and had been undetected when the totals of the year were carried over for the following year. Thus this error affected all the accounting of ensuing years. The abbot of Barbery evidently did not catch it. See de Maricourt, 'Une Abbaye,' 15–16.

21. *Confessions*, 2e partie. Livre IX. 1762 (Paris, 1864) 545.

22. de Maricourt, 'Une Abbaye', p. 6. About 1767, Jean-Jacques Rousseau under an alias, was given haven, by the prince of Condé in the Château of Trie, then later in a turret of the abbey.

Spiritual Direction of Women at Port-Royal

F. Ellen Weaver

IT IS TEMPTING to speculate on how monastic history would have judged the reform of the cistercian abbey of Port-Royal had the nuns not become involved with the Jansenist controversy. My own research has led me to believe that the reforming abbess, Mère Angélique Arnauld, would have been considered a heroine of the Counter-Reformation in France[1] and that her niece, Mère Angélique de Saint-Jean Arnauld d'Andilly, would have gone down in history as one of the great cistercian abbesses.[2] I have argued elsewhere for the cistercian character of the reform and of the continued loyalty of the nuns to their cistercian and benedictine heritage.[3]

The fact remains that the nuns did become involved with the Jansenists. How could it have been otherwise, considering the close family ties of the Arnaulds with the monastery and the movement? The Arnauld women provided three abbesses and numerous members for Port-Royal. Robert Arnauld d'Andilly was an influential sponsor of the father of French Jansenism, Jean Duvergier de Hauranne de Saint-Cyran, and his younger brother, Antoine Arnauld, was the theologian and polemicist of the movement. This is not to mention the relatives and friends who formed the community of gentlemen hermits known as the *Messieurs de Port-Royal*.

This convergence of monastic, counter-reformation and intellectual (the *messieurs* were scholars and theologians) influences produced a very particular spirituality of Port-Royal.[4] The treatise on *la Direction* (spiritual direction, or direction of conscience) presented here well illustrates this tradition. It also offers an aspect which is of special interest today with the focus on women and women's issues in the Church, for it is directed to women and written by a woman.

701

The manuscript is stored at the Bibliothèque de la Société de Port-Royal in Paris. A critical edition in French was published by Louis Cognet in 1955.[5] Cognet, who was until his death in 1971 the leading scholar of Port-Royal and knew the Port-Royal collection intimately, made the following comment on authorship:

> This text was copied by the lawyer Le Roy de Saint-Charles (1736–1803) from a manuscript which was found in a packet of writings which originally came from Port-Royal. This copy is found today at the Bibliothèque de la Société de Port-Royal, P. R. 96. It has no author's name, which proves that Le Roy, who knew very well the handwriting of the Port-Royal group, was not able to identify the writing of the manuscript. In certain regards this text makes one think of Nicole, and it would not be unworthy of his pen. However, the style is not exactly his, and I am inclined to attribute it to Angélique de Saint-Jean Arnauld d'Andilly in the last years of her life, between 1680 and 1684, at the time when the nuns, after the failure of the Peace of the Church, found themselves almost completely deprived of their usual directors.[6]

I feel even more certain than Cognet that the author is Angélique de Saint-Jean. The style is hers, the concern is hers. There is evidence in her letters that she suffered from the lack of spiritual directors that is addressed in the text.[7] Saci (Louis-Isaac LeMaitre), her cousin and preferred advisor, was often more or less in exile and she had limited recourse to him for her personal direction. As abbess of Port-Royal, an office she held from 1678 until her death in 1684, the need for confessors for her nuns was a constant concern. In 1681, upon her re-election to a second term, her first act was to write to the archbishop asking for confessors.[8] This is a constant theme in her letters. She rejoiced when M. Le Tourneux, who was sympathetic to Port-Royal, was allowed to come to confess the nuns before All Saints Day.[9] She complained to her friend Mme de Fontpertuis that ' . . . we are reduced to having neither preacher nor confessor. Our servants have had no instruction at all this Lent, any more than we'.[10] Her remarks in many places about how the community, left without spiritual direction, nourish themselves with spiritual reading and by recalling former instructions, are just like the advice given in the text.

In this concern she is in direct continuity with her famous aunts, Mère Angélique and Mère Agnes. A major feature of the reform of Port-Royal by Mère Angélique Arnauld was to assure adequate spiritual direction for herself and her community. In this, as in other respects, the reform of Port-Royal in its early stages followed closely the pattern of the counter-reformation following the Council of Trent. The seventeenth century has been called the 'golden age of spiritual direction'.[11]

It is not necessary to recount here the history of spiritual direction from its beginnings in the writings of Saint Jerome and the *Vitae* of the Desert Fathers, through its development in medieval monasticism, to the point where, in the sixteenth century, one feature of the reform within the Catholic Church was the extension of guidance in prayer and asceticism beyond monastery walls into the lives of individual lay persons. This is the point where the history of the reform of Port-Royal begins. Concern with spiritual direction for women is the central theme of the treatise *de la Direction*. Hence, before discussing the immediate context of the writing, it will be helpful to review the forms which the spiritual direction of women took at Port-Royal.

Within the monastery the superior was far more than administrator of community affairs. Port-Royal was a monastery of the Cistercian Order, juridically until 1626, and in spirit and identity to the end of its existence. As Cistercians their basic Rule was the Rule of Saint Benedict. In this Rule the superior is ideally a true father to his monks, the wisest of the elders who form the governing council of the monastery. Mère Angélique took this model seriously and attempted to be mother and counsellor to her nuns. Besides individual counselling, she gave spiritual conferences from time to time. Sometimes these were on the Rule but often they were simply informal talks.[12] When Angélique de Saint Jean became abbess in 1678 she continued the custom.[13]

Another important counsellor of the nuns within the monastery was the novice mistress. Angélique de Saint-Jean held this post from 1648 until 1669 when she became prioress. Her advice to novices is included as an appendix to the *Constitutions* of Port Royal.[14]

That within the monastery there should be guidance in prayer and the discipline of religious life for the nuns by their superiors is only to be expected. It should be noted, however, that the most important spiritual director was considered by the nuns to be the priest who served as their confessor. For these women who had very little of serious nature to confess, the confessional was the place above all where they received individual and continued guidance on the spiritual journey. This is why, when the monastery was placed under interdict from 1664 to 1669, the dispersal of the priests caused great consternation. It was at that point that the nuns took a step which was a more radical break with authority than it seems to us today: they turned to a layman, Jean Hamon, their doctor, as their spiritual director.[15]

But what of spiritual direction of laywomen by the nuns? Those with whom the nuns had earliest contact were the girls who were boarders at the monastery. These ranged from three to sixteen years of age. The custom of accepting these boarding students was a ancient one in the Cistercian Order of nuns.[16] At Port-Royal, besides teaching them 'to read and to write, to sew and do other useful work and not that which serves vanity',[17] the nuns gave these girls careful formation in christian life. The *Reglement pour le Enfants*, appended to the Constitutions and attributed to Jacqueline Pascal, reads like a Rule for nuns.[18] Some of the girls did enter the convent when they reached the proper age,[19] but many left and married. At the time of the suppression of admission to the order, between 1661 and 1669 and after 1679 until the destruction of the monastery in 1709, all boarders as well as postulants and novices were dismissed. These women who had lived at Port-Royal retained their loyalty to the Order, and the nuns kept up correspondence with them, often writing letters of spiritual direction.

There was another group of women who were close to the monastery. In the earlier times cistercian monasteries had accepted retired women, mainly of nobility, as pensioners. This had led to abuses, since the women moved in with their servants and maintained their usual style of life, which tempted the nuns to do the same. But the custom of retiring to a monastery was not easily repressed after the reform of the Orders in the seventeenth century. At Port-Royal there were widows who actually entered the Order at retirement and lived out their years as nuns. But there were others, among them Madame de Sablé and the Duchess of Longueville, who built apartments attached to the monastery, or residences as near it as possible, and lived out their years in close proximity to the nuns. In return for financial and political support these women received spiritual direction as well as benefits of ending their life piously by attending the offices and receiving the sacraments at the monastery church.

Finally there were laywomen who never lived in or near the monastery. In a 1974 dissertation, W. Ritchey Newton has shown the intricate web of relationships which made up the universe of Port-Royal. The attraction of the community was such that relatives and friends of the nuns were drawn into its orbit and often became benefactresses, seeking in return spiritual and personal advice.[20]

To all of these women the nuns gave spiritual direction. The medium was the personal letter, which was often copied and passed around in a circle of friends. In the collections of the correspondence of the three Arnauld abbesses, Mère Angélique, her sister Mère Agnès, and Mère Angélique de Saint-Jean, a substantial number are such letters of spiritual direction.[21] In this the nuns of Port-Royal were not unique. The letters of the holy women of all times include those giving guidance in spiritual life, to men as well as to women. Nor does the direction given, for example by Angélique de Saint-Jean to one of the most faithful of the friend-benefactresses, Madame de Fontpertuis, differ greatly from that given to her by Angélique's uncle, Antoine Arnauld, who was one of the major directors of the nuns themselves.[22]

It is clear that when Angélique de Saint-Jean set out to write on spiritual direction she had behind her many years of practical experience in the art. Implicitly she, as her famous aunts before her and as other nuns of the community, had for a long time been playing the role normally assigned to men, that of spiritual director in the lives of her sisters in the community—and in the world.

What distinguished this work from the tradition out of which it grows is that in it Angélique explicitly recommends that women act as directors, or that women simply take direct responsibility for their lives in this matter.

The circumstances that prompted the composition of this little treatise on spiritual direction was the renewal of the persecution of Port-Royal in 1679. The monastery had enjoyed a period of uneasy peace for ten years, during which time they had been allowed to receive boarders, postulants, and novices, and priests of the Port-Royal group had been allowed once more to enter the monastery as confessors. Now, in the course of two months, sixty-six persons were dismissed from the monastery, including the priests. Angélique de Saint-Jean was in her first term of office as abbess, and thus the search for adequate confessors to replace their spiritual fathers was her first major task. She was told that she could suggest names, but, she writes, the conditions laid down by the archbishop made a real choice impossible:

> He wants it to be a person whom we do not know and who does not know us, who had no connection with our friends, and who has only mediocre capacity, because he says we are well enough instructed. Thus we are in a situation of running great risk, because simply at random we must name people who are

unknown and ignorant and who could be very dangerous. Of the twenty-two we have named one after the other, all have refused to come. Some are afraid that it will make them suspect of Jansenism, and the others, and almost all, don't want to leave their little niche in Paris.[23]

Finally a priest was named, Nicolas Le Tourneux. He was sympathetic, but he was not given a permanent nomination by the archbishop, and by 1682 he too had left. From that time until her death in 1684 no priest who was truly suitable was found. It is no wonder that the piece she wrote would be better titled 'How To Get Along Without Spiritual Direction'.

We noted above that the specific focus on spiritual direction of women by women sets this treatise apart from others of its period and makes it relevant to our own time. There are other features which make it unique. The evidence of scholarly awareness of the history of the Church, especially of the Early Church, is a characteristic of all the Port-Royal scholarship. The final bit of advice urging one who is without a director to step back from the questions he or she would bring to the director if one were available and to 'figure out what we would say to someone revealing similar difficulties to us' has a surprisingly modern ring.

Angélique de Saint-Jean steps forth from these pages, a strong, independent woman, relying on her own good sense and on the Providence of God. She has obviously benefitted from an education very similar to that given the more cultured clergy of her time to which the scholarly work of the *messieurs* of Port-Royal has added the depth of the historical dimension. Her years of practical experience in giving spiritual direction within and without her monastery have given her confidence to speak clearly to the question of the lack of spiritual direction. She finds the answer in history, which affirms the legitimacy of her assumption of the role of spiritual director for her nuns as their abbess. But she also finds it in the inner resource of the enlightened individual conscience. Cistercians should be proud to reclaim her, and also to claim as a continuation and development of their tradition of spiritual direction this little text.

DE LA DIRECTION[24]

by
Angélique de Saint-Jean Arnauld D'Andilly

1

Nothing is more common today than to see pious people complaining that they do not receive the help they need from their directors, and that other than confession and a few bits of advice received there, they derive almost no light for the conduct of their private life. [Their directors] have no concern about giving them support and causing them to advance. They do not provide advice regarding their particular actions. As a consequence these persons are obliged to act haphazardly and find themselves abandoned to their own judgment.

2

We must admit that these complaints are not entirely without foundation for several reasons.

First. There are those who are afraid to push souls and to make suggestions. Therefore they are satisfied to see those they direct live a life that is orderly and free from serious fault.

Second. Those who could assist them most efficiently are often so loaded with work that they haven't time to get involved with the details of the lives of those whom they direct, and so they must limit their direction to hearing confession and to giving advice on important occasions.

3

The rarity of directors who are truly spiritual contributes further to making this complaint more common. For if you are seeking a director who is at all like the model proposed by Saint Francis de Sales often you can hardly find one or two in a whole province.[25] And since they have at their disposal but a limited amount of time which they can give to only a few persons, all others have to accept the guidance of rather ordinary directors from whom they cannot expect that special attention which they would like to have paid to their progress in virtue.

4

Therefore one must suppose that there are an infinite number of persons professing a life of piety who receive very little help from their confessors. How many nuns there are who are obliged to confess to the priest assigned to them, who is often less than mediocre! And how many devout women endure this same poverty, either because they live in places where there is no one available for personal counseling, or because those whom they might consult do not have the leisure to give them the attention they believe they need!

5

One should not imagine that this dearth of enlightened directors capable of advancing souls by this particular care for the details of their actions is peculiar to our time. It is about the same in every century. Can one believe, for example, that when the apostles had converted a certain number of pagans and Jews and had formed a Church, they established directors in that Church who would inquire about the particular actions of the Christians? They had done a great deal when they left a bishop and a deacon in each town. And that bishop and deacon, being responsible for the administration of the sacraments, the care of the instruction of the faithful, the collection of alms, and a multitude of exterior concerns, doubtless did not have time to give to each Christian an hour a week to direct their particular needs.[26]

6

One will rarely find that the laity ordinarily benefitted from this kind of help in the first centuries of the Church. Although there is reason to believe that the faithful consulted the pastors about the important events of their life, I do not know if one could prove that they practiced these examinations and moderations of conduct which some practice very usefully today, or that they turned to their pastors for the control of the details of their activity.

7

One does find in *The Pastoral Care* of Saint Gregory that the faithful sometimes made known to the priests their temptations, and this practice can be regarded as the equivalent of the confession of venial sins, which had not yet been established.[27] But apart from the fact that this disclosure of temptations does not seem to have been very common, and those who outlined the duties of priests did not emphasize the duty [for priests] to respond to [the faithful] who disclosed to them the movements of their conscience, the common practice of all those who care about their salvation has always been to find at least that help which the faithful derived in the time of Saint Gregory the Great from the advice of the priests to whom they disclosed their thoughts, and thus past centuries had no advantage whatsoever over this one.

8

This tradition and practice of particular direction has really come from the monasteries and it has almost never been found elsewhere. And it is true that all the founders of religious orders intended to provide this help for those who would renounce the world to embrace the religious life, and they have identified it as one of the greatest advantages of monastic life.

9

This is why there is no law more universally prescribed by the authors of monastic rules than the obligation for the monk to disclose his thoughts to his abbot in order to learn from him how to control them, and to receive light for his conduct. They all established as the foundation of religious life that the monk should do nothing except under obedience, which supposes the attention of the superior to each individual. Now the Councils of France expressly determined

that what was said of abbots in the Rule of Saint Benedict should
be understood also of abbesses.[28]

10

But, as it is certain that the founders of [religious] Orders intended
that the abbot and abbess would be the director and directress of
the conscience of all their monks and nuns, they also intended that
there would be no others except them, and I do not know if any
example can be found of monks and nuns who had directors outside
their monasteries. We do find in the seventh and eighth centuries
priests coming to hear the confessions of nuns at certain times of the
year, but outside of that confessions were rather infrequent. These
priests do not seem to have exercised any particular direction, since
that duty was always assumed by the abbess.[29]

11

I know quite well that the irregularities in the monasteries of
women, in which the superiors were even more involved than others, caused the nuns to lose the trust necessary to disclose their
thoughts to them, and they were obliged to have recourse to priests
in order to find the assistance which they no longer found in [the
women] who were their superiors.[30] But this assistance was never
very considerable. And for one monastery where the nuns had such
aid there were hundreds where no other help was available than
whatever they could find in their Rule and the good order of their
houses, from some sermons, from reading, and finally from counsels
they might occasionally receive from pious people.

12

From that I do not mean to conclude that it is not a very great
benefit to have an enlightened director who inspires us, supports
us, who keeps us from straying, who directs us to the correction
of our principal faults, who enters into the details of our activity,
and to whom we render an exact account of all our conduct. The
practice of all the monasteries which are the healthiest portion of
the Church suffices to justify the utility of this particular direction.

But what I mean to conclude is that this benefit, however great, has always been extremely rare, that most women have always been deprived of it, and that God has not ceased to sanctify an infinite number of souls in every state of life in the Church.

13

From this it follows that a soul who, because of her state of life or the place where the providence of God has put her, finds herself deprived of this particular direction, should endure this privation with the following dispositions:

First. She should consider that this privation only places her in the same condition as almost all the faithful in the Church. For where are those who have directors interested in their particular needs and effectively helpful to them? How many are there who have recourse only to unenlightened people incapable of helping them? And finally, how many are there for whom the relationship with their directors is very dangerous?

Second. And since this lack of directors is an evil which is so common and so widespread, she should not give up the desire or the hope of obtaining from God what she wishes, nor cease to ask it of him on that account. But she should pray as one prays for all things which are not absolutely necessary and essential, that is, with peace and patience and with submission to the will of God, and on the condition that the aid she is asking is advantageous for her salvation.

14

This submission should lead her not only to accept this privation with patience so long as it pleases God to leave her in this situation, but even to acknowledge that ultimately she is not sure that it is not beneficial for her, and that God is not leaving her in it because he sees it is for her good. For there are an infinite number of persons who abuse spiritual direction, who use it to authorize themselves in their attachments to their passions, who, deceiving themselves first, then deceive their directors and use their advice to confirm themselves in their illusions. How many there are who rely too much on men and for whom spiritual directors become an impediment on

their way to God? And who knows whether or not she is herself of
that number?

15

It seems to most devout women that the director has the gift of
communicating holiness; or rather that they only need someone to
tell them what they must do, and they will find the strength in
themselves to do it. In regard to their directors they are making
the same error that the Jews made with regard to the law. They
believed they could observe it by themselves; similarly these women
believe that to be very devout all they need is to have a director.
But God often convinces them of their error, as he convinced the
Jews, by making them see that often they remain just as weak and
just as imperfect with the most famous director in the world as if
they were completely bereft of help.[31]

16

Christians ought to have an entirely contrary principle, and be
persuaded that only God can truly advance souls in his way even
as only he can make them enter it; and that no man, however
enlightened he may be, can do anything but harm them unless God
uses him as an instrument to assist them.

17

This principle should dissuade them from worrying about being
deprived of the holiest and most enlightened persons when God
takes them away from them. For if this separation corresponds
to the will of God, it should bring them to conclude that these
persons, having ceased to be the instruments of Jesus Christ in their
behalf, have become incapable of serving them. And it should even
prevent them from eagerly desiring communication with persons of
piety, because, since they do not know whether [these persons] are
sent to them by God and whether God wishes to use them to aid
and enlighten them, consequently they do not know whether [such
persons] could be truly useful to them.

18

All this should cause those who find themselves in this state of privation to conclude that they should not base the hope of their advancement solely on finding a director; and without giving up the desire of having those they seem to need, they should not cease to work seriously to make progress without that assistance which God is not giving them.

19

The means to do this consists principally in two things: to use well what they have, and to compensate for what they have not. I say one must learn to make good use of the help one has, because most often [the women] who make these complaints, under the pretext of desiring a particular direction which they cannot have, neglect to use as they should the aids which they enjoy. If they really reflect on the use they have made of the lights they have received they will find that most often they have profited very little from them because they have paid little attention to them and let them easily escape.

However, such is not the fruit God wants them to derive from the instructions of their directors, but they should retain what is said, go over it in the memory, assimilate it, make use of it, apply it to their actions, and finally become more enlightened from it and not be one of those women of whom Saint Paul says, they are always learning but never attaining knowledge.[32] One truth put into practice is worth more than a hundred truths which only pass through the mind. Thus, rather than collect a great number of instructions and truths, it is better to stick to a small number and try to put them into practice; and if we do not wish to fool ourselves, we will recognize that we always learn enough for that.

20

There is no word in the Gospel which better reveals the life of the holy Virgin and at the same time the eminence of her virtue than that which says of her that she kept everything about her Son and pondered it in her heart.[33] That is to say, she lost nothing of all that God revealed to her by whatever means. All these truths made in her mind and in her heart the impression that they should have made, and that impression was not transitory but durable and permanent because she was careful not to lose any one of these truths. And since she was witness to the pilgrim life of Jesus Christ from his birth until his death, all that life of the Son of God produced fruits of sanctity in Mary, which can lead us to realize the excellence of her virtues, because everything in Jesus Christ is sanctifying, and all that is sanctifying in Jesus Christ sanctified Mary in an eminent manner proportioned to her excellent dispositions. Jesus Christ scattered his seeds in the other elect, but he poured all of them into Mary; and Mary did not lose a single one, and she received in herself the sanctifying impression of all the life and all the words of the Word incarnate.[34] All took root in the heart of Mary, was kept there, and bore fruit.

21

We ordinarily do just the opposite in regard to the few truths God has made known to us. Either we let them escape without reflecting on them, or if we taste them for a moment we let these sentiments be extinguished very soon. We are like those bad managers who do not know how to save money and who, dissipating all their goods, find themselves in less than no time reduced to poverty. So too, however rich we seem to be in light we find ourselves poor and destitute of all strength in a short while, because we have accustomed ourselves always to want new meats, and since the old truths do not satisfy our curiosity enough, our spirit does not derive from them the nourishment it should.

22

Moreover, some fail to profit from their directors because they do not want to trouble themselves to find the right time to speak to them, or to reduce what they have to say to a few words. They want their directors to anticipate their needs, to perceive when they are in a good mood, to talk to them, never to be in a hurry, to give them all the time they believe they need. And since that cannot be, they drop it all and do not manage any opportunity to learn about their difficulties. They want all or nothing, and by this they show that ultimately they have very little esteem for the guidance of their directors, because they do not want it to cost them any effort or constraint.

23

One is always poor in the world when one does not learn to live within one's means, however great they are; one is always rich when one knows how to live within them however small. It is the same with spiritual lights received from directors. One is always poor when one manages them poorly, whatever attention [the directors] give us; and one is always rich when one manages them prudently, and knows how to use wisely what [directors] tell us and the time they dispose for us. Because if they have no more time to give us this is a sign that God wishes us to be contented with what is given and to act so that it suffices.

24

A soul who does not wish to deceive herself on this point has only to make a little examination of herself and to consider how many useless truths are in her which do not bear fruit, how many defects in herself she has to correct, and how many means she has not put into practice. And then, from what she will discover from these reflections, which should be habitual, she should make a resolution to put into practice seriously these truths and these means and thus merit that God enlighten her more, either through men or by himself.

25

Since the privations which God causes us to experience during the course of the spiritual life are the effects of the will of God who sends them to us out of mercy or justice, are we not only obliged to submit ourselves to them, but, moreover, we should hear what God wants to make us understand by them and be faithful in carrying it out. For all the states in which God places us have certain duties and certain obligations and God, when he places us there, wants us to discover these and to fulfill them.

26

What, then, is God saying to a soul whom he deprives wholly
or partly of the exterior guidance coming from her director? He is
saying that by imposing on her the necessity of walking by herself
in some regard, without anyone to hold her by the hand and lead
her in her way, he is obliging her to be more watchful over herself,
to look more often to one side and the other, to excite herself since
there is no one else to do it, and that he does not want her to rely
on others.

27

Furthermore, a soul should recognize in this state of privation of
the assistance of men that everything she ever received from them
came effectively from God, that men can be helpful to her only
insofar as God wants to use them, since of themselves they are
capable only of harming her, and that God can provide for her by
other means and by himself all that she could gain from the most
excellent director in the world, provided it was not her fault that
she was deprived.

28

Therefore, it is the right time to have recourse to God, to adore
him as the unique source of all light and of all good, and to beg his
pardon for the too great attachment we have for creatures, and the
too great confidence we place in them as if they had any virtue and
any strength of themselves. As she should fear having drawn this
privation by her lack of fidelity to profit from the aids God gave
her, she should merit by a greater exactitude to her duties that he
refill this void in the manner that pleases him, because the privation
of a certain means for advancement in piety is a warning that God
gives us to try to profit more from others.

29

All these dispositions into which souls should enter should not
make them indifferent to having or not having directors who care

for them. It is good that they desire them and that they grieve about this privation which is an evil according to the ordinary lights of faith. But this grieving should be accompanied by peace, patience, and submission, and gratitude for the benefits which God bestows on them, and finally, as I have already said, by a sincere acknowledgment that we do not know if what we desire is advantageous for us. It is good to take advice when we can and to act on our own as little as possible, but since self-love can slip in everywhere often those who have the possibility of consulting abuse this facility which they have of communicating with their directors. They did not make use of their own lights, and by a certain spiritual laziness joined with excessive scruples or some human pursuit in these communications, they take pleasure in being told a hundred times what they know very well, and what they would decide without difficulty if they wished to work on it.

The way we should consult about difficulties of conscience which we would wish to go over with a director when the means are unavailable is to reduce them, insofar as possible, to something very precise. For often we do not know exactly what we want, or what worries us. We give in to vague impressions of scruples, boredom, discouragement, without well knowing the reason, and then there is nothing to do but to say with David: Why are you heavy, my soul, and why do you trouble me? Hope in God for I shall confess again his mercies; He is my salvation and my God.[35]

But when these doubts and these worries have definite objects, the best way to use the light we have in order to discern what God is expecting from us, is to figure out what we would say to someone revealing similar difficulties to us, for ordinarily we are very enlightened for others and very blind for ourselves. And thus, to silence to some extent the tumult of the passions which hinder us from discerning the truth in our own case, it is necessary somehow to consider the problems as if they were another's, and then to take for oneself the advice we would have given to that person.

It is true that a soul does not dwell as strongly in peace and assurance after these resolutions which she can take on her own as if they were taken with a director in whom she had confidence, but it is not always a bad thing to have this diffidence and to fear doing nothing worthwhile. There are many souls for whom that fear is more beneficial than the confidence they place in their directors, which is often much more dangerous. Furthermore, [this person] should find peace and repose in the thought that she is following God by acting in this fashion because God, by depriving her of particular guidance, made it necessary for her to act in this way. For I do not say that it is not good to consult when possible, but I say that when we cannot we must do what we can in another fashion, and often God makes that other way just as beneficial as the guidance of a particular director.[36]

NOTES

1. I have argued for the cistercian character of the reform of Port-Royal in F. E. Weaver, *The Evolution of the Reform of Port-Royal. From the Rule of Cîteaux to Jansenism* (Paris, 1978). One of the major scholars of cistercian life, Louis Lekai, does not agree with me. See his *The Cistercians. Ideals and Reality* (Kent State University, 1977) pp. 359–360. I respect his opinion, but am more convinced of my own as I work more in the Port-Royal papers.

2. For details on the life and role of Angélique de Saint-Jean, see Weaver, 'Angélique de Saint-Jean of Port-Royal: The "Third Superior" as "Mythographer" in the Dynamics of Reform Caught in Controversy', in *Cistercians in the late Middle Ages*, ed. E. Rozanne Elder (Kalamazoo, 1981) 99–101.

3. See note 1 above.

4. See the article 'Port-Royal' by F. Ellen Weaver in the *Dictionnaire de Spiritualité*, Vol. 13 (Paris, 1985) cols. 1931–1952.

5. The text is found appended to Cognet's article, 'La Direction de Conscience à Port-Royal,' *Supplément de La Vie Spirituelle*, Vol. III, no. 34 (15 September 1955) pp. 289–319.

6. *Ibid.*, p. 319. My translation.

7. Bibliothèque de Port-Royal, MSS Let. 358–361. This is a collection of the *Lettres d'Angélique de St. Jean* prepared for publication by Mademoiselle Rachel Gillet.

8. *Ibid.*, Let. 360, Aug. 1681.

9. *Ibid.*, 14 Aug. 1681.

10. *Ibid.*, April 1683.

11. Irenée Noyé, 'Note pour une histoire de la direction spirituelle,' *Supplément de la Vie Spirituelle*, vol. III, no. 34 (15 September 1955) p. 275.

12. A collection of these was published as *Entretiens ou Conférences de la Révérende Mère Marie-Angélique Arnauld* (Paris, 1762).

13. Her talks can be found in *Conférences de la Mére Angélique de Saint Jean*, 3 vols. (Utrecht, 1760); *Discours de la Révérende Mére Marie Angélique de S. Jean, Abbess de P.R. des Champs, Sur la Regle, de S. Benoît*, 2 vols. (Paris, 1736); *Discours de la R. M. Angélique de Saint-Jean appelles Misericordes* (Utrecht, 1735); *Reflexions de la R. Mère Angélique de S. Jean Arnauld, abbess de P. R. des Champs* (No place, 1737).

14. *Les Constitutions du Monastère du Port Royal du Saint-Sacrament* (Paris, 1665) pp. 259–285.

15. Sainte-Beuve, *Port-Royal*, 3 vols. (Paris, 1968) II:753 ff.

16. See Lekai, *The Cistercians*, p. 353.

17. *Constitutions de Port-Royal*, p. 94.

18. *Ibid.*, pp. 383–479.

19. According to the Council of Trent no one could make profession before the age of sixteen, but a girl could enter the novitiate at twelve after examination by the bishop of his delegate to be certain she had not been 'forced or enticed' and knew what she was doing. 'Reform of Regulars', *Canons and Decrees of the Council of Trent*. Original text with English translation by H. J. Schroeder, OP (St Louis London, 1950) p. 228.

20. 'Port Royal and Jansenism: Social Experience, Group Formation and Religious Attitudes in Seventeenth-Century France,' 3 vols. (University of Michigan dissertation, University Microfilms, 1974) pp. 488–547.

21. Letter collections of Mère Angélique and Mère Agnès have been published: *Lettres de la Révérende Mère Marie Angélique Arnauld*. 3 vols. (Utrecht, 1742–1744); *Lettres de la Mère Agnès Arnauld Abbess de Port-Royal*, edited by M. P. Faugere, 3 vols. (Paris, 1858). The correspondence of Mère Angélique de Saint-Jean Arnauld d'Andilly was prepared for publication in the nineteenth century by Rachel Gillet and the manuscript is conserved at the Bibliothéque de la Société de Port-Royal, MSS P. R. 358–361.

22. In the correspondence of Angélique de Saint-Jean are found 358 letters to Madame de Fontpertuis between 1674 and 1684. In the letters of Arnauld can be found 150 to Madame de Fontpertuis between 1678 and 1694. See Antoine Arnauld, *Oeuvres Completes*, 43 volumes (Paris, Lausanne, 1775–1783), Vols. II–IV *passim*. Both commend her for her serious piety but warn her against too much austerity.

23. Sainte-Beuve, III:181–182.

24. I am indebted to a Summer Research Grant from Rutgers University and a fellowship from the Ecumenical Institute at Saint John's University, Collegeville, Minnesota, for the support that made possible the annotated translation of this text.

25. The influence of Francis de Sales (1567–1622) was equalled only by that of the ignatian (jesuit) school in forming the spirituality of the seventeenth century. His *Introduction à la vie dévote*, first published in 1609, and followed by a definitive edition in 1619, was the first popular work on spiritual direction for women. It quickly became a standard in the library of the devout of France, members of religious Orders and laity alike. Francis de Sales was the first to meet the spiritual needs of Mère Angélique and was always considered as one of their spiritual fathers by the nuns of Port-Royal.

26. This development of an historical context with a reference to the early Church is typical of the style of Port-Royal, and represents that aspect of Port-Royal spirituality which I have identified as the erudite tradition. Note the accuracy of the author's detail about bishops and deacons without mention of priests.

27. The author's accuracy and knowledge of patristic sources should be noted. We find in Chapter 5, Part II of *Pastoralis curae*: '. . . when these little ones are enduring the waves of temptation they will have recourse to the pastor's understanding as to a mother's bosom'. In other aspects this treatise reflects the doctrine of Gregory the Great regarding acceptance of trials as evidence of God's love (the *flagella Dei*, see *Morales sur Job*, Sources Chrétiennes, vol. 32 [Paris 1950] pp. 121, 128–130, and many other places). Gregory the Great was a favorite of the Port-Royal group, Nicole in particular. (See *Morales sur Job*, introduction by Dom Robert Gillet, p. 14). Angélique de Saint-Jean is also accurate in stating that the practice of confession for venial sins was not established in the sixth century. See Henry C. Lea, *A History of Auricular Confession and Indulgences*, vol. I (Philadelphia, 1896) 118–120. Paul Anciaux, *La Théologie du Sacrement de Pénitence au XIIᵉ siècle* (Louvain, 1949), p. 609, mentions that as late as the eleventh century there was still much controversy about whether or not penance was a sacrament. For example, Lanfranc wrote that in the absence of a priest one could confess to any other worthy person, and in virtue of the sanctifying power possessed by the Christian who lives united to the Church that person could remit the sins of the penitent (Anciaux, pp. 31–36).

28. It would be difficult to trace her reference to the Councils of France, although it might be found in one of the works of the Port-Royal group on the so-called freedoms of the Gallican Church which were said to have been granted in the very early Councils of the Church in France. However, it is an established fact that in the Middle Ages abbesses had considerable power in France. The case of the great monastery of Fontevrault is a famous example. Here in 1106 Robert d'Abrissel united three convents of nuns and one of monks under the Rule of Saint Benedict and the

direction of an abbess. Monks and nuns professed obedience to this powerful abbess, whose shield bore the words of Christ from the cross: *Ecce mater tua*. See Patrice Cousin, *Précis d'Histoire Monastique* (Paris, 1956) pp. 288–289. Gabriel Le Bras, *Institutions ecclésiastiques de la Chrétienté médiévale*, volume 12 of Histoire de l'Eglise (Paris, 1964) pp. 465–467. In her own Order of Cîteaux, because the cistercian monks had from the beginning resented any demand on their time and services made by the nuns, a compromise had been reached in the thirteenth century whereby priests willing to serve as chaplains to the nuns would be trained by the cistercian monks to a minimum knowledge of the customs of the Order. They would then promise obedience to the abbess and serve her monastery for the rest of their lives. See Louis Lekai, *The White Monks* (Okauchee, WI, 1954) p. 242.

29. The reference to the custom of abbesses hearing their nuns' confessions is accurate. Saint Donatus, Bishop of Besançon (592–631), drew up a Rule for the convent of Jussamoutier which was founded by his mother, Flavia. The Rule, based on the Rule of Saint Caesarius of Arles and the Rules of Saint Benedict and Saint Columbanus, included directions for confession to the abbess several times daily: 'Among other observances of rule we commend this above all to the sisters, not only the junior, but the senior also, that confession be always rendered assiduously and with unceasing zeal, alike of thought, of the idle word, and of deed, or of any perturbation of the mind, and this every day, every hour, every moment; and that nothing be hidden from the spiritual mother (*matri spirituali*), because this is enjoined by the holy fathers . . . because confession liberates from death' *Regula ad virgines, c.* 23 in Oscar D. Watkins, *A History of Penance*, 2 volumes (London, 1920) 2:621. Watkins comments that this confession had nothing to do with the penance of the Church discipline, but was a practice of the devout life. Yet, the words ' . . . confession liberates from death', would seem to attach some sacramental significance to the practice. It was certainly clear precedence for the spiritual direction of nuns by the abbess. It is also certain that in time some abbesses claimed the power of absolution, even though this was severely forbidden. Pope Innocent III (1160–1216) specifically forbade the abbesses of Burgos and Palentia (spanish Cistercians) from hearing the confessions of their nuns. See Lea, Auricular Confession, 1:218 and *Dictionnaire d'Archéologie Chrétien et de Liturgie*, 'Abbess', Vol 1:col. 42. One can surmise from this much evidence of the custom that it was much more widespread than the records show, and was probably well-rooted in the traditions of the Orders.

30. The lax condition of the convents in the late Middle Ages and immediately before the reforms of the sixteenth and seventeenth centuries is well known. It was part of the intimate history of Port-Royal. One of the cistercian monasteries to which Mére Angèlique was sent to institute the reforms she had carried out at Port-Royal was Maubuisson. Here the abbess, Madame d'Estrées, sister of the mistress of Henri IV, Gabrielle d'Estrées, provided a trysting place for her sister and the monarch, and brought up her own twelve children each according to the rank of its father. Hardly one of the *matres spirituales* to whom a nun would go for spiritual direction!

31. A basic principle of Port-Royal (jansenist) theology is reflected here. In the perennial grace versus free-will debate, Port-Royal accepted the most extreme interpretation of Paul and Saint Augustine about grace; namely, that no action pleasing God can be performed without the activating grace of God. To trust in material aids and one's own ability was often compared to the Jews' reliance on the law in the writings of Antoine Arnauld.

32. 2 Timothy 3:6–7: 'For such are they who make their way into households and capture weak women, burdened with sins and swayed by various impulses, who will listen to anybody and can never arrive at a knowledge of the truth.' Familiarity with Scripture is another characteristic of Port-Royal spirituality.

33. Luke 2:51: ' . . . and his mother kept all these things carefully in her heart'. The Port-Royalists were accused of lack of devotion for the Virgin Mary. On the contrary, their devotion for her was very sound. It never took the exaggerated form

which it did in other congregations of the era, but was solidly based in Scripture, liturgy, and the writings of the Fathers. Among the Port-Royal papers conserved at the Bibliothèque Nationale in Paris is a letter written by Angélique de Saint-Jean defending the Port-Royalists against those who accused them of not invoking Mary and the saints. In it she mentions devotion to Mary as part of their heritage as Cistercians. MS BN fonds *francais* 17,778, fol. 248–249, dated 1679.

34. This passage recalls the teaching of another great master of *école française* spirituality, Cardinal de Bérulle. Berulle was a friend and guide of Saint Cyran. Oratorians, founded by Bérulle, were directors for the nuns of Port-Royal when they first moved to Paris in 1626. This counter-reformation influence is another aspect of their spirituality. For Bérulle's spirituality of the Word Incarnate (and 'Jesus in Mary'), see M. Dupuy, *Pierre de Bérulle* (Paris, 1963) especially pp. 55–56; 150–156.

35. Psalm 41 (42):6.

36. A note about the use of the feminine pronoun in this translation. In French one is not always certain that *elle* refers to a woman, since generic terms such as *âme* and *personne* are feminine. The sense of this text, and the frequent references to *femmes et filles* in the text make me certain that my translation of *elle* as 'she' rather than 'he or she' is correct.

722

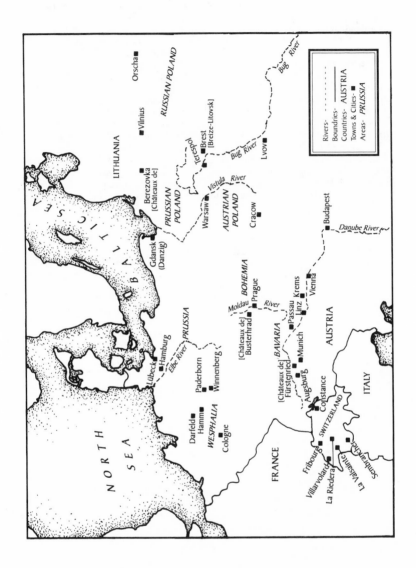

A New Branch of the Cistercian Order: The Cistercian-Trappistines[1]

† *Marie de la Trinité Kervingant* OCSO

CISTERCIAN NUNS IN FRANCE AT THE END
OF THE EIGHTEENTH CENTURY

AT THE TIME OF THE REVOLUTION, abbeys of cistercian monks were still very numerous in France. In his work *The Cistercians, Ideals and Reality*, Father Louis Lekai has given us a list of two hundred thirty-seven monasteries and, following the official statistics, the state of personnel in each of them in 1790, when all the monasteries were on the verge of disappearing. For the nuns, this systematic research based on the national Archives has not yet been done. Yet the study of certain archives, notices, monographs and a chart made about 1775 by a monk of Clairvaux show that there were a few more than a hundred houses of nuns, unequally scattered throughout the territory of France. Monasteries in the north of France were more numerous and, generally, had more personnel. In Paris itself there were four abbeys, including the royal abbey of Saint Antoine des Champs which had thirty-five religious in 1790. Their Father Immediate was the abbot of Cîteaux.

In monasteries of nuns the life was generally regular, peaceful, observant of enclosure, and fervent. Evidence on this is abundant, even if there were several exceptions.

The nuns had been less affected than the monks by the cultural evolution of the world around them. The Age of Enlightenment with its treacherous stars had hardly penetrated into the women's abbeys at all, even in those places where worldliness had been introduced to a greater or lesser degree. The trial which was approaching and would affect everyone was to bring out in a significant way that the women's faithfulness to their commitment was almost universal.

French Society

The period of political and social fever which preceded the meeting of the Estates General foreseen for 1789 developed in a kind of connivance, tacit agreement and near-harmony between the Nation and the Church. The most convinced 'patriots' felt the need of relying on the authority which the Church still had over the great majority of the french population. This was so, even though the *cahiers* (lists of grievances) of the Third Estate[2] manifested pronounced hostility toward the privileges, fiscal exemptions, and tithes reserved for the clergy and nobility. With regard to the monks, said the historian André Latreille,

> the hostility was less general or less radical than the attacks of the philosophers would lead us to believe; it was rare that suppression was intended, but the innumerable wishes for reform prove that public opinion was troubled by the decadence of monasticism and no longer accepted purely contemplative Orders having no directly useful social mission.[3]

The Revolutionary Laws and Their Religious Consequences

The Estates General opened on 5 May 1789, at Versailles. Very quickly, a process of disintegration of the established social order got under way. A few of the principal dates are as follows:

4 August 1789	Abolition of privileges, of the Church as well as of the nobility.
26 August 1789	Declaration of the Rights of Man and of the Citizen.
2 November 1789	The surrender to the Nation of all ecclesiastical property, including the monasteries.
13 February 1790	Prohibitory decree concerning pronouncement of solemn vows recognized by civil legislation. Doors open to all men and women who wished to leave the religious state. Inventory of possession.
12 July 1790	Civil Constitution of the Clergy.
27 November 1790	Oath of Fidelity to the Constitution required of priests.
10 March 1791	The pope speaks out against the oath and the revolutionary principles.

10 August 1792	The Church in France is divided; royal power is suspended.
18 August 1792	A decree of the Legislative Assembly abolishes all religious Orders.
1 October 1792	All convents are emptied, their inhabitants dispersed, their possessions sold or pillaged.

The Fate of the Expelled Nuns

Some of the nuns returned to their families, either permanently or to await the time when the storm would be over and they could resume community life. Others gathered together clandestinely. Some emigrated to England, Germany, or Switzerland.

But the storm was taking on greater dimensions. Among the nuns who had joined new groups, some were imprisoned and guillotined, as were the Carmelites of Compiègne and the group of thirty-two sisters of Orange among whom were two Cistercians of Saint Catherine of Avignon: Sisters Marguerite and Madeleine de Justamond.

For the dispersed nuns, life went along in semi-secrecy, especially if they were of the nobility. Such was the case of Rosalie de Vergèses du Mazel, called 'de Chabannes', who dressed as a peasant so that, on foot, she might reach Switzerland and the haven of peace which was established there in 1796. There, in June 1797, she rediscovered the monastic life in which she had made her vows at Saint Antoine de Paris two years before the Estates General convened. Other sisters, from other religious families, had preceded her; others would follow. Together they were to form the core group of the first Cistercian-Trappistines assembled at the monastery of the Sainte Volonté de Dieu, at Sembrancher in Valais, under the direction of Dom Augustin de Lestrange, who was then abbot of La Valsainte in the canton of Fribourg.

NEW SEEDS

The cistercian abbey of La Trappe in Normandy, reformed in the seventeenth century by Abbot Rancé, had remained fervent all during the eighteenth. With ninety-one religious, it was the largest community of the Order in France in 1789. Very highly esteemed by the people of their immediate vicinity, right up until the end of the year 1790, the monks hoped to escape the common fate. From the beginning of that year, however, one of the monks, Lestrange, had forebodings and took measures in view of a foundation in Switzerland. At the beginning of 1791, he obtained authorization from his superiors to go to Fribourg, where he received a kind welcome from ecclesiastical and civil authorities. The Senate of the canton placed at Father Augustin's disposal the ancient carthusian monastery, La Valsainte, which had been vacant for fifteen years, and offered him the possibility of bringing twenty-four companions there.

The group left during the first days of May and arrived at La Valsainte June first. In great poverty, by indefatigable labor, the monks renovated the house and prepared the land to be cultivated. Spurred on by their superior, and under the pressure of the tragic circumstances which had led them to leave La Trappe, the monks desired to perfect their fidelity to the rule of Saint Benedict by new rules going above and beyond what it required and also surpassing the rigors of Rancé's rules. These rules would never be approved by the Church.

After Father Augustin de Lestrange's motherhouse, La Trappe, had ceased to exist, he sought Rome's approval for his foundation by granting its erection into an abbey. This was accorded by the intermediary of the Nuncio at Lucerne, from whose hands he received the abbatial blessing on 8 December 1794. So it was that the canonical situation of the trappist foundation was established. A long career was to open up for the new emigrant branch of the Cistercians. During the next two centuries it was to give birth to some ninety-two monasteries of monks which exist today under the name, the Cistercian Order of the Strict Observance, and are now implanted on five continents.

The Nuns: La Sainte Volonté de Dieu

The initiative of the monks of La Trappe who had left France under the vigorous leadership of Dom Augustin de Lestrange was quite soon known by the general public in France, and the religious who had been dispersed in 1792 were not the last to take an interest in this. They had kept in their heart the desire of resuming the community life to which they had committed themselves when they were young, and they were on the alert to seize upon the slightest sign of hope. Some set out for Switzerland. From this movement was to be born a new community of cistercian nuns. Baptized 'Trappists' at first, because of their relationship with La Valsainte, these Cistercians soon became 'Trappistines', to distinguish them from their brother monks.

A short document discovered recently at Stapehill in England and written by the hand of Mother Augustin de Chabannes, traces rapidly the origin of the feminine community:

> Shortly after the establishment of our Fathers at La Valsainte, several religious women and other pious persons urged the Reverend Dom Augustin to form some sort of establishment for women. Full of zeal to come to the aid of the many religious who had been forced by the calamities of the Revolution to live in the world, he undertook this good work and had leaflets printed in Paris. In 1796, three benedictine religious and several laywomen came to Switzerland to implore him to carry this good work forward. On the thirteenth of September of the same year, they entered their little monastery; they were seven in number. It was Father Augustin who appointed a superior: a Benedictine, a simple religious in her monastery before the Revolution. The first profession took place on 17 September 1797, all this being in the hands of Dom Augustin and [done] by his authority alone. I have reason to believe that the bishop of Sion knew all about our establishment and approved of it, at least tacitly. Within the space of a year we found ourselves numbering more than sixty.[4]

This number is confirmed by the first registers found in the archives of several monasteries. These registers are of very great interest to us. The huge amount of data permits us to identify the geographical and social origin of candidates, their age, whether they persevered or not, when they made profession, when and where they died, and therefore the length of time each was in religious life.

Of sixty-two candidates who entered La Sainte Volonté de Dieu within fifteen months, twenty-eight were already religious: Benedictines, Capuchin Sisters, Carmelites, Cistercians, Poor Clares, Franciscans, Canonesses of Saint Augustine, and Ursulines. Fifteen of them would die Trappistines. Of the thirty-two unmarried women only fourteen would make profession, as would two widows. Of the total number, half of the postulants who entered would die in the Order.

A further word about the place where they assembled:

> Forty or fifty persons [wrote the Princess Louise de Condé, who had entered Sembrancher in September 1797] occupy this little ramshackle house, the four walls of which are divided inside by pine planks so as to form the principal regular places of a convent; among others, the choir, but where one is so squeezed and crammed in that it will soon be physically impossible to turn around . . . A grating separates [it] from the altar, which could

not be poorer, and this kind of chapel has indeed the advantage of reminding us of the stable in Bethlehem. All that, it is true, is perfectly suitable for the holy religious who live in this place . . . Not only is the dormitory full but already the refectory tables serve as beds, and the inconveniences that these holy souls suffer in order to give more place to those who come to serve God with them are, to their eyes, so many subjects of joy and happiness. Besides, an air of peace and contentment reigns here on their faces in a way that you cannot imagine.

In the political context, which remained alarming, the austere *Règlements* of La Valsainte, which they implored Dom Augustin to permit them to follow, were to be a sure element of unification of minds and hearts. During these first months the Father Abbot was often present, so that he himself might form the sisters to the spirit of the *Règlements*. He gave them talks each day, held chapter of faults for them, received them for confession or spiritual direction, followed each one of them in her spiritual evolution, and studied his people to discover their aptitudes and aspirations. But his monks complained about his absences, which they felt were too long.

The *Règlements* abound in minute prescriptions. The penitential character of the observances was pushed to the limit. This accounts for the multiplication and lengthening of prayers in common, the importance given to humiliations, the absolute nature of silence, the increase of work time at the expense of *lectio divina*, the reduction of time for sleep (six hours a night) and the dietary restrictions. Several quotations with respect to silence, work, and meals help us to understand better than commentaries the strict demands of the *Règlements*:

> [Silence] is looked upon as the foundation of all the regularity in this house, and the slightest infractions of it would be great faults. By these infractions one does not mean words pronounced, because that is a disorder which we do not even imagine exists, but signs accompanied by movements of the lips which help to make the sign understandable . . . All this leads to breaking silence, and comes infinitely close to it.[5]
>
> Manual work: The monk will remember that work is the first penance to which man was condemned by the Lord . . . The work of the religious [men and women] will have as its object first of all whatever there is to do in the house . . . food . . . they will weave their habits and will mend their togs . . . laundry . . . cow-shed . . . in a word, all the lowest and most humiliating exercises.[6]

Meals: The bread, with the poorest quality grain of the region . . . The drink: one should never drink wine, or beer, or cider, or any other beverage which can inebriate a person, but pure water . . . Meat, fish, eggs and butter are forbidden to all those who are in good health . . . Seasoning will never be put into our food, nor will butter, salt, honey or any kind of spice . . . but vegetables cooked in water with some salt in it.[7]

It is time to point out that this excessive *ascesis*, which went beyond human strength, was tempered in some way by the intention which ordered its exercise, and that it was to be expressed by constant and considerate charity. If the mind and the heart were turned more toward love in its two dimensions—God and others—they would be less attentive to what might be lacking to their own personal well-being. In the *Règlements* we find some gems on this subject:

Although it should reside principally in the heart, [charity] must also manifest itself exteriorly so as not to be able to go unrecognized . . . to be extremely attentive never to let anything appear which might wound charity in the slightest way.[8]

And if by frailty the slightest sign contrary [to charity] escapes us, we must make reparation at once.

There, no doubt, we find the secret of the peace and joy which appeared on the nuns' faces and in the day-to-day behavior within this new-born community. A great deal of evidence from diverse sources converges in affirming this joyful and peaceful atmosphere.

One cannot affirm, however, that the sixty persons assembled at La Sainte Volonté de Dieu had identical sentiments. Eighteen of them left the community before the beginning of the exodus across Europe. But two-thirds did not hesitate to take the plunge into the unknown.

Switzerland was, in fact, no longer a haven of peace. On Christmas Day 1797, Sister Mary Joseph wrote to her father, the Prince of Condé:

Switzerland is not escaping persecution by the French. At this moment the Directory is demanding, with arrogance and frightful despotism, the return of all the emigrants and it even appears to honor the Trappists by signaling them out and designating them in a particular way.[9]

The departure toward the east would soon be organized.

THE EXODUS ACROSS EUROPE

During the last months of the year 1797, Dom Augustin de Lestrange was following closely the political and military events manoeuvred by the Directory in France. He felt the danger that was approaching Switzerland and calculated his responsibility: more than two hundred persons had found asylum in the different houses he had opened in Switzerland: monks, nuns, religious of the Third Order, and children entrusted to their care. He had to ensure the safety of all these people.

He asked Sister Marie Joseph de Condé,[10] who in the past had received at Chantilly the Czar Paul I, when he was still czarevitch and at odds with his mother Catherine II, to ask the emperor of all Russia for places of refuge for the trappist emigrants. Before he had even received a favorable reply, Dom Augustin busied himself with organizing the departures. They would be by groups, sent out from the middle of January until 17 February 1798. So began the long march across Europe that was to last more than three and a half years.

Although the nuns were part of the total number of nearly two hundred and fifty persons, here we will speak only of their small group: forty-two persons when they left. It was to grow smaller because of deaths and departures, and then gain new members along the way. We will divide the account of this period into three parts: the journeys toward Russia and other places, two establishments in White Russia and Lithuania, and lastly the return toward the west.

The Journeys

When they left Sembrancher the nuns were divided into three 'bands' or 'colonies', each under someone responsible for the group. They were accompanied by one or two priests and several lay-brothers who were in charge of the itinerary and took care of the material aspects of the trip: baggage, buying, finding places to lodge at the stopping points, that is, monasteries or inns or other places in keeping with the general instructions of Dom Augustin, who coordinated the travels of the entire number.

The first part of the journey was arranged so that all the groups would advance toward Constance, then Augsburg, and finally Fürstenried in Bavaria, where they were to wait for the Czar's reply. The first group, consisting of eleven sisters, left on 19 January 1798, under Mother Sainte Marie Bigaux, the subprioress. The second group left the next day, under Mother Sainte Marie Laignier. Since the road going north was still open, the groups reached Constance at the end of January, and were welcomed by the Father Abbot. After a short time for rest, they were sent to Augsburg.

The third 'colony', led by Mother Augustin de Chabannes, left toward the middle of February and had a much more difficult journey. The revolutionary troops were at Bern. The sisters had to pass through the Rhone Valley and then the Rhine Valley, in the middle of March, in order finally to reach Constance, which was at an altitude of about 1500 meters and intensely cold. About 24 March the entire group was reunited at the castle of Fürstenried, where the monks and nuns spent Holy Week and Easter.

The reply of the Czar arrived about the end of March or beginning of April: fifteen monks and fifteen nuns were authorized to receive sanctuary at Orsha, in Byelorussia, in a convent of Trinitarian Fathers. That meant that there remained in Bavaria six or seven times as many brothers and sisters whose lot was far from being settled. The Father Abbot hoped later to obtain other places of sanctuary in Russia, but in the meantime he had to provide them with shelter and security.

One group of four monks and four nuns was received in an independent enclave in Bavaria. The Prince-Bishop of Freising accepted all these brothers and sisters, several of whom were unable to go any further because of poor health. They were sheltered in the Castle of Dürnast, a country house of a large benedictine abbey. The group remained there from the middle of May 1798 until the middle of April 1799. Three deaths occurred there, but also the postulants who had been accepted on the way were sent there and entrusted to the supervision of Madame de Chabannes.

At Munich the rest of the community embarked on the Isaar, a tributary of the Danube which flows into it a little before Passau. Crossing the border to Austria with the aid of a collective passport was held up by the mistrust of the border police, so that the travellers did not arrive at Vienna until the first days of June.

In the meantime, a little beyond Linz a 'colony' of nuns was separated from the others and went toward Bohemia, in the direction of Buštěrhad near Prague. This 'colony' would remain there until the middle of October. The community of visitation nuns in Vienna received them in a very fraternal way. Dom Augustin also met with kindness on the part of the Emperor Francis II, who led him to hope for a permanent place to stay in Austria. But royal ministers, disciples of the philosophy of Enlightenment, were opposed to this project. These negotiations delayed the departure for Russia of the group which was authorized to stay there. Leaving Vienna on 26 July 1798, fifteen nuns and fifteen monks led by Dom Augustin arrived at Orsha on 20 September, after a stop at Warsaw. Twelve monks and as many nuns stayed behind at the Visitation convent.

Through Sister Marie Joseph, the Father Abbot had the Czar notified of the arrival of the monks and nuns at Orsha, and requested a personal interview with him. Dom Augustin was received in a way such as he could have desired. Paul I promised him monasteries in the provinces of ancient Poland within his empire. In his kindness, he added pensions for fifty persons.

After meeting the Catholic metropolitan of Mogilev, on whom Orsha depended, the Father Abbot set out westward to organize the journey of his troops dispersed throughout Bohemia, Bavaria, and Austria, in a view of assembling them in Lithuania. Before leaving, he put the community of nuns at Orsha under the governance of Mother Sainte Marie Laignier (who had been the first superior and the first professed religious at the foundation of Sembrancher), and put the monastery under the patronage of the Holy Heart of Mary.

The Provisional Establishments

Orsha in White Russia. The community was made up of fifteen members, the majority of whom were still novices: even the novice mistress, a former Benedictine of Saint Paul of Beauvais, had not yet completed her full year of novitiate but she had the Father Abbot's confidence. There was also, naturally, Sister Marie Joseph de Condé. Regular life was begun without delay, in a setting which was already suitable for the monastic life:

> A house made entirely of brick, with all the places and workrooms necessary for a religious house [wrote one of the novices]. There was also a very beautiful garden, a pasture big enough for grazing four cows, barns, and everything that is needed for a barnyard. There was also a fine well. We had no trouble getting used to everything.[11]

But winter was coming and the cold that year, 1798–1799, was particularly intense. Byelorussia, or White Russia, was given this name because of the amount of snow there, and the temperature can go down to $-30°$ celsius. Only one room was heated; the sisters stayed there during the day. The church was not heated. The varying extremes of temperature caused terrible colds. The Father

Prior of the monks, who lodged some distance away, procured fox skins for the nuns to wrap around their hands and feet.

For ten months the Father Abbot did not show himself at Orsha and rumors circulated that he had projects for sending all his people to America, because he wanted to keep jurisdiction over the communities. Exemption was, in fact, contested by the metropolitan of Mogilev.

This instability of the abbot with regard to his projects worried Sister Marie Joseph, as did the excessively absolute importance he put on penance. She felt great uneasiness. After consulting the Father Prior and her director she decided to leave. This she did on 14 August 1799, with the novice mistress who had not yet committed herself by monastic profession.[12]

Notified of the crisis, Dom Augustin arrived in October and proposed that the novices make profession, seeing that their year of novitiate had been completed since their arrival at Orsha. Nine of them made their vows on 29 October 1799, and life went on peacefully until the following April.

The czar, disappointed by England's activity in the Mediterranean, changed his political stance and turned toward Bonaparte, whose success in Egypt had dazzled him. At the end of March he issued a *ukase*, giving legal notice to all french emigrants to leave his states within two weeks.

Lithuania. While the community at Orsha was living out its trials and joys, the three other communities, which had remained at Dürnast in Bavaria, at Buštěrhad in Bohemia, and at Vienna in Austria, knew that their days in their lands of exile were numbered. The Father Abbot intended for all of them to meet together again in Lithuania, in keeping with the czar's promise. At Dom Augustin's order, the colony in Bohemia left toward the middle of October 1798, moving in the direction of Lvov which at the time was in austrian Poland, to spend the winter there, close to Lithuania. They were given hospitality by the Benedictines there on 7 December, but two of them, including the prioress, Mother Sainte Marie Bigaux, died of infectious influenza contracted there. The superior of the Benedictines also died. Nevertheless, the sisters did not desist from their charity and continued to treat the survivors—eleven in number—in a fraternal way until July 1799.

The group of twelve sisters which had stayed with the visitation nuns in Vienna set out in the last part of November and spent the winter in Cracow in a convent of Norbertines. At the end of April 1799, they left by boat on the Vistula, and at the end of three weeks took carts and carriages to arrive in June at Brest-Litvosk, where they were lodged in a convent of Brigittines.

The colony which had passed the winter in Bavaria and had become richer by about twenty postulants or novices, responded to Dom Augustin's call and began a long roundabout trip at the end of March 1799. This journey brought them first to the important benedictine abbey of Göttweig. After staying there two weeks, the whole group of sixty monks and nuns set out on the same route as the previous group and arrived at Brest toward the end of June. Mother de Chabannes was then sent to Lvov to bring to Brest the group which had stayed with the Benedictines after the death of the two superiors.

At Brest the nuns of the three colonies were separated in two convents of Brigittines; then in October they continued on foot to a modest wooden *château* named Berezovka (from *beresa*, birch), where they then formed one single community under the direction of Mother Augustin de Chabannes. During their sojourn in Lithuania there would be five deaths among the sisters, the result of fatigue and privations experienced during their long journeys. This community was in existence scarcely six months when the *ukase* against the emigrants was issued at the end of March 1800.

The Return Westward

Two accounts of the return westward are extant, one by a novice of Berezovka and the other, incomplete, by a novice of Orsha. Here we will fuse them into a single account. While the first group had a two-weeks head-start on the second, both had similar adventures, because both groups had first to reach Brest. The first did this quickly; the second had a long snowy way to travel.

Brest-Litvosk, located on the right of the River Bug in Russian Lithuania, had opposite it on the left bank Terespol, at that time in Austrian territory. The Bug constituted a natural boundary. To go from Brest to Terespol, one needed either Austrian or Prussian passports. The former were refused to the emigrants, who found it necessary to wait for Prussian passports. But the colony no longer had the right to remain in Russia. Beneath the bridge which joined the two cities there was an island, a no man's land, neutral ground.

> A charitable man lent us a boat of which he was the master, so that we might take refuge there until we received our passports . . . We were in peace in our boat, as if we had been in a monastery. We built a fire on the island for cooking and doing the laundry. All the regular exercises were observed, holy Mass was said and

the sacraments were administered because our Fathers had their
boat alongside ours [the group of monks from Orsha had tents]
and rendered us services . . . Silence was observed as it is in our
houses and on our boats.[13]

At the end of two weeks they started out on the Vistula for Danzig.
The voyage took two months. There the sisters were given hospitality by brigittine sisters, and the brothers by brigittine brothers.
During this new exodus some novices left and there were some
deaths among the sisters.

About 20 July 1800, three vessels were put at their disposal for
their forced peregrinations by a lutheran shipowner, and the participants went to the port to await a favorable wind which would
permit them to leave. Their departure took place on 26 July.

They should have arrived at Lübeck several days later, but a
terrible storm blew up on the Baltic, separated the boats and made
almost all the passengers seasick. But on 7 August, they did dock at
Lübeck, with no losses to bewail. Following a short period of rest
the travellers set off for Hamburg where Dom Augustin had rented
two houses on the outskirts of the city: one for the monks at Altona,
to the west of the city on the banks of the Elbe, and the other for
the nuns at Hamm, to the east.

The community of nuns was at the time composed of thirty-nine
members. Of these, twenty-one had entered at Sembrancher and
eighteen of those who had entered during the travels had persevered.
The superior was Mother Augustin de Chabannes, who was soon
to be sent to England with a group of foundresses. Mother Sainte
Marie Laignier would then take charge of the community. Yet there
would be two deaths at Hamm before the transfer of the mother-
community to Paderborn.

NEW IMPLANTATIONS AND AN ADOPTION

The period spent at Hamm—six to eight months—was a crucial
time in the existence of the women's community. During this period
it would twice swarm and so be separated. One group of eight
members was designated for Westphalia, another of four members
for England. This definitive separation gave birth to two stable
communities. From them, in turn, new communities were to grow
during the nineteenth and twentieth centuries. When the mother-
community transferred from Hamm to Paderborn, which was also
in Westphalia, it had no more than twenty members.

The Foundation at Darfeld

In August 1793, three monks left La Valsainte with orders to go to Canada. The port at Amsterdam however, was closed because of the war. They returned to Antwerp where, in June 1794, the bishop procured an ancient convent of Augustinians for them, Westmalle. Twenty days later they were obliged to flee from revolutionary armies and found refuge in Westphalia, in the diocese of Münster. On property put at their disposal they constructed a building of clay masonry, along with a church. The community, directed by Dom Eugene de Laprade, soon drew new members.

In October 1800, Dom Augustin sent four nuns of Hamm to the Benedictine convent in Winnenberg to join four other sisters who had come from Danzig by land because of their poor health. They were led by Mother Edmond Paul de Barth. After several weeks of rest with the Benedictines they set out for Darfeld and arrived there the following 28 December. Dom de Laprade had arranged a second building for them, built up against the monks' enclosure wall. Gradually the monks moved to farm buildings rented by Dom Eugene, and the women's community could develop more freely.

Very soon postulants entered, and already in 1802 there were twenty professions. The following year there were twenty-one, but there were a number of deaths as well, and the number of postulants entering decreased somewhat. Between 1800 and 1810 there were eighty professions and forty-five deaths. In this year, 1810, the community consisted of thirty-four professed nuns and eight novices.

Mother Edmond Paul de Barth, a former Cistercian from Hagenau in Alsace, died 28 August 1808 and was replaced by Mother Hélène Van den Broeck, a former capuchin sister born in Brussels. In August 1809, the last survivor of the nuns who had been sent from Sembrancher to Darfeld died. By then the new community had taken root well and already had its own character.

The Foundation in England

Scarcely had the new colony sent to Westphalia begun to get organized under the benevolent authority of the prior of Darfeld than Dom Augustin thought of swarming again. In January 1801, he took advantage of a necessary trip to England to sound out the attitude of the english government and that of the trappist monks who had already settled four years earlier at Lulworth in Dorsetshire.

When he returned in February the Father Abbot was thinking about a women's foundation near the monks. Although it seems that nothing certain had been assured, when the 'general' came back to the continent he wasted no time in giving orders for the departure of a second swarm.

Led by Mother Augustin de Chabannes whom we have already met, four nuns got ready to leave Hamburg toward the middle of March. They disembarked at Saint Catherine's Docks, London before the end of the month.

A Catholic banker, Mr Wright, who generously devoted himself to rendering service to emigrants, welcomed them into his own home until the dwelling rented for them—Blyth House, Hammersmith, near London—was ready for them. They stayed there ten months. During this time the prior of Lulworth, Dom Jean Baptiste Noyer, interested their benefactor, M. Weld, in this project of a nuns' foundation. Lord Arundel of Wardour, of a family related to the Welds, placed at the sisters' disposal a house and small estate where Jesuits had formerly lived. The company had now been broken up, and Stapehill became a cistercian monastery.

Before the sisters could move in, the house needed to be put into good condition. The priests and brothers of Lulworth, located fifty miles away, busied themselves energetically with this work, while in January 1802, the sisters accepted an offer from Lady Mannock to lodge in her home, Burton House near Christ Church. They moved into Stapehill on 21 October 1802. There were, says the register, 'three professed religious, one sister admitted to profession and five novices'.[14] The first assistant to the prioress was Mother M. Josephine de Montron, who had been a professed Carmelite for sixteen years when she entered Sembrancher on 10 October 1796. The third professed was Sister Julie Favot, who had entered at Augsburg and made profession at Orsha. She died on 13 October 1803. The novice admitted to profession was Sister Teresa Lamb, of scottish origin and protestant family. She had been converted young and had previously made profession with the *Annonciades célestes* of Sens. She had joined the Trappistines at Dürnast on 20 October 1798, but circumstances had postponed her definitive commitment. Now, at this time, she was appointed mistress of novices and remained so until her death on 6 August 1831, when she was more than sixty-two years old.

By a decision of the prioress which the community approved, the monastery was dedicated to the Holy Cross. Slowly but surely the community developed, in spite of unstable and sporadic local recruitment. In 1816 it had twenty-eight members. There had been seven deaths, and of the fifty-one women who had entered, fourteen had left.

The cornerstone of this foundation was, quite surely, Mother Augustin de Chabannes who possessed solid convictions and was firm about the place of the cross of Christ in a life consecrated to God's praise. She did not lack trials. The greatest of them was the separation from the Cistercian Order imposed by Rome in 1824, at the request of the apostolic vicar of Plymouth, who feared that the community was going to die out because of the many deaths among young sisters unable to endure the excessive austerity of the *Règlements* of Dom Augustin. Mother Augustin, the last survivor of the Trappistines who had entered Sembrancher, died on 13 June 1844. She was seventy-five years old, had lived forty-seven years at La Trappe and sixty in cistercian life.

The Mother-Community Returns to Switzerland

The nuns' community which had remained at Hamm after swarming twice—to Westphalia and to England—was obliged to think about a transfer, for the houses near Hamburg had been rented only until the middle of March 1801.

As soon as the Father Abbot returned from England in February, he turned his attention to finding other places to lodge his monks and nuns who had come back from Russia. With this in mind he approached the Prince-Bishop of Paderborn. Thanks to his protection, the nuns had the advantage of being received within the city of Paderborn itself, in a former convent of Capuchins located near the cathedral. Yet, the founding community still had several stages to go through before it was to find a stable place where it could finally establish itself.

After settling at Paderborn in April 1801, a scouting group went to Switzerland in October 1802, and stopped at Villarvolard in the canton of Fribourg. There were six sisters under Mother Marie du Saint-Esprit Allard, a native of Lyon and former capuchin sister who had entered Sembrancher in July 1797. She had been sent to Darfeld, where she made profession in 1802, but Dom Augustin had called her back to Paderborn so he might entrust to her the five nuns who were to constitute the group on which would be based the reconstruction of the community in Switzerland. The new site, Villarvolard, was near La Valsainte, which the monks had received authorization to recover a short time earlier.

Six months later the prioress, Mother Sainte Marie Laignier, died at Paderborn; five other sisters had returned to God before her. Dom Augustin decided therefore to close the house at Paderborn, and told the twelve sisters who were still there to join the group at Villarvolard. They were reunited at the beginning of June 1803. The house in which they were sheltered was only rented, however. Dom Augustin obtained authorization from the Senate of Fribourg to purchase a piece of property—La Petite Riedera—located a little further north, and to add buildings to the country house which was situated in a very pleasant spot.

While the brothers of La Valsainte, aided by masons and carpenters, were putting up the church and a large building, the sisters who had left Villarvolard in August 1804, lodged in a castle called La Grande Riedera, close by the building site. There they received postulants, just as they had at Paderborn and Villarvolard. There were also some deaths: three at Villarvolard between October 1802 and August 1804, and six at La Grande Riedera between August 1804 and November 1805.

It was on 19 November of that year that the community solemnly took possession of La Petite Riedera, rejoicing that they had finally found a place of rest. The next day the bishop of Fribourg came to consecrate the newly-built church; so came into being the monastery of Notre Dame de la Sainte Trinité.

In spite of the numerous deaths the community grew, and in 1811 numbered forty-nine members. That year, a fateful one for the Trappists as we shall soon see, the sisters were forbidden to receive any more new members.

A Spontaneous Generation and its Adoption

On 2 July 1798, under the Directory, sisters met in the heart of Paris in the convent of sisters formerly called Ursulines of the Faubourg Saint Jacques. One of them was a professed nun in the Benedictines of the Blessed Sacrament; her two companions, young 'working girls' according to the register, were both twenty-three years of age. A little later a former novice of La Trappe in turn gathered together several monks and laymen who wanted to live in community.

When and how did these groups get together in Paris? No document states this exactly. It must have been quite early because by 15 March 1799, the register of religious women speaks of a sister who entered in August 1798 and left 'against the advice of the superior' (masculine). This can be none other than Père Miquel. Two police notes from 1801 and 1802 indicate the presence of Trappists of both sexes; the first mentions those in the Faubourg Saint Jacques, the second those in the Faubourg Saint Marceau. We may suppose that between these two denunciations the communities were alerted and moved. Still later, one finds them to the south-east of Paris in the forest of Sénart. In 1804 the nuns transferred again, to Grosbois, north of the forest, and there they remained until 1808.

Poor temporal administration had led to an accumulation of debts. The community changed its masculine superior twice. The sisters also changed their superior several times. Finally, in 1807, the bishop of Versailles on whom the two communities depended, called upon Dom Augustin to try to see exactly what the situation was. This resulted in the adoption of the two groups in 1808 by the Abbot of La Valsainte.

He separated the nuns from the group by transferring them to Valenton. Like their brothers at Grosbois, they were to adopt the *Règlements* of La Valsainte in place of those of Rancé, which they had been following up until that time. After all this had been decided, the Father Abbot found the means to pay all the debts, and once its financial situation had been set to rights the feminine community devoted itself fervently to its monastic life.

The various shake-ups had not put an end to their recruitment. Nevertheless, several of the foundresses had died or left. Between 1798 and 1811, that is, in fourteen years, one hundred and twenty-one persons entered, sixty-six left, there were fifty-three professions and twenty-six deaths.[15]

A curious thing is that during this year 1811 the prefect of Seine-et-Oise (Versailles) was troubled about the numerous deaths and spoke to the Minister of the Interior about it. He proposed the suppression of 'these associations which can render no service to society'. He brought up the question of their legal existence: do they really have authorization from the Emperor?[16]

Honesty obliges us to say that the *Règlements* of Dom de Lestrange were far above women's strength, and this fact was made worse by a curious practice added to the terms of monastic profession indicated by Saint Benedict. From 1802 on, the sisters introduced into their profession formula an offering of themselves as victim. Sister Saint Pétronilla drew up her profession formula on 8 September 1802 in the following way:

> I, Sister Saint Pétronilla, offer myself in sacrifice to God, as a victim for my sins and those of all men; I unite my sacrifice to that of

Jesus Christ my Saviour, in reparation and honorable amendment for the outrages against His Sacred Heart. In this spirit I promise perpetual stability in this Society, conversion of my manners and obedience according to the rule of Saint Benedict . . .[17]

In reality, the Minister of the Interior had no need to convince the Emperor that he should suppress this useless group of people: Napoleon was already convinced of it by other facts that will be recounted later. After putting a price on Dom Augustin de Lestrange's head, on 28 July of this year 1811, he decreed the closing of all trappist monasteries in the french empire.

STORMS

Internal Storm: Schism in the Cistercian-Trappist Order (1806–1808)

Following the return from Russia, several years of relative tranquillity had permitted the communities of monks and nuns of the Reform of La Trappe to attain a certain degree of stability. The hope of all of them, that is, 'to preserve their holy state' according to the formula of consecration, was being brought to realization.

But the providential man who was directing the whole affair with dexterity and devotion, and also with undeniable rectitude of intention, in his zeal did not think he could stop there. A sort of fever for foundations took hold of him and he thought he should go on with his limitless expansion. The brothers began to grow weary of this, and cracks began to appear in the structure in an indistinct way.

Contrary to the customs of the Order, Dom Augustin had given himself universal power over all the houses of his reform, of both monks and nuns. His absolute and sometimes arbitrary power was exercised in many ways: persons he moved around; property he disposed of as he wished.

A number of storm signals accumulated within the Reform of La Valsainte, of which Darfeld was the closest and most stable community in terms of the continuity of its government. One spring day in 1806 its prior, Dom Eugene de Laprade, decided to leave for London to clarify the question of pensions which the english government had accorded, at the request of Dom Augustin, to the Trappists who had come back from Russia. Dom Augustin learned that this had been done without his authorization. 'He believed he had to descend upon Darfeld and make them feel both his discontent and the weight of his master's hand.' This visit, which occurred toward the end of April or at the beginning of May, did not turn out as successfully as he had hoped. At the beginning of June he sent a new prior to the house. The subprior sent him back, even though he was a professed monk of Darfeld. The next day the subprior assembled the community for the election of a prior: Dom Eugene, absent, was elected unanimously.

Forbidden by Dom Augustin to return to Darfeld, the newly-elected prior remained in London until October, and then went back. In the meanwhile, the community had been placed under the protection of the Vicar General of Fürstenberg, who held the office of Ordinary for Münster as well as for Paderborn.

From Fribourg, Dom Augustin sent the Nuncio in Switzerland a report for the pope concerning the crisis which had become acute because of this 'brutish' (*sauvage*) election.

The dealings with the Roman Curia lasted almost two years. They were concluded by progressive steps. In October 1807, the Congregation of Bishops and Regulars suspended Dom Augustin's jurisdiction over Darfeld 'provisionally'. The following 21 June, a roman decree raising the community of Darfeld into an abbey made the break complete. This brought with it the severing of relationships between the two communities of nuns: the community of Westphalia became subject to Darfeld with Dom Eugene as its Father Immediate; the community in Switzerland remained subject to Dom de Lestrange. In 1814 the former re-adopted the *Règlements* of Rancé, whereas the latter continued to live according to the *Règlements* of La Valsainte.

The Napoleonic Storm: The Closing of the Trappist Monasteries in the Empire (1811)

Dom Augustin de Lestrange, who had enjoyed the favor of the emperor for a while, was to experience just how far a despot's wrath can go when someone has displeased him.

In May 1805, Napoleon had himself crowned king of Italy at Milan. On this occasion he received a supplication in latin verse from a trappist monk of the Republic of Genoa, entreating him for the preservation of his monastery. The monarch asked if a house could be founded by the Trappists and directed by them to serve as a hospital for his troops on their way from France to Italy. Napoleon had his Minister Portalis write to Dom Augustin that not only did he preserve the monastery of La Cervara, but he desired to found a hospice at Mont Genèvre on the road to Italy. Plans were drawn up and work was begun.

Four years later, in May 1809, the emperor signed the famous decree by which he declared the definitive joining of the Papal States to the Empire, giving as his reasons the tranquility of peoples and the dangers of the mixture of spiritual and temporal power. The morning of 10 June the decree was read publicly throughout the whole city of Rome. On the 20th, the pope replied by excommunication and on 6 July Pius VII was wafted away from the Quirinal, transferred to Florence, then to Alexandria (not far from Genoa) and finally to Savona. The abbot of La Valsainte went to visit him. Napoleon learned of this and began to have suspicions about the abbot of the Trappists. He had him imprisoned at Bordeaux while Dom Augustin was getting ready to leave for America. This transpired in May 1811.

At the end of 1810 an oath of fidelity to the Constitutions of the Empire was required of all italian parish priests. The prefect of the Apennines asked the monks of La Cervara to make this oath. They did so. When Dom Augustin learned of this he ordered them to make a public retraction, which took place on Sunday, 16 July 1811.

The Emperor lost no time in finding out how this handful of men had dared to stand up against the conqueror of Austerlitz and Wagram. A sanction followed without delay, in the form of a decree issued at Saint-Cloud on 25 July; it was as peremptory and lashing as fire from a machine gun: 'The convents of La Trappe are suppressed in all the territory of our Empire, even the one at Mont Genèvre'.

With the complicity of friends, Dom Augustin obtained a passport for Switzerland, and so escaped from the imperial police who pursued him for weeks without catching up with him. He left on horseback toward the East with a friend, arrived in Finland, and from there, went on to England and then America.

During this time, the houses of monks and nuns in France, in Belgium, in Westphalia, in Italy, and also La Valsainte in Switzerland were emptied of their inhabitants. Some were deported, some put into prison and freed only at the fall of the Empire (1815). As for the nuns, the first affected were those of Valenton, near Paris. They took refuge first in Paris, then in Brittany. The community of Darfeld was cut in two. The Germans and the Dutch found asylum in Cologne, where they worked as hired-hands in a factory; the French and Belgians ended up by finding a castle, Borsut, near Liège, where they took refuge. Only the sisters of La Riedera were left untroubled, protected as they were by the Senate of Fribourg. But they were forbidden to receive new members.

In the crucible of trial, for the three houses of nuns as well as for the monks, a future was being prepared which would progressively raise them from these ruins.

BEGINNING ANEW

August 1811 until May 1814 were almost three years of anxious waiting for events that would be favorable or unfavorable to the despot who had put an end to the laborious but peaceful existence of the Trappistines. Even if news got around more slowly then than today, nevertheless it did sooner or later reach attentive ears. Many people perceived with more or less insight that the emperor was making more and more diplomatic or military errors, and they saw his genius panic-stricken when faced with opposition or failures. His bold attempts to snap back did not succeed in giving new confidence in the future to those of his friends who were the most clear-sighted, or to the populations subject to his authority.

With a new effort, the Allies combating France entered Paris on 31 March 1814. Napoleon had to abdicate on 4 April and was exiled to the Island of Elba.

As soon as this news was known, monks and nuns who had been exiled and dispersed, particularly Cistercian-Trappists, set about trying to go back—to their monasteries, if possible, or to other places in France. The news soon reached America, where Dom Augustin was. Abandoning their attempts at foundations, which were not at all satisfying, the monks boarded ship for France in two groups.

On 26 February 1815, however, the solitary reigning on a tiny island embarked for France, and on 20 March Napoleon was at the Tuileries. He would reign there for the One Hundred Days, before having to surrender and give himself up to the English after Waterloo.

On 8 July, Louis XVIII re-entered Paris, from which he had fled during the preceding March, and re-established the monarchy for thirty years, a period called in France the Restoration.

What was the life of the trappistine nuns during this time? Each of the dispersed communities has its own history. We will trace out the principal lines in chronological order.

The Dispersed Nuns of Darfeld were separated into two groups. One took refuge in Cologne, the other at Borsut. They would never be reunited again.

As of 26 May 1814, the former returned to their monastery at Darfeld for a while under the direction of Mother Hélène Van den Broeck. The Congress of Vienna in 1815 had given Westphalia to Prussia, and the meddling police were looking for ways to make life impossible for nuns as well as for monks. In 1825 the superior of the german monks sought asylum in France. The bishop of Strasbourg kindly procured for him a former convent of Canons Regular of Saint Augustine, not far from Mulhouse. This place was called Oelenberg, or Mount of Olives. The nuns followed them there. They numbered thirty-eight at the time, and left Westphalia in January 1826. They found refuge in the large monastery of the monks at Oelenberg, separated from them by very strict enclosure. By 1814 both communities had returned to the *Règlements* of Rancè. They remained at this twin-monastery until 1895, when the nuns transferred to Notre-Dame d'Altbronn, within the limits of the village of Ergersheim in Lower Alsace (Bas-Rhin) in the diocese of Strasbourg, where they still are.

It took more time for the group which had taken refuge at Borsut in Belgium to find their orientation. Dom Eugene remained perplexed, because by the Treaty of 1815 Belgium had been incorporated into Holland, under the name The Low Countries, and was therefore governed by a protestant prince who had no sympathy for monks. Fortunately, M. de la Roussière, who had been given hospitality at la Trappe of Darfeld when he had emigrated to Westphalia, proposed an ancient monastery of Canons Regular of Sainte Geneviève at Entrammes, near Laval in Mayenne. He had acquired this house during the Empire. The monks took up residence there on 21 February 1815, and the name of the convent was changed from Port-Reinghard to Port du Salut.

At the beginning of 1816, Mlle Letourneur Laborde, a friend of the Roussière family, proposed the foundation of a monastery of cistercian nuns in another ancient priory of Canons Regular of Saint Geneviève, this one at the entrance to the city of Laval. When he was consulted, Dom Eugene approved the project, as did the bishop of Le Mans (Laval had not yet been erected into a diocese). He appointed Mother Elisabeth Piette, a professed nun and subprioress of Darfeld, as superior of a little group formed of two choir nuns, two professed lay sisters, and six postulants who had entered at Borsut. They set out for France on 16 April 1816. On Thursday, 6 June they were welcomed by their benefactress who took them to the home of M. de la Roussière where they would stay until their lodgings were ready for them. They entered Sainte Catherine de Laval the following 18 November. Dom Eugene died on 16 June at Verlaine, in Belgium.

In no time postulants came to enter and the regular life was promptly organized. Preoccupied with the sisters' health, and following suggestions of the prioress, the abbot of Port du Salut obtained from the bishop of Le Mans certain mitigations to the *Règlements* of Rancé, and the community grew so that its erection into an abbey was requested from Rome. This was accorded by a pontifical Bull on 14 April 1826. In 1859, the community transferred to Avesnières, near the gates of Laval, to the new monastery of La Coudre, and was placed under the patronage of the Immaculate Conception.

From Brittany to Normandy

The community of Valenton which had taken refuge at Tréguier and had resumed community life under the governance of Mother Marie des Séraphins de Chateaubriand (a cousin of the writer), was living among the Bretons in relative peace. After the first abdication of Napoleon it was in no hurry to leave its place of refuge. But in the spring of 1815 it decided to move, almost at the same time the fallen monarch was on his way back to France.

The community was so poor, says the chronicle, that the journey was made on foot, a donkey carrying the baggage. The Mother Prioress, we are told, intended to return to Valenton near Paris. While the sisters were on their way, an offer was made to them to buy the remains of an ancient abbey of Premonstratensians near Juay, not far from Bayeux. They took possession of the *Mons Dei, La Maison-Dieu*, Mondaye, on 8 May 1815. The chronicle notes that there were only seven nuns at the time. Between 1815 and 1827, there were fifty-six professions, but also thirty deaths, because their regime was even more strict than that of La Valsainte.

After this the register of entries was no longer kept up to date, because the community was declining from day to day, especially after the death of Madame de Chateaubriand in 1832. This caused a serious crisis which was a source of anxiety to the Order. The General Chapter of 1836 asked the Trappistines of Laval to take the community in hand rather than making the foundation they wanted to make. The situation would remain unsteady because of the great poverty. In 1845 a transfer was made under the authority of the abbot of La Grande Trappe who was still their Father Immediate.

This took them to the diocese of Chartres, to La Cour Pétral, where a benefactress had appeared who was willing to assure the sisters of a place to live and their subsistence, but not without inextricable difficulties. In 1935 the community would experience another transfer, this time to the Belgian Ardennes, to Clairefontaine, where it is today.

From Switzerland to France

When Dom Augustin de Lestrange returned from America in November 1814, he promptly gave his attention to bringing the majority of his monks back to France. Dom Eugene de Laprade, who was negotiating to buy the ruins of La Trappe (Soligny), offered to let him have the house of his profession as well as the sum which he had obtained by begging and which would cover part of the purchase price. Dom Augustin accepted this brotherly aid with simplicity and gathered together the dispersed monks at La Valsainte. When he learned of the return of the Emperor he left the continent in haste for England. After Waterloo he came back to France, and of the monks assembled at La Valsainte made two groups. One group was sent to Aiguebelle, to an ancient cistercian abbey, under the leadership of the prior, Dom Étienne Malmy, who had weathered the storm. Dom Augustin took the road to La Trappe with the other group. It was November 1815. The monks who had come back from America went to the abbey of Bellefontaine, formerly a monastery of Feuillants, and were under the direction of Father Urbain Guillet.

Dom Augustin could not leave the nuns in Switzerland. During the year 1816, between 29 February and 4 October, five successive groups of six persons left La Riedera, three for Les Forges near la Trappe in Normandy, and two for Frenouville near Caen, where offers had been made to the Father Abbot. Six months later, however, this little community of twelve persons left for Lyon, the native city of the superior, Mother Marie du Saint Esprit Allard, in order to find more effective help for their implantation. Unlike the two houses which sheltered the communities of Sembrancher and Darfeld, the house at La Riedera still stands today and has become the property of the bishops of Fribourg.

The community of Forges, opened on 19 May 1816, had as its superior Mother Thérèse Malatesta who had entered Grosbois in 1804. She had been sent to Notre-Dame de la Sainte Trinité by Dom Augustin in 1809 and had made her stability there on 21 January 1810.

Soon afterwards, the Father Abbot, who had begun to have serious difficulties with the bishop of Sées, responded to a request addressed to him and sent the superior of Forges to take possession of a former convent of Augustinians in Anjou, at Notre-Dame des Gardes. The community prospered and in 1821 Dom Augustin sent the whole community of Forges to join the sisters at Gardes so that they might escape from the jurisdiction of the bishop of Sées. The number of persons in the community was then close to ninety.

The community at Lyon developed in an analogous way and, after another transfer, settled at Vaise on the outskirts of Lyon. This community was particularly faithful to Dom Augustin, and it was there that the founder of the reform died on 16 July 1827, at the hour the nuns were singing the *Te Deum* in honor of Saint Stephen Harding, third founder of Cîteaux.

In 1834 the community of Lyon-Vaise was transferred to Maubec, near Montélimar. But the people of Lyon demanded 'their' Trappistines back, and in 1837 life was taken up again at Lyon-Vaise. In 1904, however, faced with the provisions of the laws of separation of Church and State, the community transferred to Rogersville, Canada, under the name Notre-Dame de l'Assomption.

When Dom Augustin died, there were five monasteries of nuns issued from the monastery of La Sainte Volonté de Dieu: Les Gardes, Lyon-Vaise, Altbronn, and Laval in France, and Stapehill in England. In addition, there was one adopted monastery: Mondaye. At the end of the century, they had become fourteen through seven new foundations and one adoption. In the first half of the twentieth century, which witnessed two long wars, there were nine foundations and four affiliations. Since 1945, new foundations and affiliations have brought the total to sixty-four monasteries and a little more than nineteen hundred nuns on five continents.

To what can this astonishing growth be attributed?

We are allowed to think that the Spirit of God had been actively at work and that, from the very beginning, he found generous hearts ready to listen to him. Their example drew others after them and the sap of this new branch of the Cistercian Order did not wither.

> Everything begins at present, even the past . . . History has been handed down to us . . . And history waits for the response of each one of us.
>
> René Habachi

Translated by Elizabeth Connor, OCSO

NOTES

1. This chapter is a brief summary of a volume published in French early in 1989. Entitled: *Aux origines des Cisterciennes-Trappistines: Des Moniales face à la Révolution française 1790–1816* (Paris: Beauchesne). An english translation is in preparation.

2. The Third Estate represented 98% of the french population. The privileged Clergy and Nobility formed approximately 2% of the population and possessed a great part of the territory.

3. A. Latreille, *L'Église catholique et la Révolution française*, 1: p. 82.

4. Archives of Holy Cross Abbey, Stapehill, Dorset, England; now Whitland, Wales.

5. *Règlements de la Maison-Dieu de N. D. de La Trappe . . . augmentés des usages particuliers . . . de la Valsainte*, 2:110.

6. *Ibid.*, p. 133.

7. *Ibid.*, p. 159.

8. *Ibid.*, p. 102.

9. *Correspondance de la Princesse de Condé*, published by Dom Jean Rabory, osb (Paris, 1889) p. 172.

10. Archives of La Trappe, *cote* 217, *pièce* 28, p. 3.

11. Account of the journeys of Sister Maur Miel (Archives of the Benedictines of Angers) p. 19.

12. The Princess Louise de Condé felt more attracted by community adoration of the exposed Blessed Sacrament. At the beginning of 1800 she went to the Benedictines of Warsaw, where she made profession. Threatened by the approaching imperial armies, she left for England. From there she returned to France at the time of the Restoration and founded at Paris the convent of the Benedictines of the Temple.

13. Account written by Mother Stanislas Michel, Cistercian of Sainte Catherine d'Avignon. Archives of La Trappe, *cote* 55, no.13 bis.

14. Register of entries at Stapehill, first page. This register is still in use at Holy Cross Abbey.

15. Register of entries from 1798 until 1827, preserved in the archives of the community of Maubec.

16. National Archives, Paris. F. 19 6325, no.16, July, 1811.

17. Collection of profession formulas from various places, kept in the archives at Les Gardes.

Who Shall Find
A Valiant Woman?[1]

Mary Magdalen Coppendale ocso

AT HOLY CROSS ABBY, Stapehill, in the superior's room, there hung for many years a small portrait roughly 6" x 9" of a nun in a cistercian cowl. It is a little faded after being such a long time exposed to the light. Now in safe keeping at Whitland, the portrait was given to the community in November 1844, and is drawn from memory rather than taken from life. Let us study it carefully, for it is a likeness of Madame[2] Rosalie Augustin de Chabannes, the 'eldest daughter' of Dom Augustin de l'Estrange and mother of all the nuns of La Trappe.[3] The little picture is no great work of art, but it must be a fairly faithful likeness of their foundress, otherwise the Community of Stapehill would not have treasured it.[4]

Madame de Chabannes is depicted here in old age, and the tranquility of age is seen in her features. She is seated, and one suspects, a little bowed, as her hands are clasped over a sturdy walking stick. The general attitude is reminiscent of a well-known portrait of Cardinal Newman in his old age. She wears what is recognizably the cistercian habit, though it differs slightly from that which we all wore before 1970, and in greater degree from that commonly worn nowadays. But the habit does not tell us much; it is the face we want to look at. There is nothing thin or drawn about it, high, arched brows, wide, full eyes, a long nose and small, determined chin. Yet it is the mouth that surprises; wide and straight, with slightly upturned corners which suggest that the grim terror of a prison in Revolutionary France was not the only, or even the dominant, influence in her life. There is a humorous twist to those lips, so firmly closed, yet not insensitive. Here we have no fanatic,

751

but someone with clear yet balanced priorities, a balance achieved, as so often in those truly close to God, by a sense of humor.

Marie Rosalie de Vergèzes was born at Lagogne, capital of Gevaudan, on 19 May 1769, of a family of *petite noblesse* or minor aristocracy. The baptismal register tells us that her father was noble Antoine de Vergèzes, her mother Dame Marianne de Clavel. Her godparents were a cousin and one of her sisters. The child was dedicated to Our Lady from infancy and at the age of five was sent to be educated at the historic cistercian abbey of Saint Antoine des Champs, where her elder sister was already a professed religious and directress of the boarding school. It says much for the closeness of family ties that the young Rosalie had a cousin and a sister for godparents and a sister as head of the school where she was to receive her education. Later, Madame de Chabannes herself used to tell how, when she was taken to this sister and told that she would be her mistress, she drew back and declared that 'Mama says that one sister cannot exercise authority over another'. For a child of five this suggests a firm and decided character, with its full share of an independent spirit. It also suggests that the grown-up Rosalie's gift of wise government was inherited from her mother. In the event, however, her elder sister lavished such care and affection on her that for Rosalie it became a source of temptation and she would sometimes threaten to leave the monastery. This she never did and when, having reached the age of fifteen, it was time for her to leave the boarding school, she chose to enter the novitiate. Three years later, on 3 June 1787 she made profession taking the name of Augustine and being just eighteen years of age. At this time she was given as her dowry the estate of Chabannes and it was by this name that she was subsequently known.

1787—an ominous date for a young french girl of good family to commit herself to a life in religion. The peaceful, ordered cistercian life was not long to be hers, for two years later the storm broke. The Bastille was not far from Saint Antoine, and with the storming of that ancient fortress the era of Revolution was opened. The twenty-four choir nuns and eleven lay sisters were probably under no illusion as to what this might mean for them. Saint Antoine des Champs was a royal abbey and its prestige and presumed wealth made it an immediate target for the Revolutionaries. The nuns, mostly of noble families, were natural objects of hate. In the following year (1790) the Commissioners presented themselves at the abbey to make the inventory which was the prelude to its despoliation. Unfortunately, but not surprisingly, we have no details of the suppression of the monastery or of the fate of the religious, who, driven from their home, had to take refuge elsewhere. Some of the nuns returned to their families and one would expect Rosalie and her sister to have done the same, at least as a temporary measure. What is certain is that eventually some of the community were thrown into one of the Paris jails and that Rosalie was among their number. This may indicate that they had tried to live some kind of community life, thus incurring the fanatical hatred of the revolutionaries. Whether Rosalie did so or not is impossible to tell, though such a step would be quite in keeping with her character. We know that to be imprisoned in Paris at that time meant awaiting a trial as farcical as any in a 'people's court' today. The inevitable outcome was execution. But the glory of that kind of martyrdom was not, in the providence of God, for Soeur Rosalie Augustine de Chabannes. Hers was to be a different and more protracted witness, one which has much to teach our own restless and unstable generation. On 27 July (9 Thermidor) 1794, the prison doors were opened, not for its occupants to be taken to the guillotine, but to set them free. Robespierre had fallen, the Reign of Terror was over.

Once more, silence falls over Soeur Augustine's activities. Probably she found some place where she could live unmolested for the time being. Meanwhile, another Augustine, Dom Augustin de l'Estrange, was leading his group of monks from La Trappe to safety in Switzerland, where he had been allowed the use of the deserted carthusian monastery of La Val Sainte. Austerity is relative, but by any standards the life at La Val Sainte was austere. Their fare consisted of roots and leaves and occasionally black bread, their bed was the bare ground with no covering, for they had been unable to bring much with them in their hasty flight from La Trappe. Their labor was ten or twelve hours each day of the hardest physical work, trying to render the stony soil fruitful. Far from repining, they accepted these conditions with joy and even wished to restore the primitive observance of Cîteaux. It would be difficult to see how life at La Val Sainte fell short of life at early Cîteaux, had we not Dom Augustin's word and assurance that the strictness of their regime was intended to make up for those observances of the early days of the Order, which they had not been able to revive.[5] But we should note the underlying reason for these austerities: a burning desire to compensate not merely for the points of the Rule, but even more for the impious crimes perpetrated during the French Revolution.[6]

La Val Sainte became the vital link in time, binding the Cistercian Order together in pre-and post-Revolutionary France. Unlike other

Orders Cistercians had no need to make a fresh start after the Revolution. La Val Sainte had maintained the continuity.

In spite of the poverty and hardship of life at La Val Sainte, postulants flocked in and Dom Augustin was able to send out colonies, notably to Lulworth in England, a foundation which in its short life was to play an important part in the life of Madame de Chabannes. In September 1796, it became possible for Dom Augustin to open a house for nuns in Bas Valais close to one of his houses of monks. As at la Val Sainte postulants soon arrived, for there were many nuns deprived by the Revolution of their religious life who eagerly availed themselves of the opportunity of resuming it. Evidently grape-vines operated as efficiently then as they do now. Soeur Augustine was one of those who made the still dangerous journey through France. After the hardships of this journey, which had to be made as secretly as possible, she and her companions reached Switzerland in June 1797. Madame de Chabannes has herself recorded in the earliest register of Stapehill that she entered the monastery of La Sainte Volonté de Dieu (the title of the Monastery in Bas Valais) on 21 June 1797, and received the habit on the 29th of the same month. Because she was already a religious of the Order her novitiate was shortened and she made her profession on 29 October. She threw herself heart and soul into the work of the Reform, and shortly after her profession, Dom Augustin, discerning in this young religious, not yet thirty years old, qualities of heart and mind and a gift of leadership, nominated her Superior. Thus was laid upon her a burden she would carry under every imaginable difficulty for nearly half a century until her death in 1844.

These difficulties were not slow to manifest themselves, but for a few weeks at least Madame de Chabannes and her companions were able to live according to the *Reglements de la Val Sainte*. This was no easy life either, but it did possess an element of stability which was soon to be taken from both monks and nuns. Dom Augustin's interpretation of the Rule was a very demanding one. The choir office took up more time than it had in Saint Benedict's day and the necessary manual work was both prolonged and laborious. Both these factors made inroads into the time allowed for sleep. And sleep was taken not in any airy, well-appointed dormitory, but on the floor or table, wherever there was room. For Dom Augustin would turn no-one away simply for lack of space—an act of charity which must have put no inconsiderable strain on those already living the life. One might expect many of his sons and daughters to have become neurotic under such conditions. But no, charity and joy, the only antidotes to neurosis, reigned supreme in both those rough hewn monasteries. The following is the testimony which Madame de Chabannes herself gave and which is still kept in the community archives.

I regard it as a great privilege to have an opportunity of making known my sentiments regarding my holy state. I should like to ascend the house-tops, to go into all the public places, and to cross the seas, in order to make known to the whole universe the happiness which I enjoy. It is so great that the strongest expressions could give only a faint idea of it; I am sometimes unable to contain the feelings with which it inspires me. I can easily believe that anyone who is called happy in the world, if he had once tasted the satisfaction, the peace which is found in the different practices of our holy state, would not hesitate for an instant to change his condition. Let men cease, then, to regard as unhappy victims all those who retire here. They are indeed victims, but voluntary victims, and their sacrifice is accompanied by so much sweetness that I sometimes feel afraid that I am having my reward here below. I declare and bear witness to the whole world that I do not believe there can be in existence a being happier than I am; all those austerities which so alarm everyone are my greatest consolation; those constant vigils, those long fasts, which, so they say, destroy the health, have produced an exactly contrary effect, as before I entered La Trappe I had no health, and a religious of the same Order, though, to my shame, very relaxed, I could not support even that amount of regular observance. I wish also to make known the difference in my feelings in my first and second profession. In the former, although I made it with joy, I could not resist an impression of terror which penetrated me entirely; in the second, peace, joy and happiness filled me instead. In short, we bear the yoke of the Lord with joy, and there is no day on which I would not wish to be able to add something to the austerities.

I am penetrated with so lively a gratitude at having been admitted, that I am unable to express it. I am ready to sign my declaration with my blood.[7]

That poverty and hardship often draw people more closely together can be still seen today in countries where persecution is rife, and where despite the privations vocations abound. This experience has to be borne in mind when considering the early days of Stapehill. For the religious in Switzerland hardship was compounded by the fact that many of them came from various Orders and had already been formed in a different way of life. But all were united in a great love of their calling as religious and were filled with an unbounded gratitude to God for his goodness to them.

The following letter was written by Madame de Chabannes to her mother while she was still at La Sainte Volonté de Dieu. It was in answer to one from her mother written in 1797, not long after Soeur Augustine had joined the community in Switzerland, and shows that contact was somehow kept up in those difficult times. In it Madame de Chabannes seeks to allay her mother's fears that Dom Augustin's reform would be too much for her daughter, but she in no way seeks to hide from her mother the austerity of the life.

> Yes, dear Mother, I am *too* happy, since I would never have imag-
> ined that God would have been so good as to call me to live
> in so holy an Order. If you are sad because I am so far from
> you, console yourself with the thought that one of your daughters
> is more happy than if she had been raised to the throne of the
> greatest of Kings.

She goes on to detail some of the observances: for seven months in the year there was but one meal a day, 'but there is always plenty of good soup and a portion of vegetables and dry bread.' In spite of this she has never been so well, and if occasionally she is not quite so well, what does it matter anyway? Many people in the world live just as poorly, either from necessity or avarice. Although there is normally only six hours sleep a night, are they not rewarded by being able to join their voices to those of the angels in the praise of God? Then there is the silence and the profound solitude, which we cherish in order to speak to God. Yet how many people subject themselves to such a discipline in their search for profane knowledge?

It is obvious that Madame de Chabannes had indeed devoted herself joyfully to the life as lived at La Sainte Volanté de Dieu. This love and devotion which bound the community so strongly together and which Madame de Chabannes expressed so well sprang from that characteristic devotion of the Revolutionary era—devotion to the Sacred Heart of Our Lord. It runs through cistercian history and Madame de Chabannes was to implant it in the foundation of Stapehill.

So orderly and ordered a life was not to endure for long. Early in 1798 Switzerland was suddenly invaded by the French Republican Army, from whom exiled religious could expect no mercy. Dom Augustin, now responsible for more than two hundred persons, in-cluding children who had been confided to his care, made an heroic act of faith in God's continuing providential care for those he had chosen. He led them out on what has been well termed a 'Monastic Odyssey': a journey that was to last three years and take them across Europe. No happy-go-lucky hike was this, for the journey was mostly made on foot and took them into the snowbound areas of Russia and Poland. Yet in spite of hardships and uncertainties, the Rule was kept as strictly as possible. As the details of this heroic trek have been chronicled elsewhere, there seems no need to repeat them here.[8]

It was not until late in the year 1800 that Dom Augustin, on a visit to England, learnt that the british government was willing to grant a small pension to french exiles. As he had already established a community of monks at Lulworth, he decided to send some of the nuns to England as well. Thus it was that in March 1801, Madame de Chabannes set sail for England to found there what was to become the first permanent cistercian foundation since the Reformation. It took some little time for arrangements to be made for a settled abode and in the meantime the four nuns lived at Hammersmith in London and later at Canford in Dorset. In October 1802, they were able to take possession of the small property kindly and generously given them by Lord Arundel of Wardour in a remote village called Stapehill in Dorset, about two miles from Wimborne, where before the Reformation there had been a benedictine monastery. In early days this had been a double monastery, in fact two communities, one of monks and one of nuns. From Wimborne in the eighth century Saint Walburga and Saint Lioba went to help Saint Boniface in his labors among the germanic tribes. It seems somehow very fitting that centuries later the first post-Reformation cistercian monastery in England should lie almost in the shadow of Wimborne Minster.

At the time the Trappistines arrived at their destination, the site was very isolated and the farmhouse with its cottages and outbuildings was surrounded by heathland. It would perhaps be hard for us to imagine the joy of the group of nine religious (they had already been joined by some postulants) as they took possession of their new home in October 1802, although many a displaced person in today's uneasy world who has been fortunate enough to find a secure footing in some corner could enter deeply intro the sentiments of Madame de Chabannes and her companions.

The new monastery was given the name Our Lady of the Holy Cross, the choice of Madame de Chabannes with the consent of the Community.[9] This is how she put it to her nuns in one of her Chapter talks some years later on 3 May 1811:

> The respect and veneration, I may add the love, we have for the instrument of our redemption has caused me to choose this festival for our chief patronal day. My sisters, we are the children of the Cross, the spouses of a God crucified for us—we ought then to crucify ourselves for His love, for we shall share in His glory insofar as we partake of His humiliations.[10]

Surely Saint Bernard would have recognized a kindred soul in the writer of those words! The feast of 3 May was known as the Invention of the Holy Cross that is, its discovery by Saint Helena. In another Chapter Talk we find Madame de Chabannes playing on the two meanings of the word 'invention'; in Latin, to find, in English to make, or to make up.

> We say that we are willing to suffer whatever it shall please Almighty God to send us—fine projects of valour when at the same time we are unable or unwilling to endure a small uneasiness or suffering! To imagine that in any other case we should be ready to endure anything—this is inventing crosses in our own mind and refusing to carry those which we are obliged to.[11]

By looking back over the previous decade of her life, we can see where the roots of this predilection lay. All that she had done and endured and suffered had been not to save her life in this world but, if necessary, to lose it for the sake of the 'supernal vocation' which for her, as for all Christians in due measure, is a call to the Cross. Once more a present-day parallel can be observed: in countries where Christianity is not free devotion to the Cross flourishes more than in our affluent, well-padded society. And where there is devotion to the Cross, there vocations are numerous, as they were in England in the penal times.

Life in the newly-founded monastery must have been austere. The farmhouse was small and could not have afforded much space for nine people. The pension given by the Government could not have gone far in supplying the daily necessities of food and clothing, and, of course, not all the members of the community were entitled to it. In fact the *secours du gouvernement* amounted to 16.10s. a month, which, even taking into account the difference in the value of money, would not have done much to cover expenses. The community were able to supplement this chiefly by the sale of cheese, and there were some donations to help swell the budget. Ducks were also kept and some were sold. Men had to be hired with the farm work, Barnet is a name that recurs regularly at ten shillings a week. An interesting entry occurs in August 1809: *Voyage à la mer pour des pierres*, 1s.3d.' Perhaps the local children, with whom Madame de Chabannes had very friendly relations, were sent off in the carrier's cart to Bournemouth, then a tiny fishing village unknown to the world.

The monks at Lulworth were a great help and support though their own resources were not very great. Père Antoine came over every Saturday to hear the nuns' confessions and returned to Lulworth on Monday. Until the nuns were able to purchase a cow he was accompanied by a brother carrying a barrel of milk. The monks also made shoes for the nuns and they in turn cared for the Lulworth altar linens. In 1804 Madame de Chabannes proposed to the community that someone be engaged to superintend the farm, thought he nuns continued to do most of the work themselves. Four years later Lulworth was able to spare a laybrother who, by his devoted labors, put the farm on a good footing.

In spite of all the problems inherent in a new foundation and complicated by difficulties of language and the sheer physical hardship of work on the land by those unaccustomed to it, Madame de Chabannes did not encourage any form of self-pity and she made demands on her small community. All was to be accepted in joy and love in response to God's love for us. Clearly, in her eyes a vocation to religious life was the pearl of great price for which we, and they, must be prepared to sacrifice everything, to give all in order to find all. Her Chapter Talks to novices making their petition are clear on this point.[12]

> The vocation to religious life is a grace of predilection, and second only to that of predestination according to the mind of our Father St. Bernard, and being so great, it calls for similarly great correspondence on your part. It is a vocation that is painful to nature. . . . And when at the end of the day you have fulfilled all as perfectly as possible, you must be able to say sincerely from your heart 'I am an unprofitable servant.'

And a little later

> What fidelity, fervour and zeal should you not have for all the observances which are your sure means of attaining to God. You are certain to find some things painful and difficult but as St. Benedict tells you 'Do not fly therefore in dismay from the path of salvation, whose beginning cannot but be strait and difficult. But as we go forward in our life and in faith, we shall, with hearts enlarged and unspeakable sweetness of love run the way of God's commandments.'[13]

Love of one's holy state and exactitude in following the observances were a *sine qua non* for acceptance into the community.
Madame de Chabannes may have been a little intolerant of human
weakness, but given her training in the school of adversity, this is
hardly unexpected. Yet she did not expect her religious to be grim-
faced ascetics. Impressing on a newly-clothed novice the necessity
of true humility of mind and heart she added:

> If you enter into these dispositions you will taste the happiness of
> your state infinitely more.
>   To humble myself and obey. It will be on these two points, of
> such great importance, that you will be judged. I say nothing to
> you of the sweetness which you will enjoy if you are faithful to
> them. God himself will delight in overwhelming you with them.

She even rebuked them for not showing sufficient affection for one
another, though as she herself said no one knew as she did how much
they really did love one another. Even correcting mistakes in choir
was to be done with gentleness. After all, there is joy in the passion,
as Julian of Norwich told us, and we must respond with joy. It should
not be forgotten that this devotion to the passion was closely linked
with devotion to the Sacred Heart and its accompanying aspect
of reparation which was so strong in Revolutionary France and of
which Saint Bernard, centuries earlier, had written so movingly.

Because Madame de Chabannes left no personal diaries or spiritual
notes it is possible to deduce her spirituality only from those of
her Chapter Talks which have been preserved and from scattered
references in her letters to the account she knew she would have
to give of her stewardship—an attitude of mind which very much
accords with that of Saint Benedict.[14] Her teaching seems to have
been straightforward and direct. As far as her community was concerned, she was not one to mince her words. 'They had come to
a house dedicated to the Cross, they must accept it joyfully when
it is presented to them'.[15] Was this aspect of the life emphasized at
the expense of others? An answer to this question may be found in
her choice of patronal feast. It was not the Exaltation of the Cross
on 14 September, but the Finding of the Cross which occurred in
Paschal Time amid the triumphant joy and alleluias of the resurrection. The cross would always be present to them in some form.
Indeed, true to its name, Stapehill has always had some cross to bear.
Madame de Chabannes, moreover, took her full share in carrying
the cross inherent in community life. She it was who took on the
responsibility of the rising bell, and she was in the farmyard in the

early hours of the morning loading manure. Severe she could be, yet her community loved her and loved her deeply. Perhaps, being penetrated with a deep sense of the judgments of God and of the four last things, she was no autocrat, but one of the community, living and sharing their life and labors but leading them on all the time to higher reaches of holiness and union with God.

And how was this spirituality nourished? In spite of the hard work and many difficulties, the times of reading, or *lectio divina*, to use the monastic term, were strictly kept. The library must have been small at the beginning, though Madame de Chabannes and others who had been trained in various Orders before the Revolution would already have had a stock of spiritual lore and minds already formed by their reading. We find in Madame de Chabannes' chapters quotations from Saint Bernard, Saint Augustine, Blosius, Saint Ephrem, Saint Bonaventure, Saint Thomas Aquinas and Suarez. It is tempting to wonder what she would have made of the flood of paperbacks that crowd our library shelves today! Among the earliest French works in the library at Stapehill we find Dom Augustine Baker, Bossuet, Bourdaloue, Blosius, Fenelon, Saint Cyprian, Saint Ignatius Loyola, Surin, and Scupoli, in addition to Holy Scripture, the Holy Rule, and *The Imitation of Christ.* these were all published in the eighteenth or very early nineteenth century, but whether they actually formed part of the library in those early days one cannot say. In any case, Madame de Chabannes' spirituality seems to have been essentially practical rather than bookish. In fact, the conditions of life under which she lived would inevitably have made it so.

As has been said, Stapehill was seldom to be without its cross, and for Madame de Chabannes herself difficulties must have abounded. She was in a foreign country and one which, despite the Government's willingness to accept refugees and grant them a small pension, was suspicious of foreigners and especially of Catholics. Tradespeople who spoke only their own language and were perhaps not over-scrupulous had to be dealt with. A new language had to be mastered, and she once complained that because of the difficulties of the language she could give only a short talk.[16] In the end she did indeed write very good English, and over the years the account books change from French to English. In October 1835 we find a delightful mixture:

Des paniers	12/8
Petites dépenses	8/6
Bricklaire	12/7 FR 1/2

Rick of straw   6/10
Mr. Collins' bill   £5

This is the last entry in Madame de Chabannes' handwriting. In January 1836 a new hand takes over and all is in English. Over and above all these difficulties came a series of events which must be singled out for special mention all of which cost the community dear. The first of these was the departure of the monks from Lulworth. Forbidden by the English Government to receive any postulants, as a result of the activities of an apostate monk of the house, the monks returned to France and settled at Melleray in Brittany. Although two of the monks remained behind—Père Paleman, the nun's chaplain until he died, and the 'good Brother Patrick', an invaluable worker on the farm—the departure of the monks must have meant a serious deprivation for the nuns, who had hitherto been in the normal position of a monastery of nuns within reasonable distance of a community of monks of the same Order, with all that meant of help, counsel, and support. Yet this loss was only the mild beginning, of the seven grimmest years in the history of Stapehill. And these years Madame de Chabannes had to face almost alone. Her great spirit of faith and immense fortitude must have been stretched to the uttermost.

The Lulworth monks had not been gone a year when a disastrous fire took great toll of buildings, stores, and equipment. Considering that rushlights were the normal sources of illumination, it is perhaps surprising that a fire had not occurred earlier.[17] The following account of the event is taken from the old French Chronicle of the House:

> In the year 1818 Divine Providence was pleased to afflict our monastery with a terrible calamity. On May 3rd, Feast of the Invention of the Holy Cross, our Patronal Festival, between ten and eleven o'clock at night, through an unforeseen accident the exterior buildings of our house caught fire, and in the space of two hours the guest rooms, the wash-house, the Brother's room, the bakehouse and finally, the barns, stable and cowsheds were reduced to ashes. Having but little help we were able to save hardly anything from these places which contained the provisions for our subsistence, much linen, furniture, quantities of wood and straw, all the tools for the farmwork, all these became the prey of the destructive element. It was only by a miracle—we can truly say this for it was acknowledged by Protestants who came next day to see the ruins—that the whole house was not reduced to ashes, for the flames stopped close to a pile of dry wood, and if that had

caught fire the chapel and monastery would have been entirely consumed. No one, moreover, was injured amid the great confusion and consternation. We owe our deliverance to the protection of the Blessed Virgin to whom our Rev. Mother Augustine and the community had recourse by fervent prayer while the flames were raging most violently, promising her that if she came to our aid, we, and all those who came after us, would sing the *Ave Maris Stella* every year on the same day. . . . Reverend Mother then felt inspired to throw a relic of the True Cross into the midst of the flames, and from that moment they subsided and soon after the fire was completely extinguished. A few days later while clearing and turning over the heaps of ashes, we found the relic intact only the glass having been scorched without even being broken. We continued our task until eight o'clock at night and this prolonged labor lasted the whole week. We were forced to engage men for several nights to guard the house, for it was quite open and many curious people came to see the ruins. We could not even ascertain that the fire was completely extinguished for the beams and joists were still smoking there having been a shortage of water as we had only one pump, the other having been burnt at the beginning.[18]

No natural explanation could be given for the sudden cessation of the conflagration and all believed that the house had been miraculously saved from destruction. Every year on 3 May the *Ave Maris Stella* is sung in thanksgiving after Vespers at the Altar of Our Lady of Dolours.

Things were to go from bad to worse. Between 1811 and 1824, the number of welcome postulants received into the struggling community was offset by the great number of deaths, particularly among the young religious, some of them not yet professed. What must have been Madame de Chabannes' feelings as she saw her little flock being struck down one after another, some very suddenly, some even before they had finished their noviceship. On these young ones she had felt she could count for the future of the community. Was it an epidemic of tuberculosis? It is difficult to say, though there is a note in Madame de Chabannes' handwriting to say that the two doctors who had visited the house could find nothing in the diet or the water they drank (which came from a well) that could shorten life or cause *la pulmonie*. It seems rather to have been a disease that swept over Europe, or parts of it, at that time affecting young girls particularly. The same phenomenon was found among the active teaching orders. Dom Augustin sent four nuns from Mondaye to reinforce the stricken community, but three of these also died within a few years of their arrival. Yet in some ways all was not sorrow, for all these religious died with great joy, seeing in death the fulfillment of what they had come to the monastery to seek.

Not surprisingly, news of the severe mortality rate came to the ears of the local bishop. Bishop Collingridge was at the time Vicar Apostolic of the Western District, and he was, understandably enough, seriously disturbed and decided to investigate the matter thoroughly. In the early part of 1824 he visited Stapehill and asked Madame de Chabannes for a list of all the people who had died in the house since its foundation in 1802. This he forwarded to Rome, and in the following July he returned to Stapehill bearing a rescript he had obtained from Pope Leo XII. This contained some mitigations of the Rule, most of which were afterwards adopted in the Order. In what must have been a more bitter blow, Stapehill was withdrawn from the authority of Dom Augustin and placed under the jurisdiction of the Vicar Apostolic of the Western District. The nuns, all of whom had been kept in ignorance of the bishop's intentions, received the news in stunned silence. Perhaps the good bishop was dumbfounded, too, when he interviewed the religious individually and discovered that not one of them considered their Rule to be too severe.

The damage had been done, and in being cut off from the Order, the community and more especially the superior were deprived of help and counsel from any who really understood their life. This situation was to persist for nearly a hundred years, though the life differed very little from any other trappist monastery of that time.[19] This last blow seems almost to have broken Madame de Chabannes, for she repeatedly offered her resignation to the bishop who prudently and consistently refused to accept it. There was nothing for it but to struggle on alone. It was during these years of trial that a plan was mooted to transfer the house to Ireland and negotiations were started for the purchase of a property there. In the event these fell through and though Madame de Chabannes seriously considered the project, it appears that she had a deep inner conviction that the foundation in protestant England was willed by God. Speaking in Chapter on the Feast of All Saints of the Order (13 November 1810), she said:

> There is a particular reason which makes this festival so dear to us because it was under their patronage that we were established in this little monastery[20] and it is a motive of gratitude which has led us to celebrate their festival with more solemnity. I have told you my dear sisters that this festival should be still more dear

to you than to us. Why so? Because we ourselves might have preserved our state and been established in some other country but by the effect of God's mercy we came to this Kingdom to lay the foundations of this monastery without which the greatest number of you had never entered the Order.[21]

And struggle on alone she did, against constant poverty and all the other difficulties resulting from isolation. A few gleams of comfort appeared, the monasteries of Mount Melleray and Mount Saint Bernard were founded in 1831 and 1835 respectively: Father Hawkins arrived at Stapehill, at the request of Madame de Chabannes, from La Melleray in Brittany. While in England he remained under obedience to the abbot of Mount Saint Bernard. He labored for the good of Stapehill until his death in 1866. Arriving at a time when finances were at a low ebb and much needed doing to the fabric, he set about remedying this state of things with great devotion. He himself begged money to replace the old chapel which was very damp and to him the community owed the beautiful still existing church, which has the unusual feature of two naves each with its respective altar, one for the parishioners and one for nuns.[22] The nuns, he said, must also beg and the money thus obtained enabled them to construct a dormitory and workroom. His presence must have been a great weight off Madame de Chabannes' shoulders; all the more so as age was beginning to take its toll. Growing more infirm, she was no longer able to do heavy farm work. She had always taken her share of the manual labor, going out in the early hours of the morning to load the carts with manure and taking on herself the responsibility of the rising bell each day, as we have already seen. She was no armchair theorist; like Saint Benedict she lived what she taught. By 1842, when Queen Adelaide visited the monastery, she was unable to rise from the chair. She was then seventy three years old, which in physical terms was considerably older than the same age today, and for the previous fifty years she can have known little physical comfort, yet her indomitable spirit and great faith carried her on through all difficulties. One thing it seems she had never lacked was the love and devotion of her community and this may have been the chief earthly support on which she could count. To maintain a spirit of prayer and to keep oneself in the presence of God in the face of so many troubles is no small sign of sanctity. Though a truly cistercian silence surrounds this great soul in life as in death (as one of her daughters has said), miracles have been attributed to her intercession and she was reputed a saint. Not only did her children love her, but children did too. One old lady who died in 1917 had happy recollections of harvest time and of sharing with her companions the huge apple pie that Madame de Chabannes dispensed to them.

On 13 June 1844, she died surrounded by her daughters, sad at losing her but rejoicing that now at least she would reap the reward she had so earnestly and unshakably longed for. Her body lay in the nuns' choir for some days so that all who knew her might come to venerate her remains. She was buried in the nuns' cemetery while a small vault was prepared to which six months later her still incorrupt body was transferred. The vault is now surmounted by a delicate stone cross of Pugin's workmanship. The base of the cross has an inscription which reads:

> I.H.S. This Cross was Erected in memory of our Reverend and Lady Mother Augustine de Chabanne Foundress and Ruler of this Monastery for 42 years. Here her remains rest in peace, awaiting the unchangeable and glorious Resurrection, Through Our Lord Jesus Christ. She died, fortified by the Sacraments of the Church, on the 13th June, 1844 A.D. in the 57th year of her Profession and the 76th of her life.
> Out of the Depths I cry to Thee, O Lord.[23]

Thus, out of their poverty did her community honor her, for she was indeed a valiant woman.[24]

NOTES

1. *Mulierem Fortem Quis Inveniet?* Proverbs 31:10. Who shall find a Valiant woman? (Douay translation).

2. Madame - a courtesy title much used in France at that time, possibly to allay suspicions about one's religious state. It was retained by the Society of the Sacred Heart well into the twentieth century, and corresponds to the English Mistress (cf. Mistress or Mrs Mary Ward). It is as Mme de Chabannes that Soeur Rosalie Augustine is generally known.

3. A Religious of Holy Cross Abbey, Stapehill, *La Trappe in England* (London, 1935, rpt Gethsemani Abbey, 1946) p. 69.

4. This likeness is verified by Mrs Wareham, who was a child at school during Mme de Chabannes' lifetime and was one of the children who gathered round her in the harvest field to share an apple pie.

5. Jean de la Croix Bouton, *Fiches cisterciennes* 103, p. 412: 'We should not see Dom Augustine as a master who ruled his religious with a rod of iron. The religious themselves had forged these chains. In the Chapter on the Dormitory of the *Réglements de Val Sainte* we read "Let us note in passing how ill-founded is the reproach they level against us of being more austere than the Rule prescribes, since we are obliged to compensate for those things we cannot observe and these compensations are light."' *Fiche* 103 p. 412. The *Fiches Cisterciennes* were leaflets written for the nuns on various

subjects; e.g. Holy Scripture, Liturgy, History of the Order. Those on the history of the Order were printed at Westmalle between 1959 and 1965. (Translation mine).

6. *Ibid.*

7. Stapehill Archives, quoted in *La Trappe in England*, 69.

8. See Casimir Galillardin, *Les Trappists* on l'Ordre de Cîteaux au XIXe siècles (Paris, 1844) Vol. II, Chs. XVII, XVIII. *Fiches Cisterciennes* 105, with bibliography. *La Trappe in England*, pp. 75ff.

9. *La Trappe in England*, p. 97.

10. Stapehill Archives.

11. Stapehill Archives.

12. Stapehill Archives. Note: Saint Benedict prescribes that the Rule be read to the novice three times during his probation. Each time he is solemnly asked if he intends to persevere. This is not a binding commitment but ensures that the novice knows what he is undertaking.

13. Stapehill Archives.

14. Stapehill Archives. In one of the account books there is the following entry 'August 16th 1827. Day of Election. I have made up the accounts from August 14th, 1824. May God give me grace to prepare myself for those which I owe him after so long an administration.'

15. Chapter Talk of Madame de Chabannes.

16. Stapehill Archives. Chapter Talk to a novice.

17. An old sister who died in the 1950s said that when she entered in 1885 there were still sisters who remembered rushlights being used.

18. *La Trappe in England*, pp. 107–108.

19. Stapehill was not to be reunited with the Order until 1915, although Madame de Chabannes had considered the possibility of an appeal to Rome. This evidently came to nothing.

20. 13 November 1802 is the Foundation Day of Stapehill.

21. Stapehill Archives, Chapter Talk.

22. The site of the Old Chapel was later occupied by the refectory, the community kitchen and the infirmary passage. It was in the last-named that the community sheltered during the air raids of World War II and where in consequence Vigils was frequently recited.

23. IHS. In memoriam Reverendae ac Dominae Matris nostrae Rosaliae Augustinae de Chabanne, Fundatricis et Gubernatricis huyusce monasterii per XLII annos Crux ista erectus est. At hic in pace Exuviae ejus requiescunt, immutationem ac Gloriosam Resurrectionem expectantes, per Dominum nostrum Jesum Christum. Obiit die xiij Junii, Ecclesiae Sacramentis munita, AD MDCCCXLIV, Professionis LVII Aetatis LXXVI. De Profundis clamavi ad Te Domine.

24. For many years, until about 1970, her names of Rosalie and Augustine were kept alive in the community. The cross is still in place but when the community left Stapehill the cemetery was transferred to a nearby location, thus bringing to an end an honoured custom of placing a simple vase of garden flowers on her grave each year on the anniversary of her death.

A much fuller account may be found in *La Trappe in England*, now unhappily out of print. There are also some scattered references in 'The Lulworth Trappists', an unpublished manuscript now in the keeping of Mount Saint Bernard Abbey, Leicestershire.

Cistercian Nuns Today

Elizabeth Connor OCSO

THE THREE VOLUMES on nuns of past centuries which precede these final pages have given us a series of finely nuanced portraits and described various aspects of the life of monastic women: their spirituality, their history, their juridical and social status.

We who are monastic women in the Church today are linked to these nuns of the past by the type of life we live. Though monastic values are inevitably expressed differently in various periods of history, with accents reflecting the particular time in which particular communities of nuns lived, the values themselves are unchanging and enduring. The monastic life transcends eras and cultures. Monastic women of today have inherited from their predecessors monastic mores and a monastic way of existing. But first and foremost they are united to monastic women of the past by their personal call from God, a call which, uttered in eternity, meets a desire in the depths of the heart and bestows the strength to respond. In whatever way social and historical circumstances have influenced life in the monasteries during the course of the centuries, this essential bond remains. A monastery is, above all else, a place for following God's call and seeking him, for preferring nothing to the love of Christ, and for becoming a stranger to the ways of the world.

The pages which follow will endeavor to give a sketch of monastic women of the Cistercian Order of the Strict Observance as we find them in this last decade of the twentieth century. But first, a rapid summary of their history since the French Revolution seems opportune. It is, in fact, essential if we are to understand the evolution which is now taking place in the Order.

RESTORATION OF CISTERCIAN-TRAPPIST LIFE
IN FRANCE AFTER THE REVOLUTION

When Dom Augustin de Lestrange, the intrepid former novice master of La Trappe and founder of the Val Sainte community, finally returned with his followers to France after the downfall of Napoleon, they were few in number. Yet his band of monks and nuns had succeeded in keeping the Cistercian-Trappist life alive during the troubled Revolutionary times. Now, after the incredible hardships they had suffered during the exile that had taken them to Russia and back, they faced still more difficulties in re-establishing monasteries in their homeland. France, however, was ready for a new flowering of religious and monastic life, and the monks and nuns had waited a long time for this moment.

To recount the history of the nineteenth-century restoration of Cistercian-Trappist communities would be to tell of two different observances already being practiced before the monks and nuns could cross the French border: Lestrange's rule for the Val Sainte, exceedingly severe and never approved by Rome; and the regulations of Rancé, adopted by the followers of Dom Eugene de Laprade of Darfeld.[1] It would be to recount how, after the return to France, an initial single congregation made up of the houses of both observances gave way to the formation of two distinct Congregations in 1847: the Congregation of Sept-Fons, or the 'Old Reform', and the Congregation of La Trappe, the 'New Reform'.[2] Finally, it would be to explain how, in 1892, these two Congregations, along with the Belgian Trappists united to form the 'Order of Reformed Cistercians of Our Lady of La Trappe'.[3] The Constitutions for the new Order were drawn up the following year. They reaffirmed the basic principles of the twelfth-century Charter of Charity and the early Cistercian customs according to Rancé's interpretation.[4] Though documents of these historic days say little about the nuns specifically, feminine monasteries of both the 'Old Reform' and 'New Reform' were incorporated into the new Order.[5]

In 1898 the Trappists were able to acquire the Abbey of Cîteaux, on which they conferred the title 'archabbey'. Shortly afterwards, in 1902, the name 'La Trappe' was dropped definitively from the title of the Order, henceforth known as the 'Order of Reformed Cistercians or Cistercians of the Strict(er) Observance'.[6]

The desire to return to the original inspiration of the Cistercian Fathers had been a driving force for the exiled monks and nuns during and after the Revolution. In 1814, Dom Eugene de Laprade, abbot of Darfeld, had sent a circular letter to his dispersed religious, exhorting them to persevere:

> What the Lord asks of us is that we should walk in the footsteps of our holy Founders. . . . What better could you do than apply yourselves as faithfully as possible to the practice of this Holy Rule, with deep humility, love of God and neighbor, evangelical simplicity, and the spirit of wisdom and discretion. . . .[7]

The First Communities of Nuns

Three groups of Cistercian-Trappistine nuns returned to France in 1816, founding the communities which would become Les Gardes, Laval, and Lyon-Vaise.[8] Two other communities existed outside France: Holy Cross Abbey at Stapehill, in England, founded in 1802; and the community of German-speaking sisters—also followers of Dom Augustine—at Our Lady of Mercy, Rosenthal, Germany.[9] By the time the Order of Reformed Cistercians was formed in 1892 there were thirteen houses of nuns, all but one of them located in France.[10] The monks, on the other hand, already had houses in the United States, Canada, the Middle East, China, Algeria, Jugoslavia, and even Australia, as well as in Europe.[11]

Ironically enough, it was the anti-clerical laws in France at the turn of the century which led to the foundation of communities of cistercian nuns outside the country. Several communities went into temporary exile or established places of refuge either in Europe or abroad, as a precaution against possible expulsion. When the political situation again became stable some houses of refuge were closed, but others were maintained and, in time, became autonomous monasteries.[12]

During the nineteenth and early twentieth centuries, communities were often founded in conditions of great poverty. Nuns leaving their mother-house to form a new community sometimes arrived at their destination only to find that nothing had been prepared for them. They unpacked their bundles and laboriously began to make their new home liveable.[13] This often took years. Sometimes the nuns were obliged to ask the General Chapter for aid, or even for permission to beg in order to keep body and soul together.[14] They worked hard: farm work, first of all, but also industries which varied according to local circumstances. Some nuns made liturgical vestments or altar breads, others cheese or chocolate, still others woven goods, silk (from the silkworms they grew), or even wigs and artificial flowers.[15]

The nuns spent long hours in choir each day, not only singing Mass and the canonical Hours, but also reciting the Little Office of the Blessed Virgin and, on prescribed days, the Office of the Dead. The hour for rising was 2 AM, earlier on feastdays, and monastic churches were unlikely to be heated in winter. The lay sisters, who made up a considerable part of the community and could be distinguished by their brown habits from the choir nuns in white cowls, said their simplified Office of *Paters* and *Glorias* in the fields, kitchen, laundry, or wherever obedience happened to lead them.

Days so filled with liturgical prayer and work left little time for *lectio divina*, an essential element in the life of a Cistercian, but the Gospel, the Rule, and writings of the saints furnished spiritual nourishment which helped the nuns seek God within the framework of their daily life,[16] all the details of which were specified by the *Usages*. Silence, strict enclosure, fasting, and general austerity were rigorously observed.

TWENTIETH CENTURY

By World War Two the number of nuns' monasteries had reached twenty-six. In houses in Belgium, Spain, Japan, Canada, Ireland, Switzerland and England,[17] the life closely resembled that of the nineteenth century, even though both Constitutions and the Book of Usages had been re-edited after the promulgation of the 1917 Code of Canon Law.[18] In the 1950s, however, the first stirrings of a profound evolution could be detected. At the same time, a new period of expansion began.

Monastic Renewal

The first changes concerned practical points: abridgement of choral Offices, a more balanced diet, a bit more sleep for the religious. These common sense measures seemed rather revolutionary to some members of the Order at the time, but they were made in view of one single goal: to foster the spiritual life of the communities. The changes paved the way for the renewal which followed the Second Vatican Council.

In 1959, Dom Gabriel Sortais, Abbot General, convoked all thirty-eight abbesses of the Order to a meeting at Cîteaux. It was the first time in history that such a meeting had taken place.[19] True, in the Middle Ages the burgundian abbey of Tart had held annual 'chapters' for the houses of its filiation,[20] and for centuries 'chapters' had been held annually for the houses of the spanish filiation of Las Huelgas.[21] But these assemblies in no way represented all the cistercian nuns of their times, and could make decisions only concerning minor details pertaining specifically to the nuns. The practice among the Cistercians since the first houses of nuns had been established had been for the Abbots' Chapter to make all decisions about monastic observance, not only for the monks but also for the nuns. This was still the practice in 1959, when the abbesses assembled at Cîteaux.[22]

It should be remembered that in 1959 cloistered nuns were still bound by very strict rules of enclosure. Even to have such a meeting was considered a privilege. At Cîteaux, several aspects of religious life which would later be highlighted by Vatican II were already stressed by the Abbot General; fidelity to the spirit of the founders, formation, subsidiarity, for example. In talks to the abbesses, Dom Gabriel encouraged them to assume more fully their responsibility for governing their communities and gave them counsel for their spiritual life.[23]

During the late 1960s, the introduction of several important changes had considerable impact on daily life. Communities which so desired—and were capable of doing so—could convert their dormitories into simple, private cells.[24] A Decree on Unification doing away with the distinction between choir nuns and lay sisters was put into effect.[25] In 1969, the Roman Instruction *Venite Seorsum* constituted a breakthrough with regard to enclosure. Cloistered, contemplative nuns could now attend sessions and meetings pertaining to their vocation. Grills in the church and parlors were no longer obligatory,[26] and from 1971 on, each community of Cistercian nuns of the Strict Observance could decide for itself whether its grills were to be kept or replaced by a simpler type of material separation.[27]

During the years immediately following Vatican II, religious Institutes were seeking to define their identity and their specific nature. Although it was generally realized that the task is all but impossible, since identity is inseparable from the intangible spirit of the Order, the efforts were not unprofitable. All religious life has one fundamental purpose: to follow Christ by living the Gospel. In seeing the Rule of Saint Benedict as the practical interpretation of the Gospel for them,[28] Cistercians today are one with the first Cistercians, who were not really 'founders' but simply desired to live the Rule more faithfully and authentically, and by doing so to live a life of charity, of love of God and neighbor.

The introduction of pluralism into monastic observance was still another innovation of the 1960s and was to have far-reaching impact on the life of the communities.[29] But how could pluralism be reconciled with the uniformity of observance prescribed in the *Charter of Charity*? There would seem to be a contradiction. Yet uniformity was subservient to charity and, in practical application, built-in flexibility already existed. Texts of Aelred of Rievaulx, for example, show this; and during the nineteenth century, as we have seen, two observances co-existed in one Congregation.[30]

At the time when the *Charter of Charity* was written, monasteries existed within a limited geographical and cultural area. When pluralism was adopted in 1969, the Cistercians of the Strict Observance had houses in most parts of the world and in many different cultural milieux. Usages which had been drawn up for houses in France—twelfth and thirteenth-century France—were raising problems when put into practice on other continents or in other climates. The possibility of a pluralism of customs, combined with unity of vision concerning monastic values, provided a way of adapting monastic usages to local conditions. At the same time, it was in keeping with a fundamental element of the structure of the Cistercian Order: the autonomy of the monasteries.

Liturgy, Private Prayer and Lectio Divina

If cistercian life was characterized in the nineteenth and early twentieth centuries by lengthy choral Offices, long hours of manual work, and exact observance of detailed Usages, it is characterized during the post-Vatican II period of renewal by the importance given to *lectio divina* (so long the 'poor relation'), personal prayer, and the internalization of monastic values. These form a whole. It is difficult to imagine how a nun could profit from her *lectio* and personal prayer if she has not grasped the meaning of silence, solitude, obedience, and other monastic values. The *ascesis* implied in the practice of monastic observances is likewise necessary, for, as always in the monastic life, *theoria* and *praxis* go hand in hand.

The Vatican II Constitutions *Dei Verbum* on Revelation, and *Sacrosanctum Concilium* on the liturgy, opened doors for the restoration of the Word of God to its central place in the christian life and, *a fortiori*, in the monastic liturgy. Time gained by the elimination of superfluities in the Office became available for meditation and *lectio*, so that the nuns' personal prayer life develops differently than in the past. *Lectio divina* has been given much attention in recent years. Entire meetings have been devoted to it.[31] So great is its value to the monastic life that it might be called the specific activity of the monastic person. Like prayer, it forms the *locus* in which the monk or nun lives and breathes. *Lectio*, private prayer, and liturgy must remain in delicate balance if the nun is to respond to her vocation and enter ever more deeply into the Mystery of Christ. To be able to hear what the Lord wishes to say to the heart requires patience and perseverance. A special formation for *lectio* is therefore necessary, and it is normally begun in the novitiate.

Monastic authors, especially the Cistercian Fathers, have a favored place in the nuns' reading. Vernacular editions of Cistercian Fathers are facilitating familiarity with the teaching not only of the 'Four Evangelists of Cîteaux'—as Dom Anselme Le Bail, pioneer of Cistercian studies, called Saint Bernard, Saint Aelred of Rievaulx, William of Saint Thierry and Blessed Guerric of Igny—but of other cistercian authors also. The return to cistercian and monastic sources, and the desire to live by the same spirit as the early Cistercians did, are like north on the compass of renewal. Strange to say, they represent a drastic change from the immediate past.

During the 1920s when Dom Anselme, abbot of Scourmont, was advocating study of the Cistercian Fathers and their teachings, he met with suspicion and lack of comprehension on the part of many abbots. Nevertheless, the first steps were leading forward. In 1924 the General Chapter stated that:

> in principle . . . [it] . . . praised and encouraged the return to the specifically cistercian sources of the spiritual life in the Order, and accepted favorably the desire which had been manifested to publish a collection of easily accessible books which would include: 1) a series of the most practical works of spirituality of our Fathers, preferably—though not exclusively—those dating from the twelfth to fifteenth centuries; 2) a series of biographies of our Blessed and monographs of our monasteries. . . .[32]

The Chapter recognized that the liturgy and the law of the Order also needed more study. Dom Anselme 'stated that he was ready to centralize all the efforts for these different series'.[33] This he did, admirably. He also began, in 1934, the first monastic periodical in the Order, the *Collectanea OCR*.

The lines quoted above from the Acts of the 1924 General Chapter show that the theological importance of the Cistercian Fathers had not yet been fully appreciated. 'Practical works of spirituality' were what interested the abbots most in an era when detailed usages characterized monastic observance. Only gradually would the Cistercians' monastic theology be allotted its proper place, and its essential bond with monastic observance be recognized.

Formation

Vatican II insisted on the necessity of solid formation for religious.[34] Life in a monastery implies a break with the world. This has always been so, but young people who have grown up in an age of technology and rapid change no doubt experience this break in a more acute way than did young women in past generations. Because living in a monastic community does mean being cut off from situations and relationships which contribute to the acquisition of human maturity, the degree of an applicant's maturity has to be given careful attention. Girls do not enter the monastery as young as they did in the past. A number of monasteries require candidates to finish their education and to earn their living for at least a year before entering the novitiate. Discernment of vocations, though often difficult, is all important. The happiness of the individual nun and the quality of the community depend on it.

Each community tries, in proportion to its potential, to give its new members a rounded doctrinal and spiritual formation. The novitiate program is to include fundamental instruction on Scripture, the Rule of Saint Benedict, and liturgy. Guidance in the monastic and spiritual life is provided, and every effort is made to help the novice grasp the inner meaning of the observances she practices in her daily life. Formation is geared from the inside out, so to speak: monastic values, and their concrete expression in exterior monastic observances.

Once a novice has made her first vows, her formation continues in the monasticate. The junior professed are entrusted to an experienced nun who helps them not only to orientate their reading and study but also to make the adjustment to life in the community once they have left the novitiate. The young sister needs to find a new balance between prayer, *lectio*, and work, and to learn a new type of solitude. It is not a time for her to be left exclusively to her own resources.

Still another aspect of renewal is ongoing formation in the communities. Numerous sessions on Scripture, theology, the Rule, and the Fathers, provide ample opportunities for nuns to pursue studies in keeping with their monastic vocation. And it is important that their studies be related to their monastic vocation. Therein is the key to the success or failure of formation programs. A nun must learn to integrate her studies into her monastic search for God, into the whole of her monastic life. As Saint Bernard said, 'Order implies that we give precedence to all that aids spiritual progress; application, that we pursue more eagerly all that strengthens love more'.[35]

Work

In the Rule of Saint Benedict it is written that everything necessary for community living should be found in the monastery so that the monk will not have to go out, because this is not good for his soul.[36] Up until the twentieth century this prescription of the Rule was carried out quite rigorously. Monasteries of nuns, as well as those of monks, generally had farms, poultry yards, extensive gardens and orchards, as well as workshops where various domestic crafts were practiced. The sisters did the haying and harvesting, and lived principally off the products and revenues of their property. Today, few monasteries can provide for all their needs as they formerly did. Furthermore, in a society where 'time is money' it is often not expedient for them to try to do so. In an era of large scale enterprises, some communities have been obliged to give up their small farms and seek other means of earning their living. Some have turned their efforts to cottage industries. As we have already seen, these are nothing new. But now, as small industries—or large— supplant agricultural work as the principal means of earning a living, they are taking on new importance, and the question of how to maintain a type of work which fosters the contemplative life is a real one which needs study.

As in the past, a number of nuns' communities make altar breads and liturgical vestments, two occupations which go well with the monastic way of life. Some monasteries have long been known for the excellence of their chocolate or cheese. Now such industries are being increasingly mechanized, in view of reducing work hours— often necessary because of diminishing personnel—and increasing production. Here and there technological work of one kind or another has been introduced, or nuns do work for local companies. The adoption by communities of industrial techniques or sophisticated equipment has arisen in most cases from economic necessity, but it does present a number of questions. Will time be gained or will the new methods devour more work hours than former methods did? Will the nun become subservient to the machine? If traditional physical, outdoor work is replaced by industrial or technological occupations, will the nun fall prey to nervous fatigue which cannot be easily neutralized during the rest of her monastic day? The possible repercussions on her prayer life and *lectio* need to be considered. Awareness of these dangers is already a step towards finding solutions which are in keeping with monastic tradition and do not compromise what is essential in the monastic life.

Government of the Order

Monks and nuns together make up the Cistercian Order of the Strict Observance. One Order, but two Chapters: the General Chapter of Abbots and the General Chapter of Abbesses. The first General Chapter of Abbesses took place in Rome in 1971. Since then, the Abbesses' Chapter makes decisions concerning the nuns' monastic life and observances, except for matters pertaining to universal canon law which require approval of the Holy See. Abbots and abbesses began to meet together at regional conferences, monks and nuns began to work together on liturgy, formation, and other areas. The two Central Commissions of the Order (of Abbots and Abbesses) now jointly prepare their respective General Chapters. The preparation of renewed Constitutions after Vatican II led to collaboration by monks and nuns on all levels of the Order: superiors, grass roots, and commissions. The common sustained effort culminated in the establishment of the definitive text of the Constitutions for both monks and nuns at the 1987 General Chapters in Rome. These Constitutions were approved by the Holy See at Pentecost 1990, during the year of the ninth centenary of Saint Bernard's birth. The quasi-unanimity with which the vast majority of articles of the constitutions were accepted by both abbots and abbesses well showed that the communities of monks and nuns of the Order share the same tradition and patrimony, and are united by a bond of charity and common doctrine and law.[37]

A World-Wide Order

Having begun to reach out to distant lands following World War II, nuns of the Cistercian Order of the Strict Observance are present in many parts of the world. A statistical study by Sister Kathleen Waters[38] demonstrates how the nuns' branch of the Order has developed since 1950. During the period 1950-1990, the number of monasteries increased from 27 to 60, representing an increase of 122% in forty years. The total number of nuns in the Order in 1949 was 1,441; at the end of 1993; it was 1,886.

In 1990, 28% of the nuns' monasteries were non-western. If foundations in the making are counted, by the year 2000 more than one-third of the nuns' houses will be non-western. These statistics are global. When they are broken down according to continents or countries, one sees that monasteries are growing rapidly in Africa, South America, and the Far East, whereas in some Western countries the number of new members has declined sharply during the last twenty years.

Expansion is a complex matter, because each continent and each country presents its own particular context. The type of foundation made in any country depends to a large extent on whether the country is at peace or at war, whether it enjoys economic stability or turmoil, to what extent the Church is numerically present in the country, and many other considerations. Bishops from developing countries frequently ask cistercian communities to make foundations in their dioceses, so that when nuns are in a position to make a foundation they most frequently look towards the southern hemisphere.

Experience during this period of expansion has led to new ways of proceeding, once a new foundation has been decided upon. Implantation in Latin America, Africa and Asia has given rise to a new consciousness that life in the foundations should express the Cistercian spirit in a way adapted to the culture of the country. Awareness of the prerequisites for inculturation has also grown, so that foundations are planned and brought to realization in new ways.[39] The group of foundresses may be smaller than it was formerly. When a project for a foundation is adopted, a small pilot group may be sent out to study the situation, and to live in the chosen place as a monastic 'cell'. Plans are then made for simple, sometimes temporary buildings, leaving options open for the future. When the foundation is planned for a developing country or orientated towards a specific goal,[40] the foundresses study the culture of the place to which they will be going. They also study the language if it is different from their own and, in a very practical way, investigate possibilities or earning a living in the new location. These new ways of making a foundation could not be foreseen before nuns had actually experienced the implanting of cistercian life in developing countries. It is very possible that other modalities may be required in the future by other circumstances which have not yet appeared on the horizon.

Hospitality

Not all cistercian nuns go off to a foundation or belong to a new community blazing a new trail. Those who remain at home, however, also have a trail to blaze, the trail of Tradition passing through the land of the late twentieth century. They do so first of all by faithfully living their monastic life in community, and striving to internalize its values. They do so by sharing their monastic prayer with those who come to the monastery, and by sharing the monastic atmosphere of silence and recollection. More and more, monasteries are becoming places of peace in a hurried world, places where a person can put aside the 'busy-ness' of life for a while and return to what is essential. Most monasteries of Cistercian nuns have made efforts to provide retreat houses that are conducive to prayer. Monastic churches have been renovated to permit seculars attending the liturgy to participate more fully. Groups come to the monasteries—many different kinds of groups—for a day, for a week, for a retreat. Some monasteries have special quarters where groups of young people can come with a retreat master for a few days. These monasteries seem to draw young people spontaneously by the warmth of their hospitality. They feel at ease there, and accepted. They like to pray with the nuns. Some of them come back again and again. Sometimes they decide to stay.

Liturgical prayer itself expresses a new openness to the world and its needs. The problems and events which strike anguish into the hearts of men and women of our time find echo in the bidding prayers. The nun's concern for the world is in no way contradictory to her separation from it. It is not necessary for her to know all the details of complex international situations or of world catastrophes in order to pray for peace and charity on earth, and that all may come to accept God as their Father and one day enter into the eternal happiness destined for humankind created in the image of God. The nun's role is to 'gather the whole world into the depths of her love', as Saint Aelred of Rievaulx said.[41] She learns to do this by practicing the good works of monastic observance in the school of charity and service of the Lord which the monastery is.

CONCLUSION

This Epilogue has given several of the most prominent features of the life of nuns of the Cistercian Order of the Strict Observance as the world spins rapidly toward the end of the second millennium of the christian era. The subjects touched upon—and, necessarily, each one in a summary way—do not represent all the major monastic practices or values. Other points could have been dealt with: community, humility, silence, and speech. As with any sketch, filling in is necessary. Most of what has been said concerns exterior aspects of cistercian life. All these things are important, very important, because monastic life is of this world. But these lines that have been drawn will have meaning only if they are seen against the background of the nun's personal call from God, her search for God, and her desire and will to prefer nothing to the love of Christ.

NOTES

1. Bernard Martelet, OCR, 'Dom Eugène de Laprade', in *Collectanea OCR* 10 (1948) 199-209. Also, Louis Lekai, O. Cist., *The Cistercians, Ideals and Reality* (Ohio: Kent State University Press, 1977) 185.

2. Louis Lekai, *The Cistercians*, 186-188. Vincent Hermans, OCR, *Commentarium Cisterciense Historico-Practicum in Codicis Canones de Religiosis* (Rome, 1961) 443: The Decree *Kalendis octobris*, October 3, 1834, the same which stated that monasteries of nuns '*a iuridictione Episcoporum non erunt exempta*' (n. 11), united all the existing houses of Trappists and Trappistines, those following the customs of the Valsainte and those following the customs of Rancé, in the *Congregatio Monachorum cisterciensium Beatae Mariae de Trappa*. See also, Vincent Hermans, *Actes des Chapitres Généraux des Congrégations Trappistes au XIXe siècle. 1835-1891* (Rome, 1975) [63] - [69]: The Apostolic Decree *Licet Monachi* separated the Trappists into two Congregations: the Sept-Fons Congregation, or 'Old Reform', following the constitutions of Rancé, and the Congregation of La Trappe, or 'New Reform', following no longer the rules of Lestrange, but 'the Rule of Saint Benedict with the primitive Constitutions of the Cistercians approved by the Holy See, *salvis praescriptionibus quae hoc decreto continentur*' (n. 1 of the Decree) p. [68].

3. An extraordinary General Chapter, convoked by Leo XIII, opened in October 1892. The decisions of this Chpater were ratified by the Decree *Romae convenerunt*, December 8, 1892. This decree was followed up by a Brief of Leo XIII, March 17, 1893. See Hermans, *Commentarium* . . . pp. 449-453. The name of the new Order was *Ordo Cisterciensium Reformatorum Beatae Mariae Virginis de Trappa* (n. 3 of the Brief). The Belgian, or Westmalle, Congregation, had been erected by a Decree of March 18, 1836. See Hermans *Commentarium*, 444.

4. Louis Lekai, *The Cistercians*, 189.

5. Vincent Hermans, *Commentarium*, 452. The Brief of March 17, 1893, stated, '*De monialibus nihil innovamus, quoad ea quae hisce Litteris non obstant*' (n. 11).

6. Vincent Hermans, *Commentarium*, 453-456. Leo XIII's Apostolic Letter of July 30, 1902, *Ad perpetuam Rei Memoriam*, changed the name of the new Order to *Ordo Cisterciensium reformatorum seu Strictioris Observantiae*.

7. Bernard Martelet, *Dom Eugène*, 205: *Exhortation aux religieux et religieuses.* . . .

8. For a summary of the nuns' return to France, see Mère Marie de la Trinité Kervingant, *Des Moniales face à la Révolution française. Aux origines des Cisterciennes-Trappistines* (Paris: Beauchesne, 1989). *Sixième Partie: Les recommencements*, pp. 303-354, and particularly *Chapitre IV. Un regard retrospectif*, pp. 355-366. The first three communities were
—Notre-Dame des Gardes

The sisters, who had come from La Riedera, in Switzerland, first settled at Forges near la Trappe, in 1816. They transferred to Notre-Dame des Gardes in 1818 (See Kervingant, *Des Moniales*, 345-349.

—Laval
The French-speaking nuns, who had been at Darfeld-Rosenthal after their return from Russia, subsequently dwelt at Borsut castle near Liège before returning to France and taking possession of the ancient Saint Catherine's Priory at Laval in 1816. (Kervingant, *Des Moniales*, 301 & 315ff.

—Lyon-Vaise
A second group from La Riedera settled first at Frenouville in 1816. The nuns transferred to *rue de Cuire*, Lyon, in 1817, and finally to Lyon-Vaise in 1820. (Kervingant, *Des Moniales*, 349-351).

9. Obliged to leave their monastery, the nuns of Our Lady of Mercy went first to Cologne and eventually to Oelenberg in 1826. They transferred again, to Altbronn, in 1895. (Kervingant, *Des Moniales*, 314.) Holy Cross Abbey, Stapehill, Dorset, England, was founded in 1802, with Mother Augustin de Chabannes as superior. The nuns were withdrawn from the jurisdiction of Dom Augustine de Lestrange in 1824 and placed under that of the Vicar Apostolic for the Western District of England. See *La Trappe in England*, by a religious of Holy Cross Abbey (London: Burns Oates and Washbourne, 1946) 83ff and 112-114.

10. In 1892, the nuns' houses were as follows:
Old Reform: Laval, Oelenberg, Ubexy (a foundation of Laval), Mâcon.
New Reform: Les Gardes, Lyon-Vaise and its three foundations: Maubec, Espira-de-l'Agly (today Echourgnac) and San Vito (later to transfer to Grotta-Ferrata (1898) and finally to Vitorchiano (1957); Maubec's two foundations: Blagnac (1852), later transferred to Le Rivet, and Bonneval (1875); St-Paul-aux-Bois, descendant of Gomerfontaine, a thirteenth-century cistercian monastery destroyed during the Revolution; La Cour-Pétral, a community which had its origin at Valenton and had moved to Mondaye where the nuns were joined by several members of the Laval community. The Cour-Pétral community is now located at Clairefontaine in Belgium.

11. Jean de la Croix Bouton, *Histoire*, 461-464.

12. Several examples: Lyon-Vaise transferred to Rogersville, New Brunswick, Canada, in 1904, and took the name Notre-Dame de l'Assomption de l'Acadie. The community of Espira-de-l'Agly moved to Herrara, Spain, in 1905. When it became possible for the nuns to return to France in 1923, Espira could not be repurchased, so the nuns settled at Notre-Dame de Bonne Espérance, Echourgnac, formerly a monks' monastery. Bonneval founded Notre-Dame du Bon-Conseil, at Saint Romuald, Québec, Canada, in 1902. Laval opened an annex house in Blitterswijck, Holland, in 1903, as a place of refuge. The nuns were recalled to Laval in 1920. See *Collectanea OCR* 5 (1937) 126. The community of St-Paul-aux-Bois, expelled in 1904, took refuge in an abandoned brewery at Fourbechies, Belgium. The nuns lived there until 1919, when they transferred to Notre-Dame de la Paix at Chimay. See brochure *De Gomerfontaine à N.-D. de la Paix*, 1266-1966 (Chimay, 1966). The nuns of Mâcon moved to Brazil in 1909, near a foundation of monks from Sept-Fons. Dom Chautard recalled both monks and nuns in the late 1920s. The nuns remained for a time in Belgium, at Feluy and then at Soleilmont, before returning to France where they joined sisters from Maubec who had taken over the monastery of Chambarand. Formerly a monks' monastery, Chambarand was one of the few sacrificed in Dom Chautard's discussions with Clemenceau concerning the anti-clerical laws. See Bernard Martelet, ocr, *Dom Chautard, Abbé de Sept-Fons* (Paris: Editions Paulines, 1982) 131-132.

13. For example, see *Collectanea OCR* 6 (1939) 121-124, on the foundation of Ubexy.

14. Vincent Hermans, *Actes des Chapitres Généraux . . . : Acta capituli generalis 1841*, p. [37] and elsewhere . . . ; *Actes de la Congrégation de La Trappe* 1876, Session VII, p.

[426]; *Actes de la Congrégation de La Trappe* 1877, Sessions II and III, p. [429] - [430]; 1890, Session III, p. [546].

15. Jean de la Croix Bouton, *Histoire de l'Ordre . . . Fiches 'cisterciennes'*, p. 456. Some of the nuns' occupations were: cheese (Maubec, Ubexy, Mâcon); chocolate (Bonneval); artificial flowers and wigs (Fille-Dieu); embroidery (Espira and the Cour-Pétral); the cultivation of silkworms and making of silk (Maubec). The Constitutions of 1836 stated that 'the sisters will apply themselves preferably to the most simple kinds of work, such as spinning, sewing, etc. As far as they will be able, they will help to make the bread, take care of the garden, do the cooking and laundry and other household tasks, and avoid superfluous work which would have no other goal but to satisfy vanity and curiosity; they will never do embroidery, especially with gold or silver thread, unless it is for people outside'. (Quoted by the Comte de Charency, *Histoire de l'Abbaye . . .* 2: 763 (my translation).

16. Vincent Hermans, *Actes des Chapitres Généraux*, p. [484]: The General Chapter of the Congregation of La Trappe, 1887 (Session VII), deplored 'some devotional practices which are to the detriment of regular exercises and essential practices'. For *lectio divina* in the nineteenth century, see Etienne Goutagny, '*Lectio divina* chez les cisterciens des XIXe et XXe siècles', in *La Lectio Divina. Rencontre des Pères-Maîtres et Mères-Maîtresses du Nord et de l'Est de la France*. Mimeographed (Tamié, 1979) 336-343. 'L'Imitation de Jésus-Christ et le Combat spirituel sont, avec l'Ecriture sainte et la Règle, la bibliothèque privée du bon religieux', in the words of the author of the *Directoire Spirituel* published by the Order in 1869 (Paris: Ch Douniol, Libr.-Ed., 1869) 493.

17. Stapehill re-entered the Order in 1915 (see *La Trappe in England*, p. 166) and, in turn, founded Glencairn, in Ireland, in 1932 (*ibid.*, 168-171). See also Kilian Walsh, *Women who Keep God's Vigil* (Dublin: Clonmore and Reynolds, 1964) Chapter 6, pp. 45-50. Two cistercian monasteries which had continued uninterruptedly since the Middle Ages entered the Order of Cistercians of the Strict Observance during this period: Soleilmont, in Belgium (see E. Connor, 'Ten Centuries of Monastic Life', in *Distant Echoes* [Kalamazoo: Cistercian Publications, 1984] 251-267) and La Fille-Dieu, in Switzerland (see Robert Loup, *Mère Lutgarde Menétry* [Fribourg en Suisse: Editions St-Paul, 1942] 166-183). La Grâce-Dieu, near Besançon, entered the Order in 1921, thus keeping alive the flame of the famous centuries-old community of Port-Royal. During this period the first spanish house entered the Order: Santa Maria de San José, Alloz (1923); the first Japanese house, Our Lady of the Angels, was founded in 1898 at Hokkaido; and nuns took over the monastery of Igny in 1929.

18. The revised Constitutions were approved by the Holy See in 1926, and by order of the 1933 General Chapter were published along with revised Usages which had been drawn up by the abbots and adopted at their 1932 Chapter. These Usages were approved by the Holy See in 1933. See Preface of the 1934 *Usages of the Cistercian Nuns of the Strict Observance* (Westmalle, 1948).

19. By 1959 the thirty-eight houses of nuns included one in the United States, one in Africa, seven in Spain, four in Japan, and one in both Germany and Holland.

20. Jean de la Croix Bouton, Benoît Chauvin, et E. Grosjean, 'L'Abbaye de Tart et ses Filiales au Moyen-Age,' in Benoît Chauvin, ed., *Mélanges à la mémoire du Père Anselme Dimier, 2: Histoire cistercienne. 3. Ordre. Moines* (Arbois, France, 1984) pp. 19-61. A. Dimier, 'Chapitres généraux d'Abbesses cisterciennes', in Cîteaux 9 (1960) 267-271. The last extant Acts of the Tart Chapters date from 1302.

21. Anselme Dimier, *Chapitres généraux*, 271-275. José Maria Escriva de Balaguer, *La Abadesa de Las Huelgas. Estudio Teologico Juridico* (Madrid, 1974) 6ff.

22. The Abbots' Chapter continued to exercise this authority until the First General Chapter of Abbesses in 1971. See *Minutes of the Sessions of the 61st General Chapter. Cistercians of the Strict Observance* (U.S. regional Conference. Printed in U.S.A., 1969) pp. 148-156, for a discussion of the Abbesses' *vota* expressed at their 1968 meeting at Cîteaux.

784   *Elizabeth Connor*

23. These conferences were mimeographed and communicated to participants at the meeting.

24. *Compte rendu des séances du Chapitre général de 1967. Ordre des cisterciens de la Stricte Observance* (Westmalle, 1967). See heading: *Cellules individuelles,* vote 2, p. 139.

25. *Decree on Unification* (of the communities). SCRIS 16545/65. See the Second Vatican Council Decree *Perfectae caritatis,* on the adaptation and renewal of the religious life, n. 15 (Washington: National Catholic Welfare Conference, 1965) 11-12. Also, Pope Paul VI's Motu proprio *Ecclesiae Sanctae,* Norms for Implementation of Four Council Decrees (Washington: National Catholic Welfare Conference, 1966) II, v, pp. 34-35, on implementation of n. 15 of *Perfectae caritatis.*

26. *Venite seorsum. Instruction on the contemplative life and on the enclosure of nuns.* SCRIS (Typis polyglottis Vaticanis, 1969). Norm 4 admits possibilities for effective separation in parlors and church other than grilles. p. 27. Norm 12 (p. 30) permits attendance at meetings, though somewhat reluctantly.

27. *Acts of the General Chapter of the Feminine Branch. 1971. Order of Cistercians of the Strict Observance* (Printed in U.S.A., 1971), Vote 23, p. 6.

28. *Declaration on the Cistercian Life.* In *Minutes of the Sessions of the 61st General Chapter, 1969* (Printed in U.S.A., 1969) Appendix 16, pp. 275-276.

29. *Ibid. Statute on Unity and Pluralism.* Appendix 19, pp. 279-280.

30. Aelred of Rievaulx. *Speculum caritatis* III.31.75 and III.35.95, in *Aelredi Rievallensis Opera Omnia.* I. Opera Ascetica (Turnhout, Brepols, 1971). *Corpus Christianorum Continuatio Mediaevalis I:* 141 and 151. English translation by E. Connor, *The Mirror of Charity,* CF 17 (Kalamazoo, 1990) 272-273 and 286-287. Vincent Hermans, *Actes des Chapitres Généraux,* p. 3, speaking of the Decree *Kalendis Octobris,* 1834, stated, 'Les deux Observances existant avant 1834 avaient pu garder certaines libertés. En effet, le texte du Décret de 1834 avait dit: *"Quod vero ad jejunia, precationes, et cantum chori pertinet, aux Sancti Benedicti regulam, aut Constitutiones Abbatis de Rancé, ex recepto more cuiusque monasterii, sequantur"*' (n. 8).

31. Report of *Recontre des Pères-Maîtres et Mères-Maîtresses bénédictins-cisterciens du Nord et de l'Est de la France.* Mimeographed (Tamié, 1979); Chronicle of the meeting appeared in *Collectanea OCR* 41 (1979) 351-356. Also, *Session sur la Lectio Divina, with Père Edmond Mikkers,* OCR (Maredret, 1980). Summary in *Lien Vivant,* periodical of the Union des contemplatives de la Belgique, n. 38 (1980) 4-25.

32. *Décisions et Définitions du Chapitre Général des Abbés* OCSO, *1924.* 'Informations diverses', n. 3. Documents communicated to abbots of the Order.

33. *Idem.*

34. Decree *Perfectae caritatis,* n. 18. See *Ecclesiae Sanctae,* II.vii.

35. Bernard of Clairvaux, *Sermo super Cantica* 36.3; Leclercq, *Sancti Bernardi Opera,* 2 (Roma: Editiones Cistercienses, 1958) 5; English translation by Kilian Walsh, CF 7:176.

36. Rule of Saint Benedict, chapter 66.

37. *Constitutions and Statutes of the Monks and Nuns of the Cistercian Order of the Strict Observance and other legislative documents* (Rome, 1990) CST 71.1, p. 58 and CST 72.1, p. 59.

38. Kathleen Waters, OCSO, 'La Situation de l'Ordre dans 10 ans. Analyse quantative', in the Minutes of the Canadian Regional Conference, Abbaye Saint-Benoît-du-Lac (1990) 5-10.

39. See *Constitutions and Statutes of the Monks and Nuns of the Cistercian Order of the Strict Observance and other legislative documents* (Rome, 1990). *Statute on Foundations,* 27-37.

40. The Monastery of the Paix-Dieu, France, was founded by Notre-Dame des Gardes in 1970, with an ecumenical goal in view.

41. Aelred of Rievaulx, *De institutione inclusarum,* n. 28. In *Aelredi Rievallensis Opera Omnia,* 1:661.

Epilogue

On Eagles' Wings: Symbols of Spiritual Motherhood in the Writings of the Early Cistercian Fathers

Colman O'Dell OCSO

Declare this to the sons of Israel: You yourselves have seen what I did with the Egyptians, how I carried you on eagle's wings and brought you to myself.

Ex 19:4

IN THESE WORDS the God of Israel described his leadership of his chosen people out of bondage into the land he had promised them as their own. The sight of an eagle hovering over its nest, inciting the young eaglets to try their wings, then catching them on her own back and supporting them when they falter, must have been a familiar sight to the nomadic shepherds of the near East. Even today, visitors to the more remote regions of the Holy Land report seeing such incidents.

When the compiler of the book of Deuteronomy wished to describe the Exodus events, he wrote, 'As an eagle watches over its nest, hovers above its young, spreads its pinions and takes them up, and carries them upon its wings. The Lord alone led him, no alien god at his side' (Dt 32:11-12 NEB). Followers of the monastic way of life have long identified themselves with the israelites in their desert experiences. Conscious of their need for the incitement and support that only God's leadership could supply, they have also been very much aware that this leadership was one of love, completely

787

devoted to their own good. As the cistercian abbot John of Ford
(1140?-1214) described it:

> love attracts them either to advance or to strive to advance towards
> a simple principle of unity. They follow the leadership of love. . . .[1]

The love of God and the desire for unity with him formed the
driving force that inspired the early cistercian writers and their
immediate successors. Since most of them were abbots, they wished
their own leadership of their communities to resemble God's leadership of his chosen people. These men in the early years of the Order
of Cîteaux often expressed their thoughts about their 'leadership
of love', as well as their ideas on many other monastic values, in
maternal symbols.

TYPES OF MATERNAL SYMBOLS

When we analyze the use of these symbols, we find that the texts
in which they occur fall into several distinct yet closely related types:
texts which speak of Christ or God as mother; the soul of the
Christian as mother of Christ; the monastic community as mother;
the religious superior or spiritual guide as mother; the Church as
mother; and the Blessed Virgin Mary as mother of the church or
of Christians. The last two types have been minutely examined in
the documents of Vatican Council II, and we will not attempt any
analysis of this relationship here, beyond stating that very beautiful
examples abound in the early cistercian writings.[2]

In this paper, we will concern ourselves with the first four types of
maternal figures, giving examples, stating some of the characteristic
features these images display, and offering a possible explanation for
their frequent occurrence. By way of conclusion, we will make some
suggestions as to how these writings may be of benefit to people of
our own troubled times, particularly to men and women following
the monastic life-style.

Christ or God as Mother

Though an abundant scriptural and patristic foundation exists for
regarding God or Christ as mother, many people in our western
civilization experience a feeling of uneasiness when faced with the
concept of a maternal deity.[3] The early Cistercians had no such
hesitation, and we find Saint Bernard writing to a novice:

If you feel the stings of temptation, lift your eyes to the serpent on the staff, and draw life from the wounds of Christ. He will be your mother, and you will be his son. The nails which cleave his hands and feet, must also pass through yours.[4]

In his fourth sermon of Psalm 90, the saint says:

> For, as the mother-bird, on observing the approach of a hawk, spreads out her wings in order that her young ones may enter under them and there find a safe asylum; so does the infinite and ineffable loving-kindness of our Lord prepare itself to shelter us, expanding its bosom, as it were, and opening wide its arms. . . . He remembers our weakness and overshadows us with His wings . . . will foster us like a mother, and communicate to us the warmth of His own bosom. . . . We are warmed and cherished there, as young birds under the wings of their mother, lest, if we wandered abroad, charity should grow cold, and thus we should suffer a spiritual death.[5]

In speaking of the paradoxical wisdom of God which reconciles apparently contradictory things, Bernard writes that, 'The wisdom of God, like a partridge, feeds young which she has not bore; like a hen, she gathers her chickens under her wings; like an eagle, she forces them to flight'.[6] Commenting on our Lord's agony in the garden, Bernard says that Jesus showed fear and weakness so that the mother-bird might share in the weakness of her little ones.[7] The references to a mother-bird recall the gospel verse (Mt 23:37) in which Jesus compared himself to a mother hen who tries to protect her wayward chicks by concealing them under her wings. This verse occurs in the context of the passion narrative, and other references to Christ as mother are often connected with his wounds or with his death on the cross. For instance, Aelred of Rievaulx (1110-1167), in his first sermon on the Pasch, writes:

> The ones who will most perfectly taste and see the kindness of the Lord are the ones who meditate and consider Jesus Christ on the cross as if he were in their very presence. They will see his sacred arms stretched out as if to embrace them, those sweet breasts extended as if to refresh them.[8]

Gilbert of Hoyland (+1172) also compares the wounds of Christ to breasts from which we may drink wine and milk in order to be fully conformed to his image.[9] Gilbert says:

> He [Christ] himself begets, is himself in labor, shares the same nature and himself is born of us. All natural kinships derive from

him. Spiritual kinships are also initiated in him, that no one can boast over him on the score of love, and no one vie with him on the score of equality.[10]

Earlier, in the same sermon, Gilbert writes that 'According to his own admission, he is in person my father and mother and brother'.[11]

In commenting on the Song of Songs, the cistercian writers liberally employed the figure of a mother nourishing her children at her over-flowing breasts, protecting them from harm, and promoting growth, especially in the Christ-life.

The Soul of the Christian as Mother of Christ

This concept appears in several of the Cistercian Fathers, but it is most vividly expressed by Guerric of Igny, who writes:

> Brethren, this name of mother is not restricted to prelates, although they are charged in a special way with maternal solicitude and devotion: it is shared by you too who do the Lord's will. Yes, you too are mothers of the Child who has been born for you and in you, that is, since you conceived from the fear of the Lord and gave birth to the spirit of salvation. Keep watch, holy mother, keep watch in your care for the new-born child until Christ is formed in you who was born for you. . . . So you, brethren, in whom the faith that works through love has been born of the Holy Spirit, preserve it, feed it, nourish it like the little Jesus until there is formed in you the Child who is born for us; who not only by being formed and born, but also by living and dying gave us a form to be the model of our formation.[12]

Thomas Merton, in commenting on those sermons of Guerric which include references to spiritual motherhood, notes how important these maternal figures are to Guerric's doctrine of the life of grace in the soul, and to the concept of the restoration of Christ's image within us—a doctrine of vital importance to all Cistercians.[13]

The Monastic Community as Mother

The motherhood of the monastic community, closely linked with the concept of the Church as mother, is beautifully expressed by Gilbert of Hoyland, when he writes of the community's treatment of a wayward member, who seems to have been under the influence of the 'noon-day devil'. Recalling the raising to life of the only son of the widow of Nain, Gilbert writes:

That son is dead who is crushed by the weight of either tedium or despair, who possesses no lively devotion, no fervor of spirit, who although he does not abandon the precepts of the Law and hides himself in the lap of the Rule, nonetheless languishes in a cold and moribund affection and feels no sweetness in our holy work. . . . He must be cherished in the soft and womanly bosom of his mother, that he may not become rebellious and be broken by excessive sorrow. He should not be found outside the embrace of his mother's bosom, lest perhaps the true Elijah should fail to take him to his upper room. Consider those whom Christ raises to life; everywhere he grants this gift, thanks to the tears of women. So he raised the widow's son, and the brother of the holy women; so, at the prayers of her parents, he raised their daughter. Raise also this dead brother of ours, good Jesus, from his mother's bosom. . . . Then is restored to his mother the son she had lost before, while she did not retain his affection but wept over his dead devotion. He returns to us renewed, after you have clothed him with yourself.[14]

Here, too, we find reference to renewal in Christ's image.

Saint Aelred likewise speaks of the maternity of his community of Rievaulx. His biographer, Walter Daniel, says:

He [Aelred] turned the house of Rievaulx into a stronghold for the sustaining of the weak, the nourishment of the strong and whole; it was a house of piety and peace, the abode of perfect love of God and neighbor. Who was there however despised and rejected, who did not find in it a place of rest? Whoever came there in his weakness and did not find a loving father in Aelred and timely comforters in the brethren? Hence it was that monks in need of mercy and compassion flocked to Rievaulx from foreign peoples and from the far ends of the earth, that there in very truth they might find peace and 'the holiness without which no man shall see God'. And so these wanderers in the world to whom no house of religion gave entrance, came to Rievaulx, the mother of mercy, and found the gates open, and entered by them freely, giving thanks unto their Lord. . . . This house is a holy place because it generates for its God sons who are peacemakers.[15]

This maternal imagery stamps all cistercian thinking on the relationships that should exist between the various monasteries, and it is not without significance that the motto of the Order is 'Cîteaux, our Mother'.

The Superior or Spiritual Director as Mother

It is in regard to their function as superior or spiritual director that the cistercian writers most frequently employ maternal figures.

We shall cite only two examples here. The first is taken from Saint Bernard's preface to his five books of advice to his former subject, Pope Eugene III:

> It has occurred to me to write something which might edify, delight or console you. . . . Two opposites, your majesty and my love, vie to dictate my style. Love draws me on; majesty holds me back. . . . What if you have ascended the throne? Even if you were to walk on the wings of the wind, you would not escape my affection. Love knows no master. It recognizes a son even though he wears the tiara. . . . It is true that I have been freed of maternal obligation towards you, but I am not stripped of affection for you. You were once in my womb; you will not be drawn from my heart so easily. Ascend to the heavens, descend to the depths, you will not escape me. I shall follow you wherever you go. . . . Therefore, I will instruct you, not as a teacher, but as a mother, indeed, as a lover. I may seem more the fool, but only to one who does not love, to one who does not feel the force of love.[16]

Our other example is taken from Guerric of Igny, commenting on how the wisdom of Solomon was displayed in his method of determining who was the real mother of a child disputed by two women (1 Kgs 3:16-27). Referring to Christ as Solomon, Guerric says:

> Lord Solomon, you call me mother. I profess myself to be a handmaid. I am Christ's handmaid; be it done to me according to your word. And indeed I will show myself a mother by love and anxious care to the best of my ability; but I will always be mindful of my condition.[17]

We have chosen these two particular passages, because they seem to contain in germ the basic characteristics, not only of the spiritual motherhood of the superior or director, but of the types of motherhood we mentioned above.

CHARACTERISTICS OF SPIRITUAL MOTHERHOOD

A Specific Vocation

Guerric states that he has received a distinct call from Christ to fulfill the role of spiritual mother. A person does not assume these duties on one's own initiative. Monastic literature abounds in stories of holy persons who have fled the responsibilities of spiritual parenthood, seeking some remote hideaway or little-known monastery where they could pursue a life of peace and contemplation; and who could not be persuaded to take up their charge as superior or spiritual director unless commanded to do so by legitimate authority. The role of spiritual mother does not depend on blood relationships, or on a person's own self-estimation of suitability for the task. It depends on the will of God. The early Cistercians often commented on the verse in which Jesus states that those who do the will of his Father in heaven are his mother, brothers, and sisters (Mt 12:50).

Obligation of Care

It is little wonder that people have shunned the obligations of spiritual parenthood, as we saw Saint Bernard mentioning in his advice to Pope Eugene III. It has as its chief activity the exercise of 'anxious care', as Guerric expressed it. This anxiety implies no lack of trust in God's providence, or mistrust of the good will of one's spiritual children. Rather the term indicates an attitude of lively concern for the spiritual advancement of each 'child' towards union with God in love. This calls for constant vigilance, prayer, and a healthy interest in everything that influences or affects one's spiritual children. Saint Bernard has a great deal to say about the necessity of constant care by those who have the responsibility of spiritual leadership. He writes that,

> . . . since the Lord commands us to 'Watch and pray, so that you do not enter into temptation', it is clear that without this twofold activity of the faith, and the constant care of those who guard them, neither the city nor the Bride can abide in safety.[18]

Both he and Gilbert of Hoyland excoriate those who fail in this watchful care, acting instead only out of self-interest or to secure their own advancement.[19] Bernard writes of such people that:

> Neither the peril of souls nor their salvation gives them any concern. They are certainly devoid of the maternal instinct . . . About the ruin of Joseph they do not care at all. . . . There is no pretense about the true mother, the breasts that she displays are full for the taking.[20]

Adam of Perseigne (+1221), in listing the six essentials for acquiring newness of life in monasticism, includes 'the dutiful anxiety of the master regarding the novitiate' as his fifth requirement, and says that 'the master's affectionate care' is what is most instrumental in teaching the novices the importance of obedience.[21]

Care Must Include Affection and Tenderness

As Saint Bernard makes clear in the preface to his advice to Eugene III, the care of a spiritual mother is not exercised from some detached vantage point, or with a cold, intellectually-remote attitude. It demands a degree of tenderness towards the ones being cared for. Like all true relationships of love, the heart enters into the exchange as well as the mind. John of Ford has left us a graphic description of this attitude of tender, gentle care. In commenting on the verse in which Jesus compares himself to a mother hen, the abbot writes:

> To take an example which the Wisdom of God used of himself, we see how the hen yearns over her chickens, how tenderly and how often she gives birth. The keener her affection, the harsher her voice. . . . What are we to make of the way she passes, as it were, wholly into love, and shows this not only by rasping her voice, but by fluffing out her feathers, by drooping her body, by anxiously running to and fro, by brooding over her chicks with selfless devotion. Do we not also find that sheep, the meekest of animals, in dealing with their lambs, put forth the full force of their affection? They bleat tenderly, they provide sweet nourishment, they lead them about continually, they defend them vigorously. Soon they mount horns, and they are armed with these for the safety of the lambs, even at the cost of their own death.[22]

Abbot John also comments on the pericope of Christ embracing the little children who come to him (Mt 19:13):

> We see in the gospel, too, how when Jesus was talking about little children, he commanded the little ones to come to him, explained to them the kingdom of heaven, and then even tenderly embraced a little child himself. . . . How greatness shrinks itself to the scale of children, or rather, how it pours itself forth and spreads itself wide! How he yearns over them, as a mother bird over her young!. . . . You direct the way of your little ones towards yourself, dear Jesus, as if you walked ahead of them.[23]

Here we have a perfect example of the 'leadership of love' of which Abbot John wrote.

Spiritual motherhood, while it must be tender, must always be supernatural in character, not disintegrating into mere cuddling or babying. Aelred of Rievaulx, the most affectionate of superiors, cautioned those whose words and actions may be sweet only on the surface:

Anyone who wishes to have that holy sweetness in words which is pleasing to God must keep two considerations in his thoughts and in his heart, holiness as a standard for himself and compassion towards his neighbor. . . . If it is milk and honey he wishes to have on his lips, by 'honey' we might understand 'holiness', and since 'milk' is a sign of motherly love and feeds little children, moving a mother's feelings toward her child, by 'milk' we might understand 'compassion'. Nothing makes a man speak to another tenderly, kindly, and gently, like compassion, though compassion without holiness is moral softness.[24]

His sister, the recluse for whom he wrote a rule of life, he warned not to turn her cell into a school, and describes what can happen to the recluse who does so:

Never allow children access to your cell. [The recluse who turns her cell into a school] sits at her window, the girls settle themselves in the porch; and so she keeps them all under observation. Swayed by their childish dispositions, she is angry one minute and smiling the next, now threatening, now flattering, kissing one child and smacking another. When she sees one of them crying after being smacked, she calls her close, strokes her cheek, puts her arms around her neck and holds her tight, calling her: 'My own baby girl, my own pet.' There before her eyes, even though she may not yield to them, the recluse has worldly and sensual temptations, and amid all, what becomes of her continual remembrance of God?[25]

Aelred himself possessed both 'milk and honey on his tongue'. His biographer Walter Daniel wrote that even though he was seriously ill a great deal of the time, he had a little cot built where his monks could gather about him, and, Walter says:

Every day they came . . . twenty or thirty at a time, to talk together of the spiritual delights of the Scriptures and of the observances of the Order. There was nobody to say to them, 'Get out, go away, do not touch the Abbot's bed'; they walked and lay about his bed and talked with him as a little child prattles with its mother.[26]

We note that the topic of their conversation was spiritual in nature, and the purpose was to lead the monks to union with God, the moving force of any spiritual motherhood.

The Cistercian Fathers frequently commented on the verse from Saint Paul's epistle to the Galatians: 'My little children, with whom I am in labor until Christ be formed in you' (Gal 4:19). The spiritual mother must not spare herself in any way, or avoid any means, no matter how painful it may be to herself, to secure this union with Christ for his or her children. Sometimes this may take the form of necessary discipline or corrections which may be more painful to the spiritual mother than to the charge. Spiritual motherhood entails a love which does not overlook faults, but which tries to correct them, if possible, recalling the verse of scripture that states that the Lord chastises those he loves (Pr 3:12).

Implicit Personal Holiness

One cannot give what one does not possess, or lead where one traveled. Not only must the spiritual mother be careful about the welfare of those for whom one is responsible, but one must be careful of one's own soul, to be sure that Christ is being formed in it. When speaking of the soul as the mother of Christ, Guerric said above that the office of spiritual mother was not restricted to prelates. In another sermon, addressed to his monks, Guerric states:

> If you will faithfully receive the Word from the mouth of the heavenly messenger you too may conceive the God whom the whole world cannot contain, conceive him however in your heart, not in your body. And yet even in your body, although not by any bodily action or outward form, nonetheless truly in your body, since the Apostles bids us glorify and bear God in our body. . . . Behold the unspeakable condescension of God and at the same time the power of the mystery which passes all understanding. He who created you is created in you, and as if it were too little that you should possess the Father, he also wishes that you should become a mother to himself. 'Whoever,' he says, 'does the will of my Father, he is my brother and sister and mother.' O faithful soul, . . . open to the Word of God an ear that will listen. This is the way to the womb of your heart for the Spirit who brings about conception. . . . You also, blessed mothers of so glorious an issue, attend to yourselves until Christ is formed in you.[27]

There is no more effective method for the spiritual mother to employ in exercising the 'leadership of love' than the example of personal holiness, and Adam of Perseigne makes it the fourth essential factor for a novice master to possess. He says, 'So lofty must be the life of superiors that the demeanor of the subordinates may be fashioned after their example'.[28]

Yet there must be nothing artificial or assumed about this good example. It must spring from real virtue, and be inspired by love of God and of the spiritual mother's charges. A modern Cistercian,

Thomas Merton, who himself seems to have fulfilled the require-
ments for a spiritual mother, writes of how to discern if one's love
for another is authentic:

> All true love is closely associated with three fundamental human
> strivings: with creative work, with sacrifice, and with contempla-
> tion. Where these three are present there is reliable evidence of
> spiritual life, of love. And the most important of the three is
> sacrifice.[29]

Christ—The Exemplar of Spiritual Mother

As in all other roles in Christian life, Christ must be the norm and
exemplar for the spiritual mother. As Merton stated, the greatest
evidence of love is the degree of sacrifice one is willing to make
for the loved one. Christ himself said that there is no greater love
than to lay down one's life for one's friends (Jn 15:13), and then
proceeded to practice what he preached.

A necessary concomitant of the willingness to make sacrifices is
the humble acknowledgement of one's weakness and inability to
accomplish anything without the help of God's grace. Isaac of Stella
(1100-1178?) wrote of 'mother grace':

> 'It was grace that saved you with faith for its instrument.' Grace,
> then, is the mother that brings Jesus to birth in our hearts; grace
> that forestalls the unworthy; grace that is the unseen depth that
> gives birth and growth to the length, breadth and height that is
> seen. Justice may seem to answer this mother roughly with 'Nay,
> woman', though it is said with loving-kindness and full of charity,
> 'Why do you trouble me with that?' Nonetheless, Mercy has its
> way. The Apostle sums it all up in the words: 'It was not thanks
> to anything we had done for our own justification; in accordance
> with his own merciful design he saved us.' 'Mother' grace was
> there through whom faith, the first of the virtues, is created.[30]

Isaac reminds superiors that no one should be wise in his own eyes,
but instead imitate Christ who was 'meek and humble of heart'. Even
when spiritual mothers have done all that they can do, they should
still say 'we are unprofitable servants'. Like Bernard and Gilbert,
Isaac had no time for spiritual mothers who did not keep guard
over their own souls and those of their charges. He says, rather
ironically:

> . . . they have become worldly businessmen though their election
> was supposed to set them up as teachers of the spiritual life.

Colman O'Dell

They take care not to go too far into the desert, and, instead of leading, they drive their flocks . . . Enemies to themselves, they try to be friends to others . . . So, my brothers, they are worthy to hear it said: Do what they say, do not imitate their actions. The community whose superior spends his time traveling about dealing with secular affairs and what is foreign to his vocation and yet manages to force his subjects to keep to the regular life seems to me to resemble a handsome man who goes around with his head where his feet ought to be.[31]

MONASTIC LIFE—A MATRIX

Having examined some of the characteristic features of spiritual motherhood as the early Cistercians saw it, let us now turn to the question of why maternal symbols occur so frequently in their writings.[32] Perhaps the basic answer lies in the monastic life-style itself. The Order of Cîteaux was only one stream of a general current towards monastic reform which reached its height at the beginning of the twelfth century. An analysis of the background and the implications of this movement for monastic history lies beyond the scope of this present study, and has, in any case, been brilliantly documented by a host of eminent scholars. We note, however, that the reform had as one of its ideals a return to the sources of monasticism and a revitalizing of many traditional monastic practices which had fallen by the wayside in the course of centuries as monks had taken the line of least resistance and adapted themselves to new trends in order that no one should be deprived of the reputation of being a true monk.

We shall look now at some of those monastic practices to see which may have provided source material for maternal imagery.

Lectio

As Dom Jean Leclercq and many other scholars have pointed out, the practice of monastic reading was an essential part of the monk's life, and is an object of study in its own right. The early Cistercians, rejecting a trend towards intellectual pursuits and the analytic study of philosophy and theology which was giving rise to scholasticism, made a conscious effort to pursue the method of *lectio*.[33] Here the aim is not the pursuit of intellectual knowledge itself (*scientia*), but rather a spiritual wisdom (*sapientia*). The two sources for reading in this method were Holy Scripture and the writings of the Church Fathers.

Holy Scripture

Even a cursory search in any reliable concordance for words related to mothers or maternal characteristics quickly reveals that the Bible holds a wealth of references. For the monk, Holy Scripture takes precedence over all other reading matter for *lectio*. Hence the early Cistercians were constantly coming into contact with maternal figures. So thoroughly did the early Cistercians steep themselves in Holy Scripture that they finally came to the point where they not only 'thought', but 'talked' Scripture.

For these men, certain passages of Scripture held a special significance for their exercise of spiritual leadership. Because they looked to Christ as their example, the Gospels naturally loomed large, as did the works of Saint Paul and the other apostles. Jesus himself had compared the trials of his apostles to those of a woman in labor (Jn 16:21), and these cistercian abbots could sympathize with them, for they also were endeavoring to establish a new Order in the face of much opposition and misunderstanding.

The monastic search for *sapientia* led them to devote much attention to the wisdom books of the Bible—books in which wisdom receives a feminine personification and is referred to as a mother. In the figure of the 'valiant woman' of the Book of Proverbs, they could see an image of the Virgin Mary, the Church, or even their own monastic community. John of Ford refers to Scripture as a mother for us, and Aelred calls it 'the womb of God'.[34] The Song of Songs, upon which so many of these early Cistercians wrote beautiful commentaries, is replete with maternal symbols.

In view of this attitude toward Scripture, the early Cistercians would have no hesitation in using maternal figures to express virtues such as tenderness, gentleness, patience, loving-kindness, mercy, and 'anxious care'.

Church Fathers

In the minds of the Cistercian Fathers, the constant reading of Scripture was inseparably linked with the reading of the works of the Church Fathers, who had written commentaries on the various books of the Bible. Though the writings of all the great Fathers were probably utilized, Augustine, Gregory the Great, Ambrose, and Origen exerted the most influence, with Augustine claiming pride of place. Maternal figures were used by all these Fathers,[35] especially Augustine, whose Christmas sermons find many echoes in those of Guerric.[36]

Liturgy

The Order of Cîteaux made a conscious effort to simplify its liturgical practices, in order that the monks might not only 'get through' or 'say' a vast quantity of prayers, devotional offices, and extra-liturgical material, but that they might 'pray' it in their hearts as well as 'say' it, and might enter into the whole vast cycle of Christ's incarnation: his birth, death, and resurrection. Following his 'leadership of love' in the liturgy, they too could be born, live in obscurity, preach the word 'in and out of season' in their Divine Office, be crucified with him, go down into the tomb, rise gloriously on Easter Sunday, and ascend with him to the right hand of the Father, to come again on the Last Day. Many of their sermons in which maternal figures appear are related to the Annunciation, Christmas, and Pascaltide.

The saints too, especially Peter and Paul, showed them how to exercise their 'leadership of love', and gave them encouragement in their task of 'anxious care'. For those lay brothers who could not read, or for monks in monasteries which owned few books, the liturgy served as a chief source of *lectio*; the various lessons at Vigils, the short readings at the little hours, and the canticles of Lauds and Vespers took the place of private reading. And always there were the psalms, which most of the monks knew by heart and which were the prayers of Christ himself, according to some interpretations.[37]

On the great Feasts of Sermon, there would be monastic Chapter for the whole community at which the abbot would comment on the feast and its implications for his spiritual charges. These sermons, usually edited for dissemination beyond the walls of the monastery, constitute the main body of the writings of the early Cistercians which we are fortunate enough to have preserved, and there we find maternal imagery. These sermons also gave the abbots occasion to remark on how their spiritual children were attending to their spiritual mother's words. Some would sleep quietly, their heads nodding piously as if lost in thought. Others would snore loudly, some would fidget if the sermon were extended, others would make mental notes on points where the abbot's interpretation did not agree with their own.[38] These descriptions give us a feeling of deep personal contact between the abbot and his monks, and a sense of true family spirit.

Monastic Tradition

The whole of monastic tradition emphasizes the close ties that should link the spiritual father or mother, and his or her children.

This is especially true in cenobitic monasticism. Saint Pachomius, usually given credit for being the organizer of this spiritual way of life, is often presented as being a harsh disciplinarian who ran his huge monastic establishments on the lines more of a military operation than of a family. Nevertheless, his biography speaks of his 'maternal care' for the souls of his monks, especially in his capacity for discernment of spirits.[39]

Though the Rule of Saint Benedict makes no specific use of maternal figures, all the characteristics of spiritual motherhood we have mentioned above find expression in its lines, particularly in those sections of the Rule which speak of the Abbot. Monastic scholars are convinced of the intimate link between the Rule of Saint Benedict and the Rule of the unknown Master. The Master document says that the abbot:

> . . . should in himself exemplify for his charges that norm of humility which the Lord presented to the apostles who were quarreling about the first place, namely, when he took a child by the hand and brought him into their midst, saying: If anyone wants to be great among you, let him be like this. Therefore whatever the abbot enjoins his disciples to do for God, he himself should first do, and thus when he gives any orders the members will follow in line wherever the head leads them. He should have such love and kindness toward all the brethren that he will not prefer one to another, and will combine in himself the characteristics of both parents for all his disciples and sons by offering them equal love as their mother and showing them uniform kindness as their father.[40]

We do not know whether the early Cistercian Fathers had read the Rule of the Master.[41] The Order of Cîteaux had as one of its primary aims a return to a more authentic living of the Holy Rule of the patriarch of western monasticism, as Saint Benedict is called. Had they known of it, they would have been interested in such a document which emphasized a deep personal relationship between the abbot and his monks. We recall that, in many ways, Cîteaux was reacting against Cluny, which tended to assume the character of a vast bureaucracy. Cîteaux envisaged its various monasteries as a family of daughters, stemming from a common mother, independent in their own sphere, but linked by the bonds of charity. The Order was ruled, not by one official who held the reins of power in his own hands, but by a General Chapter of abbots, meeting as equals to reach a solution to their problems, precedence being given to the abbot of Cîteaux and the superiors of its earliest daughter houses. This sort of governing body enhanced the family spirit, in which both obedience and humility could be fostered to the best advantage.[42]

Current Trends in Monastic Spirituality

At the time of the early Cistercian Fathers whose works we have been examining, a wave of devotion to the humanity of Jesus had already begun, and these writers contributed greatly to its development. Saint Bernard is often credited with being the focal point of this devotion, which was to flower slightly later in the cult of the Sacred Heart, the Precious Blood, the Wounds of Christ, and in a deepening love and respect for the Blessed Sacrament and the Holy Eucharist.[43] In all of these devotions, maternal figures play a prominent part, and, as men of their time, the Cistercian Fathers meditated on points of doctrine. This often took the form of a deep personal love of the monk for the Virgin Mary, and for Mother Church, which we cannot examine in the present study.

Interest in the lives of the saints found expression in the beautiful prayers of Saint Anselm to Jesus, the Virgin Mary, and to Saints Peter and Paul, and included maternal imagery.[44] In this respect, the Cistercians were merely following a trend in spirituality, and enlarging upon it.

Women in the Audience of the Early Cistercians

In the last few years, an enormous number of scholars have turned their attention to the relationships between monastic men and women. In theory, the early Cistercians sought to avoid the responsibility of spiritual direction of women, but, in point of fact, they were forced by circumstances to assume this charge.[45] As a result, many of their letters, sermons, and instructions were either intended for women or ultimately found their way to such an audience.

Like all good speakers and writers, the early Cistercians spoke of what appealed to their hearers or readers; hence maternal imagery would prove useful to their purpose. It was often necessary to comfort the anxious mother of a prospective novice, worried that her son would not be able to bear the harsh regime of early Cîteaux. We find Saint Bernard writing to one such mother that he himself will be father and mother to her son, making the way straight before him, and the rough places smooth.[46]

As a corollary to this, we remember that, in the case of Saint Aelred, at any rate, these men corresponded with women of their own families or women of the same social circle, who may have had as much influence on them as the abbots had on their feminine relations. We know almost nothing about the family life of most of these early Cistercians, but, at least in the case of Saint Bernard, the mother of the family exercised a tremendous influence on all her children. When speaking of spiritual direction, the abbots would find it natural to recall her, and employ figures which typified her.[47]

Manual Labor

The early Cistercians aimed at following the Holy Rule which states that 'they are truly monks when they live by the works of their hands'. In the twelfth century, work usually meant agricultural pursuits, especially the raising of sheep or cattle, or the tending of vine—both of which involve a vast amount of effort. The monks had before their eyes living models of the mother hens, ewes, and toilers in the vineyards which appear in their writings. Their agrarian world in many ways resembled that of Jesus, his disciples, and the Church Fathers. These early Cistercians could identify themselves more easily with these authors than we in our technological, mechanized age are able to do.

The long hours of back-breaking toil shared by all who were physically able to lend a hand, served as opportunities for shared experiences that built a family spirit in the community. The short breaks in the routine for haying, plowing, and reaping gave the monks an excellent chance to share these experiences with one another and with their abbot on a very personal basis. Issac of Stella, in his sermons, often mentions these times and uses them to comment on spiritual matters.

We are apt to have a mental picture of these early monks of Cîteaux as solitary cowled figures, roaming through graceful cloisters, in quiet garths or gardens, kneeling in high-vaulted churches, lost in contemplative repose. In reality, the monks were laboring to construct these cloisters and churches by sheer muscle power, while, at the same time, struggling to wrest their daily sustenance from newly-cleared land that often resisted their efforts to the point that they were forced to abandon everything they had accomplished and move to another site to start all over again. In moments like this, they had great need of maternal tenderness, understanding, sympathy, and compassion from their spiritual leader, who bore each one's cross as well as his own.[48]

THE MESSAGE OF SPIRITUAL MOTHERHOOD FOR OUR TIME

What can people of our day learn from these early Cistercians when they write of spiritual motherhood? In spite of the fact that we live in the technological, mechanized, over-refined environment of modern western civilization, we all have great need for the 'anxious care' that only a spiritual mother can bestow. This is especially true when it comes to the matter of caring for the Christ-life in the human souls. We have the duty of nourishing its growth by all the means that God provides. Few people in the modern world do not have access to the Bible for meditative reading, if they are willing to take only a moment from their ordinary routine.

Psychologists have noted that people of our age are much more sensitive to pain than were the people of past times, and the thought that God will console and strengthen them like a mother can be of great assistance in helping them to keep up their efforts to fulfill their spiritual, moral, and civic responsibilities.

The picture of maternal love and care that these Cistercians present is an attractive one, though sometimes the figures they employ may seem earthier than we are comfortable with.[49] Many of the images of maternal love, care, and tenderness may be of use to those who are dedicating their lives to the promotion of the family and the right-to-life movement.

For religious, especially contemplatives, these writings can be a source of inspiration to redouble their prayers and sacrifices for all people and their needs. They, with Saint Paul, should be in labor until Christ is formed in every living soul. This care and the need for it will never cease as long as there are people on earth who are wandering aimlessly in the desert, like the ancient Israelites, and who desperately need to be carried 'on eagles' wings' and incited to try their own wings by a hovering mother bird. With Aelred of Rievaulx, may every religious, especially every member of the Order of Cîteaux, be able to say, as our last words, 'God who knows all things knows that I love you all as myself; and, as earnestly as a mother after her son, "I long for you in the heart of Jesus Christ."'[50]

NOTES

1. John of Ford, *SC 14.6; Sermons on the Final Verses of the Song of Songs*, 1, CF 29, Translated Wendy Mary Beckett (Kalamazoo, 1977) 258.

2. See 'Lumen Gentium', *Vatican Council II: The Conciliar and Post-Conciliar Documents*, edited Austin Flannery, op (Dublin: Dominican Publications, 1975) 413-423.

3. For a thorough discussion and additional references, see *Julian of Norwich: Showings*, Translated Edmund Colledge, OSA, and James Walsh, SJ (New York: Paulist Press, 1978) 8-11, 84-94.

4. Letter 378; *Letters of St Bernard of Clairvaux*, Translated Bruno Scott-James (London: Burns Oates, 1953) 449.

5. *St Bernard's Sermons for the Seasons and Principal Feasts of the Year*, 1, Translated A Priest of Mount Melleray (Westminster; Newman Press, 1921) 160.

6. 'Sermon for the Feast of St Andrew', *loc. cit.* Vol. 3, p. 45.

7. Saint Bernard, *Sentences*, 2.47. Quoted by Jean Leclercq, Introduction, to *The Influence of St Bernard: Anglican Essays*, Edited Sister Benedicta Ward, SLG (Oxford: SLG press, 1976) xvi.

8. PL 195:272.

9. Gilbert of Hoyland, Treatise 6.6-7, *Treatises, Epistles, and Sermons*, CF 34, Translated Lawrence C. Braceland, SJ (Kalamazoo, 1981) 52, 53.

10. Gilbert, Sermon, Bodleian 87; CF 34: *Ibid.*, 155, 156.

11. *Ibid.*, 155.

12. Guerric of Igny, Third Sermon for Christmas, *Liturgical Sermons*, 1, CF 8 (Spencer, 1970) 52, 53.

13. Thomas Merton, *The Christmas Sermons of Blessed Guerric of Igny* (Trappist, Kentucky: Abbey of Gethsemani, 1959) 15-22.

14. Gilbert of Hoyland, *SC 16.8; Sermons on the Song of Songs*, 2, CF 20, Translated Lawrence C. Braceland, SJ (Kalamazoo, 1979) 213.

15. Walter Daniel, *Life of Ailred of Rievaulx*, Translated and edited by F. M. Powicke (New York: Oxford University Press, 1951) 36, 37.

16. Bernard of Clairvaux, *Five Books on Consideration: Advice to a Pope*, CF 37, Translated John D. Anderson and Elizabeth T. Kennon (Kalamazoo, 1976) 23, 24.

17. Guerric of Igny, *Sermons 1:* 52.

18. Bernard of Clairvaux, SC 76.8, *On the Song of Songs*, 4, CF 40, Translated Irene Edmonds (Kalamazoo, 1980) 116.

19. For Bernard's reaction, see SC 76.1-3; CF 40: 121-123. For Gilbert, see *Treatise* 7/1; CF 34: 57-65.

20. Bernard of Clairvaux, SC 10.2-4; *On the Song of Songs*, 1, CF 4, Translated Kilian Walsh, OCSO (Spencer, 1971) 62-63.

21. Letter 5; *The Letters of Adam of Perseigne*, 1, CF 21, Translated Grace Perigo (Kalamazoo, 1976) 101.

22. John of Ford, SC 14.6; 258, 259.

23. *Idem*, 3-2; CF 29: 101.

24. PL 195:325.

25. Aelred of Rievaulx, *Inst incl* 4-5; *Treatises and Pastoral Prayer*, CF 2, Translated Mary Paul Macpherson, OCSO (1971) 49, 50.

26. Walter Daniel, *Ailred*, p. 40.

27. Guerric of Igny, Second Sermon for the Annunciation, *Liturgical Sermons*, 2, CF 32, Translated Monks of Mount Saint Bernard's Abbey (Spencer, 1971) 44, 45.

28. Adam of Perseigne, *Letter 5*; CF 21: 101.

29. Thomas Merton, *The Power and Meaning of Love* (London: Sheldon Press, 1976) 4.

30. Isaac of Stella, Sermon 10; *Sermons on the Christian Year*, 1, CF 11, Translated Hugh McCaffery, OCSO (Kalamazoo, 1979) 87.

31. *Ibid.*, 89.

32. See Caroline Walker Bynum, 'Maternal Imagery in Twelfth-century Cistercian Writings', *Noble Piety and Reformed Monasticism: Studies in Medieval Cistercian History*, 7, CS 65 (Kalamazoo, 1981) 68-80.

33. For background material on *lectio*, see Jean Leclercq, OSB, *The Love of Learning and the Desire for God: A Study of Monastic Culture*, Translated Catherine Misrahi (New York: Fordham University Press, 1961); M.-D. Chenu, OP, *Nature, Man and*

Society in the Twelfth Century, translated Jerome Taylor and Lester K. Little (Chicago: University of Chicago Press, 1968); *Collectanea Cisterciensia* 41:4 (1979) completely devoted to the topic of *lectio*.

34. PL 195: 325.

35. See Carolyn Bynum Walker, *Jesus as Mother: Studies in the Spirituality of the High MIddle Ages* (Berkely-Los Angeles: University of California Press, 1982) 125-129 *et passim*; and Yves M. J. Congar, OP, *I Believe in the Holy Spirit* 3, trans. by David Smith (New York, 1983) 155-164.

36. See Augustine, *Sermons for Christmas and Epiphany*, Translated Thomas Comerford Lawler (Westminster: Newman Press, 1952).

37. See Thomas Merton, *Bread in the Wilderness* (New York: New Directions, 1953).

38. For a sermon of this type see Isaac, Sermon 14, *Sermons* 1, CF 11: 113-118.

39. See Adalbert de Vogüé, *Community and Abbot in the Rule of St Benedict*, 1, CS 5/1, Translated Charles Philippi (Kalamazoo, 1977) 122.

40. *Rule of the Master*, CS 6, Translated Luke Eberle, OSB (Kalamazoo, 1977) 113.

41. The authorship of the Rule of the Master is a highly controversial subject. For a discussion of ancient monastic rules see Adalbert de Vogüé, OSB, *'Sub Regula uel Abbate'*, *Rule and Life: An Interdisciplinary Symposium*, CS 12, edited M. Basil Pennington, OCSO (Spencer. 1971) 21-63.

42. See Louis Lekai, O. Cist., *The Cistercians: Ideals and Reality* (Kent, Ohio: Kent State University Press, 1977). It is regrettable that the english translation of the History of the Order *Fiches*, distributed to the nuns of the Order of Cistercians of the Strict Observance has not been published.

43. See Jean Leclercq, *et al.*, *The Spirituality of the Middle Ages*, The History of Christian Spirituality, 2 (New York: Seabury, 1968). The authors discuss the major trends and devotions of this period. Also see, Pierre Pourrat, *Christian Spirituality in the Middle Ages*, 2 (Westminster: Newman Press, 1953). The *Fiches* of the Order on the topic of liturgy also contain much valuable material.

44. See *The Prayers and Meditations of Saint Anselm*, translated Benedicta Ward, SLG (Harmondsworth-Baltimore: Penguin, 1973) 141-156. The prayer to Saint Paul, especially, abounds in maternal figures. See also Walker, *Jesus as Mother*, 113-115.

45. See Bede K. Lackner, 'Early Citeaux and the Care of Souls', *Noble Piety*, pp. 52-67. Also Lawrence C. Braceland, SJ, 'Nuns in the Audience of Gilbert of Hoyland', *Simplicity and Ordinariness*, CS 61 (Kalamazoo, 1980). Also Lawrence C. Braceland, SJ, Introduction to his translation of Gilbert of Hoyland's *Sermons on the Song of Songs*, 1, CF 14: 3-32.

46. Saint Bernard, Letter 112; *Letters*, p. 169.

47. The Cistercians of the Strict Observance formerly commemorated Blessed Aleth, the mother of Saint Bernard, on 23 May.

48. For a modern personal reaction to such a situation, one may consult some of the elder monks of Saint Joseph's Abbey, Spencer, Massachussetts about their experiences during and after the disastrous fire that destroyed the trappist monastery of Our Lady of the Valley at Valley Falls, Rhode Island on 21 March, 1950.

49. See the the passage from Aelred's first sermon on the Pasch, note 8 above, for example.

50. Walter Daniel, *Ailred*, p. 58.

CONTRIBUTORS

CLAIRE BOUDREAU, OCSO, a nun of Mount Saint Mary's Abbey, Wrentham, Massachusetts, is presently director of novices and vocations at Our Lady of the Angels monastery, Crozel, Virginia. She holds degrees from Seton Hill College and the Université de Laval.

JEAN DE LA CROIX BOUTON, OCSO, a monk of Aiguebelle, is secretary of the Historical Commission of the Order of Cistercians of the Strict Observance. Well known in the Order for his historical studies, he has published, among other things, four volumes (in French) on the history of cistercian nuns.

RITAMARY BRADLEY, SFCC, holds a doctorate from St Louis University and is Professor Emerita of English at St Ambrose College. The co-founder and for many years co-editor of *Mystics Quarterly*, she is also well known for her numerous articles on medieval women mystics.

AMANDERS BUSSELS, OCSO, a monk of the belgian abbey of Achel, has served his monastery as master of chant, lector in theology, and prior. A founder of the Guild of Saint Lutgard, he is editor of a flemish language review, *Sint Lutgardis Tijdschrift*.

ANN MARIE CARON, RSM, is Assistant Professor of Religious Studies at Saint Joseph College, West Hartford, Connecticut and active in the Liturgy Commission of the Archdiocese of Hartford. In addition to her studies on medieval mystics, she has written an article on 'Women Deaconesses: Historical and Contemporary Explorations'.

GERALDINE CARVILLE specializes in the historical geography of her native Ireland. In recognition of her work on the Irish Cistercians, she has received the *Benemerenti* Medal and Diploma from Pope John Paul II. Among her nearly thirty publications are *Holy Cross*

Abbey, Duiske Abbey, and *The Occupation of Celtic Sites in Ireland by the Canons Regular of St Augustine and the Cistercians.*

MARTINUS CAWLEY, OCSO, a native of Australia, studied at the Gregorian University, Rome, and the École Biblique, Jerusalem. The founder of a series of local histories of monasteries and of translations of cistercian hagiographical texts, he also takes an interest in the theology of food and is known in his community, Our Lady of Guadalupe Abbey, Lafayette, Oregon, for recycling and gleaning.

ELIZABETH CONNOR, OCSO, entered the Abbey of Notre Dame du Bon Conseil in Québec after receiving undergraduate and graduate degrees in Classics from Johns Hopkins University. In addition to her studies on the history of the Order, she is a member of the Law Commission ocso and a former associate editor of *Cistercian Studies Quarterly.*

MARY MAGDALEN COPPENDALE, OCSO, entered Holy Cross Abbey, Stapehill, Dorset, in 1940, after training as a teacher. With the community, she moved from the southwest of England to south Wales and presently lives very near the ruins of the first welsh cistercian abbey, Whitland, whose name her community now shares.

ALFRED DEBOUTTE, C.SS.R., a native of Flanders in Belgium, holds degrees in the Humanities from Brugge and a doctorate in theology from Rome. Until 1969, he was Professor of Theology at Louvain and spiritual director to Redemptoristine nuns at Bruges. In addition to his scholarly works, he has served as secretary and as president of the Guild of Saint Lutgard, and has worked to establish missions for the poor and homeless.

BRIGITTE DEGLER-SPENGLER is editor-in-chief of *Helvetia Sacra,* a multi-volume handbook on the history of the Church in Switzerland. A specialist in the history of women religious, she has published numerous articles on Benedictine, Cistercian, Dominican and Poor Clare nuns, beguines, and tertiaries.

MARTHA DRISCOLL, OCSO, a native of Staten Island, entered the Abbey of Vitorchiano in 1975, after studying history and theater. She served as organist and coordinator of ecumenical relations for her monastery, and is at present superior of the indonesian foundation of Gedono.

CHARLES DUMONT, OCSO, a monk of the Abbey of Scourmont, Belgium, has served as editor of *Collectanea Cisterciensia* and co-founder of *Cistercian Studies Quarterly*. Well known as an authority on Aelred of Rievaulx, Fr Charles has published widely in cistercian spirituality and taken an interest in Mère Louise de Ballon as a witness of the traditional bernardine spirit.

†MARIE DE LA TRINITÉ KERVINGANT, OCSO, studied at the Lycée and the Université de Caen (Normandy) before entering the Ursulines and, a number of years later, the cistercian abbey of Notre Dame des Gardes in Anjou. After serving as novice mistress and abbess, she spent her 'retirement' in researching the history of the Order. Her *Des moniales face à la Révolution française* (1989) is being translated for publication in English.

MARGOT KING obtained her Ph.D. at the University of California at Berkeley in Comparative (medieval) Literature and her early training at the University of Saskatchewan and the University of Toronto. Her interest in the (then) largely unknown female eremitical tradition led her to found Peregrina Publication. Her journal, *Vox Benedictina*, and a series of books on medieval women religious writers, originally called Matrologia Latina, and—more recently—her calendar of medieval women have become well known in scholarly and feminist circles.

†MAREN KUHN-REHFUS, at the time of her unexpected death in September 1993, was *Oberarchivrätin* (Director of Archives) at the Staatsarchiv of Sigmaringen—the first woman to hold this post in Baden-Württemburg. Born in 1938, she studied at the universities of Heidelberg, Berlin, and Tübingen, from which she received her doctorate in history. In addition to her extensive work on cistercian nuns, she published on the history of the Hohenzollerns and Upper Swabia.

BEDE K. LACKNER, O.CIST., Professor of History at the University of Texas-Arlington, is a monk of the Abbey of Our Lady of Dallas, Irving, Texas. A native of Hungary, Fr Bede studied at San Anselmo in Rome, Marquette University, and Fordham University, where he was a student of Jeremiah F. O'Sullivan. Among his many publications is *The Eleventh-century Background of Cîteaux*.

MAUREEN MCCABE, OCSO, a cistercian nun of Mount Saint Mary's Abbey, Wrentham, holds a Diploma of Biblical Studies from the

Institut Catholique of Toulouse. In addition to baking and teaching Scripture in her community, she services as novice mistress.

BRIAN PATRICK McGUIRE specializes in the study of medieval spirituality, most recently late medieval. After receiving a D. Phil. degree from Oxford, he moved to Denmark, where he is presently professor of medieval history and Latin at the Centre for Medieval Studies at Copenhagen University. Among his many publications are *Friendship and Community: The Monastic Experience, 350–1250,* and *The Difficult Saint.*

†EDMUND MIKKERS, OCSO, a native of the Netherlands, was a monk of Achel, Belgium, and chaplain to the cistercian nuns of Klaarland. After studying theology and history at Achel and the Gregorian University in Rome, he taught theology and, with Roger DeGanck, was co-founder and for many years editor of *Cîteaux: Commentarii Cistercienses,* and published widely on cistercian history and spirituality.

JOHN A. NICHOLS, co-editor of Medieval Religious Women, is Professor of History at Slippery Rock University in Pennsylvania. A graduate of Geneva College, Fairleigh Dickinson University, and Kent State University, he has published extensively on the cistercian nuns of England and on iconography.

COLEMAN O'DELL, OCSO, received a Master's degree in zoology from Pennsylvania State University before entering Mount Saint Mary's Abbey, Wrentham. Since that time she has concentrated on patrology, Scripture, and the history of the Cistercian Order. Sr Coleman has also written a number of plays and poems.

MIRIAM SCHMITT, OSB, a Benedictine of Annunciation Priory, Bismarck, North Dakota, received a bachelor's degree in finance from St Louis University, an Master of Arts in Liturgical Studies from Saint John's School of Theology, Collegeville, and a Master of Science degree in institutional administration from Notre Dame. She has concentrated on the theology and spirituality of women monastics, and services as adjunct professor at two United Methodist Academies for Spiritual Formation.

EDITH SCHOLL, OCSO, serves the community of Mount Saint Mary's Abbey, Wrentham, as organist and composer as well as gardener. Her musical works have been performed at the International Medieval Studies Congress in Kalamazoo, and her earlier study on

Mechtild of Magdeburg, 'To Be a Full-grown Bride' appears in volume two of the Medieval Religious Women series.

LILLIAN THOMAS SHANK, OCSO, co-editor of Medieval Religious Women, entered cistercian life after studying nursing. One of the founding members of Our Lady of the Mississippi Abbey, Dubuque, she has served as manager of the abbey's candy factory, infirmarian, bookkeeper, and tractor driver as well as teacher of monastic history.

MANUELA (GERMANA) STROLA, OCSO, entered the abbey of Vitorchiano in 1966, after studying Classics. Holding diplomas in Scripture and Theology, she teaches in her community and also serves as organist.

LUCIA (PAOLA) TARTARA, OCSO, received a degree in Classics from the University of Padua before entering the abbey of Vitorchiano, where is has served as novice mistress, sub-cellarer, and manager of the card department.

MARY ANN SULLIVAN, OCSO, studied at the Catholic University of America before entering Mount Saint Mary's Abbey. In 1964, she was a founding member of Our Lady of the Mississippi Abbey, where she has taught the history of the Order, served as cellarer, sacristan, and gardener, and studied iconography.

CHRYSOGONUS WADDELL, OCSO, a monk of Gethsemani Abbey, studied music at the Philadelphia Conservatory of Music and liturgy and theology at Sant' Anselmo, Rome. His publications range from *Liturgy OCSO* to twelfth-century spiritual writers, including Peter Abelard, and seventeenth-century monastic reform.

ELLEN WEAVER (Weaver-Laporte) received her Ph.D. in historical theology and liturgics from Princeton University, with a specialization in the post-tridentine Gallican Church. After teaching in the Department of Theology at the University of Notre Dame a number of years, she retired to Paris to pursue her research on seventeenth-century french intellectual history. Among her numerous publications, in both French and English, is *The Evolution of the Reform of Port-Royal: From the Rule of Cîteaux to Jansenism* (Paris, 1978).

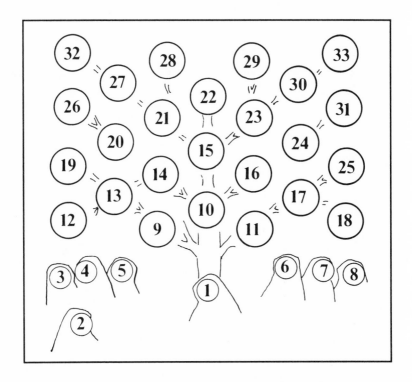

Key to Frontispiece on page (ii) in the front of the book.

1- Humbelina
2- Jeanne de Marotte
3- St Gratia
4- St Maria
5- St Hedwig
6- St. Franca, abbess
7- Hildegard of Bingen
8- Elizabeth of Schönau
9- Lutgard of Aywières
10- Juliana of Mont Cornillon
11- Beatrice of Nazareth
12- Sybil of Gages
13- Elizabeth of Wans
14- Ida of Nivelles
15- Elizabeth of Spalbeek
16- Genta, abbess

17- Agnes of Sanzinnes
18- Ozilia of La Ramée
19- Yolanta of Aywiéres
20- Ida of Léau (Lewis)
21- Yvetta of Huy
22- Ida of Louvain
23- Elizabeth of Tubbac
24- Sophie of Hoven
25- Eve (recluse)
26- Elizabeth of Hoven
27- Udewolte
28- Alice of Schaerbeek
29- Christina of Nazareth
30- Catherine of Parc
31- Alice, abbess
32- Hildegunde
33- Irmendrude

813

TREE OF CISTERCIAN NUNS

Name [Bibiliotheca Hagiographica Latina reference]
Monastery
+date of death; day of liturgical commemoration
Source of information

Agnes of Sanzinnes, Blessed
nun of Mont Cornillon; she died at Salzinnes / Salsen (Belgium)
13th century; 21 January
Life of Juliana of Mont Cornillon

Alice (Aleydis) of Schaerbeek, Blessed
nun of Ter Kameren La Cambre) (Belgium)
+1250; 12 June
AA SS June 2:471
Chrysostomus Henriquez, *Quinque Prudentes Virgines* (Antwerp 1630) pp. 168–198

Alice of 's-Hertogendal ('s-Hertogenbosch), Blessed : abbess of Valduc/'s-Hertogenbosch (Belgium)
c. 1200; 5 May
AA SS May 1:438
Thomas of Cantimpré, *Bonum universale de Apibus* (Douai, 1627) 2:10

Beatrice of Nazareth, Blessed [BHL 1062]
prioress of Nazareth (Belgium)
+1268; 29 August
Henriquez, *Quinque Prudentes Virgines*, 1–167.
Leonce Reypens, *Vita Beatricis. De Autobiografie can de Z. Beatrijs van Tienen O.Cist, 1200–1268* (Antwerp, 1964), reproduced and translated in Roger De Ganck, *The Life of Beatrice of Nazareth* (Kalamazoo, 1991).

Catherine of Vrouwenpark (Parc-aux-Dames), Blessed [BHL 1701]
  nun of Parc-aux-Dames, Louvain
  c. 1300; 4 May
  AA SS May 1:532–534
  Caesarius of Heisterbach, *Dialogus Miraculorum*, 2:25
  Thomas of Cantimpré, *Bonum universale*, 296.

Christina of Nazareth, Blessed
  nun of Nazareth
  13th century; 10 March
  The Life of Beatrice of Nazareth

Elizabeth of Hoven (Klosterhoven), Blessed
  nun of Hoven (Germany)
  +1240; 15 October (27 August)
  AA SS April 1:698
  Caesarius of Heisterbach, *Dialogus Miraculorum* 5.45

Elizabeth of Schönau, Saint (BHL 2485)
  Benedictine abbess of Schönau
  +1164; 18 June
  AA SS June 3:604–643 (3rd edn: CK)

Elizabeth of Spalbeek, Blessed (BHL 2484)
  nun of Herkenrode (Belgium)
  + 1316?; 19 October
  Catal. cod. hag. Bibliot. r. Bruxellensis 1:362–378

Elizabeth Tubbac, Blessed
  nun of Roosendael (Belgium)
  +1560; 19 November
  de Raisse, *Ad Natales Sanctorum Belgii J. Molani Auctarium*
  (Douai, 1626)

Elizabeth of Wans, Blessed
  nun of Aywières
  +1250; 1 July
  Thomas of Cantimpré, *Bonum universale* 2:50, n. 4
  Vita Lutgardis, AA SS (3rd edn) June 4:188, n. 5; 209, n. 21;
  AA SS July 1:5

Eve (Eva), Blessed
      recluse at Liège
      + 1264?; 25 June
      Life of Juliana of Mont Cornillon

Franca, Saint [BHL 3092, 3093]
      abbess of Pittolo
      + 1218; 25 April
      AA SS April 3: c. 383–404 (3d: 383–407)

Genta (Gentla), Blessed
      abbess of Florival (Belgium)
      +1247; 22 (23) March
      Henriquez, *Quinque Prudentes Virgines* 1.10 Thomas of
      Cantimpré, *Bonum universale* 1.11, n. 3; 7.10

Gratia and Maria, Saints
      Saracen converts (Zoraida and Zaida),
      martyred with their brother, Bernard of Poblet (Spain)
      + 1180; 2 September (23 August)
      Manrique, *Annales Cistercienses* (1642)
      2:277–279, 382; 3:69–70, 90–95.
      AA SS August 4:452–463

Hedwig, Saint (BHL 3769)
      widow, foundress of Trebnitz (Trzebnica, Poland)
      + 1243; 15 October
      (canonized 1267)
      AA SS Oct 8: 198–270
      Manrique, *Annales Cistercienses* 4:511–513

Hildegard, Saint (BHL 3927–3933)
      Benedictine abbess of Bingen
      seer, writer, musician
      + 1179; 17 September
      AA SS Sept 5:670–606

Hildegundis (*alias* Joseph), Blessed (BHL 3936-3849)
        monk of Schönau (Germany)
        +1188; April 20
        Caesarius of Heisterbach, Dialogus Miraculorum 1.40
        AA SS 2:782-790; (3rd edn) 780-788

Humbelina, Blessed
        prioress of Jully, sister of Saint Bernard
        +1141 ?; 12 February (21 August)
        Vita prima Bernardi 1.6.30; PL 185:244-245.
        Life of bl. Peter, Prior of Jully; PL 185:1264-1265

Ivetta (Yvette, Jutte, Ibeta) of Huy Blessed (BHL 4620) recluse
        +1228/29; 13 January
        AA SS January 1:863-887 (3rd ed Jan 2:145-169)
        Manrique, *Annales* 3:251-253; 4:321-324

Ida of Léau (Lewes, de Leeuwen, Lewis), Blessed (BHL 4144)
        nun of La Ramée (Belgium)
        + c. 1250; 29 October
        AA SS October 13:100-124, with additions 124-135
        Henriquez, *Quinque Prudentes Virgines* 440-458

Ida of Louvain, Blessed (BHL 4145)
        nun of Roosendael (Belgium)
        + c. 1300; 13 April
        AA SS April 2:155-189
        Henriquez, *Quinque Prudentes Virgines* 299-439

Ida of Nivelles, Blessed (BHL 4146-4147)
        nun of La Ramée
        +1231; 11 December
        Henriquez, *Quinque Prudentes Virgines* 199-297

Irmentrude, Blessed
        nun of Deytkirchen (Diekirch)
        29 May
        Caesarius of Heisterbach, *Dialogus miraculorum* 12.43

Juliana of Mont Cornillon, Blessed (BHL 4521)
    Augustinian canonness; prioress of Mont Cornillon
    +1258; 5 April
    AA SS April 1:443–477; (third edition) 435–475
    Henriquez, *Lilia Cistercii* (Douai 1633)
    The Life of Juliana of Mont Cornillon, translated by Barbara
    Newman (Toronto: Peregrina Press, 1988)

Lutgard of Aywières, Saint (BHL 4950)
    + 1246; 16 June
    AA SS June 3:231–263 (3rd edn.

June 4:187–210)
    The Life of Lutgard of Aywières, text and translation by Mar-
    tinus Cawley (Lafayette, Oregon: Guadalupe Abbey, 1987);
    translation by Margot King (Toronto: Peregrina Press, 1991)
    Thomas Merton, *What are These Wounds?* (1950)

Maria (see Gratia and Maria)

Ezille of La Ramée, Blessed
    3 January
    Life of Juliana of Mont Cornillon

Sophie, Blessed
    abbess of Hoven
    19 September
    Caesarius of Heisterbach, *Dialogus Miraculorum* 10.16.
    Gallia Christiana 3:757

Sybil (Sybille) de Gages, Blessed
    nun of Aywières
    +1250; 9 October
    The Life of Lutgard, AA SS June 4:187–188, 201
    AA SS October 4:567–569
    Manrique, *Annales Cistercienses* 4:114, 271.

Udewolte, Blessed
    nun of Walberberg (Germany)
    12 August
    Caesarius of Heisterbach, *Dialogus Miraculorum* 11.31

Yolanta of Aywières, Blessed
   10 December
   Life of Lutgard 2.12; AA SS June 4:198, n.12

The editors express their heartfelt appreciation to the Rev'd Chrysogonus Waddell ocso *for his help in tracing references to these nuns.*